Food Hawkers

T0362143

Street vendors are ubiquitous across the world and throughout history. They are part of almost any distribution chain, and play an important role in the marketing of consumer goods particularly to poorer customers. Focusing on the food trades, this multi-disciplinary volume explores the dynamics of street selling and its impact on society. Through an investigation of food hawking, the volume both showcases the latest results from a subject that has seen the emergence of a significant body of innovative and adventurous scholarship, and advances the understanding of street vending and its impact on society by stimulating interdisciplinary and cross-disciplinary discussions. Covering a time span of approximately two millennia, from antiquity to the present, the book includes chapters on Europe and Asia, and covers a diverse range of themes such as the identity of food sellers (in terms of gender, ethnicity, and social status); the role of the street seller in the distribution of food; the marketing of food; food traders and the establishment; the representation of food hawkers; and street traders and economic development. By taking a dynamic approach, the collection has enabled its contributors to cross disciplinary boundaries and engage in discussions which extend beyond the limits of their own academic fields, and thus provide a fresh appreciation of this ancient phenomenon.

Dr Melissa Calaresu teaches early modern European history at Gonville and Caius College, Cambridge, and has written on the Grand Tour, historical and autobiographical writing, urban space, reform to revolution, and most recently, the making and eating of ice cream in eighteenth-century Naples. She is co-editor of *Exploring Cultural History: Essays in Honour of Peter Burke* (2010), *New Approaches to Naples c.1500–c.1800: The Power of Place* (2013), and the catalogue for the Fitzwilliam Museum exhibition, *Treasured Possessions from the Renaissance to Enlightenment* (2015).

Danielle van den Heuvel is Senior Lecturer in early modern European history at the University of Kent. Her publications include the award-winning *Women and Entrepreneurship. Female traders in the Northern Netherlands, 1580–1815* (2007), and cover retailing, food markets, and informality in the context of the Dutch Republic and beyond.

Food Hawkers

Selling in the streets from antiquity to the present

Edited by
**Melissa Calaresu and
Danielle van den Heuvel**

Routledge
Taylor & Francis Group

LONDON AND NEW YORK

First published 2016
by Routledge
2 Park Square, Milton Park, Abingdon, Oxon OX14 4RN

and by Routledge
711 Third Avenue, New York, NY 10017

First issued in paperback 2018

Routledge is an imprint of the Taylor & Francis Group, an informa business

British Library Cataloguing in Publication Data
A catalogue record for this book is available from the British Library

Library of Congress Cataloguing in Publication Data
Names: Calaresu, Melissa, editor. | Heuvel, Danielle van den, editor.
Title: Food hawkers : selling in the streets from antiquity to the present /
edited by Melissa Calaresu and Danielle van den Heuvel.
Description: Farnham, Surrey, UK; Burlington, VT: Ashgate, [2016] |
Series: The history of retailing and consumption |
Includes bibliographical references and index.
Identifiers: LCCN 2015038653 | ISBN 9781409450429 (hardcover: alk. paper) |
ISBN 9781315582665 (ebook) | ISBN 9781472404008 (epub)
Subjects: LCSH: Street-food vendors–History. | Street vendors–History.
Classification: LCC HF5458.F66 2016 | DDC 381/.456413009–dc23
LC record available at http://lccn.loc.gov/2015038653

ISBN 13: 978-1-138-32970-6 (pbk)
ISBN 13: 978-1-4094-5042-9 (hbk)

Typeset in Times New Roman
by Out of House Publishing

Contents

7   The street food sector in Vietnam: serious business for female
    entrepreneurs   165
    ANNEMARIE M.F. HIEMSTRA

8   Rethinking street foods: street food hospitality in contemporary
    Calcutta   186
    MANPREET K. JANEJA

9   Negotiating gendered spatial boundaries: women's food
    hawking in Penang, Malaysia   208
    ANJA K. FRANCK

Colour plates

Figures

Tables

Contributors

Melissa Calaresu is a lecturer in history at Gonville and Caius College, Cambridge, and has written on the Grand Tour, historical and autobiographical writing, urban space, reform to revolution, and most recently, the making and eating of ice cream in eighteenth-century Naples. She is co-editor of *Exploring Cultural History: Essays in Honour of Peter Burke* (2010), *New Approaches to Naples c.1500–c.1800: The Power of Place* (2013), and the catalogue for the Fitzwilliam Museum exhibition, *Treasured Possessions from the Renaissance to Enlightenment* (Philip Wilson, 2015).

Ivan Day is an independent social historian and curator, who specialises in the recreation of period food in historical settings. His work has been exhibited at the Getty Research Institute, Minneapolis Institute of the Arts, the Bard Graduate Center, the Metropolitan Museum of Art, the Museum of Fine Arts, Houston, Chatsworth House and Kenwood House. He is a consultant to the National Trust and English Heritage. Recent books include *Eat, Drink and be Merry: The British at Table 1600–2000* (Philip Wilson, 2000), *Cooking in Europe 1650–1850* (Greenwood Press, 2008), *Over a Red Hot Stove: Essays in Early Cooking Technology* (Editor) (Prospect Books, 2009) and *Ice Cream* (Shire, 2010).

Anja K. Franck is a senior lecturer at the School of Global Studies at the University of Gothenburg. She holds a PhD in economic geography from the same university. In her PhD thesis she examines Malaysian working-class women's labour market decisions in the context of export-orientation and rapid economic development. Particular emphasis is placed upon the factors that influence women's move from the formal to the informal economy over the life course. In her current research she focuses upon various aspects of temporary labour migration in the Southeast Asian as well as European region – devoting particular attention to the role of the migration industry and corruption during the migration process.

Annemarie M.F. Hiemstra is an assistant professor in work and organisational psychology at the Erasmus University Rotterdam, where she completed her PhD thesis on fairness in personnel selection. As a consultant,

Annemarie has advised numerous profit and non-profit organisations in the area of human resource management and development. Currently, she is the course director of the minor Cross Cultural Psychology. Her research interests include cross-cultural psychology, personnel selection and psychometrics and she has published on these topics in national and international outlets.

Claire Holleran is a lecturer in classics and ancient history at the University of Exeter. She is the author of *Shopping in Ancient Rome: The Retail Trade in the Late Republic and the Principate* (Oxford University Press, 2013), and co-editor of *Demography and the Graeco-Roman World: New Insights and Approaches* (Cambridge University Press, 2012) and *A Companion to the City of Rome* (Wiley-Blackwell, 2013).

Manpreet K. Janeja a social anthropologist and Associate Professor at the Department of Cross-Cultural Studies and Regional Studies, Copenhagen University. Her work straddles the anthropology of trust, food and eating, cities, migration, law and religion. She is the author of *Transactions in Taste: The Collaborative Lives of Everyday Bengali Food* (Routledge 2010, 2013), co-editor of *Imagining Bangladesh: Contested Narratives* (SAMAJ-EASAS 2014), and *Ethnographies of Waiting* (forthcoming with Bloomsbury). Her next book-length project, provisionally titled *The Aesthetics of School Meals: Distrust, Risk and Uncertainty*, is in the works. She has been a Eugénie Strong Research Fellow in Social Anthropology at Girton College, University of Cambridge; a Visiting Scholar at the Centre for South Asia, Stanford University; and currently holds a Visiting Fellow appointment at the Department of Social Policy, London School of Economics.

Deborah L. Krohn teaches Italian Renaissance decorative arts and cultural history at the Bard Graduate Center: Decorative Arts, Design History, Material Culture, in New York City, where she is associate professor. She holds a BA and MA from Princeton University, and a PhD from Harvard University. She is co-editor and co-curator of *Salvaging the Past: French Decorative Arts from the Metropolitan Museum of Art* (Bard Graduate Center/Yale 2013) and *Dutch New York between East and West: The World of Margrieta van Varick* (Bard Graduate Center/Yale 2009), and is also a contributor to the exhibition and catalogue of *Art and Love in Renaissance Italy* at the Metropolitan Museum of Art (2008–2009). She is the author of articles on Italian Renaissance art and patronage, the history of collecting, and culinary history, and a book, *Food and Knowledge in Renaissance Italy: Bartolomeo Scappi's Paper Kitchens* (Ashgate, 2015).

Tom Stammers is a lecturer in European cultural history at the University of Durham, and in the academic year 2014–2015 he was the resident Deakin Fellow at St Anthony's College Oxford, where he completed his book manuscript entitled *Collection, Recollection, Revolution: Scavenging the Past* *in Nineteenth-Century Paris.* The book traces the transformation of the profile of the private collector in the wake of the French Revolution, and explores the contribution of private collectors to debates about the function and meaning of national heritage. Current projects include a study of collecting and cultural politics among French monarchs in exile, an essay collection on the legacy of the art historian Francis Haskell and an investigation of visual literacy and connoisseurship at the Louvre in the long nineteenth century. He has published several articles and reviews in *French History*, *French Historical Studies* and *The Journal of the History of Collections*, and is a regular contributor as reviewer and feature-writer to the arts journal *Apollo*.

Danielle van den Heuvel is a senior lecturer in early modern European history at the University of Kent. Her research has an interdisciplinary focus and centres around two main themes: the impact of institutions on groups in the margins of early modern society, and life in city streets before industrialisation. In this context she explores topics such as the informal economy, women's work, food markets and ambulant trading. She is the author of *Women and Entrepreneurship: Female Traders in the Northern Netherlands c.1580–1815* (Amsterdam, 2007) and several articles on food and retailing in *SIGNS*, *Continuity and Change*, *Explorations in Economic History* and *The Historical Journal*.

Series editor's preface

It is increasingly recognized that retail systems and changes in the patterns of consumption play crucial roles in the development and societal structure of economies. Such recognition has led to renewed interest in the changing nature of retail distribution and the rise of consumer society from a wide range of academic disciplines. The aim of this multidisciplinary series is to provide a forum of publications that explore the history of retailing and consumption.

Gareth Shaw, University of Exeter, UK

Acknowledgements

This edited volume originates from a conference held in Cambridge in 2010. The aim of the conference was to bring together scholars from different disciplinary backgrounds in order to discuss the sale of foodstuffs, fresh and prepared, on the streets in history and the present. The conference was made possible by generous support from the Economic History Society, the Trevelyan Fund of the Faculty of History of the University of Cambridge, and by financial and organisational support by the Centre of Research in the Arts, Social Sciences and Humanities of the University of Cambridge. We would like to thank Anna Malinowska from CRASSH, in particular, for the indispensable administrative support she provided. During the conference, as well as during the completion of this book, we greatly benefited from the comments and insights shared during the conference by its participants. There are a number of contributors we would like to thank individually. Jakob Klein, Jan Lucassen and Evelyn Welch played a pivotal and stimulating role as discussants in the shaping of our ideas on the role of food hawkers in history and contemporary society. We would also like to thank Gracia Clark, Philip Kelleway, Katie Scott and Psyche Williams-Forson for their contribution to the conference. Laurence Fontaine and Giorgio Riello provided us with some early and helpful comments at the World Economic History Congress in Utrecht in 2009. In turning the conference papers into a book, other people and institutions have been immensely helpful. Petra Barran of KERB provided an image of a twenty-first-century London food vendor and Ivan Day provided the beautiful photograph of three penny licks from his collection for our introduction. We would like to thank Stuart Palmer for creating the index. Our editor at Ashgate, Tom Gray, has been extraordinarily patient, and we would like to thank our copy editor, Rebecca Willford, at Routledge for her help in the final stages of the volume. Danielle would like to thank the British Academy and Girton College, Cambridge, for funding precious research time which enabled organising the conference and finishing this book.

Introduction

Food hawkers from representation to reality

Melissa Calaresu and Danielle van den Heuvel

Across the world, until very recently, most people living in cities bought their food in streets and markets. The history of those who sold this food and what was sold on the street, raw or ready-made, is almost entirely absent in historical writings. The history of food has focused almost exclusively on the serving and eating of food indoors and sitting down. Recipe books, menus, majolica plates, carving knives, and pastry cutters, almost entirely from elite contexts, have provided some of the evidence. The history of consumption has focused on the buying and selling from shops. Insurance records, bill heads, store fronts and interiors steer the historian into the shop rather than out on the street. Historical studies on markets have the tendency to focus either on the buildings in which the selling of food took place, or on just a few branches of food selling, mainly the provision of raw meat and fresh fish. The mobility of the food hawkers makes them particular difficult to track. In turn, the lack of material evidence means that there is almost nothing which survives of their activities.[1] For the early modern period, there are few traces in museum collections of the trestle tables, awnings which sometimes shaded them, pots and pans in which to fry things or keep things warm, or the containers (possibly made out of paper, pewter, or jute) in which food was weighed out or served.

Food hawkers, however, have been the subject of intense and sustained ethnographic interest from the early modern period until today and their representation in pamphlets, paintings, songs and photographs is an important source for historians, even if often bound to conventions of depicting the marginal, exotic and picturesque. In turn, the study of food hawkers in contemporary societies by anthropologists, psychologists and development economists can reveal the details of selling food on the street for a living which historians of earlier periods cannot detect or discern easily. The rhythms of life on the street are revealed by such studies – for example, the seasonality of foods sold, the temporality of their movements (and their customers') by day or by night, and the spatial politics of pitches. In turn, contemporary research on food hawking reveals the economic and social aspirations of food vendors in developing societies. This collaborative volume proposes to pull together the research strands and emphases of different disciplines focused on the present and the past in order to enliven and extend our understanding of selling food, fresh and prepared, on the street from antiquity to the present.

Food hawking in food history

There has been new and recent interest in food in historical writing on antiquity to the modern age. Historians of different backgrounds have shifted their attention to food as a factor of great importance in historical processes.[2] Economic historians are no longer focusing solely on food provision and distribution, but also on diets and calorific intake, and their impact on economic development.[3] Nevertheless, the vendors of foodstuffs play only a marginal role in the majority of their studies. Cultural histories of food including, most recently, a six-volume series, show the range of these interests and the ways through which food can tell us about, for example, social relations, political strategies and religious lives.[4] More traditional historians of food had focused on the preparation and serving of food, and their focus remains the kitchen and the table. Some of these new cultural histories have extended out their interests to 'eating out', as an alternative to the convention of 'eating in', and this has become part of an important historiography on what defines the modernity of modern life and sociability.[5]

Any study of 'eating out' first requires some knowledge of kitchens and the preparation of food in the home but domestic kitchens are notoriously difficult to reconstruct before the eighteenth century, and only exceptionally in elite contexts.[6] For example, kitchen utensils and tableware rarely appear in extant medieval inventories from England and the kitchen does not always appear as a designated place for food preparation in early modern English and French inventories.[7] Most households in European cities did not have fully functioning kitchens until later in the eighteenth century (although this chronology still depends on geography) and the majority of inhabitants in cities had limited ability to prepare hot food in their homes. Eating out for many, therefore, was a necessity, unless as one historian suggests, they were happy to subsist on a diet of cold food.[8]

Historians of eating out up to the end of the eighteenth century, like historians of kitchens for the same period, have traditionally had very little to go on, other than the evidence created by elite contexts, for example, guildhall feasts and princely banquets.[9] For non-elite contexts, historians have focused on those fixed places such as cookhouses, chop houses and taverns which generated various kinds of documents as well as visual and literary representations.[10] In studying representations, the food sometimes gets lost in the interpretation as historians get distracted by the symbolic resonance of these more 'popular' places, often as sites of crimes and misdemeanours; for example, the oyster becomes a sign of sexual lasciviousness in a Dutch tavern painting or the greasy sauces of French inns in British Grand Tour accounts become reflections of the oleaginousness of the natives. These representations, as we will see below, require caution when used as sources for food history but remain important to our understanding of 'eating out'. Nonetheless, historians of eating (and drinking) out have focused on those fixed places outside of the home which served hot food and drinks to a variety of publics. The drinking of coffee at tables in coffee houses, in turn, has been linked to new kinds of modern sociability before 'the invention of the modern restaurant' at the end of the eighteenth century, even if this interpretation has now been tempered by studies of taverns performing similar functions in early modern Europe.[11]

In historical accounts of eating out, buying food on the street most often appears as a last resort for the poorest of inhabitants of cities, serving the most basic of foodstuffs.[12] There is little consideration of the convenience of street food. We know that most urban households bought their food supplies from markets and street stalls, to be eaten or cooked at home, into the modern period and also that the street vendors sold a range of goods including what we might consider 'luxuries'. An engraved grid of hawkers on the streets of Rome from the early seventeenth century by Ambrogio Brambilla (Figure 0.1) shows that Romans could not only buy household goods such as fans and birdcages but essential cooking ingredients such as a dried biscuit and fortified wine for sauces (*mostacioli fini* and *mosto cotto*), ready-to-cook foodstuffs such as peeled chestnuts (*marroni fini*) and cleaned tripe (*tripa bianca*) as well as ready-to-eat foodstuffs such as cooked pears (*O pere cotte calde*).[13] In turn, coffee, which was once the drink of a discerning elite in late seventeenth-century London, was served on the street by ambulant vendors in eighteenth-century Paris (Figure 0.2).[14] It's clear that a variety of 'street luxuries' were available on the streets to serve poor and rich alike, even if as the nomenclature of the shop and dining room did not always transfer to the street; as Henry Mayhew notes, for mid-nineteenth-century London, 'The sweet-stuff maker was never called a confectioner'.[15]

Few historians have been able to take account of the kinds of customers that street hawkers might have served before the modern period. There is no doubt that the poorest inhabitants, from the ancient to the early modern periods, perhaps living at the very top of buildings and without a hearth in the largest cities, had only limited access to cooking facilities and were therefore obliged to buy hot prepared food from the street.[16] However, there has to be room to consider that some were buying food on the street for convenience, often during or after working hours. For modern historians of food as well as social scientists, this pattern is easily documented and acknowledged from the nineteenth century.[17] However, for the medieval period, for instance, historians can only suggest such a pattern. Martha Carlin has argued that cookshops are not simple indicators of poverty in medieval English cities. Instead, she believes that the high number of cookshops in some larger English cities is correlated to a high density of single-adult households; cookshops, open

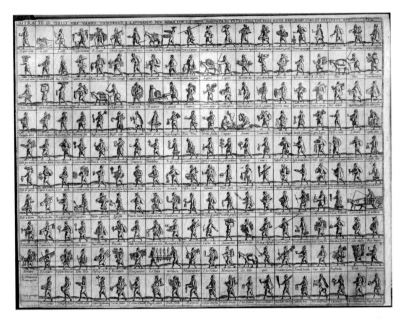

Figure 0.1 Ambrogio Brambilla, *Ritrato de quelli che vano vendendo et lavorando per Roma con la nova agionta de tutti quelli che nelle altre mancavano sin al presente* (Rome, 1612). Pepys Library, Magdalene College, Cambridge.

Figure 0.2 David Allan, 'Pont Neuf, Paris', from *A Collection of Dresses by Da. Allan Mostly from Nature, 1776*, Aberdeen Art Gallery & Museums Collections.

Figure 0.3 Female pancake seller, Gillis van Scheyndel, 1630–1706, engraving. Rijksmuseum Amsterdam.

day and night, were patronised by working men, often serving them hot food after the end of the working day at night.[18] Therefore, the assumption that urban poor were and are fed primarily by street food masks the variety of goods available for sale on the street and the social status of the customers who bought them and this needs to be challenged. In turn, this assumption also leaves little room for the pleasure of eating out on the streets or a consideration of differences in climate between, for example, northern and southern Europe. Recent research shows that the inhabitants of Naples from all social groups in the eighteenth century enjoyed eating ice cream on the street in the heat of the summer, just as inhabitants of Barcelona and Madrid clamoured for iced drinks from street vendors in the same period.[19] In fact, the street sellers of sweets, watermelon slices, and ice creams alongside puppeteers and story sellers all appeared in the same urban spaces connected to plebeian entertainment in European cities into the modern period. Although more difficult to discern, the pleasure as well as the convenience of shopping for and eating food on the streets by the greater population should be included in any historical consideration of food-hawking.

Evidence of the preparation, selling and serving food on the street in historical contexts, however, is sparse, if one compares it to what survives for the serving and eating of food sitting down at a table, for example, in a sixteenth-century Italian palace. Much, of course, can be learned from visual and literary evidence from the past such as this sketch of a Dutch pancake seller (Figure 0.3).[20] There are, however, no 'street' equivalents of the large and elaborate majolica *rinfrescatoio*, for keeping bottles cool beside the banqueting table, with scenes from Greek mythology on its sides and which has survived in the Fitzwilliam Museum collection, or of the printed manual, *Il Trinciante*, by Vincenzo Cervio of 1581, with precise details for the carving and serving of meat in front of banquet guests.[21] Until very recently, there were no recipe books of street food, no manuals about the preparation of food on the street, and very few of the utensils to prepare and serve the food which survive. How, for instance, did street vendors keep their lemonade cold or their coffee hot and how was it sold to customers?[22] Were the containers in which they sold food and drink on the street disposable or washed after every use? Images from up to the nineteenth century help us to know more about the equipment which was used to serve food on the street, even if the material culture does not survive with a few exceptions. Modern collectors of penny licks, in which ice cream was served on the street in nineteenth-century London, have ensured their survival in museum collections (Figure 0.4). Extraordinarily, in the middle of the nineteenth century, Henry Mayhew, driven by ethnographic as well as commercial interests, carefully recorded the process by which some of the food was made and the equipment owned by street vendors – the number of knives owned by the street butcher, the cloths of the cheese-seller, and the urns of the coffee-man, even if little of what he recorded survives in museum collections.[23] One wonders whether modern museums of advertising have also collected the disposable containers in which take-away food has been served in the twentieth century.[24] Of course, the sparseness of the evidence for eating out reflects its convenience, and therefore street food and the practices around its preparation have to be recovered in other ways by food historians. Literary and visual representations of food-hawking remain the most important source for this recovery, even if the interest of those who depicted street selling, until recently, were driven less by an interest in food than by an interest in people.

Representation of selling food on the street and the problem of the 'picturesque'

The history of selling food on the street is necessarily linked to the history of its representation. The tradition of representing 'street-cries' from the fifteenth century in Europe is a rich as well as a complex source for the historian of food-hawking and it is here where one often begins.[25] The complexity of such representations derives from contrasting desires to

Figure 0.4 Glass penny licks, nineteenth century, English, Ivan Day Collection. Photo
© Ivan Day.

record the variety of selling on the street against the power of what later
is called the 'picturesque', that is, the tradition of depicting street sellers
as poor, marginal, exotic, even deformed or deranged.[26] It was precisely in
the eighteenth century that this tradition reached its peak and wider public
with the engravings of street-cries in London and Paris, a tradition which
was extended and mutated into the nineteenth century.[27] Even the work of
Henry Mayhew on the London poor, despite its rhetoric of accuracy and
his use of statistics and questionnaires, cannot pull itself away entirely from
this tradition and inspired a number of Victorian writers including Charles
Dickens.[28] As we shall see, the problem of the 'picturesque' does not go away
in the modern period, even in contemporary essays and books on street
food and street markets.

   Travel, a desire for the authentic, and nostalgia have all been driving forces
behind an interest in the representation of street food and markets in the past
and today. An expanding world and the ethnographic interests of Europeans
from the late sixteenth century spawned an interest in depicting different peoples from across the globe as well as a variety of types closer to home, including those who worked on the streets. The public for travel accounts expanded
through the early modern period, and, in turn, travel continued to generate
images of street sellers, especially as emblems of an authentic popular culture.[29] By the early nineteenth century, visitors to Paris, Milan, Naples and
New York could not only buy engravings of street sellers from these cities
but the same images were printed on fans, plates and handkerchiefs as well.[30]
The weekly readers of Mayhew's articles from 1851, later published in four

volumes, as *London Labour and the London Poor*, were also interested in the authentic voices of those living in their own city and Mayhew believed that he could get them even closer to the street. As Mayhew writes, his 'street biographies' of life in nineteenth-century London 'come from the lips of the people themselves'.[31]

By the end of the nineteenth century, there was a growing public for literary accounts about life on the street in growing metropolises including direct social criticism such as Matilda Serrao's *Il ventre di Napoli* [*The Underbelly of Naples*] (1884). Later writers used this material more darkly to critique urban poverty, homelessness and criminality in the first half of the twentieth century, such as George Orwell in *Down and Out in London and Paris* (1933). A few years later, the first book solely devoted to street markets in London was published. Described as a 'photographic report', *The Street Markets of London* (1936) by Mary Benedetta, with photographs by Laszlo Moholy-Nagy, was meant to be 'a truthful record of objectively determined fact'. In a foreword, Moholy-Nagy writes: 'To many peoples' minds the street market still suggests romantic notions of showmen, unorganised trade, bargains and the sale of stolen goods.'[32] Despite his protestations, this photo-reportage shows the longevity and endurance of the picturesque when representing street sellers into the twentieth century, for example, in Benedetta's description of a fight which breaks out between two women or his photograph of an 'Oriental Perfume Seller'.[33] Here, however, the book is organised by specific markets across the city rather than by individual characters such as Madeleine or by certain products such as in Mayhew. In fact, the emphasis on place in Benedetta's book is not without reason; it was one of the first guidebooks to urban markets in London and it ends with directions to specific markets including suggestions for public transportation.[34]

Street markets have since become important travel destinations in Europe and abroad, and the search for authenticity continues in travel guidebooks into the twenty-first century. For example, the Shire guide to London markets in 1987 has less of an emphasis on the literary and the personal in the descriptions of the street sellers, but the photographs which accompany the text continues this earlier tradition of street 'characters'.[35] The most recent guide to London markets, published by Cadogan, plays precisely on the idea of the authentic, for example, assuring prospective visitors to a certain section of Portobello market that some stallholders have been trading for years and that 'despite the large number of tourists ... locals make good use of the food stalls'.[36] There are also explicit references throughout the guide to the pleasure of buying and eating food on the streets, especially in comparison to shopping at a supermarket.[37] In fact, the introduction to the Cadogan guide also includes a section on 'save our markets' – political in its criticism of out-of-town superstores and its call for responsible consumer practices, hopeful in the power of farmers' markets, in particular, as a means for urban regeneration, and nostalgic for 'genuine' street culture lost to the gentrification and touristification of street markets.[38] The power of the picturesque, however, is not entirely dissipated and nor can we underestimate the extent to which food hawkers themselves participate, and participated, in its construction for the tourist industry; one Mexican taco seller confessed that he had deliberately misspelled his signs to attract business from tourists.[39] Street markets, in London and elsewhere, continue to be tourist destinations. Tourists continue to search for the authentic, although modern travellers seem to be more interested in the food than the food sellers. Modern tourism has, in fact, produced a number of books with street food as their focus and which function as both travelogue and recipe book. Despite the mobility of food vendors and the ephemerality of street food, these books have documented the preparation and service of food on the street today in incredible detail.[40]

Some recent accounts of street food do, however, also indulge in a kind of nostalgia for a simpler life, evoked by the memory of the ice cream cone or hot dog eaten as a child. As one food writer reveals: 'Anyone who knows street food as a child can recall the promise of pleasure that certain foods evoke. Street foods tap into our nostalgia for the past, simpler times, for holidays and fairs.'[41] This nostalgia has found its way into a number of recent books with descriptions of hot dogs eaten during baseball games or late nights out ending with a kebab. These books attempt to record late twentieth-century urban life but they are also critical of the globalised food service economy. As the 'cultural critic' (and founder of the Pret A Manger sandwich chain), Kevin Jackson, writes in his book, with photographs, *Fast: Feasting on the Streets of London*: 'The point is not to produce another diatribe against fast food, but to winkle out something of what it all looks and feels and, yes, smells and tastes like to eat on the "hoof"'.[42] In a section on the fast-food restaurant, McDonalds (entitled, 'The Scottish restaurant: The devil and all his works'), the author tries to reclaim and recover, in contrast, the authentic 'fast' food experience.[43] Street food has seen a revival in the last decade with new food markets in London and elsewhere and these books reflect this revival (Figure 0.5).[44] A recent book (again with photographs) heralds the arrival of the 'street food revolution' and proclaims the food vendors as 'new food heroes'.[45] While food is the focus of many of these books, with photographs depicting individual dishes, the vendors and their stories are also of interest. In this way, there is an extraordinary continuity between those early images of street vendors as the 'Cries' of European cities and the most recent travel accounts, photographic essays and recipe books on street food.

The social and economic implications of street food selling

When we turn from the way street vendors and their foods are 'consumed' by different audiences to the issue of the identity of food sellers, the trope of the picturesque is firmly replaced by that of marginality. Interestingly, we find this reflected in the work by social scientists and historians alike. As we have seen, historians of food have paid relatively little attention to the selling of foodstuffs in the street. Similarly, historians of markets tend to focus on

Figure 0.5 Yum Bun Traders, part of London's KERB street trader collective. Photo
© Andrew Corbett (2013).

the architecture of market halls, the social and geographical place of markets
within urban space, and the more general role of markets in distribution systems.[46] The individuals selling food in these markets are largely overlooked in
such works.[47] This is different, however, for historians of women, and especially historians of women's work. Alice Clark, one of the pioneers in the history of women's work, in her 1919 work on working women, pointed to the
variety of roles women played in food selling during the pre-industrial period.
As the provision of food and drink was traditionally associated with women's
domestic role, she suggests that trades such as baking and brewing were long
seen as a 'natural' domain for women. At the same time, Clark observes that
in many food trades, including baking but also butchering, women mostly
worked as assistants to their husbands, and when they were involved in a
trade independently, such as the fish trade, they were mostly active in the less
profitable segments. Indeed, she claims, most low-capital food ventures, such
as regrating (the buying up and re-selling of small quantities of foodstuffs)
and hawking, have been dominated by women since the Middle Ages.[48]

Almost a century has passed since Clark wrote on the market trades and
the role of women in them, but her main findings are widely replicated in
more recent historical studies covering pre-industrial Europe. Many of these

studies stress not only the numerical dominance of women in food markets, but also their relatively weak position in terms of income, independence and lack of a 'formal career', as well as their disputable reputation.[49] For instance, it has been suggested that women in the fish trades of both late medieval Cologne and the Dutch town of Den Bosch owed their rights to trade to family status rather than to their own merit.[50] Poverty is also highlighted in these studies: the pudding wives of early modern Salisbury were found to be of very limited means, as were the Leiden food hawkers of the fifteenth and sixteenth centuries.[51] Finally, female hucksters and regraters in fourteenth-century Exeter suffered from a reputation more dubious than their male counterparts, one similar to the character of the proverbial fishwives of seventeenth-century Holland.[52] Interestingly, a recent study on early modern Edo (present-day Tokyo) confirms this relationship for a major city outside the Western hemisphere.[53] In many cases, these findings come with negative connotations, and as such profoundly differ from the more 'romantic' associations with marginality as seen so often in the representation of food vendors. Their origination, in a context in which feminist scholarship aimed to explain the weak position of women in the economy of the West in the twentieth century and debated whether women's economic role prior to the process of industrialisation had known a 'Golden Age', probably explains the rather different appreciation of 'marginality'.

Strikingly, social scientists reported similar findings on food vendors for contemporary developing economies. Since the 1960s and 1970s they have studied food markets in Africa, Asia and Latin America. Those who operated in these markets are mostly seen as 'marginal' groups, and included poor urban women and newly-arrived rural migrants, often working in what is generally seen as part-time and low-revenue work, while suffering from harassment and a lack of legal protection. In this discourse these jobs are generally referred to as 'casual jobs', thereby implicitly stressing the unprofessional character of these trades, and as such resonating ideas also present in much of the earlier historical work on this topic.[54] Similarly, many social scientists, like the historians discussed above, also initially believed that processes of modernisation were influential in shaping the size and the character of street trading. However, rather than seeing modernisation as a factor that ultimately led to the decline of women's economic independence, as several historians did, the early studies on street selling in developing economies suggested that modernisation, while initially having a deteriorating effect, would in the end result in the betterment of the position of food sellers.

Despite their differences in how processes of modernisation affected food vendors, historians and social scientists did agree on what was the crucial factor in determining who worked as street food vendors and what position they had in the trade: regulation and, in particular, how regulation of the food trades impacted on access to the sector.[55] Whereas historians mostly pointed to the role of craft guilds, which ruled much of the European urban economy before 1800, social scientists identified state legislation and the role of taxation and licensing as culprits for the marginal position in which many street food vendors found themselves.[56] In the same way as the (increasing) exclusivity of craft guilds hampered women to set up a food stall independently in a permanent market in pre-industrial Europe, the increasingly complicated web of regulation, and the cost involved in buying 'legality' through a licence and paying taxes, meant that twentieth-century street vendors in Africa, Asia and Latin America also had great difficulties entering the 'formal' street food sector. The result was, as we have seen above, a mixture of poverty and marginality in which women featured more heavily than men.

More recently scholars and policymakers have started to question the idea that the excessive regulation of market trades, and its main consequence, for example, that large groups of vendors operating unregulated, or informally, is necessarily a negative one. Evidence from both historical and contemporary economies shows that the difference between regulated and unregulated sales activities, or formal and informal worlds, is not always as black and white as it was long thought to be.[57] They also question whether it is possible to formalise all unregulated activities and stress that with regulation should come social protection for the vendors.[58]

At the same time we should not assume that rents, permits, taxes, harassment and policing do not negatively impact on the vendors' livelihood, both in the distant past and the present, nor that this is a problem particular to 'pre-industrial' societies. Newspapers very regularly report on conflicts between local authorities and stall holders regarding rents and licensing, for instance in the case of suddenly rising rents at various farmers' markets in East London and Essex in 2012.[59] More prominent still is the harrowing story of the Tunisian vegetable seller Mohammed Bouazizi, the face of the Arab Spring, whose sufferings became world news after he set himself alight as a result of constant harassment and humiliation by government officials, confiscations of his merchandise and sales gear, resulting in insurmountable debts.[60] While these stories continue to point to the precarious situation in which many food vendors find themselves in developed and developing economies, as several chapters in this volume show, there is more to street food vendors than their poverty and marginality.

Without neglecting or downplaying the financial struggles of food vendors, more recent studies point not only to the great variety among street vendors, but also to their work as being more than simply a survival strategy.[61] Scholars increasingly acknowledge that the type of foodstuffs sold (fresh or prepared, exotic or indigenous) greatly mattered for food vendors, not only in terms of earning potential, but also in terms of access to a particular trade and its esteem.[62] Similarly, in-depth studies of past and present food markets reveal complex labour relations in which sellers may be active as self-employed vendors, or as entrepreneurs employing wage workers to do the selling for them, either from a stall, or as hawkers in the street. Such findings highlight the complexity of food vending and the different situations in which vendors may find themselves. The recent surge in street food enterprises in the United Kingdom, as mentioned above, is a poignant example. While some vendors may have entered into food selling after having lost a more conventional job during the 2008 economic crisis, others ended up as street food vendors as a way to obtain a more fulfilling lifestyle.[63] Equally, while many seem keen to move up and transform their businesses into restaurants, some are content with keeping it small and flexible.[64]

We still have a long way to go to fully understand the workings of food markets in the past and present. The variation in how food markets operate seems to be caused by a complex web of economic, social and cultural factors such as gender roles, concepts of space, and perceptions of what makes for a satisfying life. However, in the quest for a better understanding of the sale of food in the streets a dialogue between scholars from the humanities and the social sciences, as presented in this volume, may indeed be particularly fruitful. The configuration of market spaces (both in the actual and perceived qualities of such spaces) seems to greatly influence the character of the food trades and the people involved in historical and contemporary contexts, albeit in different ways.[65] Moreover, where historians may be unable to unearth direct evidence on the sellers' perceptions of their work, social scientists can glean their motives and ideas about the food trades through interviewing sellers. Interestingly, the insights obtained through interviews point to a sense of self-worth, agency and empowerment that would probably not have been revealed had we looked at their economic profiles alone.[66] Historians, on the other hand, may be able to shed more light on phenomena observed by scholars of contemporary societies, such as the implications of the move to more formalised spaces of food selling in the form of food halls, which shows a remarkable overlap with the building of market halls in Europe and North America from the eighteenth century onwards.[67] We hope that this volume offers stimulating new directions for further inter- and intra-disciplinary research into the sale of foodstuffs on streets across the globe.

Notes

1 On the difficulty of capturing the history of street life more generally, see Fabrizio Nevola, 'Street life in early modern Europe', *Renaissance Quarterly* 66 (2013), pp. 1332–1345.
2 The 2013 theme of the 82nd Anglo-American Conference of historians was food in history, reflecting its growing importance in current scholarship.
3 See E.A. Wrigley, *Continuity, Chance and Change: The Character of the Industrial Revolution in England* (Cambridge, 1988); Robert Fogel, *The Escape from Hunger and Premature Death, 1700–2100: Europe, America, and the Third World* (Cambridge, 2004); Craig Muldrew, *Food, Energy, and the Creation of Industriousness: Work and Material Culture in Agrarian England 1550–1780* (Cambridge, 2011).
4 See the six-volume Cultural History of Food series, edited by Fabio Parasecoli and Peter Scholliers and published by Berg (London/New York, 2012).
5 See the ground-breaking study by Rebecca Spang, *The Invention of the Restaurant: Paris and Modern Gastronomic Culture* (Cambridge, MA, 2000), Rachel Rich, *Bourgeois Consumption: Food, Space and Identity in London and Paris, 1850–1914* (Manchester, 2011), and also Beat Kümin, 'Eating out before the

restaurant: Dining cultures in early modern times', in M. Jacobs and P. Scholliers (eds), *Eating Out in Europe: Picnics, Gourmet Dining and Snacks since the Late Eighteenth Century* (Oxford, 2003), pp. 71–87, who argues here and elsewhere for commercialised sociable eating before the industrial period (see also his chapter on eating out in Beat Kümin (ed.), *A Cultural History of Food in the Early Modern Age* (London, 2012). The Berg series includes a section on 'Eating Out' in each of its six volumes.

6   Deborah L. Krohn, 'Picturing the kitchen: Renaissance treatise and period room', *Studies in the Decorative Arts* 16/1 (2008–2009), pp. 20–34, and Deborah L. Krohn, *Food and Knowledge in Renaissance Italy: Bartolomeo Scappi's Paper Kitchens* (Farnham, 2015).

7   See Martha Carlin, 'Fast food and urban living standards in medieval England', in Martha Carlin and Joel T. Rosenthal (eds), *Food and Eating in Medieval Europe* (London, 1998), pp. 42–43, and Sara Pennell, 'Family and domesticity: Cooking, eating, and making homes', in Beat Kümin (ed.), *A Cultural History of Food in the Early Modern Age* (London, 2012), p. 131.

8   Raffaella Sarti, *Europe at Home: Family and Material Culture 1500–1800*, trans. Allan Cameron (New Haven/London, 2002), p. 163.

9   See, for example, Paul Freedman, 'Eating out', in Ken Albala (ed.), *A Cultural History of Food in the Renaissance* (London/New York, 2012), pp. 103–109.

10   See, for example, the excellent chapters on the sixteenth and seventeenth centuries by Hazel Forsyth and on the eighteenth century by Edwina Ehrman in the catalogue accompanying the 1999 Museum of London exhibition: *London Eats Out: 500 Years of Capital Dining* (London, 1999), pp. 13–65.

11   See Brian Cowan, *The Social Life of Coffee: The Emergence of the British Coffeehouse* (New Haven/London, 2005), Emma Spary, *Eating the Enlightenment: Food and the Sciences in Paris* (Chicago, 2012), and Beat Kümin, *Drinking Matters: Public Houses and Social Exchange in Early Modern Central Europe* (London, 2007).

12   For an important exception, see Hazel Forsyth, 'Street food – gingerbread, sugar-loaves and mechanical vending machines', in *London Eats Out*, pp. 28–29. See also Sara Pennell, '"Great quantities of gooseberry pie and baked clod of beef": Victualling and eating out in early modern London', in P. Griffiths and M.S.R. Jenner (eds), *Londinopolis: Essays in the Cultural and Social History of Early Modern London* (Manchester, 2000), pp. 228–249.

13   For an interactive version of the Brambilla image, see my translation of the grid as part of the 'Treasured Possessions from the Renaissance to the Enlightenment' exhibition at the Fitzwilliam Museum (24 March to 6 September 2015): www.fitzmuseum.cam.ac.uk/gallery/treasuredpossessions/discover/streetcries.html.   On the availability of 'luxury' household goods in seventeenth-century Rome, see Renata Ago, *Gusto for Things: A History of Objects in Seventeenth-Century Rome* (Chicago, 2013). On 'street luxuries' and for a further discussion of the Brambilla image, see Melissa Calaresu, 'Street "luxuries": Food hawking in early modern Rome', in Ivan Gaskell and Sarah Anne Carter (eds), *The Oxford Handbook of History and Material Culture* (Oxford, forthcoming).

14   On plebeian coffee consumption on the streets of Naples, see Melissa Calaresu, 'Making and eating ice cream in Naples: Rethinking consumption and sociability in the eighteenth century', *Past and Present* 220/1 (2013), pp. 35–78, at pp. 74–76.

15   Mayhew notes that street sellers of comestibles were often called by the name of the product that they sold, recording, 'he's a sweet-stuff', and '*You* can go in, Fishy' (Henry Mayhew, *London Labour and the London Poor* (Oxford, 2012), p. 51 and p. 54). For a description of 'Mush' who sold mushrooms in Lewisham Market in the 1930s, see Mary Benedetta, *The street markets of London* (London, 1936), p. 70. A similar tradition existed in nineteenth-century Greece (Antonia-Leda Matalas

and Mary Yannakoulia, 'Greek street food vending: An old habit turned new', in A.P. Simopolous and R.V. Bhat (eds), *Street Foods*, vol. 86 of *World Review of Nutrition and Dietetics* (Basel, 2000), p. 5). Mayhew's descriptions of London street life were first published as weekly instalments from 1851 and were then collected in four volumes in 1861. The first volume includes 'Street-sellers of Eatables and Drinkables'.

16 See Chapter 1 in this volume.

17 See Peter Scholliers, 'Eating out', in Martin Bruegel (ed.), *A Cultural History of Food in the Age of Empire* (London/New York, 2012), pp. 108–114; Irene Tinker, 'Street foods into the 21st century', *Food and Human Values* 16/3 (1999), pp. 327–333. This is also confirmed in the chapters in this volume on street vending in contemporary Vietnam, India, and Malaysia (Chapters 7, 8 and 9).

18 Carlin, 'Fast food and urban living standards in medieval England', pp. 49–51. See also Alban Gautier, 'Eating out in the early and high Middle Ages', in Massimo Montanari (ed.), *A Cultural History of Food in the Medieval Age* (London/ New York, 2012), pp. 91–106.

19 Melissa Calaresu, 'Making and eating ice cream in eighteenth-century Naples: Rethinking consumption and sociability in the eighteenth century', *Past and Present* 220/1 (2013), pp. 35–78.

20 See, in particular, Chapters 2, 3 and 5 in this volume.

21 The trilobite maiolica cistern with the Triumph of Galatea or Amphitrite, c.1550–70, in the Fitzwilliam Museum, Cambridge, is described and illustrated in Julia E. Poole, *Italian Maiolica* (Cambridge, 1997), pp. 74–75. On Cervio's book, see Freedman, 'Eating out', pp. 105–106. See also Allen J. Grieco on 'Meals', in Marta Ajmar-Wolheim and Flora Dennis, *At Home in Renaissance Italy* (London, 2006), pp. 244–253.

22 Sara Pennell, 'Four hundred years of keeping food hot', in Philippa Glanville and Hilary Young (eds), *Elegant Eating: Four Hundred Years of Dining in Style* (London, 2002), pp. 68–71.

23 These statistics were collected and published in Henry Mayhew's *London Labour and the London Poor* (4 vols, London, 1861–1862).

24 There is no discussion of the material culture of the preparation and serving of the hot dog, although there are photographs of mobile hot dog stands, in Bruce Kraig and Patty Carroll, *Hot Dog Cultures in America: Man Bites Dog* (Plymouth, 2012).

25 See Chapter 1 in this volume.

26 Melissa Calaresu, 'From the street to stereotype: Urban space, travel and the picturesque in late eighteenth-century Naples', *Italian Studies* 62/2 (2007), pp. 189–203.

27 See Chapter 6 in this volume, as well as Vincent Milliot, *Les 'Cris de Paris', ou, Le peuple travesti: Les représentations des petits métiers parisiens (XVIe–XVIIIe siècles)* (Paris, 1995) and Sean Shesgreen, *Images of the Outcast: The Urban Poor in the Cries of London* (Manchester, 2002).

28 See the introduction by Robert Douglas-Fairhurst of Mayhew, *London Labour and the London Poor*, p. xxxviii.

29 Melissa Calaresu, 'Costumes and customs in print: Travel, ethnography, and the representation of street-sellers in early modern Italy', in Jeroen Salman, Roeland Harms and Joad Raymond (eds), *'Not dead things': The Dissemination of Popular Print in England and Wales, Italy, and the Low Countries, 1500–1820* (Leiden/ Boston, 2013), pp. 181–212.

30 On Naples, see Melissa Calaresu, 'Collecting Neapolitans: The representation of street life in late eighteenth-century Naples', in Melissa Calaresu and Helen Hills (eds), *New Approaches to Naples c.1500–c.1800: The Power of Place* (Farnham, 2013), pp. 175–202.

31 Mayhew, *London Labour and the London Poor*, p. 3.
32 Laszlo Moholy-Nagy in Benedetta, *Street Markets of London*, p. vii. On its value as entertainment, see also the review of the book by G. Elliott Anstruther in the *Catholic Herald*, 9 October 1936, p. 4.
33 Benedetta, and Moholy-Nagy *Street Markets of London*, p. 64 and facing p. 82.
34 Benedetta, *Street Markets of London*, pp. 185–195.
35 Debra Shipley and Mary Peplow, *London Street Markets* (Aylesbury, 1987).
36 Phil Harriss, *London Markets* (1st edn 1996, London, 2002), p. 60.
37 Harriss, *London Markets*, p. 60.
38 Harriss, *London Markets*, pp. 13–18. The author includes a reference to Mayhew, comparing the few traders on Lambeth Walk today to the 104 in Mayhew's day (p. 13). A recent analysis of farmers' markets in America lauds their humanising and bonding effects on small towns, creating 'real community' (Helena Norberg-Hodge, Todd Merrifield and Steven Gorelick, *Bringing the Food Economy Home: Local Alternatives to Global Agribusiness* (London, 2002), pp. 80–81). See also: I. Techoueyres, 'Food markets in the city of Bordeaux', in P.J. Atkins, P. Lummel and D.J. Oddy (eds), *Food and the City in Europe since 1800* (Aldershot, 2007), pp. 239–250; Robert Doisneau, *Paris Les Halles Market*, edited by Vladimir Vasak (Paris, 2011).
39 Miriam Muñoz de Chávez, Adolfo Chávez Vilasana and Igor E. Vuskovic, 'Sale of street food in Latin America', in Simopolous and Bhat, *Street Foods*, p. 149.
40 See, for example, the Lonely Planet Guide, *The World's Best Street Food: Where to Find It & How to Make It* (Melbourne/London, 2012). See also the book of photographs by food and travel photographer, Jean-François Mallet, *Take Away* (San Francisco, 2009), and Hande Bozdogan, *Street Foods of Turkey*, with photographs by Ahmet Tozar (Singapore, 2011).
41 Rose Grant, *Street Food* (Impact, 1989), p. 1.
42 Kevin Jackson, *Fast: Feasting on the Streets of London* with photographs by Richard Heeps (London, 2006), blurb on the back cover.
43 Jackson, *Fast*, pp. 104–105. For similar sentiments, see also the introduction to Kraig and Carroll, *Hot Dog Cultures in America*.
44 See, for instance, the London initiatives KERB (www.kerbfood.com/) and Street Feast (www.streetfeastlondon.com/). Street food has even moved into restaurants with many establishments advertising proudly that they serve or even specialise in street foods including Mexican tacos and Vietnamese noodle soups (for the latter, see Chapter 7 in this volume).
45 Richard Johnson, *Street Food Revolution: Recipes and Stories from the New Food Heroes* (London, 2011), with photographs by Laura Edwards.
46 See, for example, Luisa Barosso, Maria Ida Cametti, Maurizio Lucat, Silvia Mantovani and Luciano Re, *Mercati coperti a Torino: Progetti, realizzazioni e tecnologie ottocentesche* (Turin, 2000); James Schmiechen and Kenneth Carls, *The British Market Hall: A Social and Architectural History* (New Haven, 1999); Donatella Calabi, *The Market and the City: Square, Street and Architecture in Early Modern Europe* (Aldershot, 2002); Isabel Obiols and Pere Ferrer, *The Boqueria Market: The Most Typical Market of Catalonia* (Barcelona, 2004); Manuel Guàrdia and José Luis Oyón (eds), *Fer ciutat a través dels mercats. Europa, segles XIX i XX* (Barcelona, 2010); Roger Scola, *Feeding the Victorian City: The Food Supply of Manchester, 1770–1870* (Manchester, 1992); Ian Mitchell, *Tradition and Innovation in English Retailing, 1700–1850: Narratives of Consumption* (Farnham, 2014).
47 An exception is Helen Tangires, *Public Markets* (New York, 2008) which includes a full chapter on street vendors. This work, however, mainly comprises photographs.
48 Alice Clark, *Working Life of Women in the Seventeenth Century* (London, 1992), pp. 207–221.

49 Sue Wright, 'Churmaids, huswyfes and hucksters: The employment of women in Tudor and Stuart Salisbury', in Lindsey Charles and Lorna Duffin (eds), *Women and Work in Pre-Industrial England* (London, 1985), pp. 100–121; M. Howell, *Women, Production and Patriarchy in Late Medieval Cities* (Chicago, 1986); Maryanne Kowaleski, 'Women's work in a market town: Exeter in the late fourteenth century', in Barbara Hanawalt (ed.), *Women and Work in Pre-Industrial Europe* (Bloomington, 1986), pp. 148–149.

50 Howell, *Women*; Jenneke Quast, 'Vrouwenarbeid omstreeks 1500 in enkele Nederlandse steden', *Jaarboek voor vrouwengeschiedenis* 1 (1980), pp. 46–64.

51 Wright, 'Churmaids, huswyfes and hucksters'; Howell, *Women*.

52 Kowaleski, 'Women's work'; Rudolf M. Dekker, 'Women in revolt: Popular protest and its social basis in Holland in the seventeenth and eighteenth centuries', *Theory and Society* 16 (1987), pp. 337–362.

53 S. Kobayashi and M. Sugiura, 'Street sellers and street markets of early modern Edo', unpublished paper presented at World Economic History Congress, Utrecht, 2009; Miki Sugiura and Shinya Kobayashi, 'Street sellers and second-hand clothing dealers: Comparative study on the marginality in urban retail trade in early modern Edo and Amsterdam', in A. Tamura, T. Kawana and H. Uchida (eds), *Marginality, Nation and Modernity Reconsidered* (forthcoming 2015).

54 See Keith Hart, 'Informal income opportunities and urban employment in Ghana', *Journal of Modern African Studies* 11/1 (1973), pp. 61–89.

55 Interestingly, while increased control and regulation is widely discussed in works that describe the rise of market halls in nineteenth-century Europe and America, in such works there is little discussion of how this affected the access to the food traders for different types of vendors. See Jon Stobart, *Spend, Spend, Spend: A History of Shopping* (Stroud, 2008), pp. 118–124 and the works mentioned in footnote 46 above.

56 The most prominent work on this topic is Hernando de Soto, *The Other Path: The Invisible Revolution in the Third World* (New York, 1989).

57 See, for instance, the contributions by Guha-Kashnobis, Kanbur and Ostrom, Hart, and Chen, in Basudeb Guha-Khasnobis, Ravi Kanbur and Elinor Ostrom (eds), *Linking the Formal and Informal Economy: Concepts and Policies* (Oxford, 2006), pp. 75–92. See also G. Brunelle, 'Policing the monopolizing women of early modern Nantes', *Journal of Women's History* 2 (2007), pp. 10–35; A. Montenach, 'Formal and informal economy in an urban context', in Thomas Buchner and Philip R. Hoffmann-Rehnitz, *Shadow Economies and Irregular Work in Urban Europe, 16th to 20th Centuries* (Vienna, 2011), pp. 91–106.

58 Martha Alter Chen, 'Rethinking the informal economy: linkages with the formal economy and the formal regulatory environment', in Guha-Khasnobis *et al.*, *Linking the Formal and Informal Economy*, pp. 75–92; Sally Roever, 'Formalizing street vendors: Presentation at dialogue on formalization of the informal', October 2013: http://wiego.org/resources/formalizing-street-vendors-presentation-dialogue-formalization-informal. Accessed 10 April 2016.

59 *East London and West Essex Guardian*, 23 July 2012.

60 'Tunisia suicide protester Mohammed Bouazizi dies', BBC News website, 5 January 2011: www.bbc.co.uk/news/world-africa-12120228. Accessed 10 April 2016.

61 Including Chapters 4, 7 and 9 in this volume.

62 Irene Tinker, *Street Foods: Urban Food and Employment in Developing Countries* (Oxford, 1997); Danielle van den Heuvel, 'Partners in marriage and in business? Guilds and the family economy in the urban food markets in the Dutch Republic', *Continuity and Change* 23/2 (2008), pp. 217–236.

63 See for example Tim Lewis, 'Breadwinners to breadmakers', *Observer*, 22 April 2012: www.theguardian.com/lifeandstyle/2012/apr/22/baking-e5-bakehouse-bread. Accessed 10 April 2016.

64 See Victoria Stewart, 'From street to seat: The food vans moving into restaurants', *Evening Standard*, 20 September 2013: www.standard.co.uk/goingout/restaurants/from-street-to-seat-the-food-vans-moving-into-restaurants-8828990.html. Accessed 10 April 2016.

65 See Chapters 4 and 9 in this volume.

66 See Chapter 7 in this volume.

67 For previous successful attempts at comparing trends in historical and contemporary street vending see Laurence Fontaine (ed.), *Second-Hand Circulations from the Sixteenth Century to the Present* (Oxford, 2008) and Danielle van den Heuvel, 'Selling in the shadows: Peddlers and hawkers in early modern Europe', in Marcel van der Linden and Leo Lucassen (eds), *Working on Labor: Essays in Honour of Jan Lucassen* (Leiden/Boston, 2012), pp. 125–151.

1 Representations of food hawkers in ancient Rome

Claire Holleran

With perhaps as many as a million inhabitants at its height (c.100 BC–AD 200), ancient Rome was the largest pre-industrial city in the Western world.[1] Feeding this considerable population was a mammoth task and a complex distribution network developed in order to ensure a regular supply of food in the city; food hawkers were a central component of this distribution network and no doubt a common sight on the streets of the city. Yet street trade is by its very nature ephemeral, and given the organic nature of the goods sold, food hawking in particular would leave little trace in the archaeological record. Compared to some of the cities considered in this volume then, the evidence for food hawking in ancient Rome is partial and somewhat sketchy. Nevertheless, the presence of hawkers in the city can be inferred from a variety of surviving material, including literary and legal sources, together with artistic representations of food vendors. As is so often the case, however, this ancient material is far from documentary evidence of the past. Ancient literature and art present images or representations of hawkers that are constructed according to the context, genre, and intended audience of the material in question.

This chapter begins by placing the evidence for food hawking in Rome into the wider context of the urban economy. This is done through a study of comparative material drawn from better-documented cities, which indicates that the phenomenon of street selling is intrinsically linked to the wider social and economic environment in which such vendors operate, and in particular, to the availability of work in urban centres. After establishing that the social, economic, and demographic conditions of Rome would likely have encouraged the widespread presence of food hawkers in the city, the chapter goes on to explore the various types of evidence for such hawkers in more depth. It begins with written descriptions, before going on to look at visual portrayals of vendors; it considers what this material suggests not only about food hawkers, but also about how these traders were viewed by those who created this material. Not all the representations are drawn directly from the city of Rome – some refer to Italy and the wider Roman world – but all can be taken as illustrative of the place of food hawkers in Rome, where the greater size of the population and the particular conditions of the labour market most likely resulted in higher numbers of vendors thronging the streets. The chapter thus argues that despite the partial nature of our evidence, food hawkers were an integral part of the distribution network in Rome, and must have been a very visible, audible, and striking feature of the streets and public spaces of the ancient city.

Food hawkers and the urban economy: a comparative perspective

To a certain extent, the presence of food hawkers in antiquity is hardly surprising, since such traders were a characteristic feature of pre-industrial retail. Indeed, as Calaresu notes, most Italians continued to buy, and very often to eat, their food on the street well into the nineteenth century.[2] Furthermore, the Mediterranean climate of Italy and many other areas of the Roman empire encouraged a culture of outdoor living; in Rome, for example, winters could be cold, but they were generally short and the climate was conducive to living – and thus trading – outside, especially if there were spaces that were shaded from the sun. There were, however, a series of more complex factors related to the particular social, economic, and demographic structure of Rome that encouraged the spread of food hawkers in the city.

In the late Republic and early empire in particular, ancient Rome was a centre of migration. In the first century BC, Italians flocked to the city in large numbers; the motivation for this population movement is disputed and much discussed, but the growth in the urban population was rapid, with estimates ranging from an average of 5,000 to 10,000 new migrants per year over the course of the century.[3] Seasonal mobility within Italy also caused the population of the city to swell at certain times of the year.[4] The population of Rome may well have reached as many as one million in the first century BC, a staggering figure for a pre-industrial city and one not reached again in the Western world until London in around 1800.[5] With a high mortality rate typical of pre-industrial urban populations, Rome relied on continual structural migration to maintain this population until at least the late second century AD, with the imperial city drawing people from a much larger Mediterranean-wide hinterland. This large and constantly changing population had a significant impact upon many aspects of life in the city.

Rome was, for example, very densely populated. Space was at a premium and many people lived in cramped accommodation, packed into overcrowded, multi-storey apartment blocks. Conditions were doubtless grim for many residents, particularly those who lived on the upper floors, where lodgings apparently worsened.[6] When they were not sleeping, residents must have preferred to spend their time elsewhere, primarily outside on the streets and in the public spaces of the city. Cooking facilities within apartment blocks were also limited, and although residents could cook on portable braziers, many probably relied primarily on cookshops or street vendors to provide them with cooked food. The streets thus became an extension of the home.

It was here that people ate their meals, rolled dice, and played board games scratched into pavements, made offerings at neighbourhood shrines, collected water at basins, and gossiped on street corners. Food hawkers were very much a part of this world, and they must have jostled for space with a myriad of other users of the street, including a wide variety of other workers, such as barbers, teachers, prostitutes, fortune tellers, and beggars.[7]

The structure of the urban economy was such that there were also many people on the streets searching for casual employment. In fact, comparative evidence drawn from other better-documented cities suggests that there was probably a significant overlap between this group and the food hawkers in Rome. This can be indicated by drawing parallels between ancient Rome, nineteenth-century London, and Lagos, a contemporary city in the developing world.[8] *Prima facie*, these comparisons may seem entirely arbitrary, but while these three cities are clearly very different, they have been selected because they share some key common characteristics. They are all exceptionally large cities by their contemporary standards; they all draw migrants on a vast scale, resulting in rapid urban growth; and they are all primarily political and administrative centres.

Intrinsically linked to these factors is another well-documented characteristic of our comparative cities: a working population that far outstrips the formal employment opportunities available. This results in a significant proportion of the population finding work within what is now classed as the informal economy; hawking food is one of the most common occupations undertaken by such workers. Henry Mayhew's remarkable work, for example, documented the lives of street traders in nineteenth-century London, and found that the majority of them sold food or drink, including fresh fruit, vegetables, fish, coffee, pies, baked potatoes, and other hot food.[9] The hawkers came from among the poor of the city and were by and large unable to find other work, or could not do so due to illness, age, or disability; selling was preferable to begging or the workhouse. London food hawkers were not, however, a homogenous group, but were internally stratified into a hierarchy of sellers; some of the richest traders had carts and donkeys, others had fixed stalls, while the poorest tended to sell goods from trays. Some hawkers were also indebted to other sellers or were in their employment. Others resorted to selling when other work was unavailable, such as the man interviewed by Mayhew who worked as a bricklayer's labourer in summer and a potato seller in winter.[10] The number of street traders working at any one time was therefore linked to the nature of the labour market in the city and the availability of work.

A similar picture emerges from the contemporary city of Lagos in Nigeria, where in recent years the formal employment market has failed to keep pace with the rapid population growth. At least half of the labour force is thought to work in the informal economy, with the majority relying on work as day labourers or as sellers of purchased or scavenged goods in order to make a living.[11] Yet entering this sector is not necessarily to be seen as a last resort;

studies of contemporary food hawkers in other areas, including Hiemstra's study of Vietnamese food hawkers in this volume, indicate that it is often the result of a deliberate choice.[12] Indeed, the informal economy is neither marginal nor peripheral, but has significant potential for job provision and income generation.[13] Street trading, and in particular food hawking, is popular as a means of generating an income because it offers workers relative autonomy, requires minimal initial capital investment and little technical knowledge, and can provide a decent profit. Furthermore, street traders provide an essential service, distributing food and other goods at low prices to urban residents with a low income.

An analogous situation can be posited for Rome, where the economic opportunities available were rather restricted, especially for new migrants who may not have been part of established networks in the city. The presence of slaves and freed slaves (referred to as freedmen, although including women) in particular impacted upon the work available for the freeborn in the city. The households of the elite, for example, were staffed primarily by slave or freed labour. The number of slaves owned was a clear indicator of a family's wealth and status, and domestic work was unlikely to have been widely available to the freeborn in Rome. Nor were there many administrative opportunities, since dependent members of a household were usually charged with running the houses and estates of their owners or former owners.[14] Slaves and freedmen dominated even within the administration of the imperial household. Dependent labour was also widely employed in production and commerce in Rome. Slaves were often trained in a craft or a skill and then employed in a workshop connected with the household; if they were manumitted, they were able to continue working as freedmen in their respective crafts. This is not to say that all work in Rome was undertaken by dependent labour, but the presence of slaves and freedmen in the city undoubtedly affected the opportunities available to the freeborn. Yet there were hundreds of thousands of workers in ancient Rome at any one time. There was no benefits system to provide a safety net for those unable to work, and although free grain was distributed in the city, the amount was insufficient to feed a family and by no means all the population were eligible to receive the grain.[15] What then did these workers do?

This is where our comparative cities can act as valuable heuristic tools. The institutional infrastructure of Rome was unique, but residents faced similar restrictions in the availability of work to those in our comparative cities, albeit for very different reasons. Our comparative cities demonstrate the likely outcome of such a scenario, namely a reliance on casual work and the development of a significant informal economy; with particularly high rates of migration, the problem must have been especially acute in Rome of the first century BC. Thus in Rome also, many of the residents were likely to have been reliant on casual work, primarily in the building trade and porterage.[16] Skilled and unskilled work on both public and private building projects, together with the movement of goods on and off boats or carts at the wharves or gates of the city (a particularly important task after the implementation of Caesar's ban on carts within Rome during daylight hours) absorbed many of the freeborn workers in Rome.[17] The urban labour market was also likely to have been linked to the agricultural calendar; workers from Rome could have been engaged seasonally in agricultural labour in the vicinity of the city, while conversely, rural labourers may have drifted to Rome to find work outside of times of high agricultural demand.[18]

Yet when such work was unavailable, undesirable or physically impossible due to disability or ill health, workers in Rome must have looked for other opportunities to earn a living, and hawking was no doubt a popular option. As in our comparative cities, retailing could act as a survival strategy, absorbing the jobless and the underemployed. Food hawking was probably particularly popular, since it required little investment; fresh food could be purchased on a daily basis, suiting those whose access to capital was limited, enabling them to 're-invest' the previous day's profit. Such patterns of purchase also alleviated problems of storage, an important issue for those living in cramped lodgings. Furthermore, fresh food items such as fruit, vegetables, and prepared meals were particularly suited to sale from stalls or by ambulant hawkers, since by necessity they had a quick turnover, and given the concentration of consumers in Rome, there was a guaranteed market for food items.

The comparative evidence suggests, however, that the desperate individual hawking food merely to survive is only part of the picture. Not all sellers are independent, nor are they uniformly poor; indeed, some contemporary food hawkers make a deliberate choice to enter this sector, and make decent profits. In Rome also, some food hawkers were probably successful sellers who were able to build up profitable businesses; it was presumably these workers who were able to record their occupations on funerary monuments, or commission the stone reliefs of their stalls which provide such valuable evidence of their trade. Other hawkers were in the employ of others, as in the case discussed by the legal writer Ulpian of a baker who sent out an *institor* (an agent) to sell bread elsewhere.[19] Cookshops also often sent out sellers to hawk hot food, thus expanding the potential market for their goods.[20] Some vendors may even have extended credit to other hawkers to enable them to purchase stock, a practice which is well-documented in our comparative cities.[21] Such agreements were probably made orally, and leave no trace in our sources, but if evidence of such arrangements were available, it is probable that we would be able to detect a complex network of credit relationships among sellers in Rome.

Ancient literary representations

While the structure of the urban economy of Rome suggests that food hawkers were likely to have been commonplace in the city, the ancient evidence for their existence, and particularly for their organisation, is not always easy to find. Furthermore, the available evidence is very often flawed, presenting a stylised representation of food hawkers rather than an accurate reflection of reality. One significant factor which affects literary representations of food hawkers in particular is that there is no definitive term in either Latin or ancient Greek to denote street vendors. The figure of the hawker is relatively commonplace in literature, but the idea of such vendors is rather under-conceptualised, something which is reflected in the terminology.[22] Thus in Latin various generic or makeshift terminology is employed, including *ambulator*, the primary meaning of which is someone who walks about, particularly idly or for pleasure;[23] *circitor*, which derives from the verb *circumeo* (to go round) and has numerous meanings, including simply a person who goes round, a watchman or overseer;[24] *circumforaneus*, which describes movement around a forum or more generally, from town to town;[25] *circulator*, a term also used to describe entertainers such as jugglers, sword-swallowers, fire-eaters, snake exhibitors, and philosophers;[26] and finally, *institor*, a formal legal term which primarily denotes Roman business managers.[27] The last term is the most formal designation of hawkers, since the other words are primarily part of the world of 'Vulgar Latin'; as Ulpian states, *institores* are commonly known as *circitores* (*volgo circitores appellamus*).[28] In ancient Greek, *kapelos*, a generic term for retailers, is used to refer to hawkers.[29] The lack of specific terminology can make the identification of food hawkers in ancient literature difficult, since the context in which a term appears is crucial to understanding the mode of retail described. Furthermore, hawkers are not always defined by any particular term and so not all literary references can be uncovered through searches of specific words within databases, the most straightforward means of analysing the appearance of particular terms within the considerable corpus of surviving ancient literature.[30] Given the ambiguous nature of much of the terminology, few of the terms appear within the epigraphic record either.

Yet despite the issue of terminology, numerous food hawkers can be identified in ancient literature. We hear of sellers of figs,[31] fish,[32] vegetables,[33] grapes,[34] milk,[35] and hawkers of prepared food such as bread,[36] and hot food, including sausages, pastries, and dishes prepared with chickpeas.[37] Food hawkers appear in a variety of surviving ancient literature covering a wide range of genres, including letters, political and legal speeches, histories, plays, novels, love poetry, epigrams, and satire. The genre of a text is perhaps the most immediate consideration in how food hawkers are portrayed, as we might expect portrayals to be exaggerated for comic reasons in writings such as satire or epigrams, or for rhetorical reasons in, for example, political or legal speeches. Our surviving references are, however, too few to make any meaningful distinction between representations in different genres. Similarly, our references are found across a wide chronological span, ranging from the second century BC to the fourth century AD, yet are so scattered that any significant diachronic analysis of representations of food hawkers is impossible. In any case, food hawkers are portrayed in much the same vein across literary genres and chronological periods in the Roman world; they are for the most part portrayed negatively, or appear as incidental characters in the background of descriptions of other peoples or events.

If, as I have argued, food hawkers were such a ubiquitous part of the Roman street scene and a fundamental component of the distribution network of the city, why do they not appear more frequently in our literary sources, and why, when they do appear, do they tend to be portrayed negatively? There are numerous possible explanations for this. In terms of ancient literature, food hawkers are somewhat peripheral to the interests of most genres of poetry and prose, and although they may appear as background characters, their presence is taken as a given and not elaborated upon further. Furthermore, food hawkers were outside of the social world of the elite authors who produced our literature. Ancient literature essentially reflects the concerns of a tiny minority of wealthy, literate Romans; such people would not generally be found purchasing their food from hawkers in Rome. In fact, the elite ideal was self-sufficiency; food should be supplied directly to a household in Rome from a suburban or country estate, and purchasing food in the city implied that an estate was unable to meet the needs of the household adequately. Even staple items such as bread, which could not practically be imported into the city on a daily basis, should be produced within the household; hence Cicero derides Piso for buying his bread in public, the implication being that he does not have the means to produce bread within his own home.[38]

While the reality does not necessarily reflect the elite ideal – Ovid, for example, advises his readers to purchase food in the city and *pretend* that it was supplied directly from a suburban estate[39] – when such food was acquired in the city, it was more likely to be purchased from places such as *macella* than from food hawkers. *Macella* were purpose-built food markets that sold expensive delicacies to a wealthy clientele, and were particularly suited to the supply of quality food on the scale required for elite dinner parties, crucial events in the demonstration and acquisition of social and political status in Rome.[40] For smaller household meals and snacks, food hawkers may well have been used, but any such purchasing would have been done by dependents from the household, and so on the whole, direct engagement on the part of the elite with food hawkers was likely minimal in Rome.[41]

Moreover, a general disdain for retailers pervades among our elite authors, since retail was equated primarily with deception and dishonesty. Cicero, for example, drawing on a Greek philosophical tradition, holds that while trade on a significant level is morally acceptable, purchasing goods solely to sell on is dishonest, since the value of the goods must be inflated falsely in order to make a profit.[42] As sellers of perishable goods, which must by their very nature be sold almost immediately, food hawkers are perhaps the ultimate example of retailers who sell goods to make a quick profit, however unfair this characterisation may be. More broadly, ancient attitudes to work in general may have influenced the representation of food hawkers in our literary sources. The Greek philosophical tradition regarded manual labour as banausic, that is, as harmful to body and soul.[43] Cicero again followed this convention in an often-quoted passage condemning manual labour, with the notable exception of agricultural work, an activity which is almost universally praised in Roman literature.[44] Cicero disapproves of wage labour in particular, arguing that selling one's labour is akin to slavery.

In practice, these attitudes were unlikely to have been prevalent outside of a narrow and privileged elite in Greece or Rome, and even within this group, the views expressed were inconsistent and not always compatible with their actions.[45] Certainly funerary commemorations recording occupations of the deceased indicate that for some sections of society at least, work was not shameful but was a central tenet of their identity. Furthermore, such reservations about manual labour or earning wages were not necessarily followed by Christian authors.[46] Yet the prevailing attitude among the elite still affects our literary record, since work was rarely discussed in a neutral fashion. In fact, references to work in Rome are very often found as part of political invective or satirical attacks; the emperor Augustus, for example, was taunted by accusations that he was descended from traders, with a banker, a rope maker, a perfume maker, and a baker among his ancestors.[47] Working for a living was not necessarily to be praised or admired. Retail was treated with particular disdain, and since food hawking was very often undertaken by some of the poorest and most marginalised in Rome, such traders were probably especially scorned. Some food hawkers were also of slave or freed status, which goes some way towards explaining their negative portrayal in our sources.[48] Food hawking was derided not only because it was in itself demeaning, but also because of the status of those who engaged in this activity; these two aspects were most likely mutually reinforcing from the point of view of the Roman elite.

Food hawkers were not likely, therefore, to have been viewed as worthy of much interest by the Roman elite; there was certainly no sympathetic character akin to Henry Mayhew to document the lives of street sellers in Rome. Furthermore, attitudes to work, and to retail in particular, significantly affected the representation of food hawkers in our literary sources. Street traders in general appear primarily as incidental characters, or as caricatures of vulgarity, as insults hurled at others. Martial, for example, degrades a certain Caecilius by accusing him of undertaking the meanest jobs in Rome, including the work of street traders.[49] Similarly, poor oratory is compared to the sales patter of street vendors. Pliny the Younger, for instance, likens Regulus' oratory to that of a seller in the forum (*circulator in foro*), while Martial compares an impersonator's poetry to the shouts of those who collect broken glass for recycling; these are not intended to be compliments.[50] Indeed, in his guide to oratory, Quintilian instructs his readers to aim at forceful oratory rather than the rapid speech of a street hawker (*circulator*).[51]

Yet although the context is pejorative, these representations of hawkers *are* useful in that they strongly hint at the performative aspect of street selling in Rome. That hawkers were active sellers of their goods is also suggested by the use of the term *circulator* to refer to both hawkers and street performers; both clearly provided an element of entertainment for their audience. This seems to be particularly true of food hawkers, who had distinctive cries to attract customers and enable them to stand out from their competitors. Seneca, for example, tells of the disturbance caused by the hawkers who frequent the bathhouse below his apartment in first-century Rome, describing the noise of the 'pastry-cooks with their varied cries, the sausage dealer and the confectioner and all the vendors of food from the cookshops selling their wares, each with his own distinctive intonation'.[52] Similarly Martial talks about the noise of the 'vendor of boiled chickpeas to the idle crowd ... the salt-fishmongers' worthless slaves and the bawling cook who hawks smoking sausages round stuffy bistros', while elsewhere he complains about the noise of traders in Rome disturbing his sleep.[53] Cicero reports how a fig seller's shout of *cauneas* (Caunean dried figs) at Brundisium was heard by soldiers embarking in ships to Parthia as *cave ne eas* ('beware going') and interpreted as a bad omen, while Calpurnius Siculus describes the loud cries of an urban milk hawker.[54]

Food hawkers appear as active sellers in surviving pictorial representations of sale also, although they are of course largely silent. A funerary monument from Narbonne, however, includes a seller's sales cry alongside his image. The hawker is depicted with a basket of fruit around his neck and next to him is inscribed the distinctive shout of '*mala! Mulieres, mulieres meae!*'. The performative aspect of the cry lies in the pronunciation of the first word. If the seller pronounced *mala* with a long 'a' in the first syllable, it would mean apples, while with a short 'a', it would mean troublesome; the second part of the phrase translates as women, my women, and the seller could thus implore 'his' women to buy his apples, or he could describe them as harmful.[55] The cries of food hawkers were no doubt a characteristic feature of the ancient city – and of Rome in particular – with sellers competing vigorously for customers. Yet in contrast to those who found the street cries of early modern London and Paris interesting enough to document and even to set to music, the Roman street cries are rarely recorded for their own sake; they are primarily remarked upon as another irritating aspect of urban life, or used as a means to malign the oratory of others.[56]

Legal sources are no more neutral in tone, and moreover, rarely show more than a passing interest in such traders. Roman Jurists were concerned primarily with the role of *institores*, many of whom were of servile status and were sent out from more permanent places to sell goods in public spaces and private homes.[57] Ulpian, for example, describes a baker sending out an *institor* daily to sell bread in a particular location, as well as tailors and cloth merchants entrusting cloth to *institores*, commonly known as *circitores*, to hawk and to sell;[58] the legal status of transactions undertaken by *institores* within the homes of the wealthy is also considered.[59] Otherwise, there is little evidence in the legal sources for the regulation or licensing of hawkers, although there does appear to be a concern with keeping the streets passable, which presumably affected the size and positioning of stalls.[60] Ambulant hawkers present less of a problem, as their mobility means that they cause only a passing obstruction. They are also more difficult to control and regulate, since their constant movement enables them to evade the authorities more effectively than vendors with fixed stalls. In any case, even if prosecutions of food hawkers had taken place in ancient Rome, there would be no police or prosecution records to provide us with additional information about these sellers.[61]

The representation of food hawkers in our ancient literary sources clearly presents a challenge, as the concerns and attitudes of our authors mean that such vendors are rarely presented in a neutral manner. We cannot, of course, counter the elite view by interviewing food hawkers from ancient Rome in the manner of those who study such vendors in contemporary cities. Nevertheless, the literary sources do at least enable us to establish the presence of food hawkers in Rome, and go some way towards revealing the performative aspect of such sellers in the city. There are, however, other types of evidence that can further illuminate the picture of vendors in Rome.

Artistic representations

Several artistic representations of food hawkers, for example, survive from the Roman world.[62] None of these visual portrayals come from Rome itself, but were primarily found in Pompeii and Ostia, whose particular histories have enabled better preservation of their Roman remains, although such depictions are equally evocative of the sellers in Rome. The pictures are not, however, to be taken as merely illustrative of Roman street sellers; as with our literary sources, these are representations of hawkers, the interpretation of which requires further thought and analysis.

Four small statuettes (c.25cm high), found stored in the remains of a carbonised chest in the house of P. Cornelius Tages at Pompeii (I.7.10–12; also known as the house of the Ephebus), are some of the more intriguing visual representations of food hawkers (see Figure 1.1);[63] as with all finds at Pompeii, these items were buried in the eruption of Vesuvius and therefore can be dated no later than AD 79. The original function of these statuettes is unknown, but since the figures hold small silver trays in their hands, it has been thought that they were used as a novel means to serve delicacies at dinner parties, with their striking appearance presumably acting as a talking point among the guests.[64] The statuettes are conventionally referred to as the *placentarii*, a late Latin term referring to pastry-cooks or confectioners. Although the name is a modern invention of the archaeologist Maiuri, the figures probably are intended to represent ambulant hawkers, perhaps of pastries or bread, although other wares could be carried on the trays.[65] These are, however, by no means realistic depictions of hawkers. The figures are heavily caricatured, and are naked, in a parody of a heroic nude; they are elderly, skinny and bearded, depicted in the process of straining to shout, with their mouths open and their hands to their throats. As in our literary sources, the performative aspect of the sellers' work is clear.

Figure 1.1 Statuette of hawker, House of P. Cornelius Tages, Pompeii (I.7.10).
Photo: Archivio fotografico Soprintendenza Speciale per i beni archeologici di Napoli e Pompei.

Perhaps most striking to a modern audience are the exaggerated phalluses of the hawkers. This feature of the figures would probably be less arresting to an ancient audience, as phallic imagery abounded at Pompeii; representations of erect phalluses in particular were common, and were not intended to be erotic images, but were thought to have apotropaic powers, protecting the residents from harm.[66] The phalluses on the hawkers, however, are not erect, and were probably intended above all to incite a humorous response in the viewer.[67] They are in fact reminiscent of the phalluses worn by actors in Old Attic Comedy and probably also in fourth-century Magna Graecia.[68] Moreover, the large phalluses are part of the overall characterisation of the hawkers; the Romans followed the Greeks in an aesthetic preference for small phalluses, and this feature thus marks the sellers out as crass figures and is a further element in their marginalisation.[69] The contrast between these statuettes and eighteenth- and nineteenth-century European representations of street sellers is striking.[70] The Roman figures were similarly expensive – made from gilded bronze and furnished with silver trays – but rather than the idealised and somewhat sentimentalised representations of later Europe, these are comic figures; they ridicule the hawkers who must have been a familiar sight on the streets of Pompeii for the entertainment of wealthy dinner party guests. The statuettes rather neatly reflect the attitudes to food hawkers in our ancient literature.

Other visual representations of food hawkers from the Roman world are more neutral in their portrayal of sellers. A frieze from the atrium of the house of Julia Felix at Pompeii (II.4), for example, depicts food hawkers as part of a series of scenes set in the Pompeian forum (see Figure 1.2). The paintings, now on display in the Museo Archeologico Nazionale di Napoli, include depictions of legal judgements and business transactions taking place, a school pupil being punished, people reading public notices, numerous mules making deliveries, people chatting, a beggar, and various scenes of sale.[71] We see, for example, men in tunics showing cloth to women, while elsewhere other women are seated on benches examining lengths of cloth held by sellers. There is a man selling metal vessels, displayed on the ground around him; he bangs the inside of one his vessels with a stick, either to demonstrate its quality or to attract attention. Behind him, a man sits at an anvil and beats a container with a hammer. A seller of shoes has marked out a space with curtains, and numerous customers are seated on benches; the seller stands in the middle of the display of shoes and appears to be in the process of mending a shoe that he is holding in his right hand.

Food hawkers, however, dominate the scenes of sale. A bread seller displays his wares on a wooden table and in a basket on the ground, while another temporary stall holds fruit and vegetables; further baskets on the floor hold what appear to be figs. Hot food is sold from a large cauldron suspended over a fire and the seller uses tongs to hold a small bowl of food drawn from the cauldron for a customer. A man is also shown seated next to a low table on which he displays his wares; it is unclear exactly what he is selling, but it may

Figure 1.2 Scenes of sale, frieze from *praedia* of Julia Felix, Pompeii (II.4). Photo: Archivio fotografico Soprintendenza Speciale per i beni archeologici di Napoli e Pompei.

be food, since a customer is passing him a bowl to be filled and on the floor are various other vessels, from one of which protrudes a serving implement.[72] Almost all of the sellers in these particular scenes are male, although many of the customers are female, suggesting that women were active participants in the community of Pompeii. Women also appear as sellers elsewhere in the town, as for example the woman shown behind a counter selling felt objects at the workshop of Verecundus (IX.7.5–7).[73]

A colonnade runs behind all the scenes, demonstrating that the setting is to be understood as the forum. The architectonic details do not exactly mirror those of the Pompeian forum, but are presumably intended to be representative, rather than a faithful reproduction.[74] A similar approach must be taken to the scenes themselves. While other depictions of trade that are found within domestic settings at Pompeii may add a fantastical or mythological element – such as the famous paintings in the House of the Vettii (VI.15.1) in which workers are portrayed as Cupids and Psyches – the artist of the forum scenes paints images that would be instantly recognisable to the ancient viewer.[75] This is genre painting, intended to represent a typical and recognisable scene, but not to document faithfully any one particular person or event.[76] Perhaps not all of these events would ordinarily take place at the same time, but the overall aim of the artist was to capture the bustling nature of the Pompeian forum through a depiction of the activities that would occur within that setting. Since the pleasure for the viewer comes from the familiarity of the scene, the artist would surely focus on the typical rather than the atypical. In a similar manner, many early modern prints of street sellers appear to have been drawn from figures posed in a studio rather than produced from sketches of genuine hawkers done on the streets, but the intention was to produce a staged representation of reality.[77] Above all, the frieze is decorative, but from our point of view, the pictures indicate the type of food that would be available for sale in the Pompeian forum, and by extension, in the public areas of other Roman towns and cities, including Rome itself; this includes fruit, vegetables, bread and prepared food.

Not all artistic representations of Pompeian hawkers are to be found in the context of genre paintings. The depiction of the riot in the amphitheatre, for example, documents a specific event in Pompeii's history, which took place in AD 59 when residents of the nearby town of Nuceria visited Pompeii to attend gladiatorial games and clashed with the townspeople in the amphitheatre.[78] In the foreground of this picture, the artist painted a number of temporary stalls, with sales areas marked out and shaded by curtains hung between trees or attached to stakes in the ground; a more permanent wooden structure can also be seen. The painting is not detailed enough to see what the vendors are selling, especially as many appear to have been overrun by rioters, but given the concentration of hungry consumers in the vicinity of the amphitheatre, many of these sellers were likely to have been food hawkers; some perhaps also sold gladiatorial programmes of the type mentioned by Cicero.[79] The pictorial evidence can to a certain extent be corroborated by the archaeological material. Traces of writing survive on the exterior of the amphitheatre at Pompeii, where traders marked out their spaces for stalls; permission to trade was granted by the aediles, local town magistrates.[80] Given the potential profits to be made, such trading spaces were probably jealously guarded, but temporary stalls would surely have been supplemented by numerous ambulant hawkers taking advantage of the demand for food and other goods generated by those attending the games.

Several stone reliefs depicting food sellers also survive. A marble relief from Ostia, for example, dating to the late second-century AD, shows a vegetable seller behind a trestle table; underneath is a large basket in which the seller must have transported the stock (see Figure 1.3).[81] The contents of the table are deliberately displayed to the viewer and include several different types of vegetables. Further vegetables are displayed on stepped shelves, which are to be understood either as resting on the table, or perhaps as part of some more permanent furniture. Thus while the trestle table clearly suggests a temporary arrangement, the shelves may hint at something more permanent here, making the context of the scene difficult to interpret. This issue is compounded by the fact that the provenance of the relief is unknown, meaning that its original function is difficult to know. The relief is small (c.50cm by 35cm), and was perhaps initially part of a funerary monument, or was intended to mark out a place of sale, forming a visual marker of the seller's usual location. It has also been suggested that it was used as a shop sign, in which case, the relief would depict the interior of a shop, rather than a market stall or a street vendor;[82] without the original context, it is impossible to fully understand the meaning of the scene. Indeed, it may have been primarily decorative in function, in the manner of the paintings from the house of Julia Felix. The features of the seller are indistinct and the clothes could be worn by either a male or female, but given the lack of a beard, the

Figure 1.3 Relief of vegetable seller, Ostia FU 2383, Fototeca Unione, American Academy in Rome.

seller is generally identified as a woman, although some ambiguity remains.[83] The seller is shown in the centre of the relief, standing behind the counter, with one hand touching the produce, and the other hand raised as though to attract the attention of passersby, with the thumb and the first two fingers extended in what was a common oratorical gesture.[84]

Figure 1.4 Relief of poultry seller, Ostia FU 2380, Fototeca Unione, American Academy
in Rome.

A second Ostian relief of a similar date shows a female poultry seller behind
a stall made out of cages in which her stock of live poultry and rabbits (or
hares) is stored (see Figure 1.4).[85] Next to the stall, two dead birds are shown
hanging from a post. Also on the stall are two bowls of fruit, perhaps figs, and
a large wooden barrel with two holes; a snail carved next to the barrel is presumably intended to indicate its contents. To the far side of the barrel sit two
monkeys who are looking directly at the viewer and are presumably intended
to attract and entertain customers, again highlighting the performative aspect
of food sale and the crossover between hawkers and entertainers. The woman
behind the counter is accompanied by an assistant, and to the side of the cages
are three male figures. One holds a dead rabbit and appears to be engaged in a
discussion with a second man beside him, who has his arms open in gesticula-
tion and is perhaps another seller. The third figure is being served by the female
seller, who hands him some fruit with one hand, while her other hand touches
the fruit in one of the bowls, a gesture similar to that adopted by the Ostian
vegetable seller. The figure being served by the woman is noticeably smaller
than the other two men, enabling the viewer to see the dead poultry hanging
behind the customer, while also emphasising the high position of the woman.
The small size of the seller may be a stylistic compromise, although it is worth
noting that this may also say something about the status of the figure, since
in Roman art, slave status is often demonstrated by size in relation to others.[86]
As with the vegetable seller, the intended function of the relief is unknown,
although a little more is known about its provenance. It was found by excava-
tors in a building along the Via della Foce at Ostia, a major route through the
city, but its original placement remains unknown.

A similar relief from second-century Arlon, this time certainly funerary in
context, shows two fruit sellers behind a trestle table covered with fruit;[87] as in

the relief of the Ostian vegetable seller, the baskets used to carry the produce are depicted underneath the table. Indeed, Kampen suggests that the trestle table was particularly associated with the sale of food, perhaps because the quick turnaround of items such as fresh fruit and vegetables meant that these were best suited to sale from temporary stalls.[88] Certainly the baskets and the trestle tables emphasise the transient nature of these stalls. Another characteristic motif of these reliefs is that the seller is placed behind a stall, creating a clear separation between them and the customer. Perhaps even more noticeable is that the sellers are all shown touching their produce, as though inviting their customers to do the same. Such motifs appear to have become part of the vocabulary of visual representations of food hawkers, and mark the vendors out once again as active sellers. The funerary relief of a hawker from Narbonne is of a different nature, since the fruit seller is shown carrying his wares in a basket that hangs around his neck on a strap, but the performative aspect of his trade is similarly highlighted, in this case by the inclusion of the hawker's cry alongside his image. Furthermore, sellers tend to be depicted wearing simple practical clothes such as tunics, while customers wear a wider variety of clothes, included the *togae* and *stolae* typical of wealthier Romans.[89] Notably, none of the surviving reliefs include any mythological elements, nor does there appear to be any hidden political or religious symbolism in the depictions of food hawkers. Thus despite the sharing of some common motifs and elements of composition, the reliefs must have been intended as realistic portrayals of sellers. They can, therefore, be taken as illustrative of the form that food stalls took, and the sorts of goods that were sold.

Such reliefs appear to be almost entirely without Greek precedents and are part of a tradition of depicting scenes of work that flourished primarily in the western part of the Roman empire in the first to the third centuries AD.[90] The majority of reliefs showing work activities were found on funerary monuments, and were thus part of the self-representation of the deceased. The Ciceronian distaste for work was clearly not shared by all, although it is notable that work as a mark of identity is most prevalent among freedmen, who could become wealthy but were excluded from many of the more traditional markers of status.[91] Funerary inscriptions recording occupational titles are also demonstrative of the pride that some took in their work; such commemorations are in fact far more numerous than artistic representations of work, since the latter were understandably more expensive to produce.[92]

Yet food hawkers seldom appear in our epigraphic record. Given that much of the terminology used to denote food hawkers in our literary sources was rather make-shift, ambiguous, and primarily a part of 'Vulgar Latin', it is perhaps unsurprising that we do not see people adopting such terms as part of their identity or self-representation. The only term that does appear in inscriptions is *institor*, a more formal legal term, but even this appears only a handful of times on funerary commemorations across the Roman empire, and never specifically referring to the sale of food.[93] The low status attached to such terms perhaps goes some way towards explaining why they rarely appear as titles on funerary monuments. Indeed, although the elite disdain for work does not appear to have been common throughout Roman society, the literary terms by which food hawkers are defined are probably not those by which the workers would have chosen to define themselves. Perhaps more pertinently, the urban economy of Rome was structured in such as way that many food hawkers were among the poorest in the city. They were, therefore, unlikely to have been in a position to pay for even the most basic of commemorations and would largely be absent from the epigraphic record, leaving no physical trace of their existence.

Conclusion

Our literary representations of hawkers are clearly subjective, since they represent the viewpoint of a wealthy elite educated in a philosophical tradition that taught them to condemn retailers as dishonest and to elevate the self-sufficient lifestyle of those who lived off the produce of their land. Hawkers appear only when they can be a useful tool to writers, for example, as a means to disparage the oratorical skills of others, as shorthand for vulgarity, or to provide background to an everyday scene; they are rarely discussed in any detail, since the character presented is one that is readily understood by their audience, requiring no further explanation. Aside from the Pompeian statuettes with the exaggerated phalluses, which rather neatly encapsulate the literary representation of food hawkers in a visual form, depictions of hawkers in paintings and reliefs are generally more neutral. They show sellers in a more realistic light as a typical part of urban street life, although these cannot be taken as 'documentary' evidence either; they are representations of sellers, appearing as part of genre paintings, or in the case of the Ostian reliefs, perhaps as place markers for stalls, as shop signs, or as images of the deceased on funerary monuments.

The ancient evidence may then be partial and not always easy to interpret, but both the literary and the visual representations indicate that food hawkers – and hawkers of a wide variety of other goods – were an integral part both of Roman street life and the urban distribution network. Fresh food, such as fruit, vegetables, and milk, were offered for sale, as were prepared food items, such as bread, sausages, and pastries. We can also see that sellers worked from behind stalls or on foot, moving around to take advantage of concentrations of consumers. Venues such as amphitheatres, theatres, bathhouses and temples were important hubs of trade, with hawkers congregating where potential customers could be found. Food hawkers were also lively sellers of their wares, encouraging customers through vocal advertisements of their products, offering colourful entertainment as well as sustenance. Although our ancient sources show little interest in the lives of food hawkers, comparative material can provide some valuable models to help explain the phenomenon of food hawking in Rome, linking the presence of such sellers to wider issues in the social and economic environment of the city. Despite the frequent vilification of hawkers in our ancient sources, and their relative invisibility in the archaeological record, with careful consideration of the evidence, it is possible to go some way towards reconstituting the place of food vendors within the wider urban economy, and to discover more about some of these most marginalised people in Roman society.

Notes

1 I would like to thank Roy Gibson, Sophie Lunn-Rockliffe, and the editors for their valuable comments on an earlier draft of this chapter. For details of any of the ancient authors cited in this chapter, see relevant entries in Simon Hornblower and Anthony Spawforth, *The Oxford Classical Dictionary*, 4th edn (Oxford, 2012).

2 Chapter 5 in this volume.

3 Migration to Rome is discussed in more detail in Claire Holleran, 'Migration and the Urban Economy of Rome', in Claire Holleran and April Pudsey (eds), *Demography and the Graeco-Roman World: New Insights and Approaches* (Cambridge, 2011), pp. 155–180. For 10,000 migrants *p.a.*, see Neville Morley, *Metropolis and Hinterland: the City of Rome and the Italian Economy, 200 BC* (Cambridge, 1996), pp. 43–44; for 5,000 migrants *p.a.*, see Walter Scheidel, 'Human Mobility in Roman Italy I: the Free Population', *Journal of Roman Studies* 94 (2004), p. 17. See also Paul Erdkamp, 'Mobility and Migration in Italy in the Second Century BC', in L. De Ligt and S.J. Northwood (eds), *People, Land and Politics: Demographic Developments and the Transformation of Roman Italy, 300 BC – AD 14* (Leiden, 2008), pp. 440–444.

4 See Cameron Hawkins, 'Labour and Employment', in Paul Erdkamp (ed.), *The Cambridge Companion to Ancient Rome* (Cambridge, 2013), pp. 339–346. For Italian mobility in the second century BC, see Erdkamp, 'Mobility and Migration', pp. 424–433.

5 For a detailed discussion of the population figures for Rome, see Elio Lo Cascio, 'La popolazione', in Elio Lo Cascio (ed.), *Roma imperiale: una metropoli antica* (Rome, 2000), pp. 17–69.

6 See, for example, Martial, *Epigrams* 2.53.8; 3.30.3; 7.20.20 (hereafter Mart.); Suetonius, *On Grammarians* 9; Juvenal, 3.198–210. For more on housing in Rome, see John Patterson, 'Living and Dying in Rome in the City of Rome: Houses and Tombs', in Jon Coulston and Hazel Dodge (eds), *Ancient Rome: The Archaeology of the Eternal City* (Oxford, 2000), pp. 273–276. On living conditions in Rome in general, see the (pessimistic) account by Alex Scobie, 'Slums, Sanitation and Mortality in the Roman World', *Klio* 68 (1986), pp. 399–433. See also Chris R. Whittaker, 'The Poor', in Andrea Giardina (ed.), *The Romans* (Chicago, 1993), pp. 272–299; Neville Morley, 'The Salubriousness of the Roman City', in Helen King (ed.), *Health in Antiquity* (London, 2005), pp. 192–204.

7 For more on the street life of Rome, see Claire Holleran, 'Street Life in Ancient Rome', in Ray Laurence and David Newsome (eds), *Rome, Ostia, Pompeii: Movement and Space* (Oxford, 2011), pp. 245–261.

8 These parallels are developed further in Holleran, 'Migration and the Urban Economy' and Claire Holleran, *Shopping in Ancient Rome: The Retail Trade in the Late Republic and the Principate* (Oxford, 2012).

9 Henry Mayhew, *London Labour and the London Poor, Volumes 1 and 2* (London, 1851). See also John Benson, 'Retailing', in J. Benson and G. Shaw (eds), *The Retailing Industry. Volume 2: The Coming of the Mass Market* (London, 1999), pp. 132–161. For street trading as a way for the marginalised to gain an income, see also Chapter 4 in this volume.

10 Mayhew, *London Labour, Vol. 1*, p. 174.

11 See, for example, Michael P. Todaro, 'Urbanisation, Unemployment and Migration in Africa: Theory and Policy', *Policy Research Division Working Paper* no. 104 (New York, 1997); Amy Otchet, 'Lagos: The Survival of the Determined', *Unesco Courier* June 1999; Geoffrey I. Nwaka, 'The Urban Informal Sector in Nigeria: Towards Economic Development, Environmental Health, and Social Harmony', *Global Urban Development* 1.1 (2005), pp. 1–11. Also see Chapters 7 and 9 in this volume for hawkers dominating the informal economic activity in South-East Asian countries. In Ghana, see Gracia Clark, *Onions are my Husband: Survival and Accumulation by West African Market Women* (Chicago, 1995).

12 Chapter 7 in this volume.

13 Kristina Flodman Becker, *The Informal Economy: Fact Finding Study* (SIDA, 2004).

14 Richard Saller, 'Human capital and economic growth', in W. Scheidel (ed.), *The Cambridge Companion to the Roman Economy* (Cambridge, 2012), p. 78.

15 Augustus effectively 'closed' the lists at just over 200,000 recipients in 2 BC (Augustus, *Res Gestae* 15; Suetonius, *Augustus* 40.2; Dio Cassius 55.10.1); in any case, eligibility was based on citizen status rather than need. For more on the calorific requirements met by the grain distributions, see Peter Garnsey, *Cities, Peasants and Food in Classical Antiquity* (Cambridge, 1998), p. 236.

16 See for example, Peter Brunt, 'The Roman Mob', *Past and Present* 35 (1966), pp. 3–27; 'Free Labour and Public Works in Rome', *Journal of Roman Studies* 70 (1980), pp. 81–100.

17 For the law on carts, see *Tabula Heracleensis*, lines 54–69.

18 For workers from Rome being employed outside of the city, see Cicero, *Letters to Atticus* 14.3.1. For the connection between the rural labour market and seasonal migration to Rome, see Hawkins, 'Labour and Employment'.

19 Ulpian, *Digest* 14.3.5.9 (hereafter Ulp. *Dig.*).

20 Seneca, *Letters* 56.2; Mart. 1.41.5–10. See n.41 for sellers being sent directly to private homes also.

21 In London, see, for example, Mayhew, *London Labour, Vol. 1*, pp. 29–34. In developing-world cities, see for example, Ray Bromley, 'Working in the Streets: Survival Strategy, Necessity, or Unavoidable Evil?', in Josef Gugler (ed.), *The Urbanisation of the Third World* (Oxford, 1988), pp. 168–169; Allison MacEwan Scott, 'Who are the Self-Employed?', in Ray Bromley and Chris Gerry (eds), *Casual Work and Poverty in Third World Cities* (Chichester, 1979), p. 119.

22 A similar phenomenon can be seen in the figure of the flatterer or parasite; such characters are familiar in Greco-Roman literature, but can be identified by a variety of Latin and Greek terms, such as *scurra, captator, parasitos, kolax* and so on.

23 For example, Cato, *On Agriculture* 5.2.6; Columella 1.8.7.2. As a hawker: Mart. 1.41.3.

24 For example, Frontinus, *The Aqueducts of Rome* 117.1.2; Petronius, *Satyricon* 53.10 (herafter Petr.). As hawker, Calpurnius Siculus, *Eclogues* 5.97 (hereafter Calp. *Ecl.*); Ulp. *Dig.* 14.3.5.5.

25 The word retains a strong sense of itinerancy, although not necessarily in reference to traders; for example, Suetonius, *Vitellius* 12.1 refers to an itinerant gladiator trainer. Also see Apuleius, *Metamorphoses* 4.13; 9.4 (hereafter Apul. *Met.*). As hawkers: Cicero, *In defence of Cluentius* 40.7; Augustine, *On the Measure of the Soul* 21.36; Historia Augusta, *Commodus* 2.8.

26 Celsus 5.27.3c; Seneca, *On Benefits* 6.11.2; *Letters* 29.7.1; 52.8; Apul. *Met.* 1.4; Paul, *Digest* 47.11.11.pr. (hereafter Paul. *Dig.*); Tertullian, *On the Prescription of the Heretics* 43.1; *Apology* 23.1. The term derives from the noun *circulo*, indicating the formation of circles or groups around oneself. As hawkers: Cicero, *Letters to Friends* 10.32.3; Petr. 68.6-7; Quintilian, *On Oratory* 2.4.16; 10.1.8; Mart. 10.3.2; Pliny, *Letters* 4.7.6.

27 See, for example, Ulp. *Dig.* 14.3. As hawkers, see for example: Cicero, *Philippics* 2.97; Horace, *Carmina* 3.6.30; *Epodes* 17.20; Ovid, *The Art of Love* 1.421; *Remedies for Love* 306; Propertius, 4.2.38; Valerius Maximus, *Memorable Deeds and Sayings* 2.7.1.8; Seneca, *Letters*, 42.8; 52.15; 56.2; Quintilian, *Declamationes* 260.13.4; Mart. 12.57.14; Juvenal, 7.221; Ulp. *Dig.* 14.3.5.4; 14.3.5.9; Paul. *Dig.* 14.3.4; Jerome, *Against Jovinian* 1.47.

28 Ulp. *Dig.* 14.3.5.4. For more on Vulgar Latin, see J. Herman, *Vulgar Latin*, trans. R. Wright (Philadelphia, 2000).

29 For example, Aristophanes, *The Birds* 1292; Plato, *Protagoras* 313c; Dio Chrysostom, 8.9; 35.4; 35.15. Following the army: Xenophon, *Cyropaedia* 4.5.42.3; Demosthenes, *Against Aristogiton* 1.46.1; Lucian, *How to Write History* 16.5; Athenaeus, *Deipnosophists* 10.38.8 (10.431d).

30 See, for example, the Classical Latin Texts database produced by the Packard Humanities Institute (http://latin.packhum.org/), containing almost the entirety of Latin literature up to AD 200, together with selected later authors.

31 Lucilius, 5.221–2; Cicero, *On Divination* 2.40.84.

32 Plautus, *The Captives* 813–16.

33 Horace, *Satires* 1.6.111–14; Petr. 6–7 (the old woman selling vegetables in this passage in fact turns out to be gathering custom for a nearby brothel). Female street vendors in early modern London were also often equated with prostitutes, see Chapter 2 in this volume. See also Mayhew, *London Labour, Vol. 1*, p.134 for prostitutes in eighteenth-century London who masqueraded as flower sellers.

34 Calp. *Ecl.* 5.97.

35 Calp. *Ecl.* 4.25–26.

36 Cicero, *Against Piso* 67.10; Ulp. *Dig.* 14.3.5.9.

37 Seneca, *Letters* 56.2; Mart. 1.41.5–10. The preparation of food often enables the highest profit margins, as value is added to raw materials through their transformation into a more saleable product.

38 Cicero, *Against Piso* 67.10.

39 Ovid, *The Art of Love* 2.263–6. See also Mart. 7.31.

40 For more on the *macella* as a luxury food market, see Holleran, *Shopping*, pp. 160–181. Also Claire De Ruyt, *Macellum: marché alimentaire des Romains* (Louvain-la-Neuve, 1983), pp. 341–350; 367–372.

41 An exception to this is door-to-door sellers, who called on the houses of the wealthy, although these rarely appear as hawkers of food; see, for example, Horace, *Carmina* 3.6.30; *Epodes* 17.20; Propertius, 4.2.38; Ovid, *Remedies for Love* 305–6; Jerome, *Against Jovinianus* 1.47. Since such sellers visit houses directly and would have found women alone, they are often portrayed as a sexual threat by our male authors.

42 Cicero, *On Duties* 1.1.50. Cicero is here following Panaetius: Peter Brunt, 'Aspects of the Social Thought of Dio Chrysostom and of the Stoics', *Proceedings of the Cambridge Philological Society* 19 (1973), pp. 26–34. For the Greek philosophical tradition see, for example, Plato *Laws* 919d–920c; *Protagoras* 313c; Aristotle *Politics* 1.9–10, although the association of retail with deceit appears already in Herodotus (1.153.1–2). See also discussion in Leslie Kurke, 'Kapeleia and Deceit: Theognis 59–60', *American Journal of Philology* 110 (1989), pp. 535–544. For the continued influence of this idea into the twentieth century, see John Benson and Laura Ugolini, 'Introduction', in John Benson and Laura Ugolini (eds), *Cultures of Selling: Perspectives on Consumption and Society since 1700* (Aldershot, 2006), pp. 13–16.

43 See Maurice Balme, 'Attitudes to Work and Leisure in Ancient Greece', *Greece and Rome* 31 (1984), 140–52. Also Brunt, 'Aspects of the Social Thought', pp. 11–12.

44 Cicero, *On Duties* 1.150–151. For Roman attitudes, see Susan Treggiari, 'Urban Labour in Rome: *mercennarii* and *tabernarii*', in Peter Garnsey (ed.), *Non-Slave*

Labour in the Greco-Roman World (Cambridge, 1980), pp. 48–64; Sandra Joshel, *Work, Identity, and Legal Status at Rome: A Study of the Occupational Inscriptions* (Norman, 1992), pp. 63–69 (in Latin literature). In general, see also Alison Burford, *Craftsmen in Greek and Roman Society* (London, 1972), pp. 12–13; 25–26; 28–30.

45 See Treggiari, 'Urban Labour', p. 57, n.2 for some inconsistencies in Cicero's own view. See also John H. D'Arms, *Commerce and Social Standing in Ancient Rome* (Cambridge, MA, 1981) for elite Romans profiting from commercial activities, at least indirectly. For the more nuanced view of Dio Chrysostom, see discussion in Brunt 'Aspects of the Social Thought'.

46 For wage labour in the early Christian tradition, see David A. Fiensy, 'What Would You Do for a Living?', in Anthony J. Blasi, Jean Duhaime and Paul-André Turcotte (eds), *Handbook of Early Christianity: Social Science Approaches* (Walnut Creek and Oxford, 2002), p. 566; Dimitris J. Kyrtatas, 'Modes and Relations of Productions', in Anthony J. Blasi, Jean Duhaime and Paul-André Turcotte (eds), *Handbook of Early Christianity: Social Science Approaches* (Walnut Creek and Oxford, 2002), p. 550.

47 Suetonius, *Augustus* 2.3; 4.2. For similar accusations levelled at the emperors Vitellius and Vespasian, see Suetonius, *Vitellius* 2.1; *Vespasian* 1.2–4; at Cicero, see Dio Cassius 46.4–5; 7.4. See also Mart. 3.16; 3.59; 7.64.

48 For example, Mart. 1.41.8; Ulp. *Dig.* 14.3.5.9.

49 Mart. 1.41.

50 Pliny, *Letters* 4.7.6.4; Mart. 10.3.2. See also Petr. 68.6–7; Historia Augusta, *Commodus* 2.8.

51 Quintilian, *On Oratory* 10.1.8; also 2.4.16.

52 Seneca, *Letters* 56.2. For more on the provision of food in bathhouses, see also Mart. 5.70; 12.19; 12.70; Juvenal, 8.167.

53 Mart. 1.41.5–10; 12.57. For the noise of Rome, see also Juvenal, 3.232–38.

54 Cicero, *On Divination* 2.40.84; Calp. *Ecl.* 4.25–26.

55 Emilio Magaldi, *Il commercio ambulante a Pompei* (Naples, 1930), p. 15.

56 For the street cries of early modern Paris, see Katie Scott, 'Edme Bouchardon's "Cris de Paris": Crying Food in Early Modern Paris', *Word and Image: A Journal of Verbal/Visual Enquiry* 29.1 (2013), pp. 59–91. In this volume, see Chapter 2 for street cries in Late Renaissance Europe and Chapter 8 for contemporary Calcutta.

57 *Institores* could technically be of any legal status (Ulp. *Dig.* 14.3.7.1), but the legal writers tend to be concerned with those of servile status. For further discussion and references, see Holleran, *Shopping*, p. 32.

58 Ulp. *Dig.* 14.3.5.4; 14.3.5.9.

59 Paul. *Dig.* 14.3.4.

60 See, for example, Mart. 7.61; Papinian, *Digest* 43.10.1.4. For further discussion, see Holleran, *Shopping*, pp. 214–215. Also see p. 32 for local magistrates granting permission to certain stallholders to trade in the vicinity of the Pompeian amphitheatre.

61 For control and documentation of street sellers in early modern London, see Chapter 2 in this volume, and for eighteenth-century Naples, see Chapter 5.

62 For approaches to Roman art in the lives of those outside of the elite sphere in Rome, see John R. Clarke, *Art in the Lives of Ordinary Romans* (Berkeley, 2003). Also Peter Stewart, *The Social History of Roman Art* (Cambridge, 2008).

63 Now in the Museo Archeologico Nazionale di Napoli: Inv 143758–61.

64 Stefano De Caro, *Il Gabinetto segreto del museo archeologico nazionale di Napoli: guida alla collezione* (Naples, 2000), p. 60.

65 Magaldi, *Il commercio ambulante*, pp. 11; 28–29; De Caro, *Il Gabinetto segreto*, p. 60. Another possibility is that these are intended to be representations of slaves

holding out trays of food for guests at dinner parties, but their coarse appearance suggests otherwise; literature of this period emphasises the physical beauty and elegant dress of table servants, something which can also be seen in late antique artistic representations of such people. Table servants are also silent, whereas the Pompeian statuettes are clearly shown in the process of shouting. For further discussion of representations of waiting staff, primarily in later Roman art, see Katherine Dunbabin, 'The Waiting Servant in Later Roman Art', *American Journal of Philology* 124 (2003), pp. 443–467.

66 See, for example, John R. Clarke, *Looking at Lovemaking: Constructions of Sexuality in Roman Art, 100 BC – AD 250* (Berkeley, 1998), p. 13.

67 For representations of enormous phalluses with humorous intent, see Clarke, *Looking at Lovemaking*, pp. 131; 134.

68 For this comic costume, see Kenneth Dover, *Greek Homosexuality* (Cambridge, MA, 1978), p. 131.

69 For the Roman aesthetic taste for small phalluses, see discussion in Clarke, *Looking at Lovemaking*, pp. 134; 136; 209–212. Also in the Greek tradition: Dover, *Greek Homosexuality*, pp. 125–135.

70 See, for example, Isabelle Baudino, 'Eighteenth-Century Images of Working Women', in Isabelle Baudino, Jacques Carré and Cécile Révauger (eds), *The Invisible Women: Aspects of Women's Work in Eighteenth-Century Britain* (Aldershot, 2005), pp. 173–182, for idealised representations of women in eighteenth-century engravings of female street sellers, particularly those of Wheatley. See also Chapter 6 in this volume for the representation of street sellers in nineteenth-century Paris.

71 Inventory numbers: 9057; 9059; 9061–62; 9064; 9066–68; 9070. For a detailed description of each of the panels, with good quality reproductions, see Salvatore Ciro Nappo, 'Fregio dipinto dal *praedium* di Giulia Felice con rappresentazione del foro di Pompei', *Rivista di studi pompeiani* 3 (1989), pp. 79–96; also Pietro Giovanni Guzzo, 'Sul fregio figurato *praedia* di Giulia Felice di Pompei (II, 4. 3)', in Marina Sapelli Ragni (ed.), *Studi di archeologia in memoria di Liliana Mercando* (Turin, 2005), pp. 102–113.

72 Identified as a food stall: Helen Tanzer, *The Common People of Pompeii: A Study of the Graffiti* (Baltimore, 1939), p. 30. Others have plausibly identified the items on the table as metal tools. See, for example, Guzzo, 'Sul fregio figurato', p. 107; Nappo, 'Fregio dipinto', p. 88. See also Magaldi, *Il commercio ambulante*, p. 25, who calls the seller a *scrutarius*, a dealer in second-hand goods.

73 The vegetable seller is the only one who could potentially be female, although the gender is disputed; Nappo ('Fregio dipinto', p. 86), for example, describes the seller as male, while Natalie Kampen, 'Social Status and Gender in Roman Art: The Case of the Saleswoman', in Eve D'Ambra (ed.), *Roman Art in Context: An Anthology* (Englewood Cliffs, 1993), p. 66 argues that the seller is female. For a detailed description of the painting of a female seller from the workshop of Verecundus, see Clarke, *Art in the Lives of Ordinary Romans*, pp. 105–112. For more on women and retail in Roman Italy, see Claire Holleran, 'Women and Retail in Roman Italy', in Emily Hemelrijk and Greg Woolf (eds), *Gender and the Roman City: Women and Civic Life in the Western Provinces* (Leiden, 2013), pp. 313–330.

74 Guzzo 'Sul fregio figurato', p. 108; Nappo, 'Fregio dipinto', pp. 94–95. It would in any case have been difficult for an ancient viewer to make out many of the smaller details in the frieze, since it was only about 60cm high and was initially displayed at a height of around 240cm from the ground. These figures are taken from Clarke (*Art in the Lives of Ordinary Romans*, p. 96), although Nappo ('Fregio dipinto', pp. 92–93) gives a height of 73cm for the frieze itself, and places it 247cm from the ground.

75 For the paintings from the House of the Vettii, see Clarke, *Art in the Lives of Ordinary Romans*, pp. 98–105.

76 For early modern examples of genre paintings of markets and street sellers, see Chapter 2 in this volume.
77 See, for example, Scott, 'Edme Bouchardon's "Cris de Paris"', pp. 65–66.
78 An event recorded by Tacitus (*Annals*, 14.17). The painting is now on display in the Museo Archeologico Nazionale di Napoli: inv. 112222. For a discussion, with further bibliography (although no mention of the scenes of trade), see Clarke, *Art in the Lives of Ordinary Romans*, pp. 152–158.
79 Cicero, *Philippics*, 2.97.3.
80 *Corpus Inscriptionum Latinarum* (hereafter *CIL*) IV 1096a–b; 1097; 1097a–b; 1115.
81 For a more detailed description of this relief, see Natalie Kampen, *Image and Status: Roman Working Women in Ostia* (Berlin, 1981), pp. 59–64.
82 See, for example, Raissa Calza, *Museo Ostiense* (Rome, 1962), p. 21.
83 For the seller as female, see, for example, Kampen, *Image and Status*, pp. 59–64.
84 Apul. *Met.* 2.21; Kampen, *Image and Status*, p. 62.
85 For more detailed discussions, see Clarke, *Art in the Lives of Ordinary Romans*, pp. 123–125; Kampen, *Image and Status*, pp. 52–59.
86 See, for example, Dunbabin, 'The Waiting Servant', p. 445.
87 Musée Archéologique Luxembourgeois, Inv. No. 49 (Pilier du Cultivateur).
88 Kampen, *Image and Status*, p. 62.
89 Kampen, 'Social Status and Gender', pp. 118–120.
90 Kampen, *Image and Status*, pp. 83–98. Also Michel Reddé, 'Les scènes de métier dans la sculpture funéraire Gallo-Romaine', *Gallia* 36 (1978), pp. 43–63. For a catalogue of Roman images of work, see Gerhard Zimmer, *Römische Berufsdarstellungen* (Berlin, 1982).
91 See Michele George, 'Social Identity and the Dignity of Work in Freedmen's Reliefs', in Eve D'Ambra and Guy P.R. Métraux (eds), *The Art of Citizens, Soldiers, and Freedmen in the Roman World* (Oxford, 2006), pp. 22–28. Also Lauren Hackworth Peterson, *The Freedman in Roman Art and Art History* (Cambridge, 2006), pp. 114–117; 190–191.
92 For a study of occupational inscriptions from Rome, see Joshel, *Work, Identity, and Legal Status*. See also Nicolas Tran, 'La mention épigraphique des métiers artisanaux et commerciaux dans l'épigraphie de l'Italie centro-méridionale', in Jean Andreau and Véronique Chanowski (eds), *Vocabulaire et expression de l'économie dans le monde antique* (Pessac, 2007), pp. 119–141.
93 See Jean-Jacques Aubert, *Business Managers in Ancient Rome: A Social and Economic Study of Institores, 200 BC – AD 250* (Leiden, 1994), pp. 30–32 for a discussion of the rarity of the title *institor* on epitaphs; the term appears three times in Italy (*CIL* VI 10007; *CIL* XI 1621 (both perfume); *CIL* IX 3027 (cobblers) and twice in the rest of the empire (*CIL* III 13523 (Britain); *CIL* III 14206 (Macedonia)). Cf. Tran, 'La mention épigraphique', p. 129.

2 Quodlibets and fricassées

Food in musical settings of street cries in early modern London*

Deborah L. Krohn

Introduction

Street cries were a common feature of the urban soundscape in early modern cities such as London and Paris, Rome and Naples.[1] The food, clothing, housewares and services being hawked by itinerant merchants played an important role in the evolving economic structures of these growing cities. In London, they also served as the inspiration for polyphonic musical settings by several composers otherwise associated with composition and performance for ecclesiastical and court patrons. Hawkers were also the subject of prints such as an English engraving from the seventeenth century which depicts male and female vendors, identified by their cries and the objects they are selling, a watchman and his dog at the centre (Figure 2.1).[2] Ballads incorporating street cries were published in broadsides, and also echo in works for the stage, performed by actors playing street vendors, common characters in English plays of the seventeenth century.[3]

Though there was presumably a shared audience for prints depicting criers and vocal works composed of cries, there are no studies that focus on the musical settings of English cries in their broader social or economic context, no less as a potential source for the history of food.[4] Prime artefacts of the emerging commercial society of early modern London, the commodification of street cries in the form of song bears witness to a complex web of cultural relations. As several of the chapters in this volume demonstrate in reference to cries from other times and places, settings of cries should not be seen simply as reflections of urban life. They are rather mediated cultural objects that have the potential to reveal more than the sum of their parts to the attentive listener. In the words of Bruce R. Smith, the songs 'domesticate the cries, bringing them in from the streets one by one and setting them to a musical continuo provided by a family of viols'.[5] Unlike later street cries, appropriated and sentimentalized by a host of nineteenth-century chroniclers and composers who were responsible for their appearance in street theatre as well as in the opera house, many of the English Renaissance settings were not published in their own day.

Figure 2.1 Cries of London, seventeenth century, English. Etching 7.32 x 10.63 in. (18.6 x 27 cm). British Museum, 1843, 0311.279.

The following discussion addresses a small group of English compositions from the turn of the seventeenth century. Though the composers – Orlando Gibbons (1583–1625), Thomas Weelkes (1576–1623) and Richard Dering (c.1580–1630) – were important figures in English musical culture, their settings of London street cries were largely forgotten until the early twentieth century, when ethnographic interest in folk songs led to their publication – in some cases for the first time – and their entrance into the performance canon. It was their appeal to a nostalgic conception of 'olden times' that led to their initial recovery, akin to the revival of La Belle Madeleine so compellingly outlined by Stammers in this volume (Chapter 6). The only comprehensive comparative study of the group of English songs links them to 'folk music', and sets out to prove their derivation from the common pool of cries with 'inherent musical characteristics'.[6] Scholars who have worked on both the texts and the tunes of the cries argue that they survive as authentic records of the tonalities and rhythms of calls used by street vendors to sell wares.[7] Other chapters in this volume demonstrate the ongoing employment of cries for selling food in the streets and reference examples of attempts to fix those cries in the historical record.[8]

The 'domestication' enacted on the cries by composers such as Gibbons transformed them from public advertisements to private entertainments, from popular discourse to more lofty forms of expression. Thus, re-constituting the object of study presents further challenges than doing so primarily through recourse to images that circulated in the form of prints. In the words of Eric Wilson, 'The representation of sound, like other modes of discourse – iconography, genre, diction, or whatever we take to be the ground of our own peculiar cultural poetics – is fundamentally tied to the material conditions of its production and of its variable receptions'.[9] By listening to these musical settings as potential transmitters not only of the cries themselves, but also of contemporary perceptions of food hawkers by their consumer audience, their thespian interpreters, and the composers who set them, we can perhaps recover some of the nuances that have otherwise faded into the silence.

If a cross-disciplinary study of the English cries is the ultimate goal, in this limited context I can do no more than raise a series of questions and sketch out potential ways to approach this broader narrative. To date, there is no parallel enterprise in music history to the work of Shesgreen or Beall, who have published studies which aggregate and make accessible the visual culture of street selling in Europe and early America.[10] One explanation for this is that a study of the musical settings does not have the benefit of a body of material evidence beyond surviving manuscript versions. Music is ephemeral, and the history of performance is haphazard and hard to document for the early modern period. What is more, we simply do not have any actual street cries – we only have the art that was crafted with and through them. Though some vocal works incorporating material from street cries were published in the early seventeenth century, such as the rounds by Thomas Ravenscroft (c.1582–1635) in the series of books *Pammelia*, *Deuteromelia* and *Melismata* which appeared in 1609, many were not. Surviving songs exist largely in very limited manuscript copies from the period. While this will be briefly addressed below, a codicological investigation into these manuscripts, surely a worthy enterprise, is not the brief here. Finally, although it is possible to re-constitute the songs fashioned from street cries based on the surviving manuscript sources for modern performance, as Frederick Bridge, followed by Philip Brett, have done, the ephemeral experience of the songs, arguably the ultimate object of study, cannot be recovered.[11]

As in art historical discussions of genre paintings that focus on the verisimilitude of the objects represented, that is, how much they can be trusted to document *how things really looked*, part of what is at issue here is the open question of the extent to which the echoes of street cries incorporated into composed, or at least formally notated, music of the late Renaissance can be trusted to document not only what the cries sounded like, but what goods, services and foods were offered for sale on the streets. What follows is a preliminary exploration of the cultural history of some of the musical settings of the London street cries, with a focus on the food-related content.

Context

Street cries were incorporated into composed music in Europe as early as the thirteenth century, establishing precedents for the group of English songs from around 1600. An anonymous French motet from the Montpellier codex (compiled c.1300) juxtaposes cries for fresh strawberries and blackberries with poetry in praise of Paris.[12] Cries also figure in a fourteenth-century South Flemish motet, as well as in Italian music beginning in the early fifteenth century. German composers made use of the melodic calls of street sellers in sixteenth- and seventeenth-century compositions.[13] But in most of these earlier examples, street cries are embedded as quotations inserted into larger structures rather than comprising the sole content of the compositions.

The various settings of cries in European languages are formally denoted by music historians as quodlibets, compositions 'in which well-known melodies and texts appear in successive or simultaneous combinations'.[14] As in other areas of artisanal or craft production, treatises which attempted to organize and categorize musical practice proliferated during the sixteenth century, so the term quodlibet effectively created a category for a type of composition which had rather porous boundaries. Coined by a German music theorist in 1544, it was originally used to describe an oral examination in German universities, but it also came to refer to the genre of humorous catalogue poems comprising lists of things – the example given in *Grove Music Online* is 'objects forgotten by women fleeing a harem'.[15] The most famous musical quodlibet is in the final movement of Johann Sebastian Bach's *Goldberg Variations* (first published in 1741), which incorporates musical quotations from a folk-song about cabbage and turnips.[16] The term fricassée is used for French quodlibets, as a page from the *superius* part-book of Jean Servin's *Meslange de Chansons…*, published in Lyon in 1578, with the title 'La Fricassée des cris de Paris' demonstrates. A five-part *chanson*, it is constructed out of calls for a variety of foods, goods, and services, juxtaposed and interwoven to create a rich tapestry of sound, in fact obscuring many of the individual cries since each part sings a different text simultaneously.[17] It is truly an aural omelette.

The term fricassée originally meant simply to fry, usually in butter, but in English cookbooks, it came to refer to a group of popular recipes that self-consciously manifest the French influence.[18] Versions of the fricassée in Gervase Markham's *The English Hus-Wife* (1615), include everything but the kitchen sink: 'Now to proceed to fricassees, or *quelquechoses*, which are dishes of many compositions and ingredients, as flesh, fish, eggs, herbs, and many other things, all being prepared and made ready in a frying pan'.[19] Sarah Longe's Receipt Book of 1610 includes a recipe 'for a white ffrigasy' which is a kind of chicken stew.[20] Not all musical fricassées or quodlibets had food as their primary subject, but the metaphorical relationships were certainly operative. In fact, the Spanish term for a musical pastiche or quodlibet was *ensalada*, or salad, another composed dish, suggesting a broad association between food and musical form. While it is tempting to draw conclusions from the applications of these culinary terms to music, there is more work to be done in order to establish what, if any, the implications might be. At the very least, it is worth noting that familiarity with particular foods was diffuse enough to warrant the generation of parallel meanings.

As several other chapters in this volume assert, cultural representations of cries are not an unmediated record of everyday life. Rather, they reflect particular interpretations of the experience of consumers and inhabitants of the urban environments where they arose, providing a critique of the phenomenon within these specific contexts and perhaps more broadly as well. They suggest a self-conscious, almost ethnographic attentiveness to details of daily life. Musical settings of street cries also reflect the aesthetic disconnection between, in this case, street vendors and presumably wealthier patrons of music.

A central question is where musical settings of the cries should be placed on the social continuum. Answers can begin to be formulated through examination of the musical genre in which the songs appear and the type of notational practice which they followed. Just as print literacy provides an index of social and economic status, musical literacy is also a marker of social class.[21] But, like reading, which exists in a separate realm from printed text, music also had a life of its own for which texts are not adequate or complete records.

With these caveats in mind, what, if anything, can the English songs tell us about foodways in Renaissance London? When we look at the texts of the songs, which ostensibly record quotations of street sellers who describe foods that they were hawking, do we learn anything about the materials of everyday life that we can't find out from other sources such as recipe collections, diaries, inventories or travel literature? How can we negotiate between the arch compositional structure of the musical settings, which even obscure the comprehensibility of the text in some cases, and their humble contents, including mackerel and mussels, cabbages and capons? Did the pieces 'work' on contemporary listeners in the same way that genre paintings of kitchens, markets, gardens and street vendors, such as Pieter Aertsen's *Market Scene* (Plate 1) or Vincenzo Campi's *Chicken Vendors* (Plate 2) pitted bravura painterly illusionism against the visceral and sensual reality of food?[22] Was it ironic to behold the coarse, repetitive cries of street vendors miraculously forged into seamless polyphonic songs? Or was it satire? Just as Renaissance painters delighted in verisimilitude and the play between nature and artifice, so, perhaps did contemporary composers strive to approach and even surpass reality in their embellishments of the cries. A useful musical parallel to the cries settings might be contemporary programme music such as William Byrd's *The battel*, an instrumental piece that appears in the 1591 *My Lady Nevell's Booke* in which various military marches and calls are cited in a medley, or the many songs which imitate bird calls or other animal sounds that were composed all over Europe in the sixteenth and seventeenth centuries.

London

In fact, the presence of street vendors in late sixteenth-century London is well documented, and the period just preceding the appearance of the cluster of songs under consideration was a time of crisis in terms of food distribution. By all accounts, by the end of the sixteenth century the streets and markets of London were clogged with men and women hawking a large variety of foods and wares. London records are full of examples of legislation, beginning in the thirteenth century and escalating into the seventeenth century and beyond, aimed at the control of street vendors, from denunciations of disruptive behaviour to attempts to limit the numbers of sellers operating in the streets.[23] Historical demographers estimate that London's population doubled, from 100,000 to 200,000, between 1580 and 1600.[24] Existing networks of food supply and distribution strained under the burden of increased population, and unlicensed extra-guild merchants filled a gap in the supply chain. In the words of Vanessa Harding, 'Market supervision was always troublesome for city government, but it now became something of a nightmare'. Regulations aimed at controlling the free commerce of foodstuffs such as fruit, milk, herbs, roots or flowers were enacted, including the specification of locations where sellers were allowed to stand, and the number of baskets they were permitted to have, presumably to reduce chaos.[25] One of the best sources documenting the chaotic nature of London markets is Hugh Alley's *Caveat*, dating from 1598. An illustrated manuscript now in the Folger Shakespeare Library, it was drawn up by a clerk-turned-informer who was presumably offering his services to the aldermen and lord mayor to control various unsavory practices. Among these practices were 'engrossing' and 'regrating', essentially buying from a legitimate market seller and re-selling at a higher price. Since women were often the ones carrying out these activities, they appear frequently in the rolls of the overseers for offences such as 'twoe baskettes cheryes engroced by an huxter' or 'certein heringe whiche were forstalled and ingroced by dyvers women'.[26] Alley describes street sellers as 'a sorte, of like greedie kind of people, inhabitinge in and about the citty, & suburbs of the same, called *Haglers, Hawkers Huxters*, and *wanderers*, uppe and downe the streetes, in buyenge into their owne handes, to rayse the prices, for their owne luker, and pryvate gayne, all kind of provisions, and *victuals*'.[27] While both men and women hawked food in the streets, the women, called 'oysterwives' or 'fishwives', were subject to greater censure and were often equated with prostitutes.[28] Thus, street cries are also a valuable source for contemporary views concerning women in the labour force. Evelyn Welch's observations concerning the cultural representation of women street sellers in earlier and contemporary Italian literary and visual sources are parallel to what Griffiths, Korda, Van den Heuvel, and others assert for seventeenth-century London and Holland. In both Italian and English contexts, legal, visual and literary sources reflect the same attitudes. Though suspicion and censure were not limited to women, with male peddlers also appearing as the object of derision, women were more likely to be associated with moral failings, their presence in the marketplace as well as their goods and services conflated with offerings of sexual favours and licentious character.[29] It is tempting to speculate that the musical settings of cries referenced these attitudes in the way they were performed, but there is too little information concerning the performance of the songs in their own day to explore how gender stereotypes may have been enacted in their interpretation by individual singers or ensembles. Some modern recorded performances do attempt to bring out humour and communicate the possible double meanings and sexual innuendo evidently coded into the cries themselves.[30]

Words and music

For London residents and visitors familiar with them, songs and ballads making use of street cries must have been like shopping lists set to music. In the group of songs, written, most probably, in the first decade of the seventeenth century, by Gibbons, Weelkes and Dering, cries for about 50 edibles form the core of the texts. There are 15 kinds of fish including: cockles, cod, eels, haddock, herring, lampreys, mackerel, mussels, oysters, periwinkle, plaice, smelts, sprats, thornback, whiting; about 12 fruits including apples, cherries, damson, gooseberries, lemons, medlars, oranges, pears, pippins, pomegranates, and strawberries; vegetables including artichokes, cabbage, cucumbers, lettuce, onion, parsnips, peascod, radish, turnips, and samphire, and including the potato which must have been a new sensation at the time and available only in London;[31] and dairy products including cheese, cream and milk, and a variety of herbs and spices including bay, garlic, juniper, rosemary, salt, and two meats: capon and sausage. According to Joan Thirsk, potatoes may have been brought from Virginia by Sir Walter Raleigh who 'left some tubers in southern Ireland where he paused on his journey back home',[32] though it is more likely that they arrived in Europe via Spanish colonists. Potatoes appear first in English cookbooks in John Murrell's *A delightful exercise for ladies and gentlewomen* (1621) but based on the evidence of their appearance in the texts of the songs, they must have been available on the streets prior to this date.[33] Along with raw materials, there are also cries for various kinds of dishes, hot and ready to eat: pies of apple, pippin, mutton, and pudding, as well as oatcakes and spiced cakes. Capons and sausage appear to have been sold cooked as well. Presumably, hot pies must have come straight from a neighbourhood oven (or were not in fact hot), so this raises the question of whether these vendors were selling on behalf of a baker's shop rather than on their own, but this must remain a speculation. As Sara Pennell has written, many of the residents of sixteenth- and seventeenth-century London did not have access to cooking facilities so purchasing cooked food would have been an important source of sustenance.[34] Samuel Sorbière, visiting London at the end of the seventeenth century, records the custom of selling 'Hot Grey Pease and Bacon' on the streets, one of several ready-to-eat options available:

> I believe they delight in'em most for Supper; for every Night there goes by a Woman crying Hot Grey Pease, and Bacon. Though I take Pease to be too windy for supper Meat, and am inclinable to believe that Hot Ox Cheek, and Bak'd Wardens, cried at the same time may be wholesomer.[35]

The variety of comestibles available in the streets mirrors what we know of the foodstuffs featured in recipe collections and cookbooks of the period. However, by no means all the products mentioned in, for example, Thomas Dawson's *The Good Housewife's Jewel*, of 1587, appear to have been sold by street sellers, whose habitual products seem to have been largely local. Dawson gives recipes for capon boiled with oranges and lemons, damsons, salads of herbs, 'water of life' and many others containing ingredients that might have been purchased on the streets of London. As Thirsk has written, culinary culture in England was becoming more sophisticated in the sixteenth century, marked by both the awareness of continental culinary collections as well as the earliest English books on food such as the 1500 *A Noble Booke of Festes Royalle and Cokery*.[36] London markets were famous for the varieties of foods available, many of which were imported from other regions as well as abroad. The London portbooks of 1567–1568 report sugar from North Africa and Genoa via Antwerp, oranges arriving as the sole cargo of a ship from Spain, and dried prunes arriving from Rouen, France, as well as large quantities of spices from the East Indies via Antwerp and Amsterdam.[37] Though not all of these foods would have been sold by hawkers, Seville oranges, lemons and pomegranates do appear in both Gibbons' and Weelkes' texts.[38]

In addition to the growing taste for foreign and exotic foods, an interest in Italian culinary knowledge is demonstrated by books that made their way to England, parallel to the fashion for Italian musicians and musical forms found in the second half of the sixteenth century in English aristocratic and court society. Both cookbooks and musical forms were aimed at an elite audience. An English translation of the Venetian cookbook first published in 1517 using material largely pirated from Maestro Martino under the title *Epulario or the Italian Banquet*, appeared in 1598. Though not, apparently, translated into English until very recently, many copies of Bartolomeo Scappi's *Opera*, published in several editions between 1570 and 1643, may be found today in English libraries.[39] Scappi was cited as an authority by Hugh Plat in his 1600 *Delightes for Ladies*. In a recipe entitled, 'How to purifie and give an excellent smell and taste unto sallet oyle', the author instructs the cook to refine the oil by beating it together it with water, then draining the water, repeating several times. He then indicates his source: 'Al

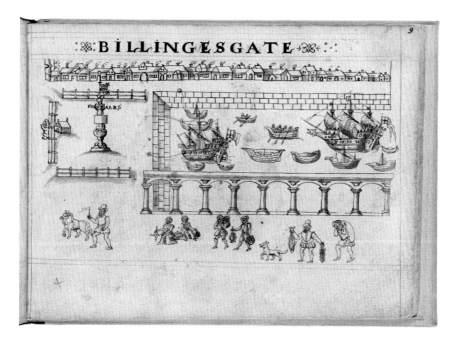

Figure 2.2 Hugh Alley (1556–1602), *A caveatt for the city of London, or a forewarninge of offences against penall lawes*, 1598. Folger Shakespeare Library Digital Image Collection, V. a. 318, fol. 9r.

this is borrowed of *M. Bartholmeus Scapius* the Master Cooke of Pope *Pius Quintus* in his privie kitchen.'[40] Several books of secrets were translated from the Italian during this period, many of which contained information about food and diet as well as remedies and medical advice.[41] Cries for the cordial water Rosasolis, as well as for Aquavitae, appear among raw materials and other consumables. Dawson's recipe for Water of Life from *The Good Housewife's Jewel* (1586–1587) includes a long list of plants and herbs, spices, sugar, dates, mutton, a coney, a capon, pigeons, larks, a dozen eggs, and a lot of mustard and white wine. After leaving the ingredients to ripen for eight or nine days, it is distilled several times before being ready for consumption, diluted in ale, beer or wine, or by itself. Given the labour and equipment necessary to produce this remedy, it is not surprising that it was commercially available.[42]

Fish was plentiful, coming from both local waters – rivers, the sea, or fish ponds, which were increasingly found in the sixteenth century – or from more distant sources. A London portbook of the 1560s lists cargoes from Amsterdam, Hamburg and Danzig.[43] Sorbiére, in 1698, observes that '*This City is well-Served with Carp, Herrings, Cod, Sprats, Lobsters, and Maccarel; of which there are such incredible quantities*, that there is a publick allowance for *Maccarel*, as well as *Milk*, to be cried on *Sundays'*. Thomas Ravenscroft's song, *Broomes for old shoes*, also based on street cries, mentions fish at Billingsgate, which was London's largest fish market, and is one of the markets illustrated in Hugh Alley's *Caveat* (Figure 2.2). Gibbons also includes a cry for 'Oysters, threepence a peck at Bridewell dock, new Wallfleet oysters'.

London's importance as a centre for food is both reflected in and reinforced by the cultural representations in song. Part of what made London a destination for visitors from other parts of England as well as from abroad was its urban spectacle, food hawkers included. Samuel Sorbiére recorded that:

> even though a friend volunteered to shew me the Princes of the Blood, the Prime Minister of State ... yet I refus'd the Civility, and told him *that I took more pleasure* to see Honest John Sharpe of Hackney, in a *White Frock*, crying *Turneps, ho, four bunches a penny*, than Sir *Charles Cottrel, making room for* an Embassadour.[44]

This suggests that the character of the food hawker, whether in music or print, was already setting the stage for a voyeuristic form of cultural tourism more recently associated with the nineteenth-century *flaneur*. Corroborating evidence for food as popular spectacle in early modern Europe is discussed in this volume by Ivan Day in his chapter on frost fairs on the frozen Thames (Chapter 3) and by Melissa Calaresu on the variety of prepared food available in the streets of eighteenth-century Naples (Chapter 5). As Calaresu suggests, many of the visual records of the Neapolitan street scenes are filtered through the eyes of the English Grand Tourists who likely connected their experiences at home with those in Naples.[45]

In addition to the cries for food, the musical settings include cries for household objects, clothing and tradesmen's services. There are also several 'songs' included, meaning text and melodic sequences generally longer than the individual cries that may already have had an independent status as ballads such as the section starting 'Sweep, Chimney Sweep' in the second part of Gibbons' *Cries*. Gibbons, alone among the other composers, embedded a well-known plainchant quotation, the 'in nomine Domini' from the Benedictus section of John Taverner's early sixteenth-century mass on *Gloria Tibi Trinitas*, into one of the viol parts. Though interrupted a few times in the course of the piece, this melodic quotation would probably have been evident to some contemporary listeners, since the same tune was incorporated into many other compositions through the end of the seventeenth century. This example of layering, where an ecclesiastical melody is embedded into a distinct and much more popular genre, is prime evidence of a kind of playful irony which calls attention to the appropriation of street cries into composed music by doing just the opposite: quoting the church tune within the secular and even bawdy realm of street cries. This subtle internal architecture suggests that the play between high and low was very much part of the composer's intention, if nothing else.

Orlando Gibbons' *Cries of London* begins with the town crier announcing the start of a new day: 'God give you good morrow my masters past three o'clocke and a faire morning.' The musical accompaniment for this section, a series of slow chords, serves as a prelude. This parallels prints (as in Figure 2.1) where the town crier is featured in the centre of the sheet, seemingly more significant than other characters since he has been placed in a larger arcade than all the other vendors. By the end of the sixteenth century, town criers or watchmen, who may have played horns as an alarm or signal, were essentially municipal musicians or waits. Their cries appear in several of the musical settings, suggesting the possibility that the songs might sometimes have been performed by professional musicians who also carried out the services of town criers when needed. Purchases of instruments by the city of London for the waits suggests that they played for various civic occasions, and may even have been available for hire for private events such as holiday celebrations in both city and country.[46]

After the introductory section, Gibbons' part-song, written for four or five voices, contains cries for fish, followed by hot pies, various kinds of nuts, vegetables, then oysters, fruit, and garlic, etc. A listener quickly realizes there is no real order to the musical juxtaposition of the individual cries, suggesting that the composer layered them based on their tonal characteristics rather than any kind of more logical taxonomy. The only symmetry comes in the bracketing of the piece by the voice of the town crier who returns in the last bars entreating, 'Twelve o'clocke, looke well to your locke, your fier, and your light, and so good night'.

The musical iterations of the cries are repetitive, almost plaintive, stressing the qualities of the items that make them marketable. In their raw form, the cries were a form of advertisement, a shrewd marketing tool, alerting potential consumers to the availability of a certain type or quality of food. Almost all foods are described as fresh, new, great, ripe, white, fine, hard, or whatever quality distinguished that particular type of fish, fruit or vegetable. The cries' emphasis on colour, texture and size suggest the visceral or sensual experience of the potential consumer. Though there is some variation in the goods and services proffered in each of the cries settings, they reflect a similar market.

Reception

Given the generally negative characterization of street vendors in London based on the prescriptive sources, namely, their illegitimacy in relation to legal commerce, and their assumed social inferiority and moral inadequacy, how can we explain the fashion to set the cries to music for performance presumably among the very people whose livelihood may well have been compromised by the itinerant sellers?

In order to answer this question, we need to look at the performance practice for songs such as this in London. Musical settings of the cries by Gibbons, Weelkes and Dering were not published until the twentieth century, and I have not yet found any references to contemporary performances of these pieces. However, their popularity in the first decades of the seventeenth century is documented by their inclusion in several manuscript compilations. There were only about 100 music books printed in England between the reigns of Elizabeth and Charles I, and there was also a great deal of imported music, but manuscript copying was probably much more pervasive.[47] Cries songs appear in eight of the 24 secular manuscripts for combinations of voices and viols surveyed by Craig Monson. This was the most common performance ensemble for consort songs of the pre-Restoration period in England.[48] The contents of these manuscripts are varied, and include pieces for instruments alone as well as for combinations of voices and instruments. The cries settings are often grouped one after the other in the manuscripts, suggesting that they were seen as a genre and may even have been performed together, though this is pure speculation.

The most well-known of the manuscripts in which cries settings appear was compiled by Thomas Myriell, who settled in London after training at Cambridge in 1616.[49] The manuscript known as British Library Add. 29372 is entitled *Tristitiae remedium. Cantiones selectissimae, diversorum tum authorum, tum argumentorum; labore et manu exaratae THOMAE MYRIELL. A.D. 1616* – the title may in fact refer to the elegiac pieces contained within it which mourn the death of Prince Henry in 1612, though recent scholarship has suggested that the title page with an engraved image does not belong to the original collection and was added at least 200 years later.[50] Since we do not have much information about the compilers of the other manuscripts in which the cries settings are found, looking at Myriell might help to situate them within their material context. Like several of his contemporaries, Myriell moved from the provinces to London and a 'more cosmopolitan, up-to-date musical life'.[51] His neighbourhood was densely populated with musicians and composers, allowing his manuscript collection to serve as an important record of the history of musical taste in the first decades of the seventeenth century. As Monson observes, 'Viewed as a whole, the corpus of vocal works reveals a somewhat traditional and highly serious bias'.[52] This suggests that the settings of the cries by Gibbons, Weelkes and Dering were distinct in the contemporary mind from the more straightforward re-use of cries in rounds or theatrical music which were easy to sing and probably did not require much musical training. Because of their relative complexity to perform, they must have been considered comparable with other vocal works included in the Myriell manuscript and thus appeared in appropriate company. It is striking to find a song based on popular material such as cries included together with music for an elite audience.

Performance

Performance ensembles for music such as the settings of the cries would have consisted of both vocalists and instrumentalists, generally viols. As can well be imagined, there was a range of musical training and talent in Tudor and

Stuart England. As David C. Price states in his study of musical patronage in the English Renaissance, 'the late sixteenth century was a time of increasing interest in and desire for the accomplishments of musical literacy'.[53] According to the leading pedagogical authors of the period such as Sir Thomas Elyot (*The Boke Named the Governour*, 1531), Baldassare Castiglione (*The Courtier*, English edition 1561) and Henry Peacham (*Compleat Gentleman*, 1622), musical skill was valued but not required for a gentleman to possess.[54] Beginning in the 1540s, music teachers are recorded consistently in upper class and royal households, but publication of pedagogical books did not flourish until later.[55] That several early seventeenth-century composers appealed to their audience by claiming in print that their music was not challenging supports the notion that not everyone was a skilled musician, and that there was indeed a market for amateur performance for which print musical anthologies such as Thomas Ravenscroft's *Pammelia*, *Deuteromelia* and *Melismata*, all published in 1609, were created. In his note to the reader, the author of *Deuteromelia*, T.R., calls it a collection of which 'almost all men are capable, that are not altogether immusicall'.[56] There were also a number of didactic manuals offering musical training for playing instruments such as the lute, viol and pandora, published between 1590 and 1620.[57]

But polyphonic songs were not simple to perform, and would have required a modicum of musical literacy at the very least. In comparison to a ballad or round by, for example, Thomas Ravenscroft, where a small number of cries are simply threaded together in sequence and would not be layered in the manner of a polyphonic song, for the Gibbons, Weelkes or Dering compositions each performer would have his or her own musical part, but would not be able to see what other singers were doing at the same moment. The parts were copied out in isolation so performers would have to be highly aware of calibrating duration and pitch with the other singers to achieve the intended harmonic structure. As a perusal of the manuscript of the individual parts for Gibbons' *Cries of London* reveals, a thorough knowledge of notational conventions would have been required for performance even if, and this is a big if, the singers may have been familiar with the actual cries from which the songs were crafted from visiting or residing in London. Though the material may have been 'popular', the artifice employed in the transformation of 'nature' into 'art' assumed a high level of musical literacy for both composer and performer alike.

In contrast, Ravenscroft's *New Oysters*, from *Pammelia*, adapts three simple cries to craft a canon (or a round) in the unison, a much less technically demanding piece.[58] Potential performers were likely aware of the challenges of singing part-songs. Thomas Morley, in his *A Plaine and Easie Introduction to Practicall Musicke*, dating from 1597, informs the reader that to sing a part-song is not possible without talent and practice.[59]

Finally, I return to the question with which I started: what do these songs have to do with food? The cries as they appear in composed music c. 1600 present a list of goods for sale on the streets that may reflect only partially the actual variety of foods for sale in that setting. We can presume that the itinerant sellers would have been savvy enough to sell items for which the market was not already saturated in other, more legitimate commercial venues like shops. Fresh seafood brought by street vendors directly from the docks would have saved consumers from travel across town. Herbs or apples or milk would have been grown or produced locally, while citrus fruit may have been more exotic. Pre-cooked or hot dishes sold on the street catered to the many servants and domestic workers in London who did not have access to kitchens or cooking equipment, or were in shared lodgings.[60]

An interest in and awareness of food as a form of identity was growing in Europe in the course of the sixteenth century. Like the increase in musical literacy, measured by the number of pedagogical texts published, a growing market for cookbooks and recipe collections suggests a similar focus on culinary sophistication. Among the manifestations of this burgeoning interest is the documentation and study of ancient dining practices by a group of doctors in Rome such as Andrea Bacci as well as Protestant theologians in Zurich.[61] Bartolomeo Scappi, the papal chef whose massive cookbook was first published in 1570, was probably influenced by the Roman antiquarian circles in which he cooked. His book includes a meticulous series of illustrations of kitchen interiors, cooking tools and implements that must be considered a kind of ethnography of the kitchen, and are the first of their kind. The fashion for things Italian in Elizabethan and Jacobean England extended to food and other types of recipes, as we see, for example, in the English translation of Alessio Piemontese's *Secrets* by William Warde in 1558, with five editions up to 1615, as well as to music, with the popular collection of Italian madrigals called *Musica Transalpina* published by Andrew Yonge in 1588.[62] But there was also a local or even proto-national dimension to the idea of food as a form of self-fashioning, as evinced by William Harrison's *Of the Food and Drink of the English* from 1587, which traces the history of English food from the classical period up to the book's date.

Musical settings of street cries from early seventeenth-century London are more than simply fashionable pieces intended to entertain across a broad social spectrum, from merchants to aristocrats, though they are that as well. From the perspective of other adaptations of cries and criers, the musical settings of the late Renaissance document one stage on a continuum. Viewed together with other cultural representations of food however, they point to an attempt to record, classify and even celebrate the chaotic culinary streetscape of contemporary London, to an awareness of food and its progress from hoof to home, from farm to fricassée, and to a contemporary nostalgia which guaranteed their re-discovery and absorption into the musical repertory in the twentieth century.

Encouraged from the top down by royal patronage, domestic musical culture thrived in late sixteenth- and seventeenth-century London. Professional groups that formed the Chapel Royal or the King's Musick, the waits or London city musicians, as well as non-affiliated individuals who played for hire, and finally gifted or not-so-gifted amateurs who played and sung for their own entertainment, flourished in London, as well as in the major university towns. The composers who created the musical settings of cries were all prominent figures in the musical elite, with their audiences drawn from royalty as well as the merchant classes. This rising mercantile sector had a voracious appetite for the non-food luxury goods mentioned in the cries, such as gloves, fine combs or perfumed waistcoats, discussed by Linda Levy Peck in the context of the rise of the London Exchange and other commercial markets.[63] It is worth noting that, in the case of the musical settings of cries, the audience was in fact consuming consumption itself. Both the performance of these songs, and their reception, are part of the rise of commercial society. As to more complex inter-relationships between cries and musical culture – the question of to what extent the settings, fixed in pen, ink and paper even if not published, might have standardized the cries themselves, rather than simply notated them, and of course the question of how they were received by contemporary listeners – one can only presume with both humour and bemusement – we await further exploration.

Notes

* I would like to thank Melissa Calaresu and Danielle van den Heuvel for their insightful comments on earlier drafts of this chapter.

1 The term 'soundscape' dates from the 1960s. See Jessie Ann Owens, 'Soundscapes of Early Modern England', in Jesse Ann Owens (ed.), *'Noyses, sounds and sweet aires': Music in Early Modern England* (Seattle and London, 2006), pp. 9ff. The term is also extensively used by Bruce R. Smith in *The Acoustic World of Early Modern England: Attending to the O-Factor* (Chicago, 1999).

2 For a nuanced discussion of prints depicting hawkers in London, see Sean Shesgreen, *Images of the Outcast: The Urban Poor in the Cries of London* (New Brunswick and Manchester, 2002). A catalogue of prints of hawkers, arranged by city of origin, is found in Karen F. Beall, *Kaufrufe und Straßenhändler/Cries and Itinerant Trades* (Hamburg, 1975). The English example illustrated here was probably inspired by Italian prints of street sellers from the late sixteenth century such as one made by Ambrogio Brambilla and engraved by Claudio Duchetti (Beall, *Kaufrufe*, p. 354, illustration on p. 355).

3 On street sellers and the stage, see the extended discussion by Natasha Korda, *Labor's Lost: Women's Work and the Early Modern Stage* (Philadelphia, 2011), pp. 144–173, and 'Gender at Work in the Cries of London', in Mary Ellen Lamb and Karen Bamford (eds), *Oral Traditions and Gender in Early Modern Literary Texts* (Aldershot and Burlington, 2008), pp. 117–135. I would like to express my thanks to Natasha Korda for sharing unpublished material, as well as for helpful bibliographic suggestions and discussion. On ballads see also Ross R. Duffin, 'Ballads in Shakespeare's World', in Owens, *'Noyses, sounds and sweet aires'*, pp. 32ff. Two plays that featured street criers, Thomas Heywood's *Rape of Lucrece* (1609) and Ben Jonson's *Bartholomew Fair* (1614), are discussed extensively by Eric Wilson, 'Plagues, Fairs and Street Cries: Sounding Out Society and Space in Early Modern London', *Modern Language Studies*, 25/3 (1995), pp. 1–42.

4 For a survey of the market for prints of the cries of London, see Sean Shesgreen, 'The Cries of London from the Renaissance to the Nineteenth Century: A Short History', in Jeroen Salman, Roeland Harms and Joad Raymond (eds), *Not Dead Things: The Dissemination of Popular Print in England and Wales, Italy and the Low Countries, 1500–1820* (Leiden and Boston, 2013), pp. 117–152.

5 Smith, *Acoustic World*, p. 64.

6 Kristine Forney Gibbs, 'A Study of the Cries of London as found in the Works of the English Renaissance Composers' (Unpublished Masters Thesis, University of Kentucky, 1974), p. ii.

7 Gibbs cites both Bridge and Gustave Reese making this assertion (Gibbs, 'A Study of the Cries of London', pp. 67–68).

8 See Chapters 4 and 6 in this volume.

9 Wilson, 'Plagues, Fairs and Street Cries', p. 39.

10 Shesgreen, *Images of the Outcast*. See also his article 'The Cries of London in the Seventeenth Century', *Papers of the Bibliographical Society of America*, 86 (1992), pp. 269–294, and an earlier book, *The Criers and Hawkers of London: Engravings and Drawings by Marcellus Laroon* (Palo Alto, 1990). See also Beall, *Kaufrufe*.

11 Frederick Bridge, *The Old Cryes of London* (London, 1921). Several of the musical settings of the Cries of London are published in Philip Brett, *Consort Songs*, 'Musica Britannica', 22 (London, 1967), and 2nd revised edition (1974).

12 Maria Rika Maniates and Richard Freedman, 'Street Cries', *Grove Music Online. Oxford Music Online*, www.oxfordmusiconline.com/subscriber/article/grove/music /26931?q=Cries&search=quick&pos=2&_start=1#firsthit (accessed 11 February 2010). For a discussion of the Montpellier Codex and the Grocheio motet in which the cries appear, see also Richard Taruskin, *The Oxford History of Western Music* (6 volumes, Oxford and New York, 2005), vol. I, pp. 236ff.

13 The Flemish motet is in Utrecht. On this, see Edward Stam, 'Het Utrechtse fragment van een Zeeuws-Vlaamse markt-roepen-motetus', *Tijdschrift van de Vereniging voor Nederlandse Muziekgeschiedenis*, 21/1 (1968), pp. 25–36. There is little written on the Italian settings, but they are mentioned in Maniates and Freedman in the *Grove Music Online* article cited above.

14 Maria Rika Maniates (with Peter Branscombe) and Richard Freedman, 'Quodlibet,' *Grove Music Online. Oxford Music Online*, www.oxfordmusiconline. com/subscriber/article/grove/music/22748 (accessed 11 February 2010).

15 Maniates *et al.*, 'Quodlibet'.

16 Thanks to Christopher H. Gibbs for pointing this out.

17 The transcription of the text is from a sound recording: *L'Écrit de Cri. Renaissance and 19th–21st Century Songs*, Ensemble Clément Janequin, Dominique Visse, Harmonia Mundi, 2009, HMC 092028.

18 For the use of the term as a verb meaning to fry in butter, see, for example, the many recipes with this instruction in the 1604 Belgian cookbook, *Ouverture de Cuisine par Lancelot de Casteau*, trans. Léo Moulin (Antwerp/Brussels,1983). The verb is also used in earlier French cookbooks such as the *Platine en Francoys* (Lyon, 1505), a French translation of the Latin by Bartolomeo Sacchi/Platina first published in Rome the 1470s.

19 Gervase Markham, *The English Housewife*, ed. Michael R. Best (Kingston and Montreal, 1986), p. 67.

20 Joan Thirsk, 'Food in Shakespeare's England', in Mary Anne Caton (ed.), *Fooles and Fricassees: Food in Shakespeare's England*, ex. cat., Folger Shakespeare Library (Seattle and London, 1999), p. 116. This is from 'Mrs. Sarah Longe Her Receipt Booke', c. 1610, in the Folger Shakespeare Library, Washington, DC.

21 For a consideration of printed cries and the popular press, see Shesgreen, 'The Cries of London from the Renaissance to the Nineteenth Century', pp. 143ff., where he states, 'Cries as forms of depiction are intensely social, with direct and potent ties to everyday life as it is lived in the streets of big cities. They take class difference, economic status, trade, labor, and money as their métier'.

22 See Margaret Sullivan, 'Aertsen's Kitchen and Market Scenes: Audience and Innovation in Northern Art', *Art Bulletin*, 81/2 (June 1999), pp. 236–266, and Sheila McTighe, 'Foods and the Body in Italian Genre Paintings, about 1580: Campi, Passarotti, Carracci', *Art Bulletin*, 86/2 (June 2004), pp. 301–323. On Campi,

see also Robert S. Miller, '"Diversi personaggi molto ridiculosi": A Contract for Cremonese Market Scenes', in Andrea Bayer (ed.), *Painters of Reality: The Legacy of Leonardo and Caravaggio in Lombardy*, ex. cat. (New York, 2004), pp. 156–158, which includes a contract for lost paintings depicting market scenes which suggest that the subject matter is more straightforward than symbolic.

23 Food was only one of many types of goods for sale on the streets. For a comprehensive summary and discussion of the historiography of early modern peddlers and hawkers, see Danielle van den Heuvel, 'Selling in the Shadows: Peddlers and Hawkers in Early Modern Europe', in Marcel van der Linden and Leo Lucassen (eds), *Working on Labor: Essays in Honour of Jan Lucassen* (Leiden and Boston, 2012), pp. 125–151.

24 On the population of London, see A.L. Beier and Roger Finlay, 'The Significance of the Metropolis', in A.L. Beier and Roger Finlay, *London 1500–1700: The Making of the Metropolis* (London and New York, 1986), pp. 1–7; also Paul Griffiths and Mark S.R. Jenner (eds), *Londinopolis: Essays in the Cultural and Social History of Early Modern London* (Manchester, 2000), p. 2ff.

25 Vanessa Harding, 'Cheapside: Commerce and Commemoration', *Huntington Library Quarterly*, 71/1 (2008), p. 9. Official attempts to regulate and control street vendors in other areas of early modern Europe are discussed in Danielle van den Heuvel, 'The Multiple Identities of Early Modern Dutch Fishwives', in *SIGNS: Journal of Women in Culture and Society*, 37/3 (Spring 2012), pp. 587–594, and Merry E. Wiesner, *Working Women in Renaissance Germany* (New Brunswick, 1986), pp. 111–147, a chapter which discusses meat, fruit, vegetables and herbs, and related products.

26 Ian Archer, Caroline Barron and Vanessa Harding (eds), *Hugh Alley's Caveat: The Markets of London in 1598* (London, 1988), p. 23.

27 Archer *et al.*, *Hugh Alley's Caveat*, p. 35.

28 For an exhaustive survey of records from the Bridewell and Bethlem Hospital Courtbooks, the Bethlem Royal Hospital Archives and Museum, the London Metropolitan Archives, among others, documenting the presence of women selling in the streets and the negative attitudes concerning them, see Paul Griffiths, *Lost Londons: Change, Crime, and Control in the Capital City, 1550–1660* (Cambridge, 2008), pp. 123–134. Many women are named in specific situations as they come in conflict with the law, presenting a different aspect of the situation from the more generic descriptions in *Hugh Alley's Caveat*. On this, see also Korda, 'Gender at Work in the Cries of London', p. 125, and Van den Heuvel, 'The Multiple Identities of Early Modern Dutch Fishwives'.

29 Evelyn Welch, *Shopping in the Renaissance* (New Haven and London, 2005), pp. 32–51; Korda, *Labor's Lost*, pp. 155ff.

30 See, for example, *Orlando Gibbons: Fantasias & The Cries of London*, Paul Nicholson and Red Byrd, Virgin Classics, 6 Junc 2000, Audio CD; also *The Cries of London*, Theatre of Voices, Fretwork, Conductor: Paul Hillier, Harmonia Mundi France, 13 June 2006, Audio CD.

31 Potatoes are mentioned in Richard Dering's 'The City Cries', in Brett, *Consort Songs*, pp. 133–147, as well as in Gibbons' 'The Cries of London', in Brett, *Consort Songs*, pp. 114–126.

32 Joan Thirsk, *Food in Early Modern England: Phases, Fads, Fashions 1500–1760* (London and New York, 2007), p. 30.

33 London: Printed [by Augustine Mathewes] for Tho: Devve, and are to be sold at his shoppe in St: Dunstons Church-yard in Fleete-street, 1621. Recipe 61: To make a paste of Potatoes. Recipe 62: To dry Potatoes. Recipe 63: To preserve Potatoes. A note in one of Hugh Plat's commonplace books reads: 'I have seene of these rootes grow in [England – crossed through] holborne as Mr. Jarrett assured mee in his owne garden, qre iff the same will grow of seedes for that were a profitable coarse' – evidence that they were grown in local gardens in the 1590. See Malcolm

Thick, *Sir Hugh Plat: The Search for Useful Knowledge in Early Modern London* (Totnes, 2010), pp. 77–78.

34 For an extended discussion of food available outside of domestic settings, see Sara Pennell, 'Great Quantities of Gooseberry Pye and Baked Clod of Beef: Victualling and Eating Out in Early Modern London', in Griffiths and Jenner, *Londinopolis*, pp. 228–249.

35 Samuel Sorbière, *A Journey to London in the Year 1698. After the Ingenuous Method of that made by Dr. Martin Lyster to Paris...*, trans. William King (London, 1698), pp. 29–30.

36 Thirsk, *Food in Early Modern England*, p. 11. She also mentions *A Proper Newe Booke of Cokerye* of 1545.

37 Thirsk, *Food in Early Modern England*, pp. 30–31.

38 In Renaissance Germany, women who sold imported oranges and lemons were forbidden from selling home-grown fruit. See Wiesner, *Working Women*, p. 120.

39 Bartolomeo Scappi, *The Opera of Bartolomeo Scappi (1570)*, trans. Terence Scully (Toronto, 2008).

40 Sir Hugh Plat, *Delightes for Ladies* (London: Peter Short, 1603), p. G5v. There is a similar recipe in Plat's *The Jewell House of Art and Nature* (London: Peter Short, 1594), p. 38.

41 Thirsk, *Food in Early Modern England*, p. 33.

42 Thomas Dawson, *The Good Housewife's Jewel*, ed. Maggie Black (Lewes, 2002), pp. 143–144.

43 Thirsk, *Food in Early Modern England*, p. 266.

44 From William King, *Journey to London*, 1698, cited in Shesgreen, *Images of the Outcast*, p. 8.

45 See Melissa Calaresu, 'Costumes and Customs in Print: Travel, Ethnography, and the Representation of Street-Sellers in Early Modern Italy', in Salman *et al.*, *Not Dead Things*, pp. 181–209.

46 Walter L. Woodfill, *Musicians in English Society from Elizabeth to Charles I* (Princeton, 1953), pp. 33–35.

47 Woodfill, *Musicians in English Society*, p. 232.

48 Craig Monson, *Voices and Viols in England, 1600–1650: The Sources and the Music* (Ann Arbor, 1982), p. 2.

49 Craig Monson, 'Thomas Myriell's Manuscript Collection: One View of Musical Taste in Jacobean London', *Journal of the American Musicological Society*, 30/3 (Autumn 1977), pp. 419–465.

50 Donna M. Di Grazia, 'New Perspectives on Thomas Myriell's Tristitiae remedium and Add. Ms.29427', *Early Music*, 28/1 (2010), p. 101.

51 Monson, 'Thomas Myriell's Manuscript Collection', p. 420.

52 Monson, 'Thomas Myriell's Manuscript Collection', p. 423.

53 David C. Price, *Patrons and Musicians of the English Renaissance* (Cambridge, 1981), p. 1.

54 Woodfill, *Musicians in English Society*, pp. 209ff.

55 Price, *Patrons and Musicians*, p. 4. On musical pedagogy, see Pamela F. Starr, 'Music Education and the Conduct of Life in Early Modern England: A Review of the Sources', in Russell Eugene Murray, Susan Forscher Weiss and Cynthia J. Cyrus (eds), *Music Education in the Middle Ages and the Renaissance* (Bloomington, 2010), pp. 103–206.

56 Thomas Ravenscroft, *Deuteromelia: or the seconde part of Musicks melodie, or melodius musicke Of pleasant roundelaies; K.H. mirth, or freemens songs. And such delightful catches* (London: Printed [by T. Snodham] for Thomas Adams, dwelling in Paules Church-yard at the signe of the white Lion, 1609), p. 4.

57 For example, Anthony Holborne, *The cittharn schoole, by Antony Holborne gentleman, and seruant to her most excellent Maiestie. Hereunto are added sixe short aers*

Neopolitan like to three voyces, without the instrument: done by his brother William Holborn (At London: Printed by Peter Short, dwelling on Breadstreet hill at the signe of the Starre, 1597).

58 *Pammelia Musicks miscellanie. Or, Mixed varietie of pleasant roundelayes, and delightfull catches, of 3. 4. 5. 6. 7. 8. 9. 10. parts in one. None so ordinarie as musicall, none so musical, as not to all, very pleasing and acceptable* (London: Printed by [John Windet for] William Barley, for R. B[onian] and H. W[alley] and are to be sold at the Spread Eagle at the great north doore of Paules, 1609), #5.

59 Cited in Woodfill, *Musicians in English Society*, p. 217.

60 Pennell asserts that, 'In an early modern version of the modern supermarket practice of supplying free recipes with unusual foodstuffs, hawkers sold novel market garden produce – early asparagus, sea kale, soft fruit – ready packaged with instructions for preparation and "dressing it up"' (Pennell, 'Great Quantities of Gooseberry Pye', p. 235).

61 Andrea Bacci, *De naturali vinorum historia, de vinis Italiae et de conviviis antiquorum* (Rome: ex officina N. Mutij, 1596). On Bacci, see Nancy G. Siraisi, '*Historiae, Natural History, Roman Antiquity, and Some Roman Physicians*', in Gianna Pomata and Nancy G. Siraisi (eds), *Historia: Empiricism and Erudition in Early Modern Europe* (London and Cambridge, 2005), pp. 335–336. One of the theologians is Johann Wilhelm Stuck, author of *Antiqvitatvm Convivialivm Libri III. In Qvibvs Hebraeorvm, Graecorvm, Romanorvm Aliarvmqve Nationvm Antiqva Conviviorvm Genera, necnon mores, consuetudines, ritus ceremoniæq[ue] conuiuiales, atque etiam aliæ explicantur, & cum ijs, quae hodie...* (Zurich: Christophorvs Froschovervs, 1582).

62 On Alessio and his popularity in England, see William Eamon, *Science and the Secrets of Nature: Books of Secrets in Medieval and Early Modern Culture* (Princeton, 1994), pp. 139–147.

63 Linda Levy Peck, *Consuming Splendor: Society and Culture in Seventeeth-Century England* (Cambridge, 2005), pp. 14ff.

3 Street cries on the frozen Thames

Food hawkers at London frost fairs, 1608–1814

Ivan Day

Between 1092 and 1814 the River Thames froze solid at least 25 times. On some of these occasions 'frost fairs' were held on the ice, creating lucrative commercial opportunities for street vendors and other casual traders. As a result of a series of particularly cold winters between 1550 and 1850, a phenomenon sometimes described as the little Ice Age, the river frequently remained frozen for months.[1] In 1608, 1683, 1715, 1739, 1789 and 1814, the fairs were extensive and are particularly well illustrated and described in contemporary printed broadsides and ballad sheets. Some of these publications were produced on presses that enterprising city printers moved from their shops into booths on the frozen river itself, therefore serving as potent mementoes of these unusual occasions. Sold to a public who were only too keen to own a permanent representation of a rare moment when normal city life had been suspended, these often crudely illustrated sheets possessed little literary merit, but the fact that they were 'printed on the River of Thames' made them well worth owning. The survival of large numbers in both public and private collections is probably due to the unusual conditions of their production, giving them an added value which resulted in a longevity not enjoyed by other classes of printed ephemera. Some of these broadsides could even be made up into packs of playing cards. One surviving in the Guildhall Library from the fair of 1683–4 is printed with instructions to play a particular game called Frost Fair Cards.[2] Another published at the same fair provides musical notation to allow the rhyming couplets describing the occasion to be sung to a catchy melody.[3]

A number of celebrated visitors to the fairs purchased souvenirs of this kind. A small ticket 'printed by G. Groom, on the ice, on the River Thames, January 31, 1684' was personally printed for Charles II and five other members of the royal family to commemorate their frost fair visit.[4] John Evelyn, who once owned this item, commented on the practice of printing these keepsakes on the ice:

> The people and ladyes tooke a fancy to have their names printed, and the day and yeare set downe when printed on the Thames: this humour tooke so universally, that 'twas estimated the printer gain'd £5 a day, for printing a line onely, at six-pence a name, besides what he got by ballads, etc.[5]

Similar mementoes were still being published on the ice during the last ice fair in 1814, when one printer, G. Davis, even issued an entire 124-page book offering a history of the London frost fairs entitled, *Frostiana: or the History of the River Thames in a frozen state.*[6] One handbill from the same event indicates why these printed keepsakes were perceived as popular memorials:

> You that walk here, and do design to tell
> Your children's children what this year befell,
> Come buy this print, and then it will be seen
> That such a year as this hath seldom been.[7]

Souvenirs printed on the ice frequently turn up in scrapbooks, or pasted onto the endpapers of family bibles. One printed on the frozen Thames for Mr. Wm. Baker Junior and dated 18 January 1715 clearly tells us its purpose,

> To tell our Offspring that those Streams
> Which gently glide along the Thames,
> Were froze so hard, that Trades were there,
> May shock their Faith, and make 'em stare,
> But when their Parents Names they see,
> They'll own for Truth the Prodigy.[8]

The survival of printed frost fair ephemera as family heirlooms testifies to the regard that these rare occasions were held in the popular imagination and are essential sources to the historian for further research on the subject.

Much has been written on the Thames frost fairs, but the nature of the commercial activity relating to food on the frozen river is only discussed superficially in passing by most authors. Thompson sporadically outlines the occasions when the Thames froze, from the earliest recorded instance in 1092 to the great freeze of 1814. His observations consist of scattered references in a work that more generally focuses on the history of London Bridge and he has little to say on the sale of food on the ice.[9] Rimbault was one of the first to recognize the value of the frost fair broadsides as rare insights into commercial activity in early modern London and he catalogued examples located in institutional libraries.[10] However, like most nineteenth-century antiquarians, he was not much interested in food vendors and offers little comment on their activities on the ice. Andrews also writes from a purely antiquarian stance and his observations on vendors at the fairs tell us very little about the nature of the hawkers or the food they were purveying.[11] More recent reviews of the literary evidence for the London frost fairs, by Currie and Reed, are general treatments aimed at a popular readership and add very little that is new to our understanding of food culture on the ice.[12] My own interest in frost fair food vendors was initiated by some research on the practice of ox roasting at these events, the results of which were published in a paper that examined this custom in a broader historical context. The current chapter includes some material on frost fair ox roasting that was not covered in that earlier essay as well as attempting to identify the nature of other food and drink offered for sale at these events.[13]

Under ordinary circumstances, street commerce was such an everyday occurrence that the activities of food vendors were not usually considered worthy of much comment. As a result of the extreme conditions the almost total suspension of normal trade meant that street sellers moved from their usual street pitches onto the ice, a space where they exploited new and lucrative opportunities for purveying their wares. Their activities, usually unexceptional and anonymous, moved centre stage. As a result they were recorded in the context of these highly abnormal events. These rare visual and literary representations of their activities on frost fair broadsides and ballad sheets offer a rich insight into the economic culture of a social class who tended to be ignored under normal conditions. London had a number of well-established terrestrial fairs such as Southwark Fair and Bartholomew Fair, which were regular features in the city calendar. Although these annual occasions are richly represented in literature, they did not generate the enormous amount of visual and descriptive material inspired by the much rarer frost fairs.

The literary and visual evidence provided by the frost fair broadsides indicates that a surprisingly varied selection of food and drink was sold from temporary canvas booths transformed into cook shops, taverns and coffee houses. Hawkers of hot pies, gingerbread, fruit and ardent spirits plied their goods on the ice at highly inflated prices. Whole oxen and other animals were roasted in front of enormous fires, usually concealed behind tall temporary fences, so that visitors could not witness the marvellous spectacle without paying an entrance fee. Those who wanted a slice of roast meat paid extra. Vendors of beverages not only sold cups of hot ardent spirits, but also expensive souvenir mugs with inscriptions that proved the drink had been consumed on the frozen river. One of the earliest references to food being offered for sale on the Thames ice is from a description of the 1608 fair: 'there were many that set up boothes and standings upon the ice, as fruit-sellers, victuallers, that sold beere and wine, shoomakers, and a barber's tent &c.'.[14]

Very little is known about the actual identity of these vendors. However, in the early eighteenth century, an anonymous female pippin seller was transformed into a celebrated literary heroine as a result of a tragedy on the river during the harsh winter of 1715–16 when the Thames froze for nearly three months. The London poet and playwright John Gay, who witnessed this ice fair, described the event in his 1716 poem, *Trivia; or the Art of Walking the Streets of London*:

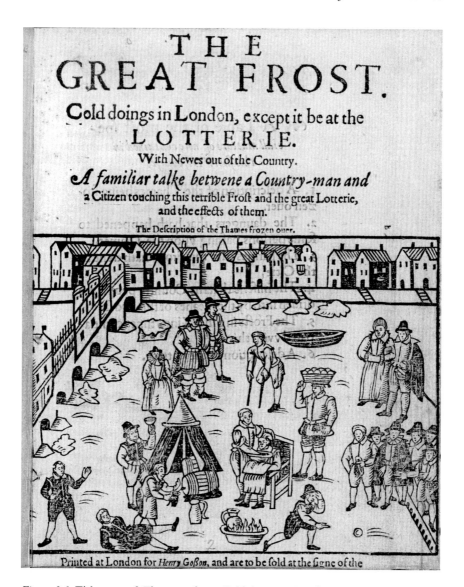

THE
GREAT FROST.
Cold doings in London, except it be at the
LOTTERIE.
With Newes out of the Country.
A familiar talke betwene a Country-man and
a Citizen touching this terrible Froſt and the great Lotterie,
and the effects of them.

The Deſcription of the Thames frozen over.

Printed at London for *Henry Goßon,* and are to be ſold at the ſigne of the

Figure 3.1 Title page of *The great frost: Cold doings in London, except it be at the lotterie. With newes out of the country. A familiar talk betwene a country-man and a citizen touching this terrible frost and the great lotterie, and the effects of them.* Letterpress and woodcut (London, 1608). Courtesy of Houghton Library, Harvard University STC 11403.

O roving Muse, recal that wondrous year,
When winter reign'd in bleak Britannia's air;
When hoary Thames, with frosted osiers crown'd,
Was three long moons in icy fetters bound.[15]

In this mock-Georgic poem, Gay uses the fair as the setting for the tragicomic death of Doll, an itinerant apple seller who falls through the ice and loses her head as the 'cracking crystal' closes violently around her neck. He relates how the unfortunate hawker's decapitated head bounces across the frozen surface as her body sinks into the river:

> Her Neck grew warpt beneath autumnal Loads
> Of various Fruit; she now a Basket bore,
> That Head, alas! shall Basket bear no more.
> Each Booth she frequent past, in quest of Gain,
> And Boys with pleasure heard her shrilling Strain.
> Ah Doll! all Mortals must resign their Breath,
> And Industry itself submit to Death
> The cracking crystal yields, she sinks, she dies,
> Her head, chopt off, from her lost shoulders flies;
> Pippins she cry'd, but death her voice confounds,
> And pip-pip-pip along the ice resounds.[16]

Gay really did witness the 1716 fair, but his account of Doll's macabre passing was not simply a journalistic report of a real event. There were frequent accidents on the ice, including a number of deaths, but Gay combined Doll's story with that of Isabella in Ludovico Ariosto's *Orlando Furioso*, a tragic heroine who suffered an equally violent decapitation. Gay had translated some of Ariosto's work into English and clearly borrowed Doll's abbreviated street cry of 'pip-pip-pip' from the horrific scene when Isabella's disembodied head utters the name of her lover as it bounces along the ground three times.[17] As a counterpoint Gay also compares Doll's violent end to that of Orpheus at the hands of the Thracian women, making an easily identifiable allusion to Dryden's translation of Virgil's Georgics.[18] In this mock-heroic, Gay's humble apple seller becomes a tragic heroine of casual commerce rather than of epic myth and her familiar street cry is metamorphosed into an Orphic hymn. The usually grey Thames, London's main arterial highway and commercial conduit, is transformed by the arctic cold into a frozen incarnation of the ancient Heber.[19] So Doll was modelled on multiple literary sources, as well as journalistic ones. There were many such accidents on the Thames ice and Gay may have had one in particular in mind when he invented the character. He deliberately uses the frost fair as an emblem of suspended normality, of magical transformation. Even a lowly peddler could become a heroine of operatic stature in such an exotic environment.[20]

It was a commonly held belief that unusually severe winters offered prognostication of disastrous events. A broadside, entitled *The English Chronicle; or Frosty Kalendar*, printed on the ice during the 1739 fair by an unknown publisher, explains: 'It is observable, that when any Frost has happened remarkably severe, it hath very soon been followed by some extraordinary

Revolution, Change or Event.' The unknown author remarks on the harsh winter of 1684:

> This was but a Year before that gracious and merry Monarch King Charles II who himself hunted a Fox upon the Thames, was taken out of the World in a very suspicious Manner; after which came in a Deluge of Popery and arbitrary Power: And this intervening Year was the most troublesome one that had been known since the Restoration, being intirely filled up with Conspiracies, Trials and Executions.

Of Gay's 1715 winter he reminds us:

> It was during this Frost that the Pretender landed in Scotland, and made his public Entry into Perth: the fatal Consequences of which too many of his Adherents are but too well remember'd at this Time, and therefore shall be omitted.[21]

The violent consequences discreetly alluded to were the beheadings which followed the 1715 Jacobite uprising, an event so recent that Doll's decapitation by the razor sharp Thames ice must have had uncomfortable resonances for many of Gay's readers.

As well as poor unfortunate Doll, nearly all the other characters in *Trivia* have something to sell and the poem's central theme explores the poet's own uncertain relationship with the marketplace. It is possible that Gay may have noticed his rival, the poet William Ellis, was reduced to peddling verse on the ice at the 1715–16 fair and may have worried that he too could be reduced to the same precarious situation as a hawker (Ellis is depicted in Figure 3.2). Gay's fluctuating fortunes as an author put him in a unique position to relate his own experiences to those of others who relied on small-scale commercial enterprises for their survival. On those rare occasions when the Thames froze over, the watermen found themselves deprived of their usual livelihood, often for months at a time. Gay describes their precarious situation, and exploits it as a metaphor for a penniless poet without patron: 'The waterman, forlorn along the shore, / Pensive reclines upon his useless oar.'[22]

A couplet from a broadside published in the year of Gay's frost fair poem explains how the watermen earned a living by other means: 'The Water-men for want of Rowing-boats, / Make use of Booths to get their Pence and Groats.'[23] The frost fairs were entirely organized by the Thames watermen, whose livelihood was threatened by prolonged hard freezes because they could not launch their boats. The coat of arms of their livery company is sometimes displayed with that of the City of London on some of the broadsides sold on the ice. Their normal activities of ferrying Londoners and goods had to be suspended until the thaw. They considered it their right to charge a fee to anyone who wanted to stroll on the frozen river and they restricted access to the landings and steps until visitors paid up. Unlike the annual London fairs held on

Figure 3.2 Unlike the ox roasting in 1683/4, which was concealed behind a tall fence, that of 1715 as depicted in this woodcut, appears to have been visible to all. Printed broadside of Thames frost fair of 1715–1716. *Mr David Hannott. Printed on the Ice, at the Maidenhead at Old-swan Stairs, Jan. 25. 1715–16* (London, 1715). Letterpress and woodcut. Guildhall Library. Courtesy of the City of London, London Metropolitan Archives P7499528.

Figure 3.3 Detail from Figure 3.2 showing the ox roasting.

terra firma, such as Bartholomew, Southwark and May Fair, all regulated by ancient royal charters, the frost fairs were opportunistic affairs that afforded the watermen a means of making a living at these very difficult times without official interference.[24] They rented out the improvised oar and canvas booths and charged other vendors for the privilege of trading on the ice. The commercial activities of watermen were strictly controlled by their livery company, which regularly updated and published their rules and constitutions. Nothing, however, is said in any of their by-laws about how they should respond in the eventuality of a total freeze. So without the benefit of any kind of charter, the watermen claimed temporary ownership and complete control of the frozen space.[25] Though of low status, they were a powerful group who were extremely defensive of their trade. In 1681 they petitioned Charles II against moving parliament to Oxford, as they believed it would have a detrimental effect on the volume of river traffic going to and from Westminster and they would lose money from a serious decrease in their passengers.[26] Londoners appear to have been sympathetic to their difficult predicament during the really serious freezes and happily paid their entrance fees to gain access to the icy river and its attractions, knowing they were helping the watermen and their families.

The intense cold forced many others into joining the watermen in new enterprises, the frozen river itself providing novel opportunities for money making. Peddlers and other vendors migrated from their usual street locations in the city to the dramatic stage of the icy Thames itself, where a holiday atmosphere prevailed and crowds of Londoners with full purses flocked to promenade on the normally inaccessible river:

> Behold the Wonder of this present Age,
> A Famous RIVER now become a Stage.
> Question not what I now declare to you,
> The Thames is now both Fair and Market too,
> And many Thousands dayly do resort,
> Ther to behold the Pastime and the Sport.[27]

Hot food and drink were a priority for visitors and many casual traders exploited this to the full. As well as the customary peddlers like Doll selling baked pippins, hot pies, gingerbread, and other warming refreshments, sail-cloth booths were transformed by the watermen into alfresco coffee houses, taverns and cook shops. The watermen used their superfluous oars to prop up the tents and booths:

> How am I filled with wonder for to see
> A Flooding River now a Road to be,
> Where Ships and Barges used to frequent
> Now you may see a Booth of fudling Tents,
> And those that us'd to ask where shall I Land ye
> Now cry, what lack ye Sir, Beer, Ale, or Brandy.[28]

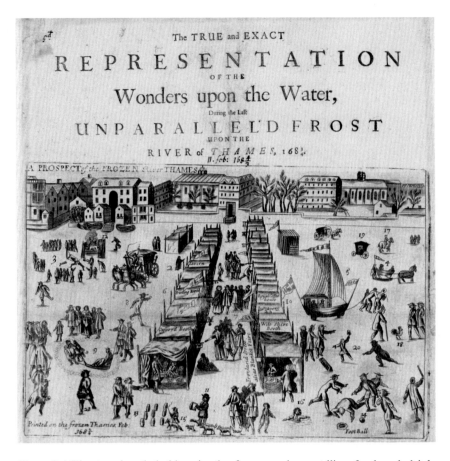

Figure 3.4 The two booth holders in the foreground are selling food and drink, though it is not possible to identify the exact nature of their wares. Note the tavern and coffee house on 'Freezeland Street'. *The True and Exact Representation of the Wonders upon the Water During the Last Unparallel'd Frost upon the River of Thames*, 1683/4 (London, 1684), British Museum 1880, 1113.1770. Letterpress and engraving. Anonymous. Published by George Croom. Courtesy of the Trustees of the British Museum.

This 'blanket fair' became a temporary microcosm of the city re-created on the river, complete with its own icy thoroughfares and alleys. The main centre of commerce of this arctic Lilliputian London was not East Cheap, but 'Freezeland Street' where traders in makeshift booths sold everything from lottery tickets to toys (Figure 3.4).

The 1715–16 fair is illustrated in a broadside woodcut issued by 'Mr David Hannott. Printed on the Ice, at the Maidenhead at Old-swan Stairs, Jan. 25. 1715–6' (Figure 3.3). Gay describes the same scene:

Here the fat Cook piles high the blazing Fire,
And scarce the Spit can turn the Steer entire,
Booths sudden hide the Thames, long Streets appear,
And num'rous Games proclaim the crouded Fair.[29]

Hannott's woodcut illustrates these activities perfectly and identifies Gay's ox roasting cook as one Cripple Atkins (see B in Figure 3.3). Illustrated broadsides from the 1715–16 fair are scarce. However, one other example, printed by John Bowles and Son at the Black Horse in Cornhill, is illustrated with a detailed panorama of the frozen Thames. It shows that as well as two separate ox roasting fires, there was another for roasting a sheep.[30]

Fortunately, many more of these publications have come down to us from the frost fair of 1683–4, which was also well documented in a number of paintings by Abraham Hondius, Jan Wyck and Jan Griffier the Elder.[31] Although the text of these hastily printed sheets was occasionally written in prose, the preferred vehicle was the rhyming couplet. Both Gay and his readership were aware of this and his mock-Georgic verse deliberately echoes the doggerel of the frost fair broadsides. One frost fair memento of 1683, entitled *God's Works is the Worlds Wonder*, describes how rapidly the frozen river was exploited for commercial purposes:

That spacious River in which they row
And where the mighty Tydes do ebb and flow;
Was then conjealed to a mighty Rock,
Where multitudes of Tradesmen there did flock
As many hundreds yet can witness well,
They built them Tents to trade, both buy and sell.

The food and drink booths were rapidly set up by the redundant watermen:

The Water men had laid aside their Boats;
Beer, Ale and Brandy, this was still their Notes.
Walk in, good Sir, here's what you can desire;
Come shew a Room, Boy, stir up the fire:
And though I do confess they sold it dear,
There was roast Beef, and other sumptuous Cheer;
There was both Coffee, Chocolet and Wine
For those that willing were to spend their Coin
But in this Fair upon the Rock of Ice,
All things were sold at an excessive price.[32]

Another broadside published in the same year makes a similar complaint about the atmosphere of unbridled commercialism that prevailed on the ice: 'What you can buy for three-pence on the Shore, / Will cost you four-pence on the Thames or more.'[33] Clearly the transformation of the Thames into a frosty wonderland, experienced perhaps once in a lifetime, lent a sense of exclusivity that added considerably to the value of any commodity sold on its icy walkways. A slice of ordinary roast beef could be purchased from any city cook shop for a few pence, but this was no everyday common-or-garden beef, but beef roasted on the frozen Thames and therefore possessed added value. For well-considered commercial reasons, ox roasting was a perennial feature of these events. It took between 12 and 29 hours to roast this large animal. This meant that the cook would not normally receive a penny from sales until the meat was ready to eat. However, an ox roasted in front of a very large fire on the ice was a different matter. It was a major spectacle guaranteed to attract a large crowd, curious to see why the fire, ox and cook did not disappear through the melting ice and join Doll at the bottom of the Thames. To capitalize on this situation, a tall wooden paling was constructed around the roasting fire to conceal the proceedings from prying eyes (Figures 3.5 and 3.6). If one had a desire to witness the ox being cooked, one would have to pay an entrance fee; if one wanted to eat a slice of beef, one forked out extra. An everyday catering event was transformed into a lucrative theatrical spectacle within its own hastily erected auditorium.[34] There is a traditional belief that at the 1683 fair Charles II and Catherine of Braganza sampled some slices of roast ox from one of these booths, though the evidence for this is doubtful as it is only described in nineteenth-century sources.[35]

However, the basic economics of ox roasting on the ice need to be considered carefully before assuming that the vendors were completely guilty of opportunist profiteering. During the cold snap, both timber and coals were transported by road rather than on river barges, so the cost of fuel rose to exorbitant heights.[36] There was also the effort and expense of carting it by sledge across the ice. It takes four to five tons of wood to cook an ox, so there was a considerable outlay in fuel and carting alone. In order to recoup their investment, the frost fair roasters could not entirely rely on sales of meat when the animal was finally cooked – thus the screened enclosure and entrance fee. At least six of the 1683 broadsides illustrate the ox roasting palisade, but the most revealing image of this event is in a little known painting by Jan Griffier the Elder (c.1685–1718).[37] Griffier shows a seated woman, perhaps the cook's wife, at the entrance to the enclosure extracting a fee from a fashionably dressed couple. This enterprise seems to have been highly successful. According to the unknown author of *A True Description of Blanket Fair upon the River Thames in the Time of the Great Frost*, it certainly attracted numerous visitors:

> Besides all these things were seen in Freezeland Fair,
> An Ox was roasted whole which Thousands saw
> For 'twas not many days before the Thaw,
> The like by now man in this present Age
> Was ever seen upon this Icy stage.[38]

Figure 3.5 The fence surrounding the ox roasting enclosure is clearly visible in the bottom right-hand corner. *Great Britain's Wonder: London's Admiration* (London, 1684). Anonymous. Engraving and letterpress. Printed by M. Haly and J. Millet. British Museum 1880, 1113.1769. Courtesy of the Trustees of the British Museum.

Roast meat was sold from other booths, though these were more orthodox in that smaller joints were rotated in front of more modest fires. Unlike the ox enclosure, their turnover was constant because cooked meat was always ready for sale. However, some roast meat hawkers also resorted to spectacles which

Figure 3.6 The palisaded ox enclosure. The spit with its great wheel is clearly visible.
Detail from *A True Description of Blanket Fair upon the River Thames, in
the time of the great Frost. In the year of our Lord, 1683* (London, 1683).
Woodcut and letterpress. Anonymous. Published by H. Brugis. British
Museum 1880, 1113.1771. Courtesy of the Trustees of the British Museum.

had the potential to attract a crowd. An unusual clockwork roasting appar-
atus, or jack, made of wood (Figure 3.7) is mentioned in one 1683 broadside
and must have attracted interest. The couplet also describes the game and
poultry it was used to cook: 'Hot Codlins, Pancakes, Duck, Goose, and Sack,
/ Rabit, Capon, Hen, Turkey, and a wooden Jack.'[39] Whole mutton carcasses
were roasted by dangling them from a string and spinning them round in
front of the fire, a delicacy marketed on the ice as 'Lapland Mutton'. At the
1715 fair 'a shoulder of mutton roasted in a string' could be viewed at the
'Sign of the Rat in the Cage'.[40] Hot codlins were roasted apples of the kind
Doll sold from her basket. They were a good buy because as well as being
sustaining they kept chilly hands warm. Hot pies were popular for the same
reason. Itinerant vendors of these foods moved from one booth to another –
wherever there was a crowd, there were potential sales. As Gay writes: 'Each
Booth she frequent past, in quest of Gain, / And boys with pleasure heard
her shrilling strain.'[41] The nature of the food sold on the frozen river differed
little to that offered by criers during wintertime on the streets of the city and
at the chartered fairs at other times of year. Hawkers just like those depicted
by Marcellus Laroon in the *Cryes of the City of London* (1687) moved from
the streets onto the ice to sell hot seasonal winter foods. Laroon included an

Figure 3.7 A joint of meat is being roasted in the booth to the left with the use of a
clockwork jack, which is just visible to the right of the cook attached to one
of the oars supporting the booth. This could well be the wooden jack mentioned in the broadside *Great Britain's Wonder* (Figure 3.5). Detail from *A
True Description of Blanket Fair upon the River Thames, in the time of the
great Frost. In the year of our Lord, 1683* (London, 1683). Woodcut and
letterpress. Anonymous. Published by H. Brugis. British Museum 1880,
1113.1771. Courtesy of the Trustees of the British Museum.

image in his collection of a female vendor crying 'Hott Bak'd Wardens Hott'
(a variety of cooking pear). His street seller is dressed in winter clothes and
carries the hot pears on her head in an earthenware pot covered with a cloth.
She could be Doll with her baked pippins.[42]

Ardent spirits and other beverages were also sold piping hot. Just like their
terrestrial equivalents, the improvised taverns and other watering holes set
up in the canvas booths displayed inn signs. At the 1684 fair, most had fairly
orthodox names like the Three Tuns, the Duke of York's Coffee House and
the Horn Tavern. Some had less delicate designations:

> Where e'ry Booth hath such a cunning Sign,
> As seldome hath been seen in former time;
> The Flying Piss-pot is one of the same,
> The Whip and Egg-shell, and the Broom by name:
> And there if you have Money for to spend,
> Each cunning Snap will seem to be your Friend.[43]

The Whip and Egg-shell sold coffee and hot chocolate, but the nature of the refreshments sold by the 'cunning snaps' at the Flying Piss-pot is not mentioned. One 1684 inn displayed the sign, 'Here's the first Tavern built in Freezeland Street'. Another, at the sign of the Phoenix, declared that it was 'Insured as long as the Foundation stand'. With the cries of the traders and the hullabaloo of the 'cheating, drunken, leud and debauched crew' who drank in the 'fuddling tents', they were noisy and boisterous places:

> And there the quaking Water-men will stand ye,
> Kind Master, drink you Beer, or Ale, or Brandy;
> Walk in, kind Sir, this Booth it is the chief,
> We'll entertain you with a slice of Beef,
> And what you please to Eat or Drink, tis here,
> No Booth, like mine, affords such dainty cheer.
> Another crys, Here Master, they but scoff ye,
> Here is a Dish of famous new-made Coffee.[44]

Some suspected that many of the wines sold in these tents were counterfeited:

> Besides rare Wines of e'ery sort,
> *White, Claret, Sherry, Mountain, Port,*
> Tho' none of't e'er had cross'd the Seas,
> Or from the Grape deriv'd its Lees,
> But made at Home, 'twixt chip and Dash,
> Of Sugar, Sloes, and Grocer's Trash,
> Of Cyder dy'd with Cochineal.[45]

Coffee, tea and chocolate were still fairly new and expensive beverages in London at this time, more likely to be served in a city coffee house than by street vendors. The coffee sold on the ice was targeted at the same moneyed class who enjoyed it in the terrestrial coffee houses and like most other commodities sold at the fair was likely to have been more expensive and therefore even more socially exclusive.

Frost fair drinking spawned a unique material culture as the fuddling booths also sold souvenir vessels to their customers, though only fragmentary evidence of these survives. A tin mug with silver mounts engraved 'Bought by Mr Gabril Tanner at Ice Fare ye 28th Janr 1683' survives in the collection of the Museum of London.[46] A very small glass mug with a silver mount engraved with 'Bought on ye Thames ice Janu: ye 17 1683/4' was acquired in 1997 by the Victoria and Albert Museum, although this object, which is only 60mm high, was probably intended as a child's toy (Figure 3.8).[47] Even items of food were saved as mementoes of the occasion. In the collection of the Museum of London there is a small piece of gingerbread, carefully wrapped and labelled as a souvenir of the last frost fair of 1814.[48] Gold plate and pewter were also sold on the ice. Vessels made of these metals were also probably engraved on request with a personal inscription, although none seem to have survived. A 1683 broadsheet describes:

> And goldsmiths' shops well furnished with plate;
> But they must dearly pay for 't that would ha' it.
> And coffee-houses in great numbers were
> Scattered about in this cold-freezing fair.
> There might you sit down by a char-cole fire
> And for your money have your heart's desire,
> A dish of coffee, chocolate, or tea:
> Could man's desire more furnished to be?[49]

Like newly fashionable tea, coffee and chocolate, many of the alcoholic beverages on offer were also sold hot and included some drinks that are now extinct. One of these was mum, a once popular ale flavoured with a complex mixture of spices and other plant materials. Most mum was imported from Brunswick in Hanover, but an English version was also brewed in Bristol. It was a powerfully intoxicating drink ideally suited to frosty weather: 'The rabble here in Chariots run around/ Coffee and Tea and Mum doth here abound.'[50]

During Gay's lifetime, gin began to creep into the proceedings. There was a Geneva tent at the 1715 fair. At the 1739 and 1814 events, gin was usually teamed up with gingerbread to make a warming combination, often being sold from the same booth or by the same hawker. This combination is referred to in a verse accompanying an engraving of the 1739–40 frost fair: 'Some Soldiers shivering in their red / Attack the Gin and Gingerbread.'[51] Gin in particular was consumed in vast quantities. A satirical print by George Cruikshank of the 1814 fair shows a makeshift canvas inn displaying a sign inscribed 'Gin and Gingerbread sold here wholesale'.[52] By this time, although gin was ubiquitous, some of the other drinks sold by the taverns had changed. A slice of roast beef or a mutton pie could be washed down with a glass of Old Tom, or 'Fine purl, good gin and rum', sold at the City of Moscow tavern and other 'fuddling tents'. Purl was a speciality of the watermen. It was hot ale flavoured with wormwood and spices, but there was also 'purl royal' for those who could afford it, a kind of wormwood wine. Watermen and colliers customarily consumed purl as a piping hot draught in the early morning, but it was also an ideal drink for warming chilled bones at a frost fair. According to Mayhew it was still being served steaming hot from purl boats moored on the river in the middle of the nineteenth century, although by his time, it usually consisted of a mug of ale fortified with gin.[53]

Gingerbread sellers were commonly present at all fairs, both of the terrestrial kind, as well as those on the frozen river. Those hawking their warming spicy cakes on the ice tended to sell their goods piping hot. Their moulded and frequently gilded wares were really edible toys for children and were marketed as such. Some were even instructive. A small piece of gingerbread in the

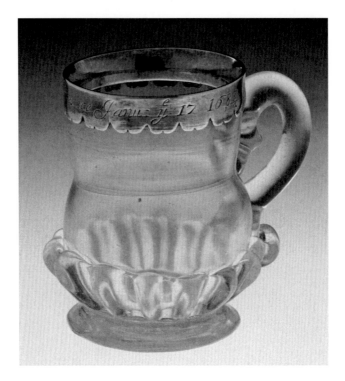

Figure 3.8 Too small for practical use, this tiny glass beer mug is embellished with a silver mount which is engraved with the words 'Bought on ye Thames ice Janu: ye 17 1683/4'. Glass, with engraved silver mount. Southwark, England, 1684. Unknown maker. V&A No. C.156–1997. Courtesy of the Victoria and Albert Museum.

Museum of London surviving from the 1814 frost fair appears to have been printed from a hornbook mould, a common genre where an entire alphabet was formed out of the spicy confection.[54] Children could learn their letters as they chewed – literally 'eating their words'. Just as common as the ginger-bread hawkers were vendors of small hot pies. Gingerbread, pies, puddings, cakes and other baked goods sold on the ice were almost certainly made by professional bakers. Large ovens were required to make all these foodstuffs in quantity and were only to be found in the city cook shops and bake-houses. It is doubtful if the low-status peddlers who sold them had access to cooking facilities of this kind. Unfortunately, there does not appear to be any evidence regarding the arrangements that vendors had for procuring their wares. Did they buy them up-front from a supplier? Or did they work on a sale or return basis? Were they organized by gang leaders or just sent out on the ice from the city cook shops and bake-houses? One 1814 illustrated broadside depicts a mutton pie seller with a portable warming stove, but this was just to keep his wares hot. They would have actually been baked in an oven in a city cook shop or bake-house.

Frost fairs were rare and extraordinary events, which provided short-lived, but intensive commercial opportunities for street vendors. The frozen river landscape acted as a magnet for the curious and large crowds of visitors from all classes were guaranteed. Unlike the orthodox London fairs which were held over just a few days in summer, some of the frost fairs lasted for the entire months of December and January, providing unusually long time spans for selling goods to large crowds of visitors. Although many decades separated each fair, the surviving evidence indicates an extraordinary uniformity and continuity regarding both the nature of the entertainments and the food available. Ox roasts in particular featured at all fairs between 1683 and 1814. There is some evidence to suggest that the city butchers controlled these spectacles. Although John Gay's 'fat cook', Cripple Atkins, cooked the ox at the 1715–16 fair, a butcher called Mr Hodgson claimed an ancestral right to slaughtering the animal and preparing it for the spit. Hodgson's father had knocked down the ox for the 1683–4 fair and he himself provided both beasts for the fairs of 1715 and 1739. Similarly, there was probably specific family control over other commercial activities on the ice. Other than these brief documentations of actual personages, very little is known about the actual identity of the ice fair vendors. Many were watermen and, although they would have been guild members, the names of specific individuals who traded on the ice are not known.[55]

In conclusion, the other-worldly atmosphere which furnished Gay's poetical imagination with a backdrop for his metamorphosis of a common street vendor into an Orphic heroine was also exploited by Virginia Woolf in her 1928 novel, *Orlando*. Woolf's frozen pippin seller sits in a sunken boat full of apples and is mummified in a transparent glacial stratum of ice 'twenty fathoms deep'. Ice fairs excited the imagination not only of the poet and novelist, but also of the thousands of visitors who swarmed on to the frozen river to spend money, eat hot food and to escape for a few hours from a domestic life that was made almost unbearable by the extreme weather. However, the drastic suspension of normal life and city trade caused by these extreme weather conditions did not prevent the enterprising and cunning from making money. Frost fairs provided unique opportunities for traders and hawkers to move their activities from the terrestrial sphere of the streets to that of the carnival atmosphere of a frozen river. Unusual spectacles such as bull baiting and horse and coach racing on the ice attracted large crowds who were only too willing to pay over the odds for hot food and warming beverages. Evelyn's short diary entry is one of the few firsthand accounts of a London frost fair to have survived and poignantly describes the dreadful conditions caused by the extreme weather. However it is the remarkable testimony, both in verse and images, provided by the popular illustrated broadsides sold on the frozen river itself, which allow us to reconstruct the forgotten culture of the hawkers of frost fair food and drink.

Notes

1   H.H. Lamb, 'The Cold Little Ice Age Climate of about 1550 to 1800', in *Climate: Present, Past and Future* (London, 1972), p. 107.

2   *An Exact and Lively Mapp or Representation of Booths and all the varieties of showes and humours upon the Ice on the River of Thames by London ... Anno Dm. MDCLXXXIII*, Guildhall Library, 28026. The British Museum also possesses a similar version of this print, which is divided up into rectangles marked with Roman numerals, but not with the hearts, diamonds, clubs and spades of the Guildhall example (British Museum 1880, 1113.1773).

3   *Wonderful News from the River of Thames. To a Pleasant New Tune* (British Museum 1880, 1113.1777).

4   Richard Thompson, *Chronicles of London Bridge* (London, 1827), p. 467. The ticket reads, 'Charles, King. James, Duke. Katherine, Queen. Mary, Duchess. Ann, Princesse. George, Prince. Hans in Kelder'. The royal party consisted of King Charles II, his brother James, Duke of York, afterwards James the Second, Queen Catherine of Braganza, Maria d'Este, sister of Francis, Duke of Modena and James's Second Duchess, Princess Anne, second daughter of the Duke of York, afterwards Queen Anne; and her husband, Prince George of Denmark. The presence of 'Hans in Kelder' – Jack in the Cellar – was probably a joke, as Princess Anne was pregnant at this time.

5   *The Diary of John Evelyn*, ed. William Bray (London, 1902), II, p. 193. Evelyn's description of the 1683 Frost Fair is one of the most detailed. In his diary entry for 24 January 1684, he disapproves of the excesses of the fair, calling it 'a bacchanalian triumph, or carnival on the water' and enlightens us to the desperate conditions from which his fellow Londoners were escaping by whiling away a few hours on the icy landscape of the river: 'The frost continues more and more severe, the Thames before London was still planted with booths in formal streets, all sorts of trades and shops furnished, and full of commodities ... Coaches plied from Westminster to the Temple, and from several other stairs to and fro, as in the streets, sleds, sliding with skates, a bull-baiting, horse and coach-races, puppet-plays and interludes, cooks, tippling, and other lewd places, so that it seemed to be a bacchanalian triumph, or carnival on the water, while it was a severe judgment on the land, the trees not only splitting as if the lightning struck, but men and cattle perishing in divers places, and the very seas so locked up with ice, that no vessels could stir out or come in. The fowls, fish, and birds, and all our exotic plants and greens, universally perishing. Many parks of deer were destroyed, and all sorts of fuel so dear, that there were great contributions to preserve the poor alive. London, by reason of the excessive coldness of the air hindering the ascent of the smoke, was so filled with the fuliginous steam of the sea-coal, that hardly could one see across the street, and this filling the lungs with its gross particles, exceedingly obstructed the breast, so as one could scarcely breathe. Here was no water to be had from the pipes and engines, nor could the brewers and divers other tradesmen work, and every moment was full of disastrous accidents.'

6   G. Davies, *Frostiana, or a history of the River Thames in a frozen state, with an account of the late severe frost and the wonderful effects of frost, snow, ice, and cold in England and in different parts of the world, interspersed with various amusing anecdotes, to which is added The art of skating* (London, 1814).

7   Cited in Edward F. Rimbault (ed.), *Old Ballads Illustrating the Great Frost of 1683–4* (London, 1844), p. xxix.

8   Item 37 in A.L.N Munby Collection (Munby.b.131), Cambridge University Library.

9   Thompson, *Chronicles of London Bridge*.

10   Rimbault, *Old Ballads Illustrating the Great Frost of 1683–4*.

11 William Andrews, *Famous Frost and Frost Fairs* (London, 1887).

12 Ian Currie, *Frosts, Freezes and Fairs* (Coulsden, 1996); Nicholas Reed, *Frost Fairs on the Frozen Thames* (Folkstone, 2002).

13 For the earlier essay, see Ivan Day, 'Ox Roasts – From "Frost Fairs to Mops"', in Ivan Day (ed.), *Over a Red Hot Stove* (Totnes, 2009), pp. 55–82.

14 Edmund Howe, *Continuation of the Abridgement of Stow's English Chronicle* (London, 1611), p. 481. The earliest depiction of a Thames frost fair is a woodcut showing the 1608 event in *The Great Frost. Cold Doings in London, except it be at the Lotterie, with Newes out of the Country* (London, 1608).

15 John Gay, 'Trivia; or the Art of Walking the Streets of London', in *Poems on Several Occasion* (London, 1730), II, pp. 357–360.

16 Gay, 'Trivia', II, pp. 381–390.

17 Regina Janes, 'Ariosto and Gay: Bouncing Heads', *English Literary History* 70/2 (2003), pp. 447–463.

18 'So when the Thracian Furies Orpheus tore/ And left his bleeding Trunk deform'd with Gore,/ His sever'd Head floats down the silver Tide,/ His yet warm Tongue for his lost Consort cry'd;/ Eurydice, with quiv'ring Voice, he mourn'd,/ And Heber's Banks Eurydice return'd' (Gay, 'Trivia', II, pp. 393–398).

19 Henry Power, 'Virgil, Horace, and Gay's Art of Walking the Streets', *Cambridge Quarterly* 38/4 (2009), pp. 338–367. Power explores Gay's relationship with street commerce and how he utilized it in re-working his classical sources. I am indebted to Dr Power in helping shape my own argument about the role of Doll in Gay's poem. For a useful collection of essays on Gay's *Trivia*, including the full text of the poem, see Clare Brant and Susan E. Whyman, *Walking the Streets of Eighteenth-Century London* (Oxford, 2007).

20 A young woman falling through the ice is depicted in a printed broadside: *God's Works is the Worlds Wonder* (London, 1683), British Museum 1871, 0812.5237. The caption describes her as, 'The Maid that fell in at Black-fryars, the Sunday before the Frost broke'.

21 *The English Chronicle; or Frosty Kalendar. Printed on the Thames*, 1739–40 (Guildhall Library).

22 Gay, 'Trivia', II, pp. 361–362.

23 *View of the Frost Fair looking towards London Bridge. Mr David Hannott. Printed on the Ice, at the Maidenhead at Old-swan Stairs, Jan. 25. 1715–16* (London, 1715–16), Guildhall Library, London Metropolitan Archives, P7499528.

24 Sybil Rosenfield, *The Theatre of the London Fairs in the Eighteenth Century* (Cambridge, 2008), p. 1.

25 *The Constitutions of the Company of Watermen and Lightermen* (London, 1708). Updated editions of this detailed collection of rules and regulations were published by the Worshipful Company of Watermen and Lightermen of the River Thames in 1730, 1732, 1790 and 1828. None of these publications contain any by-laws relating to those occasions when the river froze.

26 Tim Harris, *London Crowds in the Reign of Charles II* (Cambridge, 1990), p. 214.

27 *Great Britain's Wonder: London's Admiration* (London, 1684), British Museum 1880, 1113.1769.

28 *A True Description of Blanket Fair upon the River Thames, in the time of the great Frost. In the year of our Lord, 1683* (London, 1683), British Museum 1880, 1113.1771.

29 Gay, 'Trivia', II, pp. 367–370.

30 *Frost Fayre, Being a True Prospect of the Great Varietie of Shops and Booths for Tradesmen, with other Curiosities & humors, on the Frozen River of Thames as it appeared before the City of London, in that memorable Frost in the second year of the Reigne of Our sovereigne Lord Kinge George Anno domini 1716 Published by John Bowles*, British Museum 1880, 1113.1780.

31 Two paintings of the frozen Thames by Jacob Hondius are in the collection of the Museum of London. One executed in 1677 depicts a general view of the river with London Bridge in the background. The other represents the 1684 fair and clearly depicts the booths and crowds on the ice. An extensive panorama of the frost fair of 1739 by Jan Griffier is in the Guildhall Art Gallery, Corporation of London.

32 *God's Works is the World's Wonder*.

33 *Great Britain's Wonder*.

34 The cost of a serving of roast ox at the 1684 fair varied from 6d to a shilling, depending on the size of the slice. Prices had not changed much by the time of the last frost fair in 1814, when a slice of so-called 'Lapland Mutton', carved from a sheep roasted in front of a coal fire, was one shilling. Mutton at this time could be purchased at a butchers shop for between 3d and 5d the lb.

35 *The Mirror of Literature, Amusement, and Instruction*, Vol. 13, No. 355, Saturday, February 7, 1829.

36 In the broadside *Great Britain's Wonder* the anonymous author mentions the high cost of fuel and its means of transportation: 'Coals being dear, are carry'd on Mens backs,/And some on Sledges there are drawn in Sacks.' On 10 January 1684, John Evelyn recorded that 'all sorts of fuel so dear, that there were great contributions to keep the poor alive' (*The Diary of John Evelyn*, II, p. 193).

37 The whereabouts of this work is unknown and it is only known through a reproduction on a Christmas card published in the 1950s. I am indebted to Nicholas Reed for drawing my attention to it. A detail of the painting showing the ox enclosure is reproduced in Day, 'Ox Roasts'.

38 *A True Description of Blanket Fair*.

39 *Great Britain's Wonder*.

40 *Mr David Hannott*.

41 Gay, 'Trivia', II, pp. 386–386.

42 Robert Raines, *Marcellus Laroon* (London, 1967), p. 23.

43 *Great Britain's Wonder*.

44 *Great Britain's Wonder*.

45 *British Wonders: Or A Poetical Description of the Several Prodigies and most Remarkable Accidents that have happen'd in Britain since the Death of Queen Anne* (London, 1717), p. 24.

46 Edwina Ehrman, Hazel Forsyth, Lucy Peltz, and Cathy Ross (with a preface by Loyd Grossman), *London Eats Out* (London, 1999), p. 29.

47 V&A Museum no. C.156–1997.

48 Personal communication from Hazel Forsyth, Senior Curator of Medieval and Post-Medieval Collections, Museum of London.

49 *A True Description of Blanket Fair*.

50 *The True and Exact Representation of the Wonders upon the Water During the Last Unparallel'd Frost upon the River of Thames*, 1683/4 (London, 1684). A recipe for mum was published by John Nott in *The Cook's and Confectioner's Dictionary* (London, 1723), M53. It was brewed from a mixture of malt, ground beans and oatmeal and flavoured with various spices and herbs including spruce, cardamom, sassafras, ginger and pennyroyal.

51 The author was unable to find an original copy of this print, which is reproduced in Reed, *Frost Fairs on the Frozen Thames*, p. 27.

52 George Cruickshank, *Thames Frost Fair* (1814), author's collection.

53 Henry Mayhew, *London Labour and the London Poor* (3 vols, London, 1851), II, pp. 93–95.

54 This small piece of gingerbread bought at the 1814 frost fair displays some evidence that it was printed in an alphabet mould. The gingerbread fragment is wrapped in blue sugar paper with the handwritten inscription, 'This piece of gingerbread was

bought by my father Thos. Moxon at Frost Fair on the Thames in Janry 1814'
(Museum of London MP/L.). A number of hornbook gingerbread moulds are
illustrated in Edward H. Pinto, *Treen and other Wooden Bygones* (London, 1970),
Plate 187, opposite p. 186.

55 *Mr David Hannott.* Information on Hodgson the butcher is given on the reverse
side of the print. Surprisingly, a thorough search of the Old Bailey records
did not reveal any criminal activity resulting in court appearances during the
frost fairs.

4 Food, markets and people

Selling perishables in urban markets in pre-industrial Holland and England*

Danielle van den Heuvel

Introduction

Food markets played a central role in the economies of pre-industrial European cities. First, they provided most of the basic foodstuffs for the urban population, such as meat, fish, vegetables and fruits. Second, in these cities food markets traditionally formed a focal point of exchange between local and foreign traders, and between traders and consumers of a wide variety of backgrounds. Third, food markets provided work for a large and diverse group of workers, ranging from those engaged in sales activities, such as stallholders and hawkers, to officials, such as rent collectors and market overseers, and manual labourers, such as porters and street cleaners.

Despite the great variety of people working in these markets, our knowledge of who could be found in the urban food markets of early modern Europe has remained fairly sketchy. Research on pre-industrial food markets has mainly centred on distribution processes and questions of supply, demand and food scarcity, as in the numerous studies on food riots, mostly leaving out the individuals at the heart of the exchange from buyer to seller: the stallholder in the local market.[1] Thanks to in-depth studies on butchers' and fishmongers' guilds we have some idea of who as guild members worked in such markets.[2] Women's history has offered important insights in the large role women played in the fish trade.[3] However, we are only scratching the surface when it comes to the identities of salespeople in markets for other foodstuffs; for example the sellers of fruits and vegetables are often generically labelled 'foreigners' (meaning non-locals). More importantly, we have only a limited understanding of why we observe certain patterns of labour division in the food trades: why are fish sellers often female and why does the meat trade seem mostly run by men? What factors contribute to such a gender division of labour? How do stallholders and ambulant traders relate to each other? What about local and non-local ('foreign') traders; those of wealthier backgrounds and those of more limited means?

Understanding who worked in the urban food markets of early modern Europe is of great importance. It is widely acknowledged that retailing was one of the most important ways for women to earn a living. Retailing often came second after textiles production as the economic sector that employed most women.[4] Similarly, in pre-industrial Europe, as it has been throughout history, street selling was mainly the domain of marginal groups in society, which included immigrants and the poor, in addition to many single and widowed women.[5] Shedding light on who had access to food markets, and in what role, therefore provides an insight into the economic opportunities of those at the bottom of society.

At the same time, we should also acknowledge that the sale of foodstuffs was in the hands of people of a wide variety of socio-economic backgrounds. Previous work on this topic has for instance revealed the wealthy and powerful butchers, who provide a striking contrast to the rowdy and low-status fishwives, which appear in many works on pre-industrial fish markets.[6] Whilst the identification of these two groups point to significant social stratification among different groups of food vendors, they still paint a static and somewhat stereotypical picture of the different types of food vendor regardless of time and space. Yet, closely reading the evidence on early modern urban food markets reveals that the identities of salespeople in the various branches of food trading not only contained variation according to the branch of food trading, but also substantial chronological and geographical diversity.

One important reason for the diversity among street food vendors is, as I will argue in this chapter, the way markets were organised and governed. Food markets were subject to extensive regulation determining what products could be sold, by whom, and at what time and place. Research on modern developing economies has shown that market regulation greatly affect access to trades.[7] Although several studies on early modern street life have shed some light on market regulation, we still know remarkably little about how precisely it impacted on the make-up of the urban food trades.[8] Studying the identities of food sellers before industrialisation is especially revealing as the period between the sixteenth and eighteenth centuries is not only an era of retail 'modernisation', but also of urban 'improvement' more generally. While the former included the growing importance of shops and the transfer of (at least some) retail activities from markets to the new shops, the latter comprised extensive urban planning and redevelopment, including the cleaning up of streets and the building and reconfiguring of market halls. It may come as no surprise that these developments were accompanied by changes in the way markets were governed, greatly affecting the traders in these food markets.

This chapter aims to illuminate the ways in which market regulation affected the composition of the food trades in early modern European cities. In order to do so it seeks inspiration from studies on food selling from contemporary developing economies, a field in which the identities of food hawkers, their motives, opportunities and constraints have been extensively studied. The chapter will focus primarily on the sale of perishables, such as fresh fruit, vegetables, meat, fish and dairy. It mainly draws on evidence from food markets in two highly urbanised areas: the City of London and the cities in the province of Holland, which formed a large urban conglomerate and, with

London, the most important economic centre of the early modern Western world.[9] It builds on a wide body of materials ranging from guild and government records on the running of markets, to antiquarian studies on individual market places, and contemporary visual depictions of food markets. Within the context of this chapter, it will be impossible to provide a definitive answer to the question of how market regulation affected access to food markets for different groups. Therefore, this chapter's principal aim is to point to patterns in access to food selling in early modern cities and to suggest considerations for future explorations of food sellers in the past.

Food markets and market governance

In order to understand what determined access to the urban food markets it is pertinent to know what types of food markets existed in early modern Europe and how these were governed. Before 1800, most fresh foodstuffs were sold in city streets and marketplaces. Even though shops were gaining in popularity, open-air market places as well as (partly) covered markets remained the most important places of exchange for perishables.[10] In addition to the sale of foodstuffs in these formalised marketspaces, fresh foods were hawked through the streets.[11] Food markets, either in the open air or in designated buildings, could be centred on the sale of one product or product group or could comprise different products. In Dutch cities such as Amsterdam, The Hague and Leiden, throughout the early modern period one could find separate marketspaces allocated to the sale of products such as meat, fish and vegetables.[12] In London, on the other hand, over time markets seem to have diversified. Whereas in the Middle Ages most London food markets still focused on selling one or two types of food, by the eighteenth century many food markets combined the sale of a variety fresh products.[13] Most food markets were situated in the centre of cities, although urban expansion generally led to the establishment of suburban food markets.[14]

Early modern food markets were subject to extensive regulations on the practices of buying and selling. The historiography of food marketing between circa 1500 and 1800 reports the persistent attempts of local authorities to regulate most of the goings-on in urban marketplaces. Central to many studies on food markets is the issue of 'disorder' in the marketplace, and the authorities' attempts to eradicate this. Historians studying a variety of marketplaces through time and space, from sixteenth-century Venice to nineteenth-century Manchester, report of regulation that seems comparable in character and scope, principally covering market times, market access and market behaviour.[15]

Local authorities generally governed urban food markets, although occasionally national governments were involved in market governance.[16] Municipal governments decided when and where markets could take place, who was allowed to sell their wares in the markets, and what products could be sold. In London it was the Corporation which took prime responsibility of the governance of markets within the formal city boundaries; in the cities of Holland the local magistrates.[17] However, there was another pre-modern institution that had a very important, if not at times decisive, voice in the governing of the various marketplaces: the urban guilds.[18] Most early modern crafts and trades were governed by guilds. In many areas in pre-industrial Europe to practise a certain trade one had to become a member of a guild. Guild membership often also involved obtaining citizenship of the local community and hence many economic activities could only be practised by citizens of a particular town; this could have important implications for access to the food trades as we will read later in this chapter.[19]

The number of guilds in the food trades and the actual power these guilds had in regulating food markets differed according to time and place. In the Low Countries the numbers of guilds present in any town generally grew as the economy expanded.[20] In early modern Amsterdam, one of the largest cities in the Low Countries with a population of 220,000 in the 1740s, we find a rather substantial number of guilds in the food trades: a separate butchers' guild, a fishmongers' guild, a vegetable sellers' guild, a poulterers' guild, and a fruit sellers' guild.[21] Smaller Dutch towns often only had a local butchers' and a fishmongers' guild.[22] There is some debate about the changing function and importance of early modern England guilds, with some scholars arguing they became less important over time, and others stressing their continued powers over social, economic and political life.[23] In London, guilds, also known as livery companies, still held a prominent position in the city's economy in the seventeenth and eighteenth centuries, but there is some evidence that their powers weakened as a result of suburban growth.[24] According to Colin Smith's extensive research on the organisation of London food markets, by the eighteenth century the influence of London guilds involved in market trade, such as the butchers', fishmongers', poulterers' and fruiterers' companies, was in decline.[25]

More research into this matter is required, but it is likely that these guilds of market vendors had less power than guilds in other segments of the early modern economy. The reason for this is that the urban magistrates were highly concerned about food provision and food quality. In much of the regulation of the early modern food trades we see reflected the worries of (local) governments about food shortages, the overpricing of food and the threat of food riots.[26] Another large concern was the spread of disease, from which many of the regulations directed towards meat and fish sellers derived.[27] Food markets also created other problems for the urban authorities: they led to the crowding of streets and the blocking of thoroughfares, and lastly, the markets attracted groups of people from the margins of society, such as vagrants and other outcasts, which the cities certainly did not welcome with open arms.[28]

The involvement of multiple governing bodies in controlling the market trades resulted according to some historians in a patchy and ineffective system, in which, as Smith puts it, 'pragmatism and pluralism are the dominant shades'.[29] However, even though we cannot deny that the fragmentation of market governance may not always have contributed to the smooth running of markets, we should not underestimate the impact of the regulations the various bodies produced.[30] As we will see below, the dynamics resulting from the attempts of various regulators to control marketspaces were in fact crucial in deciding who ultimately had access to the marketplace and in what role.

The impact of guild memberships

Studies on modern-day developing economies point to a number of aspects that influence an individual's opportunities to work as a food vendor. The first is the cost of registering one's business, labelled the 'costs of formality' by the influential economist Hernando De Soto.[31] A second aspect is the types of marketspaces, for instance whether they are permanent, semi-permanent or temporary in nature, and where in a city they are located.[32] We will look closely at these issues below in order to see how they determined the make-up of markets in early modern cities, but first we need to deal with one aspect to market access which is, as far as I am aware, non-existent in modern cities: guild membership.[33]

In Dutch towns, stalls in the main food markets were often only available to citizens who had acquired membership of the appropriate guild. Only members of the Leiden butchers' guild could sell in the town's two meat halls, the stalls in the central fish market on the river Rhine were only let to members of the fishmongers' guild, and only citizens who were members of the local guild of market gardeners were able to acquire permits for selling in the central vegetable market.[34] In the City of London guild membership also brought food sellers substantial privileges. Only members of one of the London guilds, also called companies, were entitled to trade from a shop on weekdays unrestricted by market hours, and only guild members or freemen could buy and sell in retail to both citizens and strangers.[35] Contrary to the situation in the Dutch cities, however, these citizen traders were not supposed to occupy stalls in most of the central markets, as these were specifically assigned to country vendors. In the late Middle Ages members of the fishmongers' and butchers' guilds were entitled to have stalls and shops in particular markets, such as Eastcheap, the Stocks and St. Nicholas Shambles for butchers and Fish Street Hill, the Stocks and Old Fish Street for fishmongers, but it is unclear whether such privileges remained in place during subsequent centuries.[36]

Technically, the costs of obtaining guild membership could be seen as equivalent to De Soto's 'costs of formality'. For some individuals in early modern Dutch society obtaining guild membership came down to a simple payment of a fee. Community citizenship was a requirement for obtaining guild membership, but those born to a father who was already a citizen of the town were granted citizenship rights at birth, and migrants were able to purchase citizenship in return for a fee.[37] The costs of citizenship varied, and while they may not have formed an obstacle for people from the middling sorts and higher social groups, for many poor people the costs of citizenship were not as easy to overcome.[38] Moreover, for some groups obtaining guild membership was far from a simple matter, and here guilds seem to create circumstances different to those found in present-day Africa, Asia or Latin America. Guild membership was not open to everyone, even in the case of the Dutch guilds, which are generally seen as inclusive. In most Holland cities, Jewish people were excluded from guild membership, women were sometimes also explicitly excluded from membership, and generally guilds only accepted heads of households as members.[39] The latter meant that married women or for instance unmarried men and women living with their parents could not obtain a separate guild membership. Whilst this was not a direct form of gender discrimination, it is safe to assume that women suffered more from this policy than men. In the early modern economy, women overall had fewer opportunities than men as many occupations were open to men only.[40]

The actual policies on guild membership varied by market trade. Of the Dutch food sellers' guilds, butchers' guilds were most restrictive. Several butchers' guilds did not allow independent women to become members. Widows could enter the trade, but only when their deceased husbands had been guild members. In cities such as Amsterdam, Dordrecht, Haarlem and Leiden, during the sixteenth and seventeenth centuries the wives of butchers were even explicitly forbidden to work in the meat hall, except in the case of illness of their partners.[41] In Leiden butchers were denied two weeks' work (before 1656) or a three-guilder fine (after that year) if they were joined by their wives at their stalls.[42] In Amsterdam after 1613 the rules were relaxed and the assistance of wives was permissible.[43] Fishmongers' and vegetable sellers' guilds were more often open to female membership: in the city of Leiden single women and widows were accepted as members of the *warmoesiers'* guild (which monopolised the vegetable market), and in Amsterdam the city fish sellers' guild not only accepted women of all marital statuses as guild members, but even allowed both spouses of a married couple independent guild membership (and hence independent rights to a stall in the market).[44]

The corporative system in London functioned rather differently from that in urban Holland. In London, like in many other places in early modern England, becoming a citizen, or Freeman of the City, was completely entwined with entering one of the livery companies; only via an apprenticeship one could gain the rights to become a Freeman of London.[45] Guild apprenticeships were uncommon in Dutch food sellers' guilds. Completing an apprenticeship in London officially took seven years, and while a substantial share of apprentices did not complete their seven-year term, even completing part of it meant a substantial investment of time.[46] Moreover, many companies did not accept women as members or did not allow women to become independent masters unless they were widows of Freemen.[47] Finally, overseas immigrants, also called aliens, were generally barred from serving an apprenticeship.[48] The barrier to becoming a Freeman and hence also a member of one of the food traders' guilds in the City of London was consequently much higher than those in most of the Dutch market guilds.

The implications of guild entry barriers in the cities under scrutiny were that local people unable to obtain membership, either through time, financial, hereditary or gender constraints, could only operate as hawkers and hagglers, or in periodical markets.[49] However, whilst circumstances for those who were not (male) heads of households with substantial enough means to enter into a guild seem to have been worse in London, the set-up of the London markets may have allowed for more room for at least non-guild members than the markets in the cities of Holland. As we read above, the central markets were largely reserved for country vendors and as we will see later, from the late seventeenth century onwards those operating as hagglers were appointed a formal space in one of the new market halls.

Further 'costs of formality'

For a spot in most marketplaces, regardless of the requirement of guild membership, one was required to pay stall rent or acquire a permit. Rents for stalls in the market were demanded in some of the London markets from as early as the thirteenth century onwards. When the Stocks Market was erected in 1283 it was instructed that the rents collected from the stallholders should go to the upkeep of London Bridge. The stall rents remained an important source of revenue for the City throughout the early modern period. In the Dutch towns, we also find that both stall rents and revenues from the permits for street selling went to the municipal authorities.[50]

Stall rents generally varied according to the size of the stall and the product that could be sold from the stall.[51] As Table 4.1 illustrates, in seventeenth-century London large stalls for meat and fish were most expensive and cost 2.5 shillings a week. Selling other products from one of the public markets was cheaper. Bakers and gingerbread sellers only paid one-fifth of what vendors at a large meat and fish stall paid; however, their stalls were much smaller. Fruit sellers and weed and herb vendors also paid much lower sums for access to the market.[52] The price setting of market stalls and standings probably reflects a combination of economic and cultural values, in which foodstuffs such as meat and fish were more highly valued than vegetables.[53] Possibly, the fact that meat and fish stalls were permanent structures will have also added to their higher prices. Nevertheless, the addition that weeds and herbs could be sold for two shillings per week 'for the poorer sorts of country people' suggests that deliberate price diversification was in place to also accommodate the needs of those of lesser means. A purely economic way of differentiating stall rents can be found in the fish trade of the Dutch town of The Hague, and this impacted not only on the social make-up of the marketplace, but also on gender divisions. The rents for stalls in the fish market varied according to their position in the market. Stalls in the central areas of the market were the most expensive, while stalls in less-visited areas were relatively cheap and sometimes even given away for free. The annual rents of

Table 4.1 Rents at the public markets in London, 1696

Trade	Type	Size	Price	Term	Remarks
Flesh-meat or fish	Stall or standing	8ft by 4ft	2.5 s.	Weekly	
Flesh-meat or fish	Stall or standing	6ft by 4ft	2 s.	Weekly	
Provisions	Horse-load		0.16 s.	Daily	Not upon stalls, nor under public shelter
Provisions	Dosser or like		0.08 s.	Daily	
-	Cart-load	Not above 3 horses	0.3 s.	Daily	
-	Cart-load	With 4 horses	0.5 s.	Daily	
Fruit (brought by land and water)	Pricket or basket	Not above 1 bushel	0.04 s.	Daily	
Fruit (brought by land and water)	Basket, dosser, maund	Above 2 bushels	0.08 s.	Daily	To be paid by people that bring or receive them
Gardiners	Standing	6ft by 6 ft	20 s.	Annually	
Weeds and physick herbs	Standing	4ft by 2ft or 6ft by 6ft	1 s.	Weekly	For the poorer sort of country people
Bakers and gingerbread sellers	Standing	Not above 4ft by 3ft	0.5 s.	Weekly	

Source: LMA, CLA/009/01/035. NB: this excludes Leadenhall market at which traditionally higher stall rents were demanded.

stalls varied considerably with 500 pounds for a central stall to two pounds for stalls in the margins of the market.[54]

In addition to paying a stall rent for access to the food markets one sometimes also had to pay a fee to be admitted to the actual allocation of stalls. For access to the central Leiden vegetable market guild members paid two to six shillings to be included in the yearly draw through which stalls were distributed. A similar situation existed for the Leiden fish market.[55] Other costs imposed on the vendors in London were fees to be paid for weighing the consumables before they could be marketed, which came down to four pence per week.[56]

From studies on contemporary developing economies we know that financial barriers such as stall rents and obligatory sales permits could have great impact on the opportunities of marginal social groups in the retail sector.[57]

Also in the early modern food trades we find that the money demanded by government and guilds generated problems for some market vendors, despite concessions being in place. In 1654, for example, four widows sharing a stall in the Leiden fish market were unable to pay for the rent with revenues of their trade, and they were forced to ask permission for the stall to be shared with yet another widow.[58] Stallholders who were unable to pay their rent were forced to appear before court in The Hague, and also in London we find that market vendors who had not paid their dues were summoned to appear before the Common Council.[59] Moreover, another pattern found in contemporary retailing and eighteenth-century shopkeeping seems to be present in early modern food markets as well: women seem to have been more affected by higher stall rents than men. In the fish market of The Hague, for example, men generally rented the more expensive stalls and women the cheaper stalls.[60] When stalls in the market were not let, the city government allowed poorer people who otherwise operated as hawkers to occupy these stalls without paying rent; interestingly these were mostly women.[61] A comparison of female stall occupancy in the fish markets of The Hague, Leiden and Amsterdam enforces the conclusion that high stall rents impacted negatively upon women's chances in the trade. Contrary to the situation in The Hague, no price differentiation in stall rents existed at the fish markets in Amsterdam and Leiden: all stalls were available at the same price and these prices were much lower than some of those to be paid in the city of The Hague. At the same time, the shares of female stallholders in these cities formed about 70 per cent, whereas in The Hague women only formed a maximum of 20 per cent of all stallholders.[62]

It is likely that in addition to the rental fees, also the time for which a stall or a standing in the marketplace was allocated to a vendor, and the instalments in which the rents had to be paid were crucial to the openness of the trade. Previous research on flexible guild memberships in shopkeepers' guilds in the eighteenth-century Dutch Republic shows that short-term guild memberships benefited poorer people. Prices for short-term membership were significantly lower than those of permanent memberships and as a result the set-up costs for a retail business were drastically lowered. Despite the fact that these memberships did not offer such extensive privileges and had to be renewed annually, they were especially popular with women.[63] Consequently, the diversity in the length of the stall leases for the London public markets (as shown in Table 4.1) could mean that some trades were much more accessible to poorer people as it allowed them not only more flexibility, but also required less financial capital. Indeed, start-up costs are regarded, both in the past and present, to be pitfalls for budding entrepreneurs who struggle to at the same time keep the business up and running, their families fed, as well as funding the required registration costs, let alone possible investments in growing the business.[64] Time, therefore, is an important factor in determining access to the food trades in early modern Europe; however, it also impacted on the opportunities for food sellers in another way, and this is what we will turn to now.

Time constraints

Apart from the length of time that market stalls were let for, the opportunities of market vendors were also affected by other temporal constraints, such as at what times sales activities could take place.[65] We discussed above that not all market traders had equal rights, with members of the London livery companies having the most extensive entitlements as they were able to sell outside specific market times from their shops. Evidence on the London markets suggests that the number of trading days in the markets went up over time, often first unofficially and later officially through an extension of market privileges.[66] Before the late seventeenth century, most City markets were only operating on Mondays, Wednesdays and Saturdays, but from that time most markets became daily affairs. Correspondingly, market hours were being extended. From the 1670s London's markets operated from six in the morning until eight in the evening, except Saturdays when the market closed at 10 p.m., and it is suggested that on Saturday evenings markets sometimes went on until midnight.[67] These time extensions of course only affected those who had access to the city's markets, principally country vendors who were lucky enough to be able to afford a space.

In most Dutch cities on the other hand, the central markets, which were accessible only to guild members, operated on a daily basis, whereas the markets that country vendors operated from were weekly events. In Amsterdam in the seventeenth century, the central fish, fruit and vegetable markets took place every day apart from Sunday, and the other markets followed the pattern for London's markets before the 1670s: on Mondays, Wednesdays and Fridays.[68] The chronicler Simon van Leeuwen in 1672 mentions that Leiden's market days were Wednesdays and Saturdays, although he also suggests daily markets took place.[69] Other evidence indicates that from the mid-seventeenth century due to increased competition between citizen and non-citizen vendors, country people selling vegetables could only sell in the Saturday market on the edge of town. While as time progressed, London's markets seemed to have offered wider sales opportunities for all types of vendors, this evidence suggests that in some Dutch cities time restrictions were put in place for certain groups.

People who were not entitled to a stall in one of the formal markets, because they were neither guild members nor country farmers, were affected by time restrictions even more than stallholders. Urban regulation restricted both the freedom of hawkers, hagglers and street vendors to acquire goods for sale, and the freedom to sell these goods to local consumers. To protect the needs of local consumers, hucksters and hawkers could only buy from country producers after local shoppers had bought for their own consumption. Often they had to wait until the afternoon before they could buy their merchandise from the country vendors.[70] This could seriously diminish their chances of making a profit: they were left with lower-quality products as most of the high-quality commodities would have been sold in the mornings. Moreover,

even though many of the labouring classes went shopping on Saturday evenings when their wages had come in, other local householders already had
their chance to stock up on fresh foods, and as a result there were fewer customers left to be served.[71] When hawkers brought in their own wares, their
sales activities were limited in other ways. In Leiden the wives of fishermen
from neighbouring coastal towns were only allowed to hawk their catch in the
mornings, and could only sell a limited amount of fish.[72] In The Hague fish
hawkers could only sell between noon and 2 p.m. and after 7 p.m. – presumably the times that stallholders in the formal fish market were not selling.[73]

   The rationale behind such measures was the worry that any sales activities
taking place outside the open market affected not only the transparency of
commercial transactions, and hence the trustworthiness of the vendor and the
customer, but also contributed to rising prices.[74] The latter argument was for
instance also the principal motivation behind large reforms of the London
market system in the late 1590s. According to a prominent advocate of market
reform at that time, Hugh Alley, hawkers buying up produce for resale outside
the formal markets were one of the major factors causing rising food prices.[75]
Indeed, a large number of market ordinances specifically dealt with what was
seen as the greatest offences against the freedom of the markets: 'forestalling', 'regrating' and 'engrossing' in England, and '*voorkoop*' (pre-emption) in
Holland.[76] While each of these activities covered a slightly different meaning,
they all concerned buying and selling outside the set marketplaces and times,
explicitly forbidden in both London and urban Holland.[77] However, the many
complaints by citizen market vendors and the reoccurring attempts to reform
market regulation in order to suppress such activities shows that offences like
these were committed on a regular basis.[78] This may come as no surprise as we
read earlier that many non-citizen market traders had only very limited scope
to practise their trade. Additionally, guild members sometimes also resorted
to buying wares for resale from foreigners outside market hours. In 1656 for
example the Leiden city council explicitly forbade members of the local guild
of vegetable sellers and growers, the previously mentioned *warmoesiers*, to
buy their produce from country producers.[79] Vegetable growing and selling
was often a family enterprise in which husbands, wives and children worked
together in growing and marketing produce.[80] As a result, the restrictions to
buy crops off other producers mainly affected those operating a vegetable
stall on their own, such as several of the unmarried women we find renting a
market stall in the Leiden vegetable market.[81] The question remains whether
the regulation and prosecution of trading outside the official market times
was deliberately targeted against women and the poor. In their study of the
1590s London market reforms Archer *et al.* suggest as much when they con-
clude that the proposed reforms by Hugh Alley and his contemporaries were
only partly enforced and that wholesalers were much less likely to be prose-
cuted than petty traders, fishwives and hucksters; also Wendy Twaithes in her
work on the Oxford food markets concludes this was the case.[82] As with the
other forms of time restriction mentioned above, also the prohibition to buy

goods before they had come to the (official) market principally affected those who already had a weaker position in the trade: the men and, mostly, women who did not have access to a stall or standing in one of the formal market-places, and those who, like the single women in the Leiden vegetable market, had limited means to acquire goods for (re)sale.[83]

Regulating market space

In addition to time restrictions, the way markets were organised in terms of space also impacted on the opportunities of food hawkers. First, we find several restrictions concerning the use of space by vendors. For instance, in 1588 it was ordered that root sellers in London could not have more than three baskets of merchandise. This measure was taken as a way to limit the obstruction of streets and thoroughfares, but of course this also limited the vendors in the number of goods they could bring to the market.[84] Such measures seem to have been taken more regularly from the mid-sixteenth century onwards. Similarly, in 1388 it was ordered that women who sold oysters, mussels, salt fish and other victuals could only sell in the streets of London if they kept moving. Two hundred years later we find this rule repeated when it was stated that women who bought fish, oysters, mussels and cockles at the wholesale market at Billingsgate could not sell them while standing in a marketplace but had to sell them walking up and down the streets crying their goods.[85] This restriction obviously impacted on the economic opportunities of these fish traders – being mobile meant that customers were not always able to find sellers at their convenience, something that stallholders with a permanent stall did not suffer from.

Second, local governments regulated where markets took place, what size markets could be, and how market spaces should be organised. Whilst not directly influencing the spatial leeway for particular groups of vendors as in the case of the restrictions discussed above, this type of market regulation had significant repercussions on the way space in marketplaces could be used and by whom. Indeed, as in modern developing countries, access to the various marketplaces was greatly determined by the spatial configuration of markets. The set-up of the market – permanent versus temporary, size, and lay-out – and the location within the urban area, all determine who could be found in particular marketplaces.[86]

The spatial configuration of markets is for a large part determined by the size of a locality and hence the size of supply and demand. The larger the city, the more complex the system of food distribution; this generally leads to a greater desire of the authorities to regulate the marketing of food and its designated marketspaces. During the early modern period both the city of London and the cities in the province of Holland underwent significant expansion. The population of London more than tripled from 200,000 in 1600 to 675,000 in 1750.[87] While several of Holland's cities experienced some form of stagnation during the eighteenth century, over the early modern period as a whole population numbers went up. Amsterdam went from a population of 105,000 in 1622 to 240,000 one hundred years later. Leiden grew from 22,000 inhabitants in 1600, to 55,000 in 1675, and had 31,000 at the end of the eighteenth century.[88] The urban authorities tried to accommodate the greater need for foodstuffs as a result of population growth by expanding and reorganising existing marketplaces as well as by setting up new markets. A second important development which determined the spatial configuration of food markets is the rise of formal market halls, with permanent stalls and standings, which became increasingly prevalent in Europe's cities during the early modern period. In London the Great Fire of 1666 destroyed most market areas (apart from Leadenhall market) and as such it provided a unique opportunity for the authorities to create new marketspaces, most of which took the shape of a market hall.

Both the increase in population and the rise of market halls impacted on access to the food markets. However, the precise effects varied according to different types of markets, and the relationship between market size and form is therefore rather complex. On the one hand expect the expansion of food markets is expected to provide greater opportunities for traders to obtain a spot in the marketplace. On the other hand, the often simultaneous arrival of tightly regulated food halls greatly resembling shops, has been suggested to have led to an increase in peripatetic trading, implying that this led to decreased opportunities in the formal food markets.[89] Let us survey the evidence on London and Dutch food markets in order to shed light on the effects of spatial expansion and reorganisation on market access.

As I have shown elsewhere, overall in the cities of Holland we find that the larger in size marketplaces were, the more beneficial the situation was for outsiders, such as independently operating women.[90] This finding confirms the hypothesis that the increase in the size of food markets could positively impact on access. Nevertheless, market expansion and growth took different shapes and forms in the markets for different types of foods, and the extent to which markets could grow also greatly depended on physical constraints. The spatial characteristics of early modern food markets could vary substantially between cities, but also between types of trades. The set-up of the various food markets in urban Holland are a case in point. Most meat was sold from meat halls, which were large buildings with permanent stalls (see Figure 4.1). Vegetable and fruit markets, on the other hand, were more often temporary in nature and apart from a designated space in the city did not have permanent buildings (such as the meat halls) or fixtures (see Figure 4.2 and Plate 3). The stands many of the vegetable sellers used were temporary standings, such as trestle tables that were erected on the day; others sold from baskets or carts. Permanent wooden stalls in the open air were features of the fish markets in most Dutch cities, and such markets thus formed an intermediate between the static meat halls and more flexible set-up of vegetable selling (see Figure 4.3).

We have already discussed a possible implication of markets with permanent stalls: the likelihood that such stalls were available at higher rental prices

Figure 4.1 View of the meat hall in Haarlem, Romeyn de Hooge, 1688–1689. Engraving. Rijksmuseum, Amsterdam.

and therefore that access to these marketplaces was more restricted. Another consequence of fixed market stalls is the limited flexibility of such markets to respond to changes in demand. Indeed, while we observe substantial changes over time in the numbers of permits available for selling vegetables in the Leiden market, the number of spaces available in the meat and fish markets was far more stable throughout the seventeenth and eighteenth centuries. Only when the authorities decided to build new market halls, such as in the case of the new Leiden meat hall in the 1670s, the number of spaces could be significantly expanded.[91]

The question remains of how the lack of potential for expansion, either temporary or permanently, precisely impacted on access and diversity in urban marketplaces, but the static character of permanent markets at least had one possible effect: increased opportunities for monopolisation. Striking examples in this context are the Leiden meat markets and Amsterdam fish market. Evidence on stall rentals indicates that both marketspaces were monopolised by particular groups of people, leaving little room for newcomers to enter these markets. In the case of the Leiden meat market this was especially clear

Figure 4.2 Vegetable sellers and their customers as seen from the back, Harmen ter Borch, 1651. Drawing. Rijksmuseum, Amsterdam.

Figure 4.3 Detail from *View of the fish market and fountain in Leiden*, A. Delfos, 1763. Copper engraving. Topografische Historische Atlas, Erfgoed Leiden en Omstreken.

in the stall allocation of the tripe hall (*Penshal*). Whilst, as we read above, the Leiden meat hall was an almost exclusively male domain, women occupied nearly all of the stalls in the tripe hall (see Plate 4). Here, meat residues such as lard, tripe and other offal were sold, products that in many cases were provided by butchers in the neighbouring meat hall. Interestingly, the sellers in the tripe hall were mostly wives of butchers, who habitually stressed their family connection to a butcher in the meat hall or another tripe seller when applying for a place in the market.[92] Thus while there were no formal regulations on who was entitled to rent a stall in the tripe hall, in practice in many cases this came down to wives of members of the butchers' guild. In a similar manner we find that part of the Amsterdam fish market was also dominated by a small number of families. Stalls in the Amsterdam eel market, for which we have information on stallholders between 1744 and 1814, were almost exclusively rented by men and women belonging to a small group of interrelated families. We find married couples renting neighbouring stalls, as well as parents and children, siblings and cousins. Again, membership of one of the handful of families that dominated the trade was not a formal requirement, but entry to these markets for those who were not part of these families through birth or marriage appears to have been far more unusual.[93]

When comparing the composition of the Leiden tripe hall and the Amsterdam eel market to evidence on the Leiden vegetable market we find that this food market was not monopolised by small groups of families. Although we do find families who work together in the sale of vegetables, there is a far greater variety in the types of people involved in these markets. While the potential for monopolisation offered by permanent market halls and fixed stalls in open air markets impacted negatively on opportunities for newcomers and outsiders (such as those who were not related to people already active in the trade), it also had positive effects as it allowed those people who were members of the families that monopolised the trade lifelong and stable careers. Indeed, many women working in these markets had long-lasting careers, uninterrupted by for instance childbirth, which differed substantially from the portrayals of market women struggling to make a living.[94]

In a similar manner, the establishment of the new common or public markets in London had a dual effect on the position of ambulant traders. These covered markets housed only 514 fixed stalls in total and therefore provided a stark contrast to London's overcrowded markets before the Great Fire.[95] The old markets are assumed to have left substantial leeway for those without an official entitlement to a selling space, whereas the lack of 'disorder' in the new market halls meant they lost their place in the market. However, we should not overlook that in some of the new markets, such as Leadenhall's beef and herb markets, specific spaces were allocated for hagglers.[96] Surely these spaces may overall have not provided as much room as before for those operating on the fringes of the official market. Nevertheless, in the same way that formalised and permanent spaces brought security to at least some traders in the Dutch food markets, we may assume that these formal spaces for hagglers brought similar advantages in the form of entitlements to sell from these markets and hence perhaps also more secure positions in the trade. Of course, as we read above, this did come at the price of a weekly fee, and, as in the Dutch case, this meant that those who could not afford such fees will automatically have been excluded. Whether, as in the Dutch cases, family connections were advantageous in accessing these spaces is unclear. The reoccurrence of family names in the records of stallholders' rent payments in London's covered markets suggests this may very well have been the case.[97]

Market regulation and access: some concluding thoughts

This assessment of food markets in some of the most populous areas in pre-industrial Europe illustrates the complexity of access to marketplaces. It is clear that despite the fragmented governance the regulation of food markets had great impact on who sold from these markets and under what circumstances. Guild control meant that certain groups of people (including independent women and Jews) were either unable, or seriously limited in their opportunities to sell foodstuffs on a daily basis, either from a stall (in the Dutch context) or a shop (in London). In both London and the Dutch cities under scrutiny country vendors were accommodated in separate markets, but local non-citizens could often only operate as hagglers and hawkers and were seriously constrained in their activities by regulation on where and when they could operate.

An often-overlooked element in access to the food trades in the pre-industrial context is the financial cost of access to markets. Guilds demanded entrance fees and (for migrants) the added costs of obtaining citizenship rights. In addition, for those who were entitled to a stall in one of the formal markets, both guild members and country vendors, the payment of stall rents and other costs imposed on stallholders meant that some people were excluded from selling from these markets because they were unable to meet these costs. Surveying the evidence on various Dutch markets suggests that overall, women suffered more than men from high stall rents and associated costs. In the context of early modern cities, in which marketplaces over time became more and more formalised with the rise of covered markets with permanent stalls, the impact of fixed stall rents should not be underestimated. At the same time, the setting of prices for sales licences and stall rents in the London markets, which included specific rates for poor people and the opportunity for short-term leases or permits, suggests that at least some local authorities acknowledged the importance of entry-level rates as well as flexible leases.

While guild memberships, stall rents and sales permits are forms of regulation that directly impacted on access to the food trades, this chapter also laid bare regulations that indirectly affected access. We have seen that regulation on when goods could be sold and when merchandise could be acquired not only greatly affected sales potential, but also the sheer opportunities for certain people to be active as food hawkers or stallhold-ers. Especially revealing was the fact that laws prohibiting selling and buy-ing outside official market times impacted on traders' abilities to acquire goods for sale. We saw that this affected mostly those without access to a space in the formal marketplace, but it could even impact on guild mem-bers who could not provide their own merchandise, such as the single women in the central Leiden vegetable market. Similarly, the rise of fixed markets in the form of market halls enabled the monopolisation of certain trades by small groups of families, making it difficult for those without relatives in the trade to enter certain food markets. At the same time, these family monopolies also enabled certain men and women to hold lifelong and well-paid careers in the food trades, which especially in the case of women contrasts the long-standing idea that selling foodstuffs was a mar-ginal and temporary economic activity taken up purely out of desperation. For a better understanding of the composition of historic marketplaces it is therefore of utmost importance to carefully analyse the way markets are regulated, what formal or informal bodies (e.g. guilds, city councils or par-ticular families) controlled the market space, and to look beyond gender as the only defining category for market traders.

Notes

* This chapter builds upon research undertaken in the context of my PhD dissertation, now published as Danielle van den Heuvel, *Women and Entrepreneurship: Female Traders in the Northern Netherlands c.1580–1815* (Amsterdam, 2007). I should like to thank Jasmine Kilburn-Toppin for her suggestions for improvement of the chapter.

1 F.J. Fisher, 'The development of the London food market', *Economic History Review* 5 (1935), pp. 46–64; Roger Scola, 'Food markets and shops in Manchester 1770–1870', *Journal of Historical Geography* 1 (1975), pp. 153–168; John Chartres (ed.), *Agricultural Markets and Trade 1500–1750* (Cambridge, 1990); Colin Smith, 'The wholesale and retail markets of London, 1660–1840', *Economic History Review* 55 (2002), pp. 31–50; Gergely Baics, 'Is access to food a public good? Meat provi-sioning in early New York City, 1790–1820', *Journal of Urban History* 39 (2012), pp. 643–668.

2 P.E. Jones, *The Butchers of London: A History of the Worshipful Company of Butchers of the City of London* (London, 1976); Sidney Watts, *Meat Matters: Butchers, Politics and Market Culture in Eighteenth-century Paris* (Rochester, 2006); James Shaw, 'Retail, monopoly and privilege: The dissolution of the fishmongers' guild of Venice, 1599', *Journal of Early Modern History* 6 (2002), pp. 396–427.

3 Alice Clark, *Working Life of Women in the Seventeenth Century* (London, 1992), pp. 219–220; Jenneke Quast, 'Vrouwenarbeid omstreeks 1500 in enkele Nederlandse steden', *Jaarboek voor vrouwengeschiedenis* 1 (1980) pp. 46–64. Darlene Abreu-Ferreira, 'Fishmongers and shipowners: Women in maritime communities in early modern Portugal', *Sixteenth Century Journal* 31 (2000), pp. 7–23.

4 Elise van Nederveen Meerkerk, *De draad in eigen handen. Vrouwen en loonar-beid in de Nederlandse textielnijverheid 1581–1810* (Amsterdam, 2007); Van den Heuvel, *Women*.

5 Andrzej Karpinski, 'The woman on the marketplace: The scale of feminiza-tion of retail trade in Polish towns in the second half of the 16th and the 17th

century', in Simonetta Cavaciocchi (ed.), *La donna nell'economia, secc XIII-XVIII* (Florence, 1990), pp. 283–292; Maryanne Kowaleski, 'Women's work in a market town: Exeter in the late fourteenth century', in B.A. Hanawalt (ed.), *Women and Work in Preindustrial Europe* (Bloomington, 1986), pp. 145–166; T.T.-F. Lam, 'Food for the city: The role of the informal sector', *Geo-Journal Supplementary Issue* 4 (1982), pp. 49–59.

6   Jones, *Butchers of London*; Watts, *Meat Matters*; Danielle van den Heuvel, 'The multiple identities of early modern Dutch fishwives', *Signs: Journal of Women in Culture and Society*, 37 (2012), pp. 587–594.

7   Hernando De Soto, *The Other Path: The Invisible Revolution in the Third World* (New York, 1989); World Bank, *Doing Business in in 2004: Understanding Regulation* (Washington, DC, 2004).

8   Vanessa Harding, 'Shops, markets and retailers in London's Cheapside, c. 1500–1700', in Bruno Blondé, Peter Stabel, Jon Stobart and Ilja Van Damme (eds), *Buyers and Sellers: Retail Circuits and Practices in Medieval and Early modern Europe* (Turnhout, 2006), pp. 155–170; Ian Archer, Caroline Barron and Vanessa Harding (eds), *Hugh Alley's Caveat: The Markets of London in 1598* (London, 1988); Peter Stabel, 'From the market to the shop: Retail and urban space in late medieval Bruges', in Blondé *et al.*, *Buyers*, pp. 79–108; Anne Montenach, 'Formal and informal economy in an urban context: The case of food trade in seventeenth-century Lyons', in Thomas Buchner and Philip R. Hoffmann-Rehnitz (eds), *Shadow Economies and Irregular Work in Urban Europe: 16th to early 20th centuries* (Vienna, 2011), pp. 91–106.

9   In this chapter when referring to 'Holland' I mean the province of Holland (contemporary North and South Holland together). The 'Low Countries' is used when referring to the area now known as Belgium and the Netherlands.

10 This continued to be the case in the nineteenth century. Roger Scola, 'Food markets and shops in Manchester, 1770–1870', *Journal of Historical Geography* 1 (1975), pp. 153–168; Colin S. Smith, 'The market place and the market's place in London c.1660–1840' (D.Phil. thesis, University College London, 1999).

11 Montenach, 'Formal and informal economy'; Van den Heuvel, *Women*, pp. 87–134; Evelyn Welch, *Shopping in the Renaissance: Consumer Cultures in Italy, 1400–1600* (New Haven, 2005), pp. 34, 37.

12 Van den Heuvel, *Women*, pp. 87–134; Jannie Stegeman, 'Scheveningse visverkoopsters ca. 1600–1900', *Holland* 21 (1991), pp. 38–53.

13 A notable exception is Billingsgate market where food sellers only sold fresh fish. Archer, *Hugh Alley's Caveat*, pp. 1–5; Smith, 'The market place', p. 20.

14 Van den Heuvel, *Women*; Smith, 'The market place'.

15 James E. Shaw, *The Justice of Venice Authorities and Liberties in the Urban Economy 1550–1700* (Oxford, 2006); Scola, 'Food markets'; Archer, *Hugh Alley's caveat*; Smith, 'The market place'; Watts, *Meat Matters*, pp. 63–84.

16 Smith, 'The market place', pp. 14, 159–160; Danielle van den Heuvel, 'Policing peddlers: The prosecution of illegal street trade in eighteenth-century Dutch towns', *Historical Journal* 58/2 (2015), pp. 367–392.

17 Archer, *Hugh Alley's Caveat*; Smith, 'The market place'; Van den Heuvel, *Women*, pp. 91–93.

18 Cf. Harding, 'Shops'; Stabel, 'Market'; Shaw, *Justice*; Danielle van den Heuvel, 'Partners in marriage and business? Guilds and the family economy in urban food markets in the Dutch Republic', *Continuity and Change* 23 (2008), pp. 217–236.

19 Cf. Sheilagh Ogilvie, 'How does social capital affect women? Guilds and communities in Early Modern Germany', *The American Historical Review* 109 (2004), pp. 325–359.

20 Bert De Munck, Piet Lourens and Jan Lucassen, 'The establishment and distribution of craft guilds in the Low Countries, 1000–1800', in C. Lis, J. Lucassen, M.

Prak and H. Soly (eds), *Guilds in the Early Modern Low Countries: Work, Power and Representation* (London, 2006), pp. 40, 55.

21 Piet Lourens and Jan Lucassen, *Inwoneraantallen van Nederlandse steden ca. 1300–1800* (Amsterdam, 1997), pp. 56–57.

22 For example the town of 's-Hertogenbosch (population c. 12,000), Van den Heuvel, *Women*, 149.

23 Michael J. Walker, 'The extent of guild control of trades in England, c. 1660–1820. A study based on a sample of provincial towns and London companies' (Unpublished PhD dissertation, University of Cambridge, 1985); Ian Anders Gadd and Patrick Wallis, 'Introduction', in Ian Anders Gadd and Patrick Wallis (eds), *Guilds, Society and Economy in London 1450–1800* (London, 2002), pp. 1–14; Michael Berlin, 'Guilds in decline? London livery companies and the rise of a liberal economy', in S.R. Epstein and Maarten Prak (eds), *Guilds, Innovation, and the European Economy, 1400–1800* (Cambridge, 2008), pp. 316–342.

24 Smith, 'The market place', p. 152; J.R. Kellet, 'The breakdown of gild and corporation control over the handicraft and retail trade in London', *Economic History Review* 10 (1958), pp. 381–394; Gadd and Wallis, *Guilds*.

25 Smith, 'The market place', pp. 152, 162.

26 Archer, *Hugh Alley's Caveat*, p. 11; S. Rappaport, *Worlds within Worlds: Structures of Life in Sixteenth-century London* (Cambridge, 1989), p. 54.

27 Margaret Dorey, 'Controlling corruption: Regulating meat consumption as a preventative to plague in seventeenth-century London', *Urban History* 36 (2009), pp. 24–41; Jones, *Butchers of London*, pp. 80–88.

28 Cf. Harding, 'Shops'; Betty R. Masters, *The Public Markets of the City of London surveyed by William Leybourn in 1677* (London, 1974), p. 12; Paul Griffiths, *Lost Londons: Change, Crime and Control in the Capital 1550–1660* (Cambridge, 2008), pp. 98–134.

29 Smith, 'The market place', p. 160. See also Ian Archer, *The Pursuit of Stability: Social Relations in Elizabethan London* (Cambridge, 1991), pp. 134–140.

30 Cf. Van den Heuvel, 'Policing peddlers'.

31 De Soto, *The Other Path*, pp. 131–188. See also Chapter 7 in this volume.

32 See Chapter 9 in this volume.

33 In present-day developing economies we do find street vendors' associations. While these resemble guilds as they also aim to protect the interests of their members, they differ from guilds in that they do not exclude certain groups from entering a trade or other forms of monopolisation as far as I am aware. There are however also signs that street vendor organisations struggle to build democratic institutions in which the voices of all members are heard. http://wiego.org/informal-economy/occupational-groups/street-vendors.

34 Van den Heuvel, 'Partners'; see also the situation in eighteenth-century Sweden: Maria Ågren, 'Emissaries, allies, accomplices and enemies: Married women's work in eighteenth-century urban Sweden', *Urban History* 41 (2014), p. 394.

35 On the importance of guild membership in the context of retailing see Rappaport, *Worlds*, pp. 29, 31.

36 Masters, *Public Markets*, p. 13.

37 De Munck *et al.*, 'Establishment and distribution', p. 51.

38 Danielle van den Heuvel, 'Guilds, gender policies and economic opportunities for women in early modern Dutch towns', in Deborah Simonton and Anne Montenach (eds), *Female Agency in the Eighteenth-century Urban Economy: Gender in European towns, 1640–1830* (London, 2013), pp. 116–133.

39 Van den Heuvel, *Women*, pp. 152, 166; Van den Heuvel, 'Partners', pp. 221–226.

40 Van den Heuvel, 'Guilds'.

41 J.C. van Dillen, *Bronnen tot de geschiedenis van het bedrijfsleven* I (Den Haag, 1929), pp. 1272, 1269; Jenneke Quast, 'Vrouwenarbeid omstreeks 1500 in enkele

Nederlandse steden', *Jaarboek voor vrouwengeschiedenis* 1 (1980), pp. 55–57; Gabrielle Dorren, '"Want noijt gebeurt is dat een vrouw meester is geworden..." Vrouwen en gilden in zeventiende-eeuws Haarlem', in Clé Lesger and Leo Noordegraaf (eds), *Ondernemers en bestuurders. Economie en politiek in de Noordelijke Nederlanden in de Late Middeleeuwen en de Vroegmoderne Tijd* (Amsterdam, 1999), p. 145.

42 Ariadne Schmidt, *Overleven na de dood. Weduwen in Leiden in de Gouden Eeuw* (Amsterdam, 2002), p. 129.

43 J.C. van Dillen, *Bronnen tot de geschiedenis van het bedrijfsleven* II (Den Haag, 1929), p. 55.

44 Van den Heuvel, 'Partners in business'.

45 We find incorporated towns all over the country; the numbers grew strongly between 1540 and 1640, and were largest in more commercialised areas. See Phil Withington, *The Politics of Commonwealth: Citizens and Freemen in Early Modern England* (Cambridge, 2005), pp. 18–19.

46 Withington, *Politics*, 10; Patrick Wallis, 'Apprenticeship and training in premodern England', *Journal of Economic History* 68 (2008), pp. 832–861.

47 Ian Anders Gadd and Patrick Wallis, 'Introduction', in Ian Anders Gadd and Patrick Wallis (eds), *Guilds, Society and Economy in London 1450–1800* (London, 2002), p. 7.

48 Though immigrants were very often brought into London companies their privileges were rarely equal to those of indigenous citizens. Rappaport, *Worlds*, pp. 29–32, 44–47; Lien Bich Luu, *Immigrants and the Industries of London, 1500–1700* (Aldershot, 2005), pp. 143–146.

49 It is difficult to precisely determine how hagglers and hawkers differed from each other in their operations. According to the *Oxford English Dictionary*, both are itinerant vendors. In the *OED* definition of hawker, it is specifically mentioned that hawkers cry their goods, and that in the nineteenth-century they differed from peddlers in that they used carts to carry their goods, while peddlers carried their wares. Hagglers on the other hand are defined as 'itinerant vendors; hucksters' implying that they are mostly retailers, as hucksters are defined as such in the *OED* (at least before the nineteenth century). I have used the terms interchangeably, apart from when I discuss the allocation of specific spaces to hagglers in the London Public Markets, as 'hagglers' was the term used in allocating this space.

50 Archer, *Hugh Alley's Caveat*, pp. 4–5, 8. Masters, *Public Markets*, pp. 11–12. Stegeman, 'Scheveningse visverkoopsters', p. 45. The importance of securing income from stall rents is clearly illustrated by the efforts that the Mayor and Aldermen of London put into the development of plans for the new public markets in London after 1666. Cf. Masters, *Public Markets*, p. 11.

51 In fourteenth-century London citizen poultry vendors were charged 4d per foot per year. Archer, *Hugh Alley's Caveat*, p. 10.

52 London Metropolitan Archives (LMA), CLA/009/01/035. See also: Masters, *Public Markets*, p. 18.

53 Joan Thirsk, *Food in Early Modern England: Phases, Fads, Fashions 1500–1700* (London, 2007), pp. 210–211.

54 Stegeman, 'Scheveningse visverkoopsters', p. 46.

55 Van den Heuvel, *Women*, pp. 92–93, 103 and 111.

56 LMA, CLA/009/01/035.

57 De Soto, *Other Path*; World Bank, *Doing Business*.

58 Schmidt, *Overleven*, p. 132.

59 LMA, CLA/009/01/009; Stegeman, 'Scheveningse visverkoopsters', p. 48. For other examples of how the costs of formality affected the economic opportunities of early modern city dwellers, see Luu, *Immigrants*, p. 144.

60 Stegeman, 'Scheveningse visverkoopsters', p. 46.
61 Stegeman, 'Scheveningse visverkoopsters', p. 48.
62 Van den Heuvel, *Women*, pp. 98, 118.
63 Van den Heuvel, 'Guilds'.
64 See also Chapter 7 in this volume; Van den Heuvel, 'Guilds', p. 126.
65 Cf. Welch, *Shopping*, pp. 96–122.
66 Archer, *Hugh Alley's Caveat*, p. 12.
67 John Strype, *A Survey of the Cities of London and Westminster*, Volume II, Book 5, Chapter 22 (London, 1720), pp. 308–12; Smith, 'The market place', pp. 26–27.
68 Jan Wagenaar, *Beschryving van Amsterdam verkort, Vierde boek* (Amsterdam, 1788), p. 168.
69 Simon van Leeuwen, *Korte besgrijving van het Lugdunum Batavorum* (Leiden, 1672), p. 75.
70 Archer, *Hugh Alley's Caveat*, p. 6; Masters, *Public Markets*, p. 13; Harding, 'Shops'; Van den Heuvel, *Women*.
71 Smith, 'The market place', p. 28.
72 Erfgoed Leiden en Omstreken (ELO), Archief van de Gilden, Beurzen en Rederijkerskamers (Gilden), inv. no. 1215.
73 Stegeman, 'Scheveningse visverkoopsters', p. 46.
74 Harding, 'Shops', p. 166; Welch, *Shopping*, pp. 79, 93–94.
75 Archer, *Hugh Alley's Caveat*, pp. 15, 32.
76 Cf. Strype, *Survey*, pp. 308–312.
77 'Forestalling' referred to illegal activities by consumers and implied that someone went out before the market and bought goods from those who would otherwise have sold the goods in the market, 'engrossing' and 'regrating' referred to illegal activities by people who resold goods. An 'engrosser' bought up large quantities of one particular product for resale at an enhanced price, while a 'regrater' bought goods in one marketplace to sell them in another. This differentiation does not seem to have existed in the Dutch system where one generally spoke of 'voorkoop' when referring to offences such as the above. Archer, *Hugh Alley's caveat*, p. 5; Van den Heuvel, *Women*, p. 104; *Oxford English Dictionary*.
78 Strype, *Survey*, pp. 308–309; Archer, *Hugh Alley's Caveat*, pp. 23–26.
79 ELO, Gilden, inv. no. 1349.
80 Harm Kaal and Jelle van Lottum, 'Immigrants in the polder. Rural-rural long distance migration in North-Western Europe: The Case of Watergraafsmeer', *Rural History* 20 (2009), p. 112.
81 Van den Heuvel, *Women*, pp. 104–109.
82 Archer, *Hugh Alley's Caveat*, p. 26; Wendy Thwaites, 'Oxford food riots: A community and its markets', in Adrian Randall and Andrew Charlesworth (eds), *Markets, Market Culture and Popular Protest in Eighteenth-century Britain and Ireland* (Liverpool, 1996), pp. 144–145.
83 See also Archer, *Hugh Alley's Caveat*, p. 23.
84 Archer, *Hugh Alley's Caveat*, p. 12. It is unknown whether this stipulation concerned country people only.
85 Archer, *Hugh Alley's Caveat*, pp. 6, 8.
86 See for evidence on this Chapter 9 in this volume. Also Loretta E. Bass, 'Enlarging the street and negotiating the curb: Public space at the edge of an African market', *International Journal of Sociology and Social Policy* 20 (2000), pp. 74–95.
87 L.D. Schwarz, *London in the Age of Industrialisation: Entrepreneurs, Labour Force and Living Conditions, 1700–1850* (Cambridge, 1992), p. 126.
88 Piet Lourens and Jan Lucassen, *Inwoneraantallen van Nederlandse steden 1300–1800* (Amsterdam, 1997).
89 Harding, 'Shops', p. 166.

90 Van den Heuvel, 'Partners in business'.
91 ELO, Stadsarchief II (SA II), inv.nos. 1395–1397.
92 ELO, SA II, inv.nos. 77–78.
93 Compare Watts, *Meat Matters*, pp. 130–136 for similar strategies in the Parisian meat markets.
94 Van den Heuvel, 'Multiple identities'.
95 Masters, *Public Markets*, pp. 45–51. Leadenhall Beef Market: 84 stalls; Leadenhall White Market: 140 stalls; Leadenhall Herb Market: 57 stalls; Woolchurch or Stock Market: 25 stalls; Honey Lane or Milk Street Market: 140 stalls; Newgate Market: 68 stalls.
96 Also citizens who did not own a shop were offered stalls. Masters, *Public Markets*, pp. 31, 53.
97 A.V. Bebb, 'Urban food markets in early modern English cities and towns: Social and economic functionality' (Unpublished BA dissertation, University of Kent, 2014), p. 21.

5 Food selling and urban space in early modern Naples

Melissa Calaresu*

The Neapolitan revolt against Castile began on 7 July 1647 in the Market Square of Naples, after a dispute between the fruit vendors of the city and the Spanish customs office. Masaniello became the leader of the revolt against the Spanish government and, although he was killed less than ten days later, his name and news of the revolt spread across Europe for years, even after Naples' return to Spanish rule in April 1648.[1] A few years later, Domenico Gargiulo (1609–1675), otherwise known as Micco Spadaro, painted one of the most well-known images of the revolt, *The revolt of Masaniello in 1647*.[2] The figure of Masaniello, astride a horse and red-capped, and the violence of the scene have dominated interpretations of this painting. Spadaro's depiction of the revolt contrasts sharply with another painting of the Market Square by him, but which has attracted less scholarly attention (Plate 5).[3] This painting is bustling, not with a murderous crowd, but, instead, with the activity of buying and selling in the main square of one of the most populous and popular neighbourhoods in seventeenth-century Naples. It reminds us that fruit vendors protesting the raising of taxes and their customers were at the centre of this conflict.

Masaniello was a porter who worked for fish sellers (*pescivendoli*) at the *pietra delle pesce* near the market square of Naples. His father was also a porter, and his mother a prostitute. Masaniello lived on the Market Square, possibly above a duty house (*casa della gabella*) in the Lavinaro neighbourhood.[4] The Market Square was close to the port and also near the customs and duty houses of the Spanish government in the city. Micco Spadaro was better-off than Masaniello; he was the son of a sword maker, as his name suggests, and likely to have been born in the neighbourhood near the port.[5] The lives of Masaniello and Micco Spadaro were embedded in the urban fabric of the city, baptised and then married in the churches of the city, walking its streets, making chit-chat with neighbours and with street vendors. Their identities were bound, in part, by the day-to-day experience of living in the city, and food hawkers were an ubiquitous presence.[6] This chapter aims to look beyond Masaniello and to explore the dynamics of food selling and urban space in early modern Naples by studying representations of the city alongside print and manuscript tax records.

Although shops dominate the history of buying in this period, most inhabitants of early modern European cities continued to buy their food on the street – either in markets or from food hawkers. For this reason, the selling of food on the streets should form a central part of the wider cultural history of the streets, a topic which is of increasing interest to historians. In an influential article, the architectural historian Diane Favro called for the breaking down of disciplinary boundaries within urban history in order to reinvigorate an interest in the 'meaning and experience of cities', and, in particular, she highlighted the need to consider the sensorial experience of the street as well as the ephemerality and haphazardness of activities on the street.[7] Regardless of any innovations within her own discipline, cultural historians have taken up her call in the last decade. As the editors of a new volume write, the street in the early modern period should not be viewed as 'a mere backdrop for social events or social relations' or 'an outcome of town planning and architecture' but be integrated in to a wider history which takes account of 'the nature of the street as a material reality, as a starting point for studying people in the streets (and near them), highlighting the integral connectivity of the material and the immaterial'.[8] A new volume on Renaissance Florence marks the emerging and exciting field of the cultural history of urban space, a history which integrates the inside with the outside and takes account of the plebeian use of public space and its material culture.[9] Most recently, new research by Niall Atkinson and Tom Stammers, who have reconstructed, respectively, the soundscapes of early modern Florence and the commercial and cultural uses of urban space in nineteenth-century Paris, suggests the innovative ways by which the richness of street life can be uncovered as part of a wider cultural history of public space and memory.[10]

In these recent works, the material culture of the street (and its furniture) have been given greater prominence, even agency, in the active creation of civic, neighbourhood and religious identities in the early modern period.[11] Urban historians have uncovered an entire world of excrescences, overhangings, balconies, protrusions (*sporti*) and shelters (*canti*), benches and trestle tables. Neighbourhood boundaries and patrician jurisdictions are marked out on the sides and corners of palace walls. Spires (*guglie*), fountains and monuments (some made out of stone, others made out of wood and canvas) in streets and squares commemorated the end of a plague, the beneficence of a local magnate, or the marriage of a princess.[12] The commercial and political uses of the things which 'furnished' the street could be explored even further to piece together the cultural life of the street in the early modern period.[13] Nonetheless, this recent work has also recognised the need to abandon the public/private dichotomy which has dominated a lot of historical literature. As many cultural historians of early modern Europe have known for years, urban life was much messier than a clear dichotomy of public/private or inside/outside suggests – as Florentine patricians hung tapestries outside of their palace windows for public celebrations, shopkeepers sold their goods outside on temporary trestle tables and through a network of peddlers and the clatter of the street were part of the domestic soundscape.[14] However, as Favro and others have remarked, the cultural life of the street is defined by its ephemerality – between night and day, within a week, between seasons – and can not be built simply from the marking out of these boundaries, extrusions, monuments and doorways within this urban space.[15] It is the human activity and movement between and within them which also have to be captured by the cultural historian in order to reconstruct human relationships, social identities and cultural exchange within the city.[16]

The difficulties in capturing the messiness and movement of street life, a reflection of what Spiro Kostoff has written – 'urban truth is in the flow' – of course, varies from city to city.[17] The intricate work of Niall Atkinson on sound or Stephen J. Milner on town criers, for instance, is made easier by the quantity and richness of the Florentine archives and by the tradition of its citizens to record their lives in *ricordanze*.[18] For other cities in Italy, there are archival records generated by the state; for instance, in Rome, food supplies can be reconstructed through the study of the *Annona*, a system of price control by the government to guarantee the provision of basic foodstuffs such as oil and flour.[19] In the case of food sellers, the archival sources reflect attempts to control, limit and survey commercial life on the streets by municipal governments, and, in this way, the illegality and marginality of peddlers tends to be emphasised through the lens of such sources.[20] peddlers and food sellers, in particular, represent the very ephemerality of the street life we are trying to capture – either in their movements across the city, carrying their goods with them, or in the trestle tables and tripods which are set down at the beginning of the day and packed up at the end of the day. In turn, the acts of preparing and serving food on the street – the roasting of chestnuts, the boiling of *maccaroni*, the scooping out of sorbets, the cutting up of cooked tripe (Figure 5.1), the pouring out of ice-cold lemon water (Figure 5.2), and the pulling of sugar to make *frammellicco*, a kind of Neapolitan sweet (Figure 5.3) – as well as the eating of food itself represent the most ephemeral acts of all. These acts, which would have been accompanied by cries, and competed with entertainers nearby, are particularly well preserved (without the sound, of course) in visual evidence from eighteenth-century Naples.

Images of food hawkers

The wealth of visual evidence of selling food on the streets in early modern Italy is striking. For the eighteenth century, the engravings of Venetian street sellers by Gaetano Zompini, the paintings and engravings of Neapolitan street life by Pietro Fabris, as well as the countless images of lemon sellers and fish markets by Grand Tour artists such as David Allan provide rich material for the study of the representational traditions of the costumes and customs of the inhabitants of Italian cities. While recent research has focused on the production of images of street sellers for civic elites and Grand Tourists in the

Figure 5.1 Pietro Fabris, 'Venditore di Merce detta carnecotta Napolitano', in *Raccolta di varii Vestimenti ed Arti del Regno di Napoli* (Naples, 1773). © British Library Board. D-7743.h.13.

Figure 5.2 Pietro Fabris, 'Banca di Acquaiolo Napolitano', in *Raccolta di varii Vestimenti ed Arti del Regno di Napoli* (Naples, 1773). © British Library Board. D-7743.h.13.

Figure 5.3 Saverio della Gatta, 'Venditore di sorbetto'. Gouache, 1809. Inv.22903, Museo di San Martino, Naples. By kind permission of the Fototeca of the Sopraintendenza Speciale per il P.S.A.E. e per il Polo Museale della Città di Napoli.

eighteenth century, the complex reconstruction of these representational traditions should not belie the ethnographic value of these depictions of street life and, in particular, what they can tell you about the selling of food in this period. The Grand Tour market in Naples produced an enormous quantity of paintings, engravings and sketches of images of Neapolitan street sellers (some of which, in turn, also appeared on porcelain and cloth).[21] The value of these images – in particular as ethnographic sources – has not been fully appreciated by historians who, rightly, have recognised the 'exoticising' in the production of these images, in particular, of the Neapolitan poor. There is a long and continuous history of representing the so-called *lazzaroni* of Naples, which can be described as an interest in the 'urban picturesque'.[22] The representational traditions behind the images of street sellers originate, in part, from early modern genre paintings of the comic, the poor and the marginalised, but also from ethnographic studies such as costume books and street-cries. In one looks closely, there is, in fact, room for some detailed ethnographic observation within both of these traditions and, in combination with other kinds of sources, a fuller cultural history of selling on the street is possible.

Grand Tourists became increasingly interested in the popular culture of southern Italy throughout the eighteenth century and this interest comes through in the visual and literary sources of the period. Travellers were keen to attend popular festivals and to hear and see street entertainers in the square in front of the Angevin Castle, known then as the Largo di Castello. Travellers often commented on the presence of street sellers who were, no doubt, as Goethe suggested below, part of the 'theatre' of the street:

> *Pedlars, etc.* Some go about with little barrels of ice water, lemon and glasses, so that, on request, they can immediately provide a drink of lemonade, a beverage which even the poorest cannot do without. Others carry trays, on which bottles of various liqueurs and tapering glasses are held safely in place by wooden rings. Others again carry baskets containing pastries of various kinds, lemons and other fruit. All of them, it seems, want nothing better than to contribute to the daily festival of joy.[23]

Henry Swinburne, who was resident in Naples in the 1780s, describes the selling of more ordinary food stuffs to the *lazzaroni* on the streets, writing that 'the markets and principal streets are lined with sellers of macaroni, fried and boiled fish, puddings, cakes, and vegetables of all sorts'.[24] And, Neapolitan observers also echoed the Grand Tour accounts, for example, Lorenzo Giustiniani, who wrote:

> It is impossible to find among all the cities of the universe an equal to our Metropolis which can boast to have in all times of the year, day, and hour such abundance of goods, as much of necessity as of luxury, and to satisfy the desire of the greediest of people. Certainly it is a beautiful to see not only in the main streets but also in each of their side-streets (of which there are more than 1315 as stated in the *Prammatica* of 7 November 1798), so many sellers of things in their *posti fissi*, the number of which grow by the day. But one can also see from morning to night other than from these said *posti*, sellers of all kinds of things roaming the city who are called *ricattieri* [second-hand dealers] or *bazzareoti* [ambulant sellers of comestibles] and who are there for the convenience of all families who can not go out to the square or send someone to buy necessities. Fruit, vegetables of all kinds, bread, meat, fish, cheese, *paste*, and even wine are the kinds of things which they carry with them to sell in the city for the convenience of its inhabitants.[25]

As these descriptions attest, the streets of Naples, like many European cities, were crowded with street sellers. Although Giustiniani's description was part of a wider narrative about the commercial success of the city, municipal administrators continued to be concerned about the overcrowding of the streets. Giustiniani mentions the law of 1798 and today there remains an even more permanent testimonial of the government's concern, a stone tablet which was installed in the Largo di Carità in 1802, by the *Portolania*, the municipal authority responsible for selling on the city's streets, announcing the destruction of the kiosks (*barrache*) on the square and the prohibition of any kind of street selling there in the future.[26] Despite these efforts, the illegal street selling continued: one Napoleonic administrator despaired in 1814 that 'several ignorant and obstinate sellers of contraband meat continue to clutter the Largo di Carità'.[27]

Grand Tourists, however, were unlikely to venture as far as Largo di Carità, at the very end of Via Toledo, and the images of the street sellers which they took home with them were, for the most part, of the kinds of sellers which one encountered near the areas of popular entertainment, such as Largo di Castello or near the newly-built pleasure gardens, the Villa Reale, in the neighbourhood of Chiaia. In his album of watercolours drawn 'mostly from nature', the Scottish painter, David Allan (1744–1796), depicted a lemon seller crying his wares in front of a smoking Vesuvius, possibly on the newly opened promenade at the city's port and near the Market Square (Figure 5.4).[28] While Allan was particularly attentive to minute details of the clothing of his figures, his interest in the wider urban environment or the equipment used by sellers on the street appears more clearly in a sketchbook from the same period, for example, in the image of a puppeteer, entertaining a crowd (Figure 5.5).[29]

Allan's Neapolitan contemporary, Pietro Fabris (active 1756–1792) produced the greatest number and most detailed images of food sellers from eighteenth-century Naples, including an image of a sorbet seller with a puppet theatre in the background at the Largo di Castello. This image (as well as Figures 5.1 and 5.2) appeared in his *Collection of Various Costumes and Trades of the Kingdom of Naples* of 1773, a volume which was dedicated to the British emissary in Naples, William Hamilton, and targeted, in part, at the lucrative Grand Tour market.[30] However, not all of his images left his readers solely with the impression that Neapolitans spent their days eating sorbet in bare feet.

Fabris' other printed images of Neapolitan street sellers in the volume include a female vendor of *Tonninole* (a kind of mollusc) accompanied by two children selling cooked apples, a male oil vendor pouring oil through a funnel from a carafe into a small jug held by a girl, with smaller jugs hanging from his belt, a male vendor of cooked offal with a boiling pot by the side of his trestle table (Figure 5.1), a male lemon-water seller, behind a stand with two suspended canisters, one of which could be turned round with handle on its lid (Figure 5.2), a male vendor of roasted chestnuts with his roasting pot on a tripod by his side, and a male vegetable seller with a packed mule also by his side.[31] Not included in his *Collection*, but part of the same series, are some original watercolours which have survived, including an image of a fruit seller and a seller of *scagliozzi* (corn-meal fritters).[32] Fabris had a good eye for the details of what and how Neapolitan food hawkers sold on the street and

Figure 5.4 David Allan, 'Lemon cryer of Naples', from *A Collection of Dresses by Da. Allan Mostly from Nature, 1776*. Aberdeen Art Gallery & Museums Collections.

also reproduced them in paint as well as print and watercolour. For example, in a Fabris painting which has recently resurfaced on the art market, three food hawkers appear in the right-hand corner, selling some kind of cooked pastry, cooked apples and sorbet to the crowd, as a 'Turkish cavalcade' passes in front of the Royal Palace during the Carnival of 1778.[33] While the images by Fabris can be placed within the street-cries tradition which was popular with Grand Tourists, they also reveal his ethnographic interests which derive from early modern costume books.[34] The day-to-day details of cooking, serving, selling and eating food on the streets in Naples come through in his images, even if the early modern material culture of food hawking which Fabris depicts – the chestnut roaster, the *sorbettiera* for making and serving ice cream, or the cauldrons to cook or fry food – only survives in miniature in eighteenth-century nativity scenes or in the continuing use of similar equipment on streets today.[35]

Most of Fabris' images do not reveal much about the topography of the city of Naples. The Largo di Castello is the backdrop to the sorbet seller but,

Figure 5.5 David Allan, 'Puppeteer', *Naples Sketchbook*, c. 1770–1776, Pencil, pen and brown ink on paper. D5088, 4r. National Gallery of Scotland.

in general, the buildings and urban spaces are unrecognisable, barely sketched out in his engravings.[36] There are, in any case, some eighteenth-century images of particular streets and squares in Naples by other artists; the most well-known are the paintings by Antonio Joli (1700–1771) which were commissioned by Lord John Brudenell, the Marquis of Monthermer, in the 1750s and now in Lord Montagu's collection at Beaulieu.[37] Joli attends to the architectural detail of the buildings in the city, and the grandeur of the buildings tends to keep the viewer's attention. Nonetheless, Joli's streets are full of carriages, and, if you look closely, the details of Neapolitan urban life begin to come through. In Joli's painting, *Church of San Paolo Maggiore, Naples* (Plate 6), for example, there is a row of food hawkers in front of the church – from right to left, a lemon-water seller, identifiable by the lemon-leaves which decorate his stand, a man selling fruit from a trestle table, and a female vendor with her goods laid out on a cloth on the ground (Figure 5.6). Around the corner of the statue, there is another female vendor, behind a trestle table, and what looks like a pot on a tripod beside her. At the centre of the square

Figure 5.6 Detail of Plate 6: Antonio Joli, *The Church of San Paolo Maggiore, Naples*, 1756–1758. Oil on canvas, 19¼ ins x 30 ins. Palace House, Beaulieu. By kind permission of Lord Montagu of Beaulieu.

Figure 5.7 Detail of Antonio Joli, *The Gate of the Holy Ghost, Naples*, 1756–1758. Oil on canvas, 19 ins x 29¾ ins. Palace House, Beaulieu. By kind permission of Lord Montagu of Beaulieu.

is a small group which surrounds a vendor with his goods in a basket; one of them holds a scale in his hands. To the left of them is another vendor with a larger and longer trestle table, perhaps connected to the shop or tavern at the corner of the building. In another painting by Joli, *Gate of Santo Spirito, Naples*, there is a wooden kiosk to the left of it and a covered trestle table to its right. There are goods hanging from the doorways of nearby shops, and wooden counters jut out from them (Figure 5.7).[38]

Although often described as 'documents' of eighteenth-century urban life, Joli's paintings have never been integrated into a social or cultural history of the city, and the context of their production has been only considered within the representational tradition of *vedutisimo* and a history of the Grand Tour. Instead, these paintings clearly reveal the material of selling on the streets of eighteenth-century Naples – a trestle table brought out from a shop interior at the beginning of the day, a fire set to keep food warm or to cook at a moment's notice, a balance laid inside a basket as a vendor made his way around the city, the threshold of a shop doorway, under which one had to lower one's head to avoid the hanging goods, a counter to lean across to make a purchase. They also indicate the topography of selling food on the streets – under gates and archways, alongside churches, in front of shops, and moving around from one square to the next.

Antonio Joli's paintings display the details of specific places in Naples which have not so far been gleaned from maps of the period. Panoramic and topographic views of eighteenth-century Naples have been studied in relation to changing representations of the city in the history of cartography, even if closer analyses reveal, for example, food vendors and laundrywomen on the edges of two engraved images of the neighbourhood of Chiaia.[39] A closer analysis of the written 'topography' which accompanied the most famous of contemporary maps of the city, the Duca di Noia's map of 1775, reveals that the beach at Chiaia was not only a point from which to admire the picturesque activities of the locals, but also a place of work and worship for sailors transporting snow to the city.[40] While the map does not indicate exactly where the snow (which had been harvested in the hills above Vico Equense, on the other side of the bay and brought by boat) was taken when it reached Naples, we do know that warehouses or *magazzini* by the sea in Naples were used to distribute the snow to a number of licensed vendors.[41] In the paintings of the Welsh painter Thomas Jones (1742–1803), we can get close to the main wharf of the city, or Molo Grande, to see the pitted surfaces of the walls of the Custom House for Salt, or Dogana di Sale. Jones' paintings (with a not a person in sight) were made from his rooftop terrace across from Dogana di Sale, not far from the Largo di Castello where Fabris' *sorbettaro* was selling ice cream to his clients (salt was a necessary ingredient for the making and preservation of ice cream), alongside the story-tellers, puppeteers and charlatans, depicted by artists such as David Allan.[42]

As we have seen, there is rich visual evidence of urban life in eighteenth-century Naples. Most of it was created to feed the interests of Grand Tourists in search of an authentic popular culture in Naples and, therefore, compromised by the representational traditions which depicted the poor in the early modern period. Some of it was produced within a tradition of *vedutismo* or cartography with a concern for exactness but with little regard or interest for the mundane. Nonetheless, closer and coordinated study of the visual evidence reveals the activity and material of selling on the street – the essential pathways through the city as well as extensions out onto the streets, temporary or permanent, for selling food to the people of Naples. Historians are rightly cautious of reading images simply as representations of reality, but, as we shall see, they can be used in combination with other sources to contribute to a more integrated and enlivened history of selling food on the street.

Taxing consumption on the streets

Very little work has been done on consumption in the city of Naples in the early modern period.[43] Historians have been preoccupied by the misgovernment of the Spanish (and the later failure of Bourbon reforms) which matches neatly with long-standing historiographical tropes, determined, in part, by the history of the south in modern Italy, which has emphasised economic underdevelopment and the 'absence' of a middle class.[44] Only now are historians making their way, slowly, through inventories and notarial records to begin to recognise that many Neapolitans, like inhabitants of other early modern cities in Italy, also had a 'taste for things'.[45] Until very recently, in fact, a story of more ordinary buying and selling had been marginalised by a greater historical interest in the consumption of luxury goods by a bankrupt nobility.[46] This, of course, is partly determined by the sources and, in the case of peddlers by the difficulties in determining more ordinary buying and selling on the street. In any case, inventories normally document what ends up in households at key points in the life-cycle and, only very unusually, everyday consumables whose path is more difficult to trace.[47]

However, a rare survival of one attempt by the municipal government to tax commercial activities of the city survives in a printed tax register from 1692 which lists the names, occupations and positions of all street sellers by neighbourhood or *quartiere* (Figure 5.8).[48] The title of the printed work, 90 pages in length, includes those who were selling immediately outside of shops (*cacciate, e pennate delle botteghe*), those with fixed stands on street corners or in squares and who might have had secure boxes to hold their goods over night (*posti fissi*), those who had to remove their wares each night (*posti ammovibili*), and those with wooden kiosks which you can see in Joli's painting of the Gate of the Holy Spirit (*barrache*). There is also an 'and others' (*&, altro*) category which must have included ambulant sellers. This list of 977 sellers shows the array of food being sold outside of shops and on the streets by types such as the grocer (*pizzicarolo*), tavern keeper (*tavernaro*) and fruit and vegetable seller (*fruttaiolo* and *verdumaro*) as well as those selling more specific goods such as citrus fruit seller (*cetrangolaro*), chicken (and egg) seller (*pollaio*), pastry maker (*pasticciero*), pasta seller (*maccaronaro*), baker (*panettiero*) and chestnut seller (*castagnaro*). It also includes the sellers of other goods and services such as key-makers (*chianchiero*), hatters (*cappellaro*), cobblers (*calzettaro*), snow-merchants (*nevaiolo*), sword-makers (*spadaro*), and scriveners (*scrittoriaro*).[49] There are surprisingly few women in the register, five in total, and there is no clear association of women selling food or, for that matter, women selling particular kinds of food.[50] It is possible that most Neapolitan women, like in some Dutch cities, are invisible in the tax records, but involved with food preparation or working alongside their husbands, who were offically regulated by the municipal government.[51]

The register is divided up by neighbourhood, or *quartiere*, and includes the location of where the seller operates, almost always with the precise measurements of the serving or selling area (*cacciata*) and the overhead covering or awning allowed (*pennata*). While these terms are not immediately comprehensible to a modern historian, an eighteenth-century dictionary defines *pennata* as a kind of awning: the 'roof protruding over tables outside, used especially for shops'.[52] *Cacciata* does not appear in any Neapolitan dictionaries but can be used to mean 'a refreshment or small snack' so it could be used here metonymically to mean the space or surface taken up by the refreshments, that is, the trestle table.[53] The measurement usually refers to the length, although

Figure 5.8 Frontispiece of *Situatione fatta dall'Illustriss. Signor Portulano Di questa Fedeliss. Città nell'Anno 1692. De Cacciate, e Pennate delle Botteghe, Posti fissi, & ammovibili, Barracche, & altro* (Naples, 1692). Società di Storia Patria Napoletana, Naples.

sometimes the width is also indicated, and is given in *palmi* (a *palmo* in Naples was the equivalent of just over 25cm), so, for example, in the *Carità* neighbourhood, 'Pietro d'Andreano, citrus-seller, in the property (*case*) of Lorenzo della Campora, is granted a selling area (*cacciata*) of five *palmi* with an awning (*pennata*) of six *palmi*'.[54] The owner of the property is most often indicated and includes private owners as well as monasteries and churches. A stone tablet in the façade of a Neapolitan church today testifies to the use of church property by their commercial tenants and to the jurisdictional complexities of selling on the street (Figure 5.9a); it reads: 'On the first of February 1706, by decree of the archiepiscopal court of this city, it is ordered that this atrium under the stairs and the two shops on either the side of them, otherwise called *bassi*, remain "profane" and do not enjoy ecclesiastical immunity.'[55] The atrium continues to be used today and a contemporary photograph shows how goods could have been stored and how trestle tables outside of shops could have been brought in and out every day from hidden commercial spaces such as these (Figure 5.9b).[56]

A dedication at the end of the 1692 tax register confirms that it was compiled to establish the rights to sell certain goods in specific locations in the

Figure 5.9a Tablet on the façade of the Church of Santa Maria ad Ogni Bene dei Sette Dolori, Naples. Photo © Bruno Pomara.

Figure 5.9b Atrium and façade of the Church of Santa Maria ad Ogni Bene dei Sette Dolori, Naples. Photo © Bruno Pomara.

city. The *Signori portolani*, or the noble administrators of the *Portalania*, the municipal authority which controlled commercial activity on the streets, proclaimed:

> Recent experience … has made us aware how far abuses have advanced, especially by sellers of comestibles – those with *cacciate* and those who illegally sell in the middle of public squares in this most faithful of cities – impeding public commerce, giving continuous disturbance to all people, whether on foot, horse, or carriage, and in such a way … making it impossible to move forward or backward.[57]

They cite the inconvenience to priests who are obliged to carry the Host through the streets of the city, without a processional canopy (*Pallio*) because they are impeded by the awnings (*pennate*) of shops which 'make this city dark and melancholic'.[58] The selling of food was not limited to the front of shops and taverns of specific property owners. In fact, the register gives very specific and complex information about the location of stands which suggests the sharing of public space by a variety of different kinds of sellers, for instance:

> Nicola Montagna is granted a place (*posto*) to sell *Moscimao* [a kind of cured tuna *salame*] behind the little table (*tavolillo*) of Geronimo Caraviello, from where the fish begins right up to the gate of the Church of San Lorenzo to the other end where the Campanile and where the chickens (*pulli*) are situated.[59]

Montagna had a *posto* to sell bread nearby and another *posto di moscimao* at the Gate of San Gennaro, in another neighbourhood, indicating that food sellers sometimes had more than one stall and were not limited to selling just one food product.[60] More generic indications are also given, such as 'From just above the Largo of the Church of Gesù Nuovo, to the Fountain of Mont'Oliveto, a *cacciata* of 8 *palmi* and *pennata* of … *palmi* is given to all sellers listed below', but then includes very specific exceptions; the register continues that Domenico Renzullo 'can not keep carriages (*Galesse*) in the alley near him'.[61]

The register also includes what are described as *baracche* in the middle of the Market Square with indications of which kiosks faced the street or in which of the eight rows they were situated (Figure 5.10).[62] Less than 40 years after the revolt of Masaniello, there appear no fruit sellers in the square and, in fact, very few sellers of any kind of food are recorded by the *Signori Portolani*; a few chestnut and bread sellers are working alongside rows of scrap merchants (*ferrivecchi*), second-hand clothes merchants (*pannazzaro*) and cobblers (*scarparo*). While it is difficult to discern many of the products which are being sold by itinerant sellers and in the kiosks in Micco Spadaro's painting of the Market Square (Plate 5), details emerge which complement and illuminate our understanding of selling on this public square. Some of the sellers are protected by slanted wooden roofs – perhaps the *barrache* indicated in

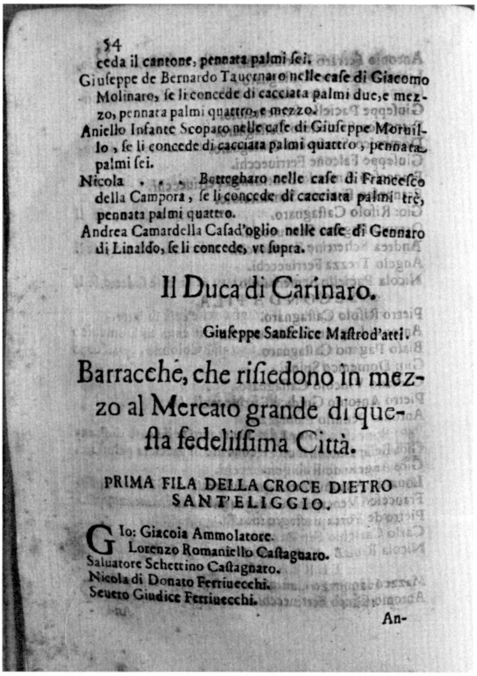

ceda il cantone, pennata palmi sei.
Giuseppe de Bernardo Taucnaro nelle case di Giacomo
Molinaro, se li concede di cacciata palmi due, e mezzo, pennata palmi quattro, e mezzo.
Aniello Infante Scoparo nelle case di Giuseppe Mornil-
lo, se li concede di cacciata palmi quattro, pennata
palmi sei.
Nicola . . . Bottegharo nelle case di Francesco
della Campora, se li concede di cacciata palmi trè,
pennata palmi quattro.
Andrea Camardella Casad'oglio nelle case di Gennaro
di Linaldo, se li concede, vt supra.

Il Duca di Carinaro.

Giuseppe Sanfelice Mastrod'atti.

Barracche, che risiedono in mez-zo al Mercato grande di que-sta fedelissima Città.

PRIMA FILA DELLA CROCE DIETRO SANT'ELIGGIO.

Gio: Giacoia Ammolatore.
Lorenzo Romaniello Castagnaro.
Saluatore Schettino Castagnaro.
Nicola di Donato Ferriuecchi.
Seuero Giudice Ferriuecchi.

An-

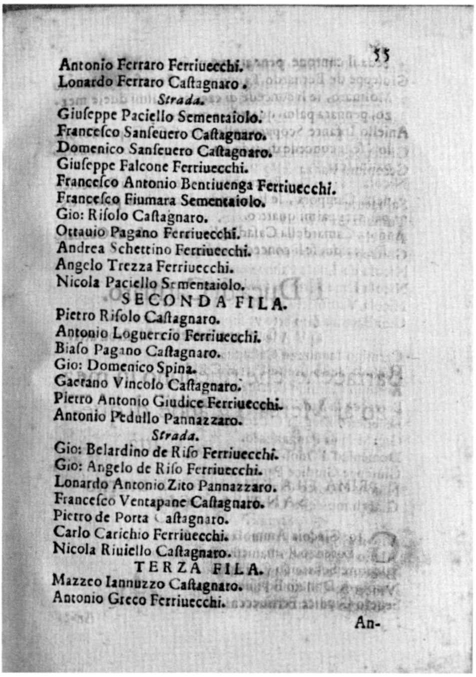

55

Antonio Ferraro Ferriuecchi.
Lonardo Ferraro Castagnaro.
Strada.
Giuseppe Paciello Sementaiolo.
Francesco Sanseuero Castagnaro.
Domenico Sanseuero Castagnaro.
Giuseppe Falcone Ferriuecchi.
Francesco Antonio Bentiuenga Ferriuecchi.
Francesco Fiumara Sementaiolo.
Gio: Risolo Castagnaro.
Ottauio Pagano Ferriuecchi.
Andrea Schettino Ferriuecchi.
Angelo Trezza Ferriuecchi.
Nicola Paciello Sementaiolo.
SECONDA FILA.
Pietro Risolo Castagnaro.
Antonio Loguercio Ferriuecchi.
Biaso Pagano Castagnaro.
Gio: Domenico Spina.
Gaetano Vincolo Castagnaro.
Pietro Antonio Giudice Ferriuecchi.
Antonio Pedullo Pannazzaro.
Strada.
Gio: Belardino de Riso Ferriuecchi.
Gio: Angelo de Riso Ferriuecchi.
Lonardo Antonio Zito Pannazzaro.
Francesco Ventapane Castagnaro.
Pietro de Porta Castagnaro.
Carlo Carichio Ferriuecchi.
Nicola Riuiello Castagnaro.
TERZA FILA.
Mazzeo Iannuzzo Castagnaro.
Antonio Greco Ferriuecchi.

An-

Figure 5.10 Situatione fatta dall'Illustriss. Signor Portulano Di questa Fedeliss. Città nell'Anno 1692. De Cacciate, e Pennate delle Botteghe, Posti fissi, & ammovibili, Barracche, & altro (Naples, 1692), pp. 54–55. Società di Storia Patria Napoletana, Naples.

Figure 5.11a and b Details of Plate 5: Domenico Gargiulo (otherwise known as Micco Spadaro), *Market Square or Piazza del Carmine of Naples, c. 1654*. Oil on canvas, 141 x 76 cm. Palacio Tavera, Fundación Casa Ducal de Medinaceli, Toledo.

the register – and others are protected by the use of old sails to shade them from the sun, described as *mantelletti* and which continue to be used to the end of the nineteenth century (Figure 5.12). Others are selling on open trestle tables, the second-hand clothes of the *pannazzari*, perhaps, draped over them. There are large baskets and crates with fruit in them, crates not dissimilar to those carried by Masaniello to the fish vendors nearby. One basket becomes a table on which what looks like fresh cheese is set. In the foreground, an old woman lays out her vegetables for sale and beside her a man shows his

Figure 5.12 Fish vendor's stall in Naples, c. 1890. Photograph, A ACA-F-011435-0000. Alinari Archives-Alinari Archive, Florence.

metalwares. In the background, a vegetable seller, with a mule by her side, rests on an upturned saddle (Figures 5.11a and 5.11b).

Spadaro depicts the street sellers, in all their variety, whom the *Portolania* was trying to tax and control – some were connected to shops, others manned stalls which leaned against city walls or alongside or under the entrances of churches, and others might have moved around the market square with their goods finding a place to set down their basket when they could. Many of these sellers were known to the municipal government, as the 1692 tax register attests, and many more would have been known to their customers, returning on a regular basis, back to the corner, kiosk or stall, where they had bought their goods before. Some of them, even those who were ambulant, would have been known by their faces, their cries, or the goods which they carried in their baskets. And, all of these food sellers would have been part of a connected 'system' of selling, which was increasingly formalised by the state into the eighteenth century.[63] Although some sellers might not appear in the 1692 document, they are present in the visual evidence from the period, integral rather than marginal to the urban economy. Some of the occupations listed in the 1692 document established themselves as guilds or *corporazioni* in the eighteenth century – for example, the citrus fruit sellers (*cetrangolari*) in 1709, the vegetable sellers (*verdumari*) in 1716, the fish sellers (*pescivendoli*) in 1729, and the chicken and egg sellers (*pollai*) in 1734 – and the documents created by their establishment should make it easier to write a fuller history of the commercial life of the city's urban spaces.[64] The 1692 register was created in response to the commercial overcrowding and disorder of the streets and to the corresponding need to establish order and, most importantly, to generate revenue. Further study of this document is required in order to produce a topography of selling in late seventeenth-century Naples. However, in combination with visual sources from the period, the extrardinary variety of the spaces and places of selling food in the city is revealed – from under awnings which protruded onto the street and slowed down the traffic, from small tables or stands surrounded by other sellers, from wooden kiosks in a row in a large market square, or simply just a space on a street corner or under an old sail held up by posts to keep out the midday sun.

Conclusion: food hawkers in the archives

The long-standing trope of Naples as dense with people, chaotic and noisy dates from the early modern period, at least, and is tied to an emerging stereotype about the *lazzaroni*, or the poorest inhabitants of the city.[65] Spadaro's 'disaster' paintings, such as the one of Masaniello's revolt, inspired and fed this interest.[66] Many descriptions of the city, such as Goethe's, at the end of the eighteenth century, included accounts of street selling in response to the same ethnographic interest which generated the prints and paintings of Pietro Fabris. What are not represented, however, are the municipal regulation and tax structure behind the selling of food. The municipal authority which controlled selling in the streets, the *Portolania*, governed all commercial activity in the streets of the city.[67] Volumes of *prammatiche* were published and republished from the late sixteenth century and updated with the arrival of a new viceroy in the seventeenth century, the establishment of the Austrian and later Bourbon governments in the eighteenth, and later the Napoleonic administration in the nineteenth. They attest to a continuing concern for greater fiscal and social order of the street.[68]

Nonetheless, the near-complete destruction of the Municipal Archives in Naples in a fire in 1946 seems to have dissuaded most historians from looking there to see how these regulations worked in practice.[69] What remains from the fire are glimpses of the municipal government's extraordinary efforts to rule and control one of the most populous cities in Europe in the early modern period. In fact, there is extensive evidence of the selling of food on the city streets, witnessed by hundreds of slips of paper folded in half lengthways and containing information related to taxes from each of the sellers. Some of them record the names of sellers and the dates on which they paid their taxes, and these appear in bundles in the archives as *affitti delle piazze*.[70] Others are more detailed and name particular sellers; they look as if they served as registration documents or licences.[71] In turn, there are two small volumes organised alphabetically by kinds of sellers, each with a specific formula for licences; these formulae, one presumes, would have been written out by the collectors of taxes. By the late eighteenth century, it is possible that the blank spaces left in printed licences, one of which survives in the archives, were simply filled out by tax collectors. These tax records suggest the extraordinary variety of food sold on the streets of Naples; for instance, under the letter 'S', *saltatori d'alici* (sellers of salted herring) and *sanguinaciari* (sellers of blood sausages) both appear.[72] The exact process by which these taxes were collected by the *Portolania* is still not known, but it is hoped that further research on this rich archival evidence will contribute to a fuller understanding of selling food in the streets in Naples.

The long-standing stereotype of chaos on Neapolitan streets, so central to descriptions of the city, even today, belies an extraordinary effort to bring order to the selling of food in the streets. As Masaniello's revolt shows, the fair, safe and constant provision of food was central to the political stability of any city in early modern Europe. The visual evidence provides one way through which we can reconstruct the material world and topography of selling in the streets. There is a lot that we cannot 'see' (or, for that matter, hear or smell). The richness of this visual material can be balanced by further study of the surviving archival material. Further study might also take us beyond the specific sites of selling food to other sites of food production and preparation – in private homes and gardens within the city and also outside of the city's walls – and to a wider network of supply from its hinterland. While, as historians, we might not be able to capture the smells and sounds of the early modern street market, we can be inspired by studies of modern-day food hawkers and, through them, try to reconstruct a more integrated history of material culture, space and social relations in the early modern city, the evidence for which resists framing this within the history of the modern shop and the dining table.

Notes

* I would like to thank the following for their help in the research and preparation of this chapter: Giuliana Buonario, Ciro La Rosa, and Bernardo Leonardi at the Municipal Archives in Naples, Gennaro Centomani and Paola Milone at the Società Napoletana di Storia Patria, Griffin Coe at the Aberdeen Art Gallery and Museum, Irene Cooper, Adam Ledgeway, and Felix Waldmann in Cambridge, Silvana d'Alessio and Giovanni Muto in Naples, Fausto de Mattia and Gaetano Damiano at the Archivio di Stato in Naples, Bruno Pomara in Valencia, and Gloria Williams at the Norton Simon Museum, Pasadena. My thanks also to the Cambridge Newton Trust, Gonville and Caius College, and the Faculty of History at the University of Cambridge for their support of my research for this chapter.

1 For an introduction to the revolt of Masaniello in English, see Peter Burke, 'The Virgin of the Carmine and the revolt of Masaniello', in Peter Burke, *The Historical Anthropology of Early Modern Italy: Essays in Perception and Communication*

(Cambridge, 1987), pp. 191–206 (first published in *Past and Present* 99 (1983), pp. 3–21). Rosario Villari's study of the origins of the revolt have been published as *The Revolt of Naples* (Cambridge, 1993). For a recent biography of Masaniello and the resonance of the revolt, as well as a full bibliography, see Silvana D'Alessio, *Masaniello: La sua vita e il mito in Europa* (Rome, 2007).

2 On this painting, see Wendy Wassyng Roworth, 'The evolution of history painting: Masaniello's revolt and other disasters in seventeenth-century Naples', *Art Bulletin* 75/2 (1993), pp. 219–234, and C.R. Marshall, '"Causa di stravaganze": Order and anarchy in Domenico Gargiulo's Revolt of Masaniello', *The Art Bulletin* 80/3 (1998), pp. 478–497. The painting is also discussed and reproduced in Giancarlo Sestieri and Brigitte Daprà, *Domenico Gargiulo detto Micco Spadaro: Paesaggista e 'cronista' napoletano* (Milan, 1994), cat. 141.

3 The painting of the market square is discussed in Sestieri and Daprà, *Domenico Gargiulo*, pp. 40–41 and pp. 292–293, and reproduced in Brigitte Daprà, *Micco Spadaro, Napoli ai tempi di Masaniello* (Exhibition Catalogue, Naples, 2002). While Marshall does not discuss the market square painting, Wassyng Roworth at least considers its visual precedents (Wassyng Roworth, 'The evolution of history painting', p. 221 and p. 225). Spadaro also painted a fair scene outside of the city walls, which is now in the Museo Correale, Sorrento, and reproduced and discussed in Sestieri and Dapra, *Domenico Gargiulo*, cat. 5, pp. 67–68.

4 On Masaniello's family origins and his social networks, see D'Alessio, *Masaniello*, pp. 62–68.

5 Documents related to Gargiulo's origins have been difficult to locate. See the entry on Gargiulo by Matteo Lafranconi in *Dizionario biografico degli Italiani* 52 (Rome, 1995), pp. 306–309.

6 On Neapolitan identity formation in the early modern period, see John Marino, *Becoming Neapolitan: Citizen Culture in Baroque Naples* (Baltimore, 2007). On the function of 'community' in the Market neighbourhood, see Burke, 'The revolt of Masaniello', p. 205.

7 Diane Favro, 'Meaning and experience: Urban history from antiquity to the early modern period', *Journal of the Society of Architectural Historians* 58/3 (1999), pp. 364–373. Of course, architectural historians had already made their own contribution to a fuller understanding of the political and religious resonance of urbanism; see, for instance, the seminal article on Rome: Joseph Connors, 'Alliance and enmity in Baroque urbanism', *Römisches Jahrbuch der Biblioteca Hertziana* 25 (1989), pp. 207–294, and Helen Hills, *Invisible City: The Architecture of Devotion in Seventeenth-century Naples* (Oxford, 2004).

8 Thomas V. Cohen and Riita Laitinen, 'Introduction', *Cultural History of Early Modern Streets* (Brill, 2008), p. 3.

9 R.J. Crum and J.T. Paoletti (eds), *Renaissance Florence: A Social History* (Cambridge, 2006).

10 Niall Atkinson, 'The republic of sound: Listening to Florence at the threshold of the Renaissance', in *I Tatti Studies in the Italian Renaissance* 16/1–2 (2013), pp. 57–84, and Chapter 6 in this volume.

11 See the excellent introduction to the volume by Georgia Clarke and Fabrizio Nevola, 'The experience of the street in early modern Italy', *I Tatti Studies in the Italian Renaissance* 16/1–2 (2013), pp. 47–55.

12 See, for example, the articles by D. Rosenthal and M. Lingohr in Crum and Paoletti, *Renaissance Florence*, pp. 161–181 and pp. 240–272. For Naples, there is an extensive literature on ephemeral festival architecture, including the *cuccagna*, a large temporary structure built for Carnival until the eighteenth century; see, for example, Franco Mancini, *Feste ed apparati civili e religiosi in Napoli dal Viceregno alla capitale* (Naples, 1968) and Silvia Cassani, *Capolavori in festa: Effimero barocco a Largo di Palazzo (1683–1759)* (Naples, 1997). There is also an extensive

anthropological literature on the *cuccagna*; see Laura Barletta, *Il carnevale del 1764. Protesta e integrazione in uno spazio urbano* (Naples, 1981) and Domeinco Scafoglio, *La maschera della Cuccagna: Spreco, rivolta e sacrificio nel Carnevale napoletano del 1764* (Naples, 1981). Further study of the material culture of the street could bring together these two approaches.

13 On the 'furnished' street in modern Paris, see M. de Thezy, *Paris, La rue: Le mobilier urbain du second Empire à nos jours* (Paris, 1976). Although this work is particularly nostalgic for the *rue traditionelle* of nineteenth- and early twentieth-century Paris – with photographs of *vespasiennes* (street urinals), ironwork entrances to the Métro, and surviving gas lanterns – it does suggest possibilities for the study of the 'street furniture' in the early modern period. My thanks to Tom Stammers for this reference.

14 Evelyn Welch has explored many of these issues in her excellent chapter on 'Place', in Evelyn Welch, *Shopping in the Renaissance: Consumer Cultures in Italy 1400–1600* (New Haven/London, 2005), pp. 123–163.

15 On the night, see Craig Koslofsky, *Evening's Empire: A History of the Night in Early Modern Europe* (Cambridge, 2011). For a study of the varied and transgressive uses and meanings of the same urban space over day and night, see Harry Cocks, 'Homosexuality between men in Britain since the eighteenth century', *History Compass* 5/3 (2007), pp. 873–874. For the regulation of urban space at night, see Michael Rocke's work based on records of the Office of the Night, which functioned between 1432 and 1501 in Florence: *Forbidden Friendships: Homosexuality and Male Culture in Renaissance Florence* (Oxford, 1996).

16 See also Donatella Calabi and Stephen Turk Christensen (eds), *Cities and Cultural Exchange in Europe, 1400–1700* (Cambridge, 2007).

17 Spiro Kostoff, *The city Assembled* (1992), cited in Favro, 'Meaning and experience', p. 364.

18 See Atkinson, 'The republic of sound' and Stephen J. Milner, '"Fanno bandire, notificare, et expressamente comandare": Town criers and the information economy of Renaissance Florence', *I Tatti Studies in the Italian Renaissance* 16/1–2 (2013), pp. 107–151. On the predominance of Florence in Anglo-American historiography of early modern Italy, see Paula Findlen, 'In and out of Florence', in Paula Findlen, Michelle M. Fontaine and Duane J. Osheim (eds), *Beyond Florence: The Contours of Medieval and Early Modern Italy* (Stanford, 2003), pp. 13–28.

19 See Jacques Revel, 'A capital's privileges: Food supplied in early-modern Rome', in R. Forster and O. Ranum (eds), *Food and Drink in History* (Baltimore/London, 1979), pp. 37–49 (which was translated from *Annales* 30 (1975), pp. 563–574).

20 As many historians of peddlers have recognised in their own research, for example, Harald Deceulaer, 'Dealing with diversity: Pedlars in the Southern Netherlands in the eighteenth century', in Bruno Blondé, Peter Stabel, Jon Stobbart and Ilja Van Damme (eds), *Retail Circuits and Practices in Medieval and Early Modern Europe* (Turnhout, 2006), pp. 171–198. See also the introduction to Laurence Fontaine, *History of pedlars in Europe* (Cambridge, 1996).

21 Melissa Calaresu, 'Collecting Neapolitans: The representation of street life in late eighteenth-century Naples', in Melissa Calaresu and Helen Hills (eds), *New Approaches to Naples c.1500–c.1800: The Power of Place* (Farnham, 2013), pp. 175–202.

22 Melissa Calaresu, 'From the street to stereotype: Urban space, travel, and the picturesque in late eighteenth-century Naples', *Italian Studies* 62/2 (2007), pp. 189–203.

23 Goethe, *Italian Journey [1786–1788]*, trans. and ed. W.H. Auden and E. Mayer (London, 1970), 18 May 1787, pp. 319–320.

24 Henry Swinburne, *Travels in the Two Sicilies* (2 vols, London, 1783–1785), II, p. 66.

25 Lorenzo Giustiniani, *Dizionario geografico-ragionato del Regno di Napoli di Lorenzo Giustiniani Regio Bibliotecario a sua Maestà Ferdinando IV Re delle Due Sicilie* (Naples, 1797–1805, 10 volumes), VI (1803), p. 376. *Ricattieri* is the Neapolitan word for *rigattieri*, or second-hand dealers, in Italian. On the *prammatiche*, see below.

26 It reads: 'Di regal ordine fattesi demolire dal Regio Tribunale della Portolania le baracche di fabbrica esistenti in questo Largo della Carità. I padroni de' circonvicini edificj son rimasti obbligati secondo la respettiva classificazione approvata dal re (D.G.) al peso dell'attuale compenso dovuto a proprietarj di quelle. Ma fra gli articoli contenuti nel regal dispaccio vi è il seguente. Dichiara il re che non debba mai più permettersi di situare posti di venditori o galessieri in questa piazza volendo che la Portolania vigili alla esecuzione di questo e ne coservi la memoria in una lapide, dove tutto ciò sia descritto, e la quale dovrà rimanere perpetuamente in detta piazza. Di real ordine lo partecipo a cotesto tribunale della Portolania, acciò ne disponga l'esatto adempimento. Palazzo 30 giugno 1802 =Giuseppe Zurlo= Quindi si è dovuta incidere in lapide tale sovrana determinazione, acciò niuno ardisca giammai di occupare in qualsivoglia modo il presente pubblico largo, sotto pena di ducati XXIV. Restando altresì vietato in perpetuo a medesimi regj Portolani di accordarvi qualsiasi concessione per quanto è ad essi cara la grazia del re n.s. Napoli 12 luglio 1802.' For a photograph of the *lapide*, see http://rete. comuni-italiani.it/wiki/Napoli/Lapide_Piazza_Salvo_d'Acquisto, at a site which attempts to record existing *lapidi* in the city. Accessed 10 April 2016. This inscription is also recorded in Oreste Albanesi, *Epigrafia napoletana* (Naples, 2015), p. 32.

27 'Nonostante i reiterati ordini per lo sgombro e nitidezza delle strade, especialmente quello di Toledo, alcuni costumaci, ed ostinati venditori di carne di nero aveano ingombrato il largo della Carità' (Archivio di Stato di Napoli (ASN), Ministero degli Affari Interni, I° Inventario, Busta 2082 (7)).

28 David Allan, 'Limon Cryer Naples', from *A Collection of Dresses by Da. Allan Mostly from Nature, 1776*, Aberdeen Art Gallery, Accession #7557, Plate 13. My thanks to Griffin Coe, Assistant Keeper of Fine Art, Aberdeen Art Gallery, for kindly providing me with reproductions of the Allan album. Although the images from this album were never published as engravings, it is likely that Allan used the images to make copies for interested buyers. On the Aberdeen album, see Francina Irwin, '"Drawn mostly from nature": David Allan's record of daily dress in France and Italy, 1779–1776', *Costume* 32 (1998), pp. 1–17. On Allan, see Peter Walch, 'Allan, David', *Grove Art Online. Oxford Art Online* (Oxford University Press, accessed 10 April 2016): http://www.oxfordartonline.com/subscriber/article/grove/art/T001861 (16 November 2014). On the new promenade and Via Marina, see Brigitte Marin, 'Sur les traces de la via Marina: Embellissements urbains et aménagements portuaires à Naples au XVIIIe siècle', *Rives méditerranéennes* 39 (2011), pp. 33–44.

29 David Allan, 'Naples sketchbook', National Gallery of Scotland, D5088. Allan used this sketchbook during his sometime residence in Naples from 1770 to 1776. There is also a very evocative sketch of a carriage making its way through the streets of Naples and an *acquaiolo* in which the faint outline of the canister to hold the water matches exactly the image from Fabris (D5088/12r). There is also a preliminary sketch of his drawing of a hot-drinks seller on Pont Neuf in Paris in the Naples sketchbook in the National Gallery of Scotland (D5088/41r), and which is reproduced in this volume as Figure 0.2.

30 Pietro Fabris, *Raccolta di varii vestimenti ed arti del Regno di Napoli* (Naples, 1773). On Fabris and his biography, see Calaresu, 'Collecting Neapolitans', pp. 182–190. The sorbet seller is reproduced in Melissa Calaresu, 'Making and eating ice cream in Naples: Rethinking consumption and sociability in the eighteenth century', *Past and Present* 220/1 (2013), p. 37.

31 Images of the chestnut seller and seller of *tonninole* have been reproduced in Calaresu, 'Collecting Neapolitans', figures 8.3 and 8.7.

32 A modern edition of the *Raccolta* includes some of the watercolours and drawings by Fabris including the fruit seller and the corn-fritter seller, in Pietro Fabris, *Raccolta di varii Vestimenti ed Arti del Regno di Napoli*, edited by Franco Mancini (Naples, 1985), respectively, Tav. VII and Tav XI.

33 The painting by Fabris, entitled, *The Carnival in Naples in 1778*, with the 'Cavalcata turca' parading through the Largo di Palazzo, oil on canvas, 188 x 340 cm, was sold on 3 December 2013 at Christie's in London: www.christies.com/lotfinder/paintings/pietro-fabris-the-carnival-in-naples-5755412-details.aspx. My thanks to Gloria Williams, Norton Simon Museum, Pasadena, for bringing this painting to my attention. On Turquerie, see Alexander Bevilacqua and Helen Pfeifer, 'Turquerie: Culture in motion, 1650–1750', *Past and Present* 221/1 (2013), pp. 75–118.

34 On these different representational traditions, see Melissa Calaresu, 'Costumes and customs in print: Travel, ethnography and the representation of street-sellers in early modern Italy', in Joad Raymond, Jeroen Salman and Roeland Harms (eds), *'Not Dead Things': The Dissemination of Popular Print in England and Wales, Italy, and the Low Countries, 1500–1900* (Leiden, 2013), pp. 181–209.

35 Calaresu, 'Collecting Neapolitans', figure 8.8. Ivan Day has an eighteenth-century *sorbettiera* from southern Italy as well as the pewter inserts to place inside and the paddles used to stir the sorbet in his private collection and depicted on his website: www.historicfood.com/Georgian%20Ices.htm. Accessed 10 April 2016.

36 Although it is not clear when the title was given, one of Fabris' paintings depicts food hawkers at Via Marina, a newly made street which connected the port with the Piazza del Mercato, in 1749 (see Marin, 'Sur les traces de la via Marina'). The painting, now known as *Venditori di vivande sulla via della Marinella*, is signed by Fabris, but undated (Calaresu, 'Collecting Neapolitans', pp. 182–183). There is greater detail of the exterior spaces of Venice in Gaetano Zompini's book of engravings: *Le arti che vanno per via nella città di Venezia* (Venice, 1785).

37 The series of paintings appear in a number of catalogues of Neapolitan paintings, including Nicola Spinosa and Leonardo Di Mauro, *Vedute napoletane del Settecento* (Naples, 1996), Tavole 31–38, and discussed on pp. 28–30 and p. 193.

38 Laundry is laid out on the railings of the balustrade between the Palazzo Reale and the Castel Nuovo, in Joli's *Palazzo Reale e Castelnuovo*, reproduced in Spinosa and Di Mauro, *Vedute napoletane*, Tav.31, p. 63. For an innovative attempt to plot public laundries on a social and cultural map of late sixteenth-century Rome, see Katherine W. Rinne, 'The landscape of laundry in late Cinquecento Rome', *Studies in the Decorative Arts* 9/1 (2001–2002), pp. 34–57.

39 The volume on Naples in the King's Topographical Collection, now in the British Library, includes four of the five views of the city engraved by Antonio Cardon, and dedicated to various dignitaries including William Hamilton (BL Maps, LXXXIII, 60c–f). The series are reproduced in Giulio Pane and Vladimirio Valerio (eds), *La città di Napoli tra vedutismo e cartografia* (Naples, 1987), p. 259. There are two views of Chiaia, both with the same title, *Veduta di Chiaia dalla parte di Ponente, Naples, 1765* [but actually 1781 because it features the Villa Reale, which was built between 1778 and 1780], showing the Villa Reale and the fountain at Chiaia. The first depicts food vendors outside of the gates of the Villa Reale, and is reproduced in Calaresu, 'Making and eating ice cream in Naples', figure 8. The second depicts women at work on the beach at Chiaia. Before the construction of the Villa Reale, a petition concerning space for washing clothes was cited in *Gazzetta universale*, 7 July 1778 (Franco Strazzullo, *Napoli: I luoghi e le storie* (Naples, 1992), p. 71).

40 *Mappa topografica della Città di Napoli e de' suoi contorni* (Naples, 1775). The publication of the map was followed by the publication of an accompanying text, Niccolò Carletti, *Topografia universale della città di Napoli in Campagna Felice*

(Naples, 1776), in which the Church of Santa Maria della Neve at Chiaia, was described as being used by sailors who transported snow to the city (Carletti, *Topografia*, p. 301). On the 1775 map, see Barbara Naddeo, 'Topographies of difference: Cartography of the City of Naples, 1627–1775', *Imago Mundi* 56/1 (2004), pp. 23–47, and also Franco Strazzullo, *Edilizia e urbanistica a Napoli dal '500 al '700* (2nd edn Naples, 1995), pp. 277–318.

41 Calaresu, 'Making and eating ice cream in Naples', pp. 55–56.

42 See, for example, 'Buildings in Naples' and 'Rooftops in Naples', both painted in April 1782 from Jones' rented room across from the Dogana di Sale, illustrated in Ann Sumner and Greg Smith (eds), *Thomas Jones (1742–1803): An Artist Rediscovered* (New Haven/London, 2003), pp. 220–221.

43 The recent exception is the work of Alida Clemente who reconstructs consumption patterns in eighteenth-century Naples, through a detailed analysis of inventories in notarial records, in *Il lusso 'cattivo': Dinamiche del consumo nella Napoli del Settecento* (Rome, 2011). For a study of prices and services in the eighteenth century, see Ruggiero Romano, *Prezzi, salari e servizi a Napoli nel secolo XVIII (1734–1806)* (Naples, 1965). For an earlier period, see also Bianca de Divitiis, 'Out of the Seggio of Nido *Apothecae* and markets in 15th-century Naples', in *Città e Storia*, II/2 (2007), pp. 381–400.

44 See the introduction in Calaresu and Hills, *New Approaches*, pp. 1–8, and Clemente, *Il lusso 'cattivo'*.

45 Echoing Renata Ago's recent work, *Il gusto delle cose: Una storia degli oggetti* (Rome, 2008), which has been translated into English by Bradford Bouley and Corey Tazzara with Paula Findlen, as *Gusto for Things: A History of Objects in Seventeenth-Century Rome* (Chicago, 2013).

46 On the way in which extremes of luxury and poverty framed earlier perceptions of Naples and persist into the modern period, see Melissa Calaresu, 'Looking for Virgil's Tomb: The end of the Grand Tour and the cosmopolitan ideal in Europe', in Jas Elsner and Joan-Pau Rubiés (eds), *Voyages and Visions: Towards a Cultural History of Travel* (London, 1999), pp. 138–161.

47 Giorgio Riello, '"Things seen and unseen": The material culture of early modern inventories and their representation of domestic interiors', in Paula Findlen (ed.), *Early Modern Things: Objects and Their Histories, 1500–1800* (Basingstoke, 2013), pp. 125–150.

48 *Situatione fatta dall'Illustriss. Signor Portulano Di questa Fedeliss. Città nell'Anno 1692. De Cacciate, e Pennate delle Botteghe, Posti fissi, & ammovibili, Barracche, & altro* (Naples, 1692). There is one copy in the Biblioteca della Società di Storia Patria, Naples. My thanks to Gennaro Centomani for his help in making this available for consultation and to Paola Milone for organising the photography. There are two other copies in Italy, one at the Biblioteca Nazionale in Naples and the other at the municipal library in Lucera. In the United Kingdom, there is a copy in the Glasgow University Library.

49 These translations are, in some cases, approximations and more research needs to be done, since the sellers might have included the selling of more and different kinds of goods than what their occupational names suggest.

50 There are two women with the same last name and both working in the Carità neighbourhood; Maddalena and Marta Magniello are both listed as *pannarazzara* which is probably similar to *pannazzàro*, a second-hand clothes seller (*Situatione*, p. 7 and p. 10). According to a modern Neapolitan definition, a *pannazzàro* is a 'rivenditore di abiti smessi in mostra su bancarella', or a seller of cast-off clothes from a booth (Dale Erwin and Piero Bello, *Modern Etymological Neapolitan-English Vocabulary – Vocabolario etimologico odierno napoletano-italiano* (Kindle edition, 2009), p. 423). This term is not used for the 22 male *revenditori* in the register. The remaining three women are listed as a *potecara*, possibly an apothecary

but there is no male equivalent listed (*Situatione*, p. 16), a *pasticcera* (*Situatione*, p. 28) and a *pizzicarolo*, Elisabetta Gaudino, although the feminine noun is not used (*Situatione*, p. 71). The register indicates that Gaudino was selling from her own house (*case proprie*). Two other women appear in the register, as aristocratic property owners who rented out premises to sellers, Comtessa dello Collo and Comtessa della Rocca (*Situatione*, p. 31 and p. 35 respectively). My thanks to the Cambridge Newton Trust Small Research Grant Scheme for the funds to compile this database and to Felix Waldmann for the creation of the database on which this initial research is based.

51 On the Dutch case, see Danielle van den Heuvel, 'Partners in marriage and in business? Guilds and the family economy in the urban food markets in the Dutch Republic', *Continuity and Change* 23/2 (2008), pp. 217–236.

52 'Pennata è un tal tetto di tavole sporto in fuori, usato sulle botteghe specialmente' (Tosco Partenio, *Vocabolario delle parole del dialetto napoletano, che più si scostano dal dialetto toscano, con alcune ricerche etimologiche sulle medesime* (2 vols, Naples, 1789), I, p. 23). A modern Neapolitan dictionary gives this definition: 'Pennàta sporgenza del tetto dal muro dell'edificio, gronda', indicating that the awning could protrude from the wall (Erwin and Bello, *Modern Etymological Neapolitan-English Vocabulary*, p. 429). My thanks to Adam Ledgeway for these references.

53 Many thanks to Adam Ledgeway for this suggestion which makes sense as the measurement for the awning should be longer than the trestle table in order to protect it.

54 'Pietro d'Andreano Cetrangolaro nelle case di Lorenzo della Campora, se li concede di cacciata palmi cinque, e pennata palmi sette' (*Situatione*, p. 7). On Italian measures, see Vincenzo De Rosa, *Tavole di ragguaglio delle misure napoletane comuni e delle consuetudinarie capuane con il sistema metrico decimale* (Cassino, 1977).

55 The tablet appears on the façade of the Chiesa di Santa Maria ad Ogni Bene dei Sette Dolori and reads: 'Nel primo di febraro 1706 Per decreto della corte arcivescovale di questa città e stato ordinato che quest'atrio scala e le due botteghe seu bassi laterali restino profani e non godano immunità eclesiastica.'

56 My thanks to Irene Cooper for bringing this to my attention and to Bruno Pomara for the two photographs reproduced here.

57 *Situatione*, p. 83. On the Portolania, see Luigi Bianchini, *Storia delle finanze del Regno di Napoli* (Naples, 1859), and Luigi De Rosa, *Studi sugli arrendamenti del Regno di Napoli. Aspetti della distruzione della ricchezza mobiliare nel Mezzogiorno continentale (1649–1806)* (Naples, 1958).

58 *Situatione*, p. 83 and p. 84. Earlier in the text, the *Portolani* also mention the growth of the *pennate*, the advancement of the *cacciate* and the introduction of *mantelletti* (which might have been the sails used to protect the tables from the sun) 'which takes over the air, and the earth underneath it, making the place dark and melancholic but also impracticable' (*Situatione*, p. 75).

59 'Nicola Montagna Posto di Moscimao, se li concede da dietro il Tavolillo di Geronimo Caraviello, dove principia il Pesce, e tira fino al primo termine a dirittura della Porta della Chiesa di San Lorenzo detto Pisce, che nell'altro termine fino al Campanile stà situato per li Pulli' (*Situatione*, p. 5). For definitions of *musciumanno* or *mosciame*, see *Vocabolario Domestico Napoletano Toscano* (Naples, 1841), p. 572, and Salvatore Battaglia, *Grande dizionario della lingua italiana* (Turin, 1961–2009), vol. X, p. 990; the term might have derived from the Spanish term for the same foodstuff, *mojama*. My thanks to Gianni Cicali and Daria Percocco for their help and to Alessandro Lucchetti for this final suggestion.

60 *Situatione*, p. 5 and p. 69. There was only one other seller of *moscimao* in Naples, Giuseppe Corvino, who had a *banca di moscimao* near the *Vicaria*, or law courts in the city (*Situatione*, p. 62).

61 'Da sopra il largo del Gesù Nuovo, fino alla Fontana di Mont'Oliveto à tutte le dette Botteghe, se li concede di cacciata palmi otto, e di pennata palmi ...

Domenco Renzullo, che non possa tenere Galesse, nel Vico à lui vicino' (*Situatione*, pp. 24–25).

62 'Barrache, che risiedono in mezzo al Mercato grande in questa fedelissima Città', *Situatione*, pp. 54–60.

63 See Danielle van den Heuvel, 'Policing peddlers: The prosecution of illegal street trade in eighteenth-century Dutch towns', *Historical Journal* 58/2 (2015), pp. 367–392.

64 Most of the statutes of the guilds survive in documents in the Archivio di Stato in Naples and remain to be studied. For the statutes of the vegetable and citrus-fruit sellers, see ASN, Capellano Maggiore Statuti e Congregazioni Busta 1184, Fascicoli 24 and 25. On the formation of these guilds, see Luigi Mascilli Migliorini, *Il sistema delle arti: Corporazioni annonarie e di mestiere a Napoli nel Settecento* (Naples, 1992), pp. 70–71.

65 The secondary literature on the persistence of this trope and stereotype is extensive. To begin, and most recently, see Francesco Benigno, 'Trasformazioni discorsive e identità sociali: Il caso dei lazzari', *Storica* 31 (2005), pp. 7–44.

66 Spadaro also painted the eruption of Vesuvius in 1631 and the plague of 1647 in Naples. Roworth describes these paintings as 'disaster' paintings (Roworth, 'The evolution of history painting'). For a discussion and reproductions of 'Eruzione del Vesuvio' and 'Piazza Mercatello durante la peste del 1656', see Sestieri and Daprà, *Domenico Gargiulo*, cats. 140 and 145.

67 On functions related to the Portolania, see Bartolommeo Capasso, *Catalogo ragionato dei libri registri e scritture esistenti nella Sezione Antica o Prima serie dell'Archivio Municipale di Napoli (1387–1806)* (2 vols, Naples, I:1876 and II:1899), II, pp. 124–129. On the feudal rights attached to the *portolania*, see Tommaso Astarita, *The Continuity of Feudal Power: The Caracciolo di Brienza in Spanish Naples* (Cambridge, 1992), p. 39. On Naples, as a capital city in the early modern period, see Giovanni Muto, 'Le tante città di una capitale: Napoli nella prima età moderna', *Storia urbana* 123 (2009), pp. 19–54.

68 See, for this period, for example, *Dizionario delle leggi del regno di Napoli, tratto da fonti delle costituzioni, capitoli, riti, arresti, prammatiche, novelle costituzioni, dispacci, e consuetudini di Napoli* (Naples, 1788).

69 The archive had brought together material generated by the city of Naples related to its government and economy, law and public order, and its relationship to the crown. Ninety per cent of the documents dating from 1387 and 1806 were destroyed, and half of what remains is partially burned and can not be easily consulted. For a printed catalogue of what the archives contained before the 1946, see Capasso, *Catalogo*. The fire is described in a typescript catalogue, compiled by Tommaso Lomonaco, now in the Archivio Storicio Municipale di Napoli (ASMUN). According to Lomonaco, the 3,000 pieces from the Municipal Archives were transferred to the Angevin Castle during the Second World War and managed to escape damage until a fire in 1946 destroyed 90 per cent of the archives (Tommaso Lomonaco, 'Archivio Storico Municipale di Napoli: Indice ragionato della Sezione Municipalita', ASMUN, p. 5). On the destruction of the Municipal Archives in Naples in 1946, see also Francesco Maria de' Robertis, 'La raccolta inedita del Migliaccio e la storia delle arti nell'Italia Meridionale dal secolo XIV al XIX', *Archivio storico pugliese* 2 (1949), pp. 192–211.

70 See, for example, ASMUN, Prima serie (1387–1805), Tribunale degli Eletti o di S.Lorenzo, Real Portolano, (1693–1798), Fasc.18, 'Portolano Affitti delle Piazze'.

71 See, for example, ASMUN, Prima serie (1387–1805), Tribunale degli Eletti o di S.Lorenzo, Real Portolano, (1748–1801), Fasc.20, 'Annona Licenze e matricole'.

72 See the volume entitled, in ASMUN, Prima serie (1387–1805), Tribunale degli Eletti o di S.Lorenzo, Real Portolano, (1780–1806), Fasc. 26, 'Licenze e Matricole 1780–1806'.

Plate 1 Pieter Aertsen (c. 1508–1575), *Market Scene*, c. 1550. 60 x 122 cm. Alte Pinakothek, Bayerische Staatsgemaeldesammlungen, Munich, Germany. Photo credit: bpk, Berlin/Bayerische Staatsgemaeldesammlungen, Munich, Germany/Lutz Braun/Art Resource, NY.

Plate 2 Vincenzo Campi (1536–1591), *Still Life with Fowl*, c. 1580, oil on canvas. Pinacoteca di Brera, Milan, Italy. Scala/Art Resource, NY.

Plate 3 The vegetable market, Hendrick Martensz Sorgh, 1662. Painting. Rijksmuseum, Amsterdam.

Plate 4 The Leiden tripe hall, Jacob Timmermans, c. 1788. Drawing. Historische Vereniging Oud Leiden.

Plate 5 Domenico Gargiulo (otherwise known as Micco Spadaro), *Market Square or Piazza del Carmine of Naples*, c. 1654. Oil on canvas, 141 x 76 cm. Palacio Tavera, Fundación Casa Ducal de Medinaceli, Toledo.

Plate 6 Antonio Joli, *The Church of San Paolo Maggiore, Naples*, 1756–1758. Oil on canvas, 19¼ ins x 30 ins. Palace House, Beaulieu. By kind permission of Lord Montagu of Beaulieu.

Plate 7 Marchande de gâteaux de Nanterre. Carle Vernet, *Cris de Paris* c. 1822. Coloured lithograph by Delpech. Cabinet des Estampes, Bibliothèque nationale de France, Paris.

Plate 8 Adrien Joly, 'Fichet rôle de Madeleine dans Le Boghey Renversé', 1813. Coloured engraving. Bibliothèque Historique de la Ville de Paris.

Plate 9 An ambulatory vendor in Hue selling noodle soup. Photo © Annemarie Hiemstra and Koen van der Kooy.

Plate 10 A stationary vendor at a local market in Hue, selling rice meals and noodle soup. Photo © Annemarie Hiemstra and Koen van der Kooy.

Plate 11 An image of the Hindu god Shiva painted on the lid of a street food (*bhel puri*) pushcart. Photo © Manpreet K. Janeja.

Plate 12 A street food vendor offering a 'home delivery' service (advertised on the painted signboard on the wall) for hot food (*ghoogni chaat*) in aluminium foil containers. Photo © Manpreet K. Janeja.

6 The myth of la belle Madeleine

Street culture and celebrity in nineteenth-century Paris

Tom Stammers

In his recent monograph on *Les Cris de Paris* ('The Cries of Paris'), Vincent Milliot has offered a bracing reinterpretation of how to read images of street sellers in early modern France. He points out the fallacy of historians who have too often treated prints as merely illustrative, rather than constitutive, of social practice. Depictions of the labouring classes evolved in tandem with pictorial conventions borrowed from dance manuals, popular chapbooks and classical aesthetics, leading to a 'theatricalization of popular behaviours'. The result was not a faithful mirror held up to the urban scene, but a concerted attempt to categorize, tame and ameliorate the poor. Milliot's provocative argument goes to the heart of our dilemma in trying to recover the lives of ordinary street sellers: what weight to attach to different genres of evidence. He decries the naivety of persistently treating visual sources as transparent windows onto the urban scene, and hence mistaking images for actual behaviours. These depictions of street traders did not function as reflections of the social fabric but as interventions upon it. As Daniel Roche argues elegantly in the preface to Milliot's study, our objective as historians should not simply be to oppose real life to its representations, but to show how these images attempted to 'transform social actors and to organise the perception of reality'.[1]

After giving a thorough chronology of how the genre evolved – from its sixteenth century beginnings to its later purification – Milliot observes that the *Cris de Paris* came to a crashing halt with the ideological and commercial upheavals of the French Revolution. The iconographic series reappeared after 1800, but for Milliot, this imagery was little more than a replication of earlier, moralizing typologies. To that extent, he posits the existence of an 'old regime of representations' that lasted well into the nineteenth century. By composing 'disembodied or idealised figures, conforming to the elite's categories of representing the social, artists and writers contributed to domesticating the image of a strange people, effacing or neutralizing its "savagery"'.[2] Milliot echoes those commentators who have emphasized that these materials disclose far more about their intended audiences and buyers than their quotidian subjects.[3] According to Sean Shesgreen, the *Cries of London* impose a highly idealized and prescriptive vision of the 'outcast' vendors: 'they are catechisms that stipulate how hawkers should behave; they are also apologies that justify why the lower orders are lower and must remain so'.[4] Studying Italian imagery, Peter Burke posits a widening social polarization across the eighteenth century, in which the 'popular' was rediscovered by the elites as an aesthetic object, an exoticized, sentimentalized and commodified 'other'.[5]

Such arguments point towards pessimistic conclusions. Elite discourse is imagined as self-referential, locked in its own matrix of interpretations, and hence inevitably distorting of the lives of the poor.[6] Milliot ends his book with a frank and wistful recognition of the 'silences' which inevitably fill up the history of the *petit peuple* ('the little people').[7] His argument is certainly persuasive for the *Cris de Paris*, conceived as a specific pictorial series. Yet part of the originality and excitement of Milliot's research comes from his desire to look beyond the hermetic self-sufficiency of the *Cris de Paris* out to other heterogeneous and unexpected sources. Indeed, in the nineteenth century characters and motifs burst out of the confines of the *Cris de Paris* tradition and circulated promiscuously across different media and genres of representation. This was certainly the case for the food hawker at the heart of this chapter: Madeleine, the *marchande de gâteaux de Nanterre* ('seller of Nanterre cakes') (Figure 6.1).

We have a paucity of biographical sources for Madeleine, but a wealth of colourful, and often contradictory, textual and artistic representations. Our only surviving contemporary likeness is an engraving based on an anonymous miniature. The most reliable observers claimed that she started her business at some point in the 1780s, and died around 1825.[8] While she was nicknamed the 'belle Madeleine', many observers remembered her as dowdy, plain, or ugly enough to 'scare a grenadier from the Empire'.[9] Her normal pitch of business was the gate of the Tuileries gardens, and certainly this was where other cake sellers congregated; yet different sources also associate her with the Champs-Elysées, the Palais-Royal and even as far to the north and the east as the Marais and the Temple district. One would be tempted to assume that these various sightings actually referred to numerous different women, were it not for the fact that she was each time identified by her trademark song. To interpret and account for these variations, we need to be alert to dissonances across genres, but also geographical and chronological shifts. The myth of the belle Madeleine was inseparable from the history of the city in which she worked and was commemorated.

The first two parts of the chapter outline the creation of Madeleine's celebrity under the Empire and the Restoration, by journalists, playwrights and artists, arguing for the permeability and heterogeneity of early nineteenth-century urban culture (1800–1830); the third and fourth situate Madeleine in the endangered universe of the *petits métiers* ('small trades'), and chart how her image was transformed and deformed in the following decades, as the commercial structures of the food trades were transformed (1830–1860). Both sections together ask how and why a common street seller

Figure 6.1 Madeleine as depicted by Frédéric Lix, based on an earlier anonymous miniature, taken from Charles Yriarte, *Paris Grotesque* (Paris, 1868). Engraving. Bibliothèque Historique de la Ville de Paris.

could be cast as a celebrity, and shed light on the unstable place of food hawkers within the Parisian 'social imaginary'.[10]

The maid from Nanterre

Who, then, was the enigmatic Madeleine? When the Irish novelist Lady Morgan visited the French capital in 1814, she was fascinated by the commercial vitality she found thronging the streets:

> Lemonade and *eau-de-groseille* ('gooseberry water') are measured out at every corner of every street, from fantastic vessels, jingling with bells, to

thirsty tradesmen or wearied messengers. Cakes are baking, soup is bub-
bling, sweetmeats are vending in every quarter, in the open streets, over
little stoves and under temporary sheds.

Yet amidst this anonymous throng, 'la Belle Magdelene' was singled out as
a distinctive personality, selling her *gâteaux de Nanterre* to children at the
'garden-gate' of the Tuileries.[11] Clearly by the Restoration the cake seller had
already become a Parisian landmark. The causes of her celebrity, though, are
harder to fathom; most observers took her fame as a fact, rather than reflecting on its origins. Jean-Baptiste Gouriet, to whom we owe the fullest portrait,
introduced his discussion:

> I name this famous woman, and that could suffice; who does not know
> Madeleine, the seller of Nanterre cakes! Her whole person is so remark-
> able that she herself, if someone should look at her intently, quickly snaps
> back at him, 'Well, what's your problem? It's really me, it's Madeleine;
> come along, my boy, I'm known in all of Paris'.[12]

Her name was connected immediately with her wares: there were abundant
references to the popularity of *gâteaux de Nanterre* in plays and novels, from
the late eighteenth century through to the Empire.[13] These were simple butter and sugar cakes, occasionally featuring currants, but belonging unambiguously to the plebeian pastries known collectively as *dariole*. Under the heading
of *dariole* were grouped brioches, butter breads, tarts, biscuits, usually fabricated in the 'dark streets of central Paris', or sometimes in the seller's home,
and sold along public squares and thoroughfares by itinerant traders for five
or ten centimes a piece.[14] Although they were a long way away from the delicacies of *pâtisserie fin* ('fine pastry'), the *gâteaux de Nanterre* merited a mention
by the doyen of restaurant critics, Grimod de la Reynière. While no competition for the heavenly achievements of the 'great men of the oven', Grimod still
conceded that 'a true Gourmand disdains nothing, and in his walking tours to
Saint-Germain and beyond, he never fails to procure these little cakes'.[15]

In her outstanding study on the birth of the restaurant, Rebecca Spang
has analysed the critical role played by self-styled *gourmands* like Grimod de
la Reynière in refashioning the 'alimentary topography' of the French capital. This entailed not only the production of new landmarks of consumption
within 'the urban gastronomic imagination' but also extended outwards to
picture the French countryside teeming with storehouses of regional produce
and culinary adventure.[16] It is arguable that a similar myth-making process
was observable for food consumed in the street as well as in the restaurant.[17]
Throughout the old regime, the expanding population of the metropolis had
been sustained thanks to a vast hinterland of provincial suppliers and commercial intermediaries.[18] The stalls of early nineteenth-century *marchands
des comestibles* ('grocery sellers') carried numerous delicacies that evoked the
outskirts of Paris, and especially towns steeped in ancient monarchical lore.

From Reims, bakers came bearing *pains d'épices* and *croquets*, which were once considered rarities, until the metropolitan bakers mastered the recipe and drove out their provincial rivals. Saint-Denis was the last refuge of the *talmouse*, a 'faded celebrity' that was still a favourite pastry among travellers who made their 'pilgrimage to the tombs of the kings'.[19]

Nanterre cakes, too, were steeped in historic associations. The village was famed as the birthplace of Sainte Geneviève, the fifth-century saint who had repelled the rampaging Huns to become Paris' patron saint. Geneviève was adored as the 'holy shepherdess', and for nearly a millennium Nanterre and its ancient churches had been flocked to by the pious and the penitent, including Louis XIII and Anne of Austria, who had drunk from the miraculous village wells. The *gâteaux de Nanterre*, according to legend, had sustained these pilgrims during their devotions.[20] Although more scrupulous scholars scoffed at Geneviève's supposed rustic simplicity – after all, the sources described her decked out in her parents' gleaming jewels – it was striking that the saint's aura still hung around the girls who sold these local delicacies. In fact, their iconography at times seemed indistinguishable; to some observers, the saint with her basket looked like a common food hawker.[21] Her sellers were nearly always recruited among rustic women. 'Some peasant women, wearing on their heads checked handkerchiefs, and carrying enormous baskets on their hips', recalled Émile de Labédollière, 'stationed themselves during Parisian promenades at the entry to the Tuileries gardens, at the Palais-Royal and offered to passers-by cakes from Nanterre'.[22]

The appearance of Madeleine – her supposed freshness, innocence and purity – made her the perfect counterpart to her cakes. Jean-Baptiste Gouriet in 1811 described her as a wholesome provincial girl, striking with a pretty white cotton bonnet, golden cross, full lips and piercing eyes. In order to draw customers in, she would place her basket on the ground and invite ladies to come forward and taste 'the joy of the people'. As if to strengthen the saintly parallel, Gouriet underlined that 'Madeleine is not married. She is a virgin of Nanterre'.[23] The 'belle Madeleine' belonged to a contemporary roll-call of female food sellers, such as the *belle jardinière* ('the fair garden-girl') and the *belle laitière* ('the fair milkmaid'), whose beauties were extolled in songs and verse in the Consulate and Empire.[24] The Bibliothèque Nationale possesses an engraving of a so-called 'belle Catherine', another maiden bringing her chaste and pastoral charms to the Parisian table (Figure 6.2).

Gouriet's main fascination with Madeleine, however, came from her song, which he patiently transcribed:

La Belle Madeleine,
Elle vend des gâteaux,
Elle vend des gâteaux,
La Belle Madeleine,
Elle vend des gâteaux
Qui sont tout chauds.

Figure 6.2 La Belle Catherine from the Cabinet des Estampes, recueil 'Métiers'. Early
nineteenth-century engraving. Bibliothèque nationale de France, Paris.

[The fair Madeleine,
She sells cakes,
She sells cakes,
The fair Madeleine,
She sels cakes,
Which are piping hot.]

In producing his vignettes of street life and street music, Gouriet drew upon
written documents and the reports of friends, but also had 'many times taken
myself to the site, remained there and listened with pen in hand'. Baffled by
the bewildering intonations and phraseology he found among the vendors, he
often had recourse to 'musical notes, especially for the benefit of individuals
who do not live in the capital'.[25]

Madeleine therefore belonged to a series of food hawkers sentimentalized and mythologized in first decade of the nineteenth century. Although Gouriet professed he was drawn to these figures not out of shallow curiosity, but a spirit of 'humanity', he was clearly fascinated by the bizarre. Madeleine's profile is juxtaposed with a blind seller of lottery tickets, a fortune-teller on the Pont Neuf, a canine choreographer and the full-throated crier of Neufchâtel cheese, who was remarkable for his ability to hold a note for up to five or six minutes. Gouriet's pen struggled to transcribe this piercing form of plebeian 'plainchant', a blast so forceful as to make the glass in the windows nearby rattle:

Froma-aaa-aaa-aaa-aaa-ge à LA CRUEME ... FROMAGES DE NEUFCHÂTEL, EN VOULEZ-VOUS DES FROMAGES![26]
[Chee-eee-eee-eee-eee-se which is CREEMY [*sic*] ... CHEESE FROM NEUFCHÂTEL, THE CHEESE YOU WANT!]

Among other female street vendors there was a fruit seller from Beauce, whose romantic past and lively refrain 'encore un quarteron, Claudine' were burned into popular memory.[27] There was also Babet the tinder seller, described by Gouriet as a 'very fat woman, always jolly, always singing', whose black skin contrasted with her brilliant white taffeta hat.[28]

For Vincent Milliot, this vein of urban ethnography represents a feeble repetition of the stereotypes of older chroniclers, like Louis-Sébastien Mercier and Restif de la Brétonne.[29] Yet this overlooks what might be novel in Gouriet's project: namely his concern with *individual* vendors, their biographies and idiosyncrasies. During the eighteenth century, a taxonomic impulse had sought to classify sections of the Parisian population along the axes of their profession or their neighbourhood. As a result, cake-sellers across the length and breadth of Paris were identified with generic musical catch-phrases, like '*deux liards, deux liards pour un sou*' or the insistent '*chaud, chaud, bon et chaud*' ('hot, hot, good and hot').[30] But following the abolition of the corporations in 1791, the emphasis shifted towards marginal professions and rogue personalities. This signalled a clear departure from both the Enlightenment obsession with tools and technologies, and also the early modern desire to crystallize in a 'harmonic, unified form' the complexities of the corporate universe.[31] The *Cris de Paris* tradition, which had formed a recognizable corpus of images for over three centuries, increasingly fragmented into the atomized and amorphous field of the *petits métiers*. In Gouriet's account, the belle Madeleine does not easily typify any one social constituency; in some ways, all that she stands for is herself.

Song collectors and antiquarians in the nineteenth century – dismissed by Milliot as mere 'folklorists' – support the view that the Empire saw the emergence of a new kind of self-referential musical sales-pitch. 'Alongside the traditional cries, a sort of collective appeal', wrote George Kastner, 'there are a mass of cries whose significance is limited to some eccentric individual, often represented by a single personage'.[32] It was this individual inventive-ness which justified Gouriet's accolade for Madeleine as an 'artist'. In 1811 Gouriet was offering a disparate anthology of 'all those who have immor-talised themselves or are still winning immortality in the streets of Paris' including contortionists, impostors and *commedia dell'arte* characters. This motley assortment testified to his fervent admiration for the street hawker, who, in whipping up custom, also managed to metamorphose into a 'poet and musician by crying his little pies, bowls or glasses', equal in ingenuity to those other 'virtuosos' who eked out a living by attracting and entertaining the crowds. In each case, Gouriet (himself a mediocre author of novels and vaudevilles) implied a shared flair for public performance, a habit familiar both to the food hawker and to the mountebank who 'makes his work out of his mouth, his hands and his feet'.[33]

The encounter between Gouriet and Madeleine could be classed as one more instance of the moralizing, idealizing impulse in treatments of the *menu peuple* ('the lower classes'). Female food hawkers had unsettled and alarmed the authorities under the old regime, due to their independence from male, corporate control.[34] The journey to Paris from the outlying villages was fraught with dangers and temptations for a female migrant, and many of the *marchands ambulantes* ('strolling dealers') were held in deep suspicion by the city authorities.[35] Throughout the nineteenth century, too, the municipal administration tried to confine ambulatory female vendors to fixed stalls, and restrain their gossip, insults and informal associations.[36] What could be more reassuring than to turn one of these potentially lawless metropolitan women into the incarnation of provincial purity and sugary saintliness?

But this assumption deprives the street seller of any agency in the exchange. If Madeleine really was a kind of performer, as Gouriet alleged, than surely she also saw the business advantages from having her profile and her songs dis-seminated in print? In this light it is striking that Gouriet reported her scheme to set up a dance hall and drinking establishment on the Champs-Elysées fea-turing 'a brilliant and select company, with cakes that are always fresh, wines that are always old, and private booths for friends of decency'.[37] There is no evidence that the dance hall ever materialized, but it does indicate Madeleine's sensitivity to the arts of publicity and self-advertisement. Gouriet's journal-ism, though, was only one early channel through which her reputation was conserved; we also need to consider Madeleine's presence on the stage, in songs and in miniatures.

The many faces of la belle Madeleine

Although according to most observers she worked largely on the other side of the city, at the Jardin des Tuileries, the theatre district around the boulevard du Temple claimed Madeleine as one of their own. Her name was invoked among the roll-call of lost talents and performers who had once delighted the Parisian crowds.[38] As in many other European cities, there were close connections in Paris between the shabby *petits théâtres* and the universe of the *petits métiers*. Most obviously, the boulevard theatres were prime sites for street hawkers to ply their goods, and the Temple area was swarming with sellers of orange syrups, roast chestnuts and cocoa. This was a mutually beneficial relationship. Dramatists borrowed the picturesque figures at the theatre door and inserted them into the action to add a splash of local colour; at the same time, canny traders re-fashioned tunes and ditties picked up from the productions to give their sales-pitches an extra twist of topicality.[39]

It is curious that Milliot, despite his concern with the 'theatricalization of popular behaviours' omits any study of how the urban trades were represented at the theatre. And perhaps this is not surprising, since there is little evidence here of moralizing discourses to improve the people. Since the mid-eighteenth century, French dramatists had experimented with putting the idiomatic and often indecent language of artisans and *poissardes* ('fishwives') on the stage.[40] With the outbreak of the French Revolution, there was a new urgency in representing the lives and concerns of ordinary citizens, and this impulse found its outlet in the *tableau populaire* in which well-known faces from the Paris neighbourhoods passed by in rapid succession. From the late 1790s onwards a crop of comic operas appeared, centring around semi-mythic Parisian women (such as the boulevard singer Fanchon la Vieilleuse, or the grasping fishwife-turned-*bourgeoise* Madame Angot), which proved enormously popular thanks to their contemporary flavour, topographic particularity and burlesque, transvestite central performances.[41] It was this genre of vaudevilles, based around fabricated anecdotes of metropolitan personalities, which helped cement the fame of Madeleine.

To take one interesting example, she appeared as the lead character in *La marchande d'amadou et la marchande de gâteaux de Nanterre*, staged at the appropriately named Théâtre Sans-Prétension in 1803. Located on the thriving boulevard du Temple, this theatre was one of the countless small dives that had emerged in the wake of the liberalization of the French stage in 1791.[42] The author of *La marchande d'amadou* ('tinder seller'), Augustin Prévost, was a deluded exponent of an avowedly popular theatre, who sought to combine patriotic uplift and moral didacticism with crowd-pleasing sketches of local life.[43] The play *La marchande d'amadou* adopted a traditional vaudeville storyline, in which the two traders, Madeleine and the cheerful tinder seller, feuded while their children fell in love and tried to win their parents' approval to marry. The action all took place within a public square, and created an impression of neighbourhood solidarity and interdependence among the minor professions. When it came to resolving their quarrel, the women had recourse to Bastringue, the *marchand de vin*, to bury the hatchet with tankards of beer and rowdy singing.[44]

The story placed a different spin on Madeleine, less a pure provincial maiden than a hard-bitten, middle-aged matriarch and foul-mouthed businesswoman. The fact that Madeleine and the tinder seller were both played by male actors doubtless created opportunities for comic impersonation and parody. Madeleine's theme song is different from the one mentioned by Gouriet, and raises the possibility that she may have owned a shop:

> Bons gâteaux de Nanterre,
> Achetez, achetez, ma pratique,
> Venez à ma boutique,
> Ils sont au beure aux oeufs,
> Qu'en mange en veut deux.
> Mes gâteaux de Nanterre,
> Ils sont faits, ils sont faits pour vous plaire,
> Mes gâteaux de Nanterre,
> Sont au lait et aux oeufs.[45]

> [Fine cakes from Nanterre,
> Buy, buy, my wares,
> Come to my shop,
> They are made with butter and eggs,
> Whoever eats one wants two.
> My cakes from Nanterre,
> They are made, they are made to please,
> My cakes from Nanterre,
> Are made with milk and eggs.]

The dialogue allowed Prévost to demonstrate his skill in capturing street slang with the same pungency as Gouriet. His spellings were anarchic, reflecting the rhythms and coarseness of popular speech. The tinder seller threatened to break Madeleine's bones, mocked her cream bonnet and accused her of poisoning all the dogs in Paris; the supposedly saintly Madeleine retorted that although her 'bitch' of a foe measured more around the hips than from head to toe, it would not need a 'strong wind' to knock her down.[46] Prévost depicted these street hawkers in line with older stereotypes about female squabbling and ferocious verbal violence.

Ironically, the cause of the dispute between the two women in the play turned on their depiction by painters in the Palais-Royal. While the tinder seller was supposedly gratified to find herself commemorated, Madeleine fumed that these pictures had made her a laughing stock.[47] Prévost's story was supported by Gouriet, who noted that 'Madeleine has been represented on numerous stages; poets have dedicated charming couplets to her, even madrigals; her portrait has been seen in nearly every display of the miniature painters in the Palais du Tribunat; her name finally shined out in letters pasted up on the walls of Paris'. One example were the images produced by Maignan at the Galerie de Foy, just up from the café d'Alexandre, where she was shown clutching her basket alongside the *quartier*'s other 'famous figures'.[48] Guidebooks to the Palais-Royal did not fail to point out her appearance in miniaturists' studios, who hung out their sketches like an 'open-air museum' to give proofs of their naturalistic skill. 'You can see there the portraits of the seller of Nanterre cakes', Jean-François Deterville wrote in 1815, noting as well 'the man with the parakeet, the fat blind man who sings in the streets, and those of lots of other original characters'.[49]

Madeleine's prominence at the Palais-Royal raises interesting questions about the place of street sellers in the social topography of Paris. Initially opened up by the Duke of Orleans in the 1780s, the Palais-Royal been a hub of political lobbying and intrigue during the revolutionary years, only to emerge under Napoleon as the pre-eminent leisure complex in the city, if not in all of Europe. It represented through its architecture and its social composition an unrivalled mingling of high and low: luxurious boutiques were juxtaposed with the shambolic and scandalous *Galérie des bois* ('wooden gallery'); *émigrés* and *salonnières* rubbed shoulders with actors, courtesans and pickpockets. It was a site that generated its own mythic personalities, including of female retailers like the *belle limonadière* ('the fair lemonade vendor') at the café Mille Colonnes, whose grace and good looks made her an object of fascination and fantasy during the Restoration.[50] Indeed, just as observers felt compelled to fill out Madeleine's life story, so too fictional scenarios and scandals were imagined for the *belle limonadière*. One story had it that she'd retired back to a domestic life in Neuilly when capricious fashion turned against her; another asserted that the fair *limonadière* had taken holy orders and shut herself away in a convent.[51]

The Palais-Royal remained a place where different classes of Parisian society collided, bartered and conversed; the iconographic schema that celebrated the local street sellers were intended to frame and encourage actual, concrete transactions. Madeleine, the tinder seller and the queen of lemonade were not just semi-mythic characters but also flesh and blood attractions for visitors to identify and interrogate. Indeed, visitors flocked to see if the real-life *belle limonadière* could live up to the alluring fashion plates (and not a few came away disappointed).[52] Hence we need to be wary of arguments that explain the creation of popular stereotypes in terms of 'othering' an alien poor; the invention of plebeian celebrities was happening across many kinds of business, in the boutique as well as in the street, and seeped into popular entertainment too. The resident Théâtre des Variétés often chose to stage neighbourhood scenes like the 1822 *Cris de Paris*, set at 4 a.m. in the central markets. Such snapshots of urban life were not especially sensitive or sympathetic to the vendors; in burlesque tradition, the great actor Odry took the part of the tinder seller, playing her as an insatiable widow who'd already worked her way through three husbands and was harassing relatives to settle her debts.[53] But parody also testified to the spell these celebrities cast over the imagination of Parisians from many backgrounds.

All the places associated with Madeleine were renowned for their social heterogeneity, from the boulevard theatres to the Champs-Elysées and the Tuileries gardens. In 1808 Pierre-Jean Nougaret marvelled at the variety of people promenading and congregating together here: 'What a difference between the people spread about in this splendid and pleasing garden!' He also pointed out that since the 1780s the Tuileries had been a favoured haunt for those desperate to be noticed.[54] The sudden increase in Madeleine's fame was rooted in the vogue of these fashionable quarters of the city, where different audiences congregated and reputations were quickly established. Just as food hawkers were drawn to these sites in search of custom, artists and shop-keepers saw the benefits of cashing-in on conspicuous local characters. For some art critics at the Salon, only 'a painter of low breeding' would dream to putting an image of a *marchande de gâteaux de Nanterre* in his shop window to demonstrate 'that he knows how to catch a resemblance'.[55] And yet a haggard Nanterre seller appears within the lithographic series of *Cris de Paris* produced in 1815 by Carle Vernet, a painter who had achieved popular and critical acclaim for his detailed battlefields and equestrian canvases. Madeleine and her wares had become a staple of the urban landscape (Plate 7).

Food hawkers were not restricted to particular, unsavoury neighbourhoods where their *dariole* cakes were baked, but took advantage of their mobility to ply their wares right across the capital. This fluidity made it hard to pinpoint them geographically or socially, and explains the diversity of different cultural forms which registered their presence. These different genres each produced their own version of Madeleine: in literary sources, she was extolled as an innocent maid, singing sweetly and selling her wholesome pastries to children, whereas on the stage, she appeared as a cantankerous but benevolent battle-axe. The circulation of divergent images and stories about her parallels her own movement back and forth across different spatial and cultural boundaries. Street hawkers like Madeleine were essentially polysemic signs, open to a host of appropriations, high and low; their songs could be heard blaring out at the market of Les Halles, or, once re-worked by Aubert or Halévy, being played by the orchestra at the opera house.[56]

This generic instability is also reflected in the miniatures of Madeleine produced by Maignan for his shop on Galerie de Foy. The originals unfortunately are now lost, but thanks to a catalogue entry from 1870, there is some reference to a composition entitled *Les chanteurs du boulevard* ('the boulevard singers'): 'Group of standing figures, among whom the author has represented himself, as well as his wife and his daughter; the other figures are the belle Madeleine, seller of Nanterre cakes, and Babet, the tinder seller.' Far from wanting to stigmatise or sanitize the hawkers, the artist chose to place his own family among the street women and their milieu. Maignan cultivated his identification with Madeleine and Babet as fellow commercial 'artists'. The fact that this portrait-cum-advertisement travelled out of the galleries of the Palais-Royal to eventually reside in an aristocratic collector's sumptuous cabinet in Florence tells its own story about the variety of buyers intrigued by 'popular' urban scenes.[57] While she was viewed as picturesque in the Empire and Restoration years, Madeleine was also recognized to be a businesswoman who knew how to make a living on the fringes of Parisian fashionable leisure.

The *petits métiers* in retreat (1830–1870)

In his compelling study of the visual satire under the July Monarchy, James Cuno interprets the depictions of street vendors in the 1820s and 1830s as serving two purposes. In one strategy, the sellers were sentimentalized and rendered 'insignificant' through a mawkish nostalgia. By carefully reproducing the prototypes laid down by the old regime, the prints of Restoration artists suggested that 'however much life may have changed since the Revolution, the city was still charming, still a centre of picturesque commerce, and still a place where the classes mingled peacefully'.[58] Alternatively, the street vendors were demonized as members of the *classes dangereuses*, the frightening mass of rootless and criminal elements swarming into the city.[59] In either case, Cuno regards these images as primarily an expression of bourgeois anxieties, and a tactic aimed at stabilizing and spatializing class relations in a time of disturbing social fluidity and transformation. A similar argument was advanced by Walter Benjamin, who regarded the taxonomic classification of the professions of Paris in the literature of the *physiologies* as a means of rendering the lower classes endearing or 'innocuous' for their middle-class readers.[60]

The example of Madeleine suggests, though, the difficulties involved in such a pictorial strategy. The attempt to fix her in a particular locale proved unsuccessful, and today it remains hard to associate her image unambiguously with any one particular market or clientele. The geographical mobility of the food hawkers, their visibility, their historical continuity and their individualism, hardly squared with the static stereotypes of the *classes dangereuses*.[61] Hawkers did not exist on the shadowy fringes of the city, but were visible in the heart of Parisian leisure; they did not belong to an undifferentiated, criminal mass, but were vividly individualized. If we consider that representations of street traders were not simple a phantasmagoria of elite interests, but were embedded in a host of local transactions, then we need to consider not just their form, but also their *content*. Nineteenth-century sources were not a pale recycling of earlier tropes, nor an outworking of bourgeois paranoia, but also acted as barometers to changing retail practices. The food hawker was fighting a losing battle against more prestigious, sheltered and comfortable rival professions.

Theatrical productions repeatedly proclaimed that the small traders were in crisis. In Prévost's piece, the tinder seller bemoans the fact that nobody sticks to their own trade anymore; the new boutiques have started to encroach on the livelihoods of others, selling ribbons and shirts alongside coal and soap, potatoes and cherries piled up with locks and thread.[62] Similarly in *Le Boghey Renversé, ou un point de vue de Longchamps* ('The upturned carriage, or a viewpoint from Longchamps') written for the Théâtre du Vaudeville in 1813, Madeleine made a cameo appearance among the cast of conjurers, chair-hirers, tailors and cane-sellers. In keeping with the *poissarde* conventions, the part was taken by a male actor, Fichet, and a costume plate survives showing his impersonation of her as a crotchety old woman (Plate 8). In the play Madeleine laughs at her faded looks, and admits frankly that her cakes are not always as piping hot as promised. But she also sings that custom is drying up:

Autrefois, en quittant Nanterre,
Sans avoir besoin de crier,
Même avant d'être à la barrière,
J'avions vendu tout mon panier.
Maintenant quelle différence!
Ma voix fait retenir les échos …
T'nez, le bon goût se perd en France;
On n' mang' presque plus d'mes gâteaux.[63]

[Long ago, on leaving Nanterre,
With needing to cry out,
Even with being at the city gates,
I had sold all my basket.
Now, what a difference!
My voice only brings back echoes …
Trust me, good taste is lost in France;
My cakes almost aren't eaten any more.]

Les petits métiers, a vaudeville staged at the Gaité in 1836, similarly depicted a community facing crisis. The play opens with an anxious conversation about a new boutique opening next door. Decked out with paintings, mirrors, mahogany, it represents the antithesis of the street peddlers with 'no doors and windows, no taxes or licences, no rents, and especially no bankruptcies'. The piece ends with a heartfelt appeal from a street urchin to the audience to show charity towards the humble traders who fear a coming storm; 'Think, gentlemen, that the smallest wind/ Could flatten their businesses.'[64]

In theatres that catered for fashionable as well as popular audiences, the message was the same: the street trades were endangered. Long before the impact of department stores, or even the sweeping transformations of Baron Haussmann, the *petits métiers* were being squeezed by harsh economic forces.[65] It is true that the municipal administration were also glad to see the back of them, for since the eighteenth century the ragged salesman lining the bridges and thoroughfares had been seen as an obstacle to traffic and a breeding ground of crime.[66] But the main challenge came from the developments within retail, as shops ornamented their premises and diversified their stock, turning women into decorative accessories at the counter.[67] By the Restoration, shop façades had been transformed from their modest old regime beginnings, giving satirists a golden opportunity to ridicule the owners' pretentions and sham gentility.[68] 'If there still exist bakers shops and *marchands de vin* in the neighbourhoods inhabited by the lower classes, almost all those in the other neighbourhoods are distinguished by frontages of gleaming iron', noted Antoine Caillot, 'of which several have cost from four to twenty thousand francs, in carpentry, metalwork, gilding and painting'.[69]

The opening decades of the nineteenth century were critical in reshaping the *pâtisserie* business in Paris. Not only did this period see the emergence of *pâtissiers-artistes* ('artist cake-makers'), such as Carême, Julien and Félix, who catered to the social elites. Cake shops that catered to every possible palate and budget multiplied in the city streets like 'Egyptian locusts or French maybugs', offering an ironic fulfilment of Marie-Antoinette's recommendation that the ravenous poor should dine on brioche.[70] Even those on the tightest budgets could find their fantasies and 'vagabond appetites' satisfied at the gleaming counters. 'At ten in the morning, the Parisian bakeries lay out their seductive and homely fineries, accessible to all purses and all digestive tracts.'[71] With the extension of shops came a scramble to sample the latest confectionary delights. According to one estimate, in 1817 there were already 40 establishments in the capital that specialized in making chocolate drops.[72] Although little more than a shack on the boulevard Saint-Denis, crowds jostled from morning until night in front of the shop of Monsieur Coupe-Toujours for a taste of his wildly popular *galettes*.[73] Most worryingly for the food hawkers, the thousands of bakeries also started to encroach on the lucrative confectionary market. It was common joke in the 1830s that it was impossible to find a Parisian baker who actually still sold an old fashioned loaf. 'If you are tenacious', noted one humorist, 'you will be presented with jam tarts, almond biscuits, little *gâteaux de Nanterre*, biscuits from Savoy; but asking for bread, impossible!'[74]

Under the old regime, corporate and municipal statutes had carefully regulated the boundaries between *boulangers* ('bakers') and *pâtissiers*, insisting that the former should not add butter and sugar to their creations. Yet from the Restoration onwards, bakeries increasingly flouted these protocols and filled their windows with an array of sweet treats. Incensed *pâtissiers* brought their grievances in a petition to the Chamber of Deputies, and found a sympathetic hearing. In 1838 deputy Lagrange thundered against 'the invasion of their profession by the bakers' which could only lead to a 'ruinous competition' which threatened to 'strip from the *pâtisserie* business a considerable portion of its profits'.[75] But these debates and subsequent petitions had no impact on the Minister of the Interior, since the *commissaire de police* effectively recognized in the Second Empire that anyone had the right to set themselves up as a cake-maker.[76] Ignoring what this unequal competition might mean for the traditional *pâtissiers*, many middle-class observers were fixated instead by the spectacle of gastronomic refinement. '*Pâtisserie* is like fashion', enthused Armand Husson in 1856, 'it is constantly perfecting its products or inventing new ones each day; the art of associating the finest pastry to the most delicious creams makes progress that is clear to see'.[77] While the *maîtres-pâtissiers* ('master cake-makers') were the primary victims of this competition, the growing diversification of bakeries would also have grim implications for street hawkers like Madeleine too.

These shifts in commercial practice are subtly captured within the iconography of the street trades. Milliot's and Cuno's arguments for the stagnation of the pictorial vocabularies of the nineteenth century are only partially true. Traces of social change can be gleaned from the modifications and omissions

Figure 6.3 Léopold Boilly, 'La Marchande de beignets', 1826. Lithograph. Bibliothèque Historique de la Ville de Paris.

that took place within this artisanal *comédie humaine*. Take the *pâtissier*, for example. Robust and flirtatious, he had been a stock character in the imagery of the old regime, whether in the celebrated set of street criers by Bouchardon in 1740 or those by Poisson in 1774. But from the 1820s he disappeared almost completely, and certainly never featured among the array of *petits métiers*. Outdoor cake selling was from this point on associated overwhelmingly with women – and old, vulnerable women at that. For instance, in his lithograph from 1826, *La marchande de beignets* ('The doughnut-seller'), Léopold Boilly highlighted the contrast between the crone who is handing out the doughy cakes and the smooth, tender faces of the greedy children who are her only customers (Figure 6.3).[78] Successive artists took a malicious delight in sketching the macaroon seller, the so-called *marchande de plaisirs* ('seller of *plaisirs/* pleasures'), whose ragged appearance was mocked by the evergreen promise

Figure 6.4 Adrien Joly, 'Des gâteaux de Nanterre, des gateaux fins' from *Arts, métiers et cris de Paris*, 1819. Coloured engraving. Cabinet des Estampes, Bibliothèque nationale de France, Paris.

of her merchandise.[79] The neglect and disdain for their outmoded goods was symbolically etched on these women's weary faces.

There's something almost sardonic, as well as sad, about the refrain of the elderly seller depicted by Joly in 1819: *gâteau de Nanterre, gâteau fin* (Figure 6.4). For as the years passed *gâteaux de Nanterre* constituted nobody's idea of *fine* pastry. The Nanterre cake seller from the 1820s onwards is invariably depicted as an old woman, both in the sleek lithographs enjoyed by the wealthy and in the crude, polychrome of the popular *imagérie d'Épinal*. Joseph Mainzer noted despondently in 1840 that the cluster of old women who still haunted the Tuileries gardens were so desperate and pathetic that their song 'provoked pity rather than appetite'. For Mainzer, these women – and the precious musical heritage they represented – were the casualties from a new branch of *pâtisserie*, in which 'the shop dethrones the street'. The food hawkers who relied on shop owners to supply their goods were subject to strictly enforced conditions: if business had been bad, they were forced to return all unsold items as well as the few coins they'd gathered; if any merchandise had been damaged in the rain, the owner had to be compensated for his loss, which could push the destitute seller into homelessness. Mainzer was horrified to learn 'what hard existence was reserved to these sad old women that we find standing for thirty years in the same place, their faces haggard and emaciated, offering their cakes to passers-by'.[80]

'Nanterre cakes were once a very profitable branch of commerce for this village', observed one traveller out to the home of Sainte Geneviève in 1836, 'but whether the quality of the produce has fallen, or rather the refined gastronomy of our era had sought out more delicate pastries, these cakes have little vogue today'.[81] His verdict is amply confirmed by other sources that suggest the pastries which delighted children in the 1800s and 1810s had sunk from view a generation later. Indeed, their earlier popularity seemed baffling to later commentators. The pieces of girdle-cake served up by the 'venerable' *pâtissier* of the Porte Saint-Denis may have been baked according to the same recipe for decades, but they were 'capable of choking a robust market porter'.[82] One dictionary entry on *gâteaux de Nanterre* from 1855 despaired that, 'the few vendors, ugly and old, who offer us today cakes dusted with grime on the quay of the Tuileries would be unable to give us the least idea of this popularity, once so dear to Parisian children'.[83] As her cakes fell out of fashion, the cult of the Madeleine herself came to be reassessed through the lens of the distressed, and distressing, vendors who still thronged around the public gardens. She was increasingly depicted not in the heyday of her fame, but as a worn-out old woman. An anonymous 1849 print presents her standing by the gates as a *type perdu*, her song inscribed underneath as another relic of times gone by (Figure 6.5).

Madeleine in the museum (1830–1870)

Increasingly marginalized by her commercial competitors, the image of the food hawker functioned as a *revenant* from a lost world. In the *Musée de la caricature* from 1838, images of Madeleine were collated alongside other street singers to chart the 'the moral existence of the people'. The volume's editor, Edouard Jaime, praised the French Revolution for endowing *le peuple* with 'its portrait, its biography', rendering a previously obscure plebeian culture visible for the first time. Yet these prints were especially valuable precisely because the street culture they depicted had receded into a distant memory. Marvelling at the France his ancestors knew, Jaime remarked in surprise: 'under the Empire, did we not accord the honours of the Salon to portraits of the belle Madeleine, the seller of Nanterre cakes, the seller of matches, the seller of ink!'. From the food hawkers to the motley circus of open-air musicians, song-smiths and *grimaciers* ('face-pullers'), a galaxy

Figure 6.5 Madeleine as 'Un type perdu', 1849. Engraving. Cabinet des Estampes, Bibliothèque nationale de France, Paris.

of picturesque types had once been considered as worthy subjects of Salon painting. Yet by the July Monarchy, these picturesque figures primarily indexed a vanished set of social relations: 'each of them recalls an era; it a signet-ring stamped in the book of the past.' Madeleine's image – like that of the acrobat or the animal entertainer – was cherished as a fond souvenir of 'childhood' and of happier times, not the kind of memory appropriate to the 'mature man'.[84]

This antiquarian condescension intensified in the following decades. As the profitability of cake selling changed, so too did Madeleine's posthumous reputation. Balzac lamented the waning of the Paris trades, as fruit-sellers, offal-mongers and chestnut vendors were all swallowed up into the 'ample flanks' of the mercenary boutiques. In a jeremiad from 1846, entitled 'What is disappearing from Paris', the novelist conflated the vanishing of these human

Figure 6.6 Gavarni, 'Achetez les gâteaux de Nanterre'. Illustration for 'Cris de Paris' in *Le Diable à Paris* (Paris, 1845–1846). Engraving. Bibliothèque Historique de la Ville de Paris.

landmarks with the demolition of the architectural fabric.[85] Later in the same periodical the caricaturist Gavarni offered a panorama of the *petits métiers*, in which the *marchande de gâteaux de Nanterre* has evolved from a sturdy young woman into a hunchbacked crone (Figure 6.6).

More tellingly, though, Gavarni's universe is populated not only by the conventional stock-trades familiar to Brossart or Bouchardon, but a surreal gallery of oddity, chicanery and exotically attired performers. Whereas Madeleine had always been noted as 'singular' or 'original', from the July Monarchy onwards the street hawker was now increasingly assimilated into the ranks of the bizarre and the 'eccentric'.[86] The attempt by Charles Yriarte to rehabilitate Madeleine as a *type*, a *célébrité de la rue* made her in same stroke a denizen of *Paris grotesque*. Indeed, images of her were filed under the rubric of 'maniacs and visionaries' in the catalogue of the Cabinet des Estampes.[87]

The clearest expression of this hostility can be found in an 1867 article from the popular illustrated journal, *La Semaine des Familles* ('The Families Weekly'). The journalist – signing only as Réné – began by recounting the story of a family who while renting a house in Nanterre had asked to sample the area's famous cakes; the landlord replied that 'he had never encountered this kind of cake except at the gate of the Tuileries, and he was completely baffled why it had been given the name of the village honoured by the name of Sainte Geneviève'. This prompted Réné to cite many other forms of false advertising – such as prunes from Tours, cherries from Montmorency or Rouen cider – in which Parisian peddlers had served up non-existent regional dishes, and proved that the nineteenth century was truly an age of *charlatans*. He then launched into a savage portrait of the so-called 'belle' Madeleine, who was actually 'very ugly', instantly recognizable by her skirt which was embarrassingly 'too short', and her 'blue stockings' which were pulled so high on her blubbery legs that they looked like coloured skittles. 'The poor old woman, who in 1830 was toothless, had been, according to one legend, young, which I am very ready to believe, and beautiful, which seems to me far less probable, and she had experienced sorrows which had driven her out of her mind.'[88]

Whatever her other traumas, she was certainly a victim of the shifting patterns of French consumption, which Réné related to the English presence in Paris after 1814. Before then, 'nobody would have dared to take up a table at the *pâtissier*, that seemed too greedy; that was the glory days of the sellers of Nanterre cakes.' But the English conquerors imported into Paris the snacking habits of London; it was the English who demanded somewhere to sit to wash down cakes with claret and Madeira, and their spending power quickly translated their whims into reality.[89] 'The shops of *pâtissiers* are today dining rooms where gold is revealed on all sides; counters, kinds of altars erected to gluttony.' Most ten-year-olds would throw a tantrum if their parents dared present them with a lacklustre *gâteaux de Nanterre*, a pastry increasingly associated not with provincial sweetness but insanitary bakers in the *faubourgs* ('suburbs').[90] Instead women like Madeleine could only hope for sales of her 'outdated cakes' to gullible juveniles and provincials: 'The open air shops and the outdoor sellers are made only for *les petites gens* ("little people").'[91]

The revulsion against *gâteaux de Nanterre* might be read as one small symptom of the revision of 'sensory thresholds' in the middle decades of the nineteenth century.[92] Tastes and smells which were previously savoured were now rewritten as dull or as disgusting, and deemed fit only for those too young or too desperate to know better. Under the growing concern over hygienic handling and preparation of foodstuffs, hawkers were remembered less as dispensers of affordable delights than potential agents of infection.[93] George Kastner claimed any idler who sampled Madeleine's cakes and the 'bitter taste of rank butter' would vow never to come back. If her cakes appeared fresh out of the oven, this was because steam wafted up from a bowl of boiling water hidden underneath the stall.[94] Of course, the retreat from street vendors was itself a bourgeois luxury, reserved for those buyers with the means to take their custom elsewhere. In her seminal work on Haussmann's Paris, Jeanne Gaillard observed that the price of sugar remained stable across the Second Empire, and that cakes and desserts featured very rarely on the working-class family's table. The boom in bakeries and patisseries was instead concentrated in the wealthier precincts of the city. While the Parisian diet diversified significantly over the 1850s and 1860s, it also became more stratified between classes, with the food hawkers pushed to the bottom rung of the social ladder.[95]

Hence outdoor sellers like Madeleine did not simply vanish in the face of stiff competition. The *petits métiers* continued to fill the cracks in the Parisian economy, and as late as 1888 there were at least 6,000 street vendors – or *marchands aux quatre-saisons* ('all year round vendors') – registered with the municipality.[96] The difference was that they were overwhelmingly associated with an older and more primitive era of consumption. Songwriter, socialist and worker-historian Pierre Vinçard was haunted in 1863 by the

> very faint memory of cake sellers who, each day, walked in the Paris of yesteryear. This *cri*, which certain sellers modulated in a melancholy way, bring back to us the joys of our first years of life which have flown away, to that age when a child had to be very unlucky and understand all the suffering of his background, since even the poorest mother always found a few centimes in her apron pocket for her young kid to go and exchange for a couple of *cornets de plaisir* or a few *macarons*.

The excitement generated by the cake seller and her song lingered faintly in Vinçard's mind. But this childish memory had been overlaid by the sight of those sad old women 'bent double under the weight of age' and hawking their pastries in filthy streets. Cakes that had once caused him to feel the sweet pains of Tantalus now aroused no emotion other than pity. Looking at such a sad woman, he felt as if the 'middle ages seemed to come back to life before us' in all its simple credulity, prejudice and ignorance.[97]

Mirroring Vinçard's transition from boyish thrills to adult aversion, Réné's 1867 article systematically subverted the early celebrations of the 'belle Madeleine'. The girl from the provinces was transformed instead into 'a ghost from past time, who walks in a world to which she no longer belongs'. Her beauty was as fraudulent as her connection to Nanterre. Far from being an icon of neighbourhood life, many had apparently asked why Baron Haussmann had not wiped her off the map 'for reasons of public utility, like a hovel of old Paris making a stain on the new one'. In common with much contemporary discourse about the urban poor, social marginality became synonymous with geographical exclusion.[98] Hence Madeleine would be expelled from the glittering precincts of the Palais Royal, and the mixed promenades of the Tuileries, to perish out at the madhouse in the suburbs.

Figure 6.7 Bertall, 'V'la le gâteau de Nanterre!'. Engraving from Alfred Nettement (ed.), *La Semaine des Familles: revue universelle et hebdomadaire*, 6 October 1866 (Paris, 1866–1867), p. 8.

'Soon she will be obliged to renounce her trade, due to lack of custom, and the curious physiologist will have to go seek the last type of the sellers of Nanterre at the Salpêtrière or at the centre for incurable women, a sort of human museum opened up to the medals of old Paris.'[99] The periodical ran as an illustration to the piece a cruel caricature by Bertall, which pictured the *marchande de gâteaux de Nanterre* as an imbecile and a degenerate, an inert and monstrous vestige of *vieux* Paris (Figure 6.7).[100]

Vincent Milliot argued that the images of street hawkers constitute a pictorial *longue durée*, 'a sort of reassuring configuration in the universe of social representations of the post-revolutionary era. At bottom the world had really changed very little'.[101] Yet the evidence here suggests that nineteenth-century images meditated as much on loss and degradation

Figure 6.8 Pierre Vidal, 'La Marchande de Plaisirs', coloured illustration in Henri Béraldi (ed.), *Le Paris qui crie. Petits métiers* (Paris, 1890). Bibliothèque Historique de la Ville de Paris.

as any sense of consoling tradition. Many of the hearty, cheerful artisans of the early modern world had aged, changed sex, or simply disappeared after 1800. In fact, the idealizing and sanitizing tone common to eighteenth-century artists was largely abandoned in order to dwell on the incorrigibly strange and perverse, especially as the street trades slipped into obsolescence. In a late attempt to revitalize the *Cris de Paris* iconography in 1890, Eugène Rodrigues painted the faded macaroon seller, the *marchande de plaisir* in acid terms (Figure 6.8):

> Her existence is dull like her merchandise. She is ageless and so to speak sexless. A figure marked by 40 to 60 years, sad, resigned, indifferent; a kind of animal overall, she carries on her body, bent-double under the weight, a long tubular box suspended on her right arm.

Surrounded by clusters of children in the text, she treads exactly the same paths as Madeleine had followed nearly a century before: 'indefatigable, she climbs the Champs-Elysées, ploughs through the Tuileries, hit the Luxembourg, the Palais-Royal and even the zoo, eternally committed to the same walk and the same itinerary. Like a horse turning in a ring.'[102]

Conclusion

What then can we learn from tracking the contemporary fame and cultural afterlife of the belle Madeleine? Her reputation emerged in a period of social disaggregation, when the unifying rubrics of the corporations dissolved to leave behind either a host of colourful, improvised *petits métiers*, precariously distinct from the morass of the urban poor. This chapter has explored her varied reception as a means of demonstrating the ongoing dynamism and instability within the depiction of street traders across the nineteenth century. Rather than a stale replay of early modern conventions – an 'old regime of representations' – nineteenth-century artists and writers like Gouriet were experimenting with novel ways of documenting street life. Moreover, these images cannot easily be reduced to a moralizing agenda of domestication or improvement. Vincent Milliot himself has persuasively argued for seeing the development of the *Cris de Paris* not as an autonomous, artistic genre, but one cross-fertilized by wider debates and auxiliary pictorial traditions. Yet we could push this logic further, and recognize that, due to its hybrid elements, urban imagery was open to appropriation for various ends by various groups and actors – including, conceivably, Madeleine herself.

The very slipperiness of la belle Madeleine – shedding and acquiring attributes as she moved between spaces, genres and periods – in part reflected the mobility of the food hawker in the nineteenth-century city. As well as trying to read these images along the grain of *class*, we need to be far more attentive to *place*. Madeleine's reputation was inseparable from urban crossroads like the Tuileries gardens, the Palais-Royal and the Temple theatres, which spawned and circulated their own mythologies. So while in socio-economic terms, food hawkers lived on the fringes, in terms of neighbourhood identity and iconography, they could occupy a central position. Their likenesses were not, as Daniel Roche once claimed of the eighteenth-century *Cris de Paris*, 'quickly banished to the lumber room of popular imagery'.[103] However, this very permeability depended on the existence of particular Parisian locales, and perished with them. The new market pressures placed on street sellers are legible within the supposedly intransitive sphere of iconography. As *boulangeries* diversified their wares and *pâtisseries* morphed into handsomely-appointed dining rooms, the depictions of Madeleine and other food hawkers acquired a tragic resonance, figured no longer as commercial agents or street performers, but as antiquarian vestiges of *vieux Paris*.

It is common in attempting to recover the lives of the poor and the marginal to assume cultural forms reflect nothing so much as the narcissistic preoccupations of the elites.[104] In this regard Milliot has undoubtedly been right to chastise any facile literalism. But his injunction to silence seems unduly defeatist. While we may struggle to retrieve the 'real' seller beneath the celebrity, Madeleine's contemporary and posthumous fame was constructed by and consumed by a range of publics. This ensured that her representation was not static, but evolved according to changing geographical locations and chronological rhythms. Even within the privileged sphere of cultural history, there might be some grounds for cautious optimism in connecting images of urban life back to the bustle of the street.

Notes

1   D. Roche, 'Preface', in V. Milliot, *Les cris de Paris, ou le peuple travesti: les représentations des petits métiers parisiens (XVIe-XVIIIe siècles)* (Paris, 1995), pp. 8–9.
2   Milliot, *Les cris de Paris*, p. 354.
3   C. Grasland and A. Keilhauer, 'La rage du collection. Conditions, enjeux et significations dans la formation des grands chansonniers satiriques et historiques a Paris au début du XVIIIe siècle', *Revue d'histoire contemporaine* 47/3 (2000), pp. 458–486.
4   S. Shesgreen, *Images of the Outcast: The Urban Poor in the Cries of London* (Manchester, 2002), p. 15.
5   P. Burke, 'Representing women's work in early modern Italy', in J. Ehmer and C. Lis (eds), *The Idea of Work in Europe from Antiquity to Modern Times* (Aldershot, 2009), pp. 177–187.
6   S Siegfried, 'Boilly's moving house: "An exact picture of Paris?"', *Art Institute of Chicago Museum Studies* 15/2 (1989), pp. 126–137.
7   Milliot, *Les cris de Paris*, p. 357.
8   C. Yriarte, *Paris grotesque: les célébrités de la rue* (Paris, 1868), p. 16.
9   J. Mainzer, 'Le pâtissier', in *Les Français peints par eux-mêmes* (4 vols, Paris, 1840–1842), IV, p. 221.
10 B. Bazcko, *Les imaginaires sociaux: mémoires et espoirs collectifs* (Paris, 1984).
11 S. Morgan, *France* (2 vols, London, 1817), II, pp. 132, 139.
12 J.B. Gouriet, *Personnages célèbres dans les rues de Paris, depuis une haute antiquité jusqu'à nos jours* (2 vols, Paris, 1811), p. 306.
13 L.A. Dorvigny, *Janot, ou les battus paient l'amende, comédie-proverbe-parade, ou ce qu'on voudra* (Paris, 1779), p. 19; Pigault-Lebrun, *L'homme à projets* (4 vols, Paris, 1819), I, p. 10; L. Prudhomme, *Voyage descriptif et philosophique de l'ancien et du nouveau Paris. Miroir fidèle qui indique aux étrangers et même aux Parisiens ce qu'ils doivent connaître et éviter dans cette capitale, contenant des faits historiques et anecdotes curieuses sur les monuments et sur la variation des moeurs de ses habitants depuis vingt-cinq ans* (2 vols, Paris, 1815), II, p. 293.
14 A. Husson, *Les consommations de Paris* (Paris, 1856), pp. 306, 309.
15 He did point out, however, that the superior examples were not cooked up in Nanterre at all, but were churned out by a baker in Neuilly, in G. de la Reynière, *Almanach des gourmands: servant de guide dans les moyens de faire excellente chère* (8 vols, Paris, 1803–1812), VIII, p. 254.
16 R. Spang, *The Invention of the Restaurant: Paris and Modern Gastronomic Culture* (Cambridge, MA, 2000), pp. 153–157, 167–169.
17 J.P. Aron, *Essai sur la sensibilité alimentaire à Paris au 19e siècle* (Paris, 1967), p. 33.
18 R. Abad, *Le grand marché. L'approvisionnement alimentaire de Paris sous l'Ancien Régime* (Paris, 2002), pp. 797–820.

19 Mainzer, 'Le pâtissier', p. 213. For an example of the desire to historicize different French pastries, see A.J. Silvestre, *Histoire des professions alimentaires dans Paris et ses environs* (Paris, 1853).

20 C. Nodier and L. Lurine (eds), *Les environs de Paris: histoire, monuments, paysages, mœurs, chroniques, traditions* (Paris, 1855), pp. 44–46.

21 Le Fongeray, 'Le coup d'état', *Revue de Paris* 10 (1830), p. 129.

22 E. de Labédollière, 'Puteaux-Courdevoie-Nanterre', *Almanach parisien* 5 (1864), pp. 77–79.

23 Gouriet, *Personages célèbres*, pp. 307–308.

24 See *Chansonnier de tous les états, ou receuil de chansons tirées des meilleurs auteurs anciens et modernes, pour et contre les tailleurs, colporteurs, marchandes de modes, lingères, dégraisseurs, épiciers, cuisiniers, boulangers et boulangères, laitières, mercières, horlogers, parfumeurs, etc etc et généralament touts les métiers, états et emplois* (Paris, 1808).

25 Gouriet, *Personnages célèbres*, pp. 17–18.

26 Gouriet, *Personages célèbres*, p. 311.

27 Yriarte, *Paris grotesque*, pp. 25–27.

28 Gouriet, *Personages célèbres*, pp. 302–303.

29 Milliot, *Les cris de Paris*, p. 355. For the ongoing vitality and development of the tableaux tradition in the nineteenth century, see K. Stierle, 'Baudelaire and the tradition of the Tableau de Paris', *New Literary History* 11/2 (1980), pp. 345–361.

30 P. Sébillot, *Légendes et curiosités des métiers* [1885] (Marseille, 1981), pp. 79–80.

31 W.H. Sewell, 'Visions of labor: Illustrations of the mechanical arts before, in, and after Diderot's *Encyclopédie*', in S.L. Kaplan and C.J. Koepp (eds), *Work in France: Representations, Meaning, Organization and Practice* (Cornell, 1986), pp. 258–288.

32 G. Kastner, *Les voix de Paris: essai d'une histoire littéraire et musicale des cris populaires de la capitale, depuis le moyen âge jusqu'à nos jours, précédé de considérations sur l'origine et le caractère du cri en général* (Paris, 1857), p. 58.

33 Gouriet, *Personnages célèbres*, pp. 1, 17–18.

34 A. Farge, *Fragile Lives: Violence, Power and Solidarity in Eighteenth-Century Paris*, trans. C. Shelton (Cambridge, MA, 1993), pp. 131–138.

35 R. Cobb, *Paris and its Provinces 1792–1802* (Oxford, 1975), pp. 14–38.

36 V.E. Thompson, *The Virtuous Marketplace: Women and Men, Money and Politics in Paris 1830–1870* (Baltimore, 2000), pp. 86–118.

37 Gouriet, *Personnages célèbres*, p. 308.

38 T. Faucheur *Histoire du boulevard du Temple, depuis son origine jusqu'à sa démolition* (Paris, 1863), p. 51. For other examples, see R. Isherwood, *Farce and Fantasy: Popular Entertainment in Eighteenth-Century Paris* (Oxford, 1986).

39 Kastner, *Les voix de Paris*, pp. 94–95; E. Texier, *Tableau de Paris* (2 vols, Paris, 1852–1853), I, p. 66.

40 A.P. Moore, *The Genre Poissard and the French Stage of the Eighteenth Century* (New York, 1935).

41 J. McCormick, *Popular Theatres of Nineteenth-century France* (London and New York, 1993), pp. 116–118. On Fanchon la Vieilleuse at the theatre, see J.L. Géoffroy, *Cours de littérature dramatique, ou receuil par ordre de matières des feuilletons de Géoffroy, précédé d'une notice historique sur sa vie* (5 vols, Paris, 1819–1820), V, pp. 321, 330–331.

42 A. Tissier, *Les spectacles à Paris pendant la Révolution: répertoire analytique, chronologique et bibliographique* (2 vols, Geneva, 2002); M. Root-Bernstein, *Boulevard Theatre and Revolution in Eighteenth-Century Paris* (Michigan, 1984).

43 A.-T., 'Prévost', in L.G. Michaud (ed.), *Biographie universelle, ancien et moderne, supplément* (85 vols, Paris, 1811–1863), LXXVIII, pp. 45–47.

44 A. Prévost, *La marchande d'amadou et la marchande de gâteaux de Nanterre, folie-parade, caricature du jour, en un acte* (Paris, 1803), p. 4.

45 Prévost, *La marchande d'amadou*, p. 7.

46 Prévost, *La marchande d'amadou*, pp. 17–18.

47 Prévost, *La marchande d'amadou*, pp. 5, 10.

48 Gouriet, *Personnages célèbres*, p. 306.

49 J.F. Deterville, *Le Palais-Royal, ou les filles en bonne fortune* (Paris, 1815), p. 120.

50 W. Scott Haine, *The World of the Paris Cafe: Sociability among the French Working Classes 1789–1914* (Baltimore, 1996), pp. 183–184.

51 A. Simonin and N. Brazier, *Arlequin au café du Bosquet, ou la belle limonadière* (Paris, 1808); E. Roch, 'Le Palais Royal', in *Paris, ou Le livre des cent-et-un* (15 vols, Paris, 1831–34), I, pp. 31–32; L. Véron, *Mémoires d'un bourgeois de Paris, comprenant la fin de l'Empire, la Restauration, la Monarchie de Juillet et la République jusqu'à l'établissement de l'Empire* (4 vols, Paris, 1853–1854), II, p. 14.

52 P. Jouhaud, *Paris dans le dix-neuvième siècle, ou Réflexions d'un observateur sur les nouvelles institutions, les embellissements, l'esprit public, la société, les ridicules, les femmes, les journaux, le théâtre, la littérature etc* (Paris, 1809), p. 57.

53 Francis, Simonin, Dartois, *Les cris de Paris: tableau poissarde en un acte, mêlé de couplets* (Paris, 1822), p. 12.

54 P.J. Nougaret, *Aventures parisiennes, avant et depuis la Révolution* (3 vols, Paris, 1808), II, pp. 111–112.

55 A. Jal, *Esquisses, croquis, pochades, ou tout ce qu'on voudra sur le salon de 1827* (Paris, 1828), p. 69.

56 M. Beurdeley, *Les petits métiers de la France d'autrefois* (Paris, 1992), p. 9.

57 *Collections de San Donato: tableaux, marbres, dessins, aquarelles et miniatures* (Paris, 1870), p. 194.

58 J. Cuno, 'Violence, satire, and social types in the graphic art of the July Monarchy', in G. Weisberg and P. Chu (eds), *The Popularization of Images: Visual Culture under the July Monarchy* (Princeton, 1994), pp. 10–36.

59 L. Chevalier, *Classes laborieuses et classes dangereuses à Paris pendant la première moitié du XIXe siècle* (Paris, 1958); G. Fritz, *L'idée de peuple en France du XVIIe siècle au XIXe siècle* (Strasbourg, 1988).

60 W. Benjamin, *Charles Baudelaire: A Lyric Poet in the Era of High Capitalism*, trans. H. Zohn (London and New York, 1973), pp. 35–36.

61 For a compelling critique of Chevalier, see B.M. Ratcliffe, 'Classes laborieuses et classes dangereuses à Paris pendant la première moitié du XIXe siècle? The Chevalier thesis re-examined', *French Historical Studies* 17 (1991), pp. 542–574.

62 Prévost, *La marchande d'amadou*, p. 11.

63 E. Théaulon and A. Dartois, *Le boghey renversé, ou un point de vue de Longchamps; croquis en vaudevilles* (Paris, 1813), pp. 19–21.

64 M. Bathelmy and E. Fillot, *Les petits métiers, tableau populaire en un acte* (Paris, 1836), pp. 3–4, 40.

65 M. Miller, *The Bon Marché: Bourgeois Culture and the Department Store* (Princeton, 1981); P. Nord, *Paris Shopkeepers and the Politics of Resentment* (Princeton, 1986).

66 D. Garrioch, *The Making of Revolutionary Paris* (Berkeley, 2002), pp. 224–225.

67 J. Jones, 'Coquettes and grisettes: Women buying and selling in Ancien Régime Paris', in V. De Grazia and E. Furlough (eds), *The Sex of Things: Gender and Consumption in Historical Perspective* (Berkeley, 1996), pp. 25–53.

68 A. Luchet, 'Les magasins de Paris', in *Paris, ou Le livre des cent-et-un*, XV, pp. 237–268.

69 A. Caillot, *La vie publique et privée des français, à la ville, à la cour et dans les provinces, depuis la mort de Louis XV jusqu'au commencement du règne de Charles X,*

pour faire suite à la vie privée des français de Legrand d'Aussy, par une Société des gens de lettres (2 vols, Paris, 1826), II, pp. 212, 219.

70 L. Huart, 'Physiologie du pâtissier', in M. Alhoy, L. Huart and C. Philipon, *Le musée pour rire, dessins par tous les caricaturistes de Paris* (3 vols, Paris, 1839–1840), III, no. 111.

71 E. Puyat, 'Les dejeuners de Paris', in *Le livre des cent-et-un*, XV, pp. 271–272.

72 B. de Châteauneuf, *Recherches sur les consommations de tout genre de la ville de Paris en 1817, comparés à ce qu'elles étaient en 1789* (Paris, 1819), p. 80.

73 P. de Kock, 'La galette', in P. de Kock (ed.), *La grande ville: nouveau tableau de Paris, comique, critique et philosophique* (2 vols, Paris, 1844), I, pp. 53–56.

74 L. Huart, 'Le Cri-Cri', in *Muséum Parisien: Histoire physiologique, pittoresque, philosophique et grotesque de toutes les bêtes curieuses de Paris et de la banlieue, pour faire suite à toutes les éditions des oeuvres de M. de Buffon* (Paris, 1841), p. 114.

75 *Moniteur*, 10 juin 1838.

76 P. Vinçard, *Les ouvriers de Paris: alimentation* (Paris, 1863), p. 95.

77 Husson, *Les consommations de Paris*, p. 306.

78 L. Boilly, *Recueil des grimaces* (Paris, 1823–1827).

79 R. Massin, *Les cris de la ville: commerces ambulants et petits métiers de la rue* (Paris, 1985), p. 38.

80 J. Mainzer, 'Le pâtissier', pp. 219–220, 222, 224.

81 G. Touchard-Lafosse, *Histoire des environs de Paris, comprenant la description des villes, bourgs et villages, sites pittoresques et curiosités naturelles, châteaux, églises, anciens couvents* (4 vols, Paris, 1834–1835), I, p. 55.

82 Huart, 'Le Cri-Cri', p. 114.

83 W. Duckett 'Gâteaux', in *Dictionnaire de la conversation et de la lecture, inventaire raisonné des notions générales les plus indispensables à tous* (16 vols, Paris, 1853–1860), X, p. 161.

84 E. Jaime, 'Le triomphe de ma mie Margot', in E. Jaime (ed.), *Musée de la Caricature ou recueil des caricatures les plus remarqués publiées en France depuis le quatorzieme siècle jusqu'à nos jours, pour servir de complément de toutes les collections de mémoires* (2 vols, Paris, 1838), pp. 1–4.

85 H. de Balzac, 'Ce qui disparaît de Paris', in *Le Diable à Paris. Paris et les Parisiens* (2 vols, Paris, 1845–1846), II, pp. 14–18.

86 M. Gill, *Eccentricity and the Cultural Imagination in Nineteenth-Century Paris* (Oxford, 2009).

87 Yriarte, *Paris grotesque*, p. 17.

88 Réné, 'La marchande de gâteaux de Nanterre', in A. Nettement (ed.), *La semaine des familles: revue universelle hebdomadaire*, 6 Octobre 1886 (1866–1867, Paris), pp. 7–8.

89 For more on the impact of English cuisine on France in the Restoration, see R. and I. Tombs, *That Sweet Enemy: The French and the British from the Sun King to the Present* (London, 2006); C. Leribault, *Les Anglais à Paris au XIXe siècle* (Paris, 1994), pp. 96–97.

90 'Finally, in the faubourgs are found obscure manufacturers of *galettes*, *gâteaux de Nanterre*, *croquets*, *plaisirs*, *chaussons de pommes*, and other cakes more or less impregnated with rancid butter and destined for the street trade' (A.-L. Joanne, *Paris illustré, son histoire, ses monuments, ses musées, son administration, son commerce et ses plaisirs. Nouveau guide des voyageurs* (Paris, 1855), p. 700).

91 Réné, 'La marchande de gâteaux de Nanterre', pp. 8–9.

92 See the collection A. Corbin, *Le temps, le désir et l'horreur. Essais sur le XIXe siècle* (Paris, 1991).

93 See V. Borie, *L'alimentation à Paris: les halles et les marchés* [1867], ed. P. Ory (Paris, 2008), pp. 21–22.

94 Kastner, *Les voix de Paris*, p. 86.

95 J. Gaillard, *Paris la ville: 1852–1870* (Paris, 1997), pp. 182, 201.

96 A. Coiffignon, *Paris vivant. L'estomac de Paris* (Paris, 1888), pp. 266–267.

97 Vinçard, *Les ouvriers de Paris*, p. 71.

98 J.M. Merriman, *The Margins of City Life: Explorations on the French Urban Frontier 1815–51* (Oxford, 1991).

99 Réné, 'La marchande de gâteaux de Nanterre', p. 9.

100 For the pervasiveness of such stereotypes in the Second Empire and after, see D. Pick, *Faces of Degeneration: A European Disorder, 1848–1918* (Cambridge, 1989); R. Nye, *Crime, Madness and Politics in Modern France: The Medical Concept of National Decline* (Princeton, 1984).

101 Milliot, *Les cris de Paris*, p. 355.

102 E. Rodrigues, 'La marchande de plaisirs', in H. Béraldi (ed.), *Paris qui crie. Petits métiers* (Paris, 1890), pp. 103–104.

103 D. Roche, *The People of Paris: An Essay in Popular Culture of the Eighteenth Century* (Berkeley, 1987), p. 72.

104 D. Rieger, 'Ce qu'on voit dans les rues de Paris: marginalités sociales et regards bourgeois', *Romantisme* 59 (1988), pp. 19–29.

7 The street food sector in Vietnam

Serious business for female entrepreneurs

*Annemarie M.F. Hiemstra**

Introduction

> Drinking and gambling till you're in over your head, but even if you are
> out of money, your kid's mother is still out there selling her wares.[1]

Street food is such a familiar sight in the streets of present-day Vietnam that
one almost overlooks it: you can eat *Pho* (noodle soup with beef or chicken)
on virtually every street corner, and in addition to soup, one finds rice meals,
noodles, cakes and sandwiches for sale. In Vietnam, street food is nearly
always sold by female hawkers.[2] As in many other developing economies,
Vietnamese women generally take up occupations that require traditional
'feminine' skills, such as cooking and sewing, and they therefore often dominate the street food sector.[3] In addition we may assume that, as elsewhere, the
street food sector allows women to work close to home, to have flexible working hours, and to enter and exit easily the job market. The sector also has
low skill requirements. However, not only do women form the overwhelming
majority of all traders, they also constitute the majority of the consumers,
making the street food sector especially significant for the female Vietnamese
population.

The number of street food stalls in Vietnam has grown extremely rapidly
since the trade was liberalized in the 1980s. Prior to 1986, all food stalls were
state-owned. By 1991, however, 99 per cent of the 55,000 food stalls in Hanoi
were privately owned, as is estimated by the Ministry of Health.[4] Given the
large number of enterprises in the food sector alone, it is not surprising that
micro- and small-scale businesses such as food stalls are of great economic
significance to the country and its people.[5] Despite impressive economic modernization and the integration of the country into the global economy over
the past two decades, the importance of these small businesses for individual families as well as the economy more widely has remained. Even though
many of the street food businesses are informal, and hence outside the control and protection of the government, they offer employment, income and

a social context for millions of households in Vietnam.[6] It is estimated that, in 2010, 82 per cent of the employment in Vietnam was in the informal sector, a large proportion of which was in street food vending.[7] Indeed, the line from the Vietnamese folksong quoted at the start of this chapter illustrates the importance of food hawking in the lives of many Vietnamese families, as well as the important economic role that female hawkers perform within these households.

Economists and policy advisors such as the International Labour Organization (ILO) for a long time considered entrepreneurial activities in the informal sector, such as street food vending, as 'income generating activities' or 'pre-entrepreneurial' rather than 'entrepreneurial'. This was because it was assumed that the income generated from such informal businesses was mainly used to cover household expenses (for example, clothing and food) rather than for reinvestment, thereby limiting the growth opportunities of the business.[8] They also dismissed the presence of a desire for growth and innovation among informal business owners and assumed that such businesses lack long-term planning.[9] The argument that income generating activities are not entrepreneurial has discouraged many researchers and policy makers from studying informal sector activities such as street food businesses.[10]

More recently however, economists and policy makers have come to acknowledge that entrepreneurship, even within the informal sector, plays an essential role in developing economies. It is increasingly recognized that entrepreneurship in the informal sector brings self-reliance, as well as economic freedom and opportunities for development for entrepreneurs and their families.[11] The ILO currently considers the promotion of entrepreneurship as one of the most effective ways to reduce problems of joblessness and poverty in developing countries.[12] Promoting entrepreneurship in micro- and small-scale businesses among women in particular is seen as a means to create employment for women that balances work and family responsibilities and that reduces disparities between women and men.[13] Women have been assigned a special role not only because they stand to benefit from entrepreneurship, being the poorer and more discriminated gender, but also because they are seen as a critical driver of entrepreneurship in light of their unique role in the household. This is especially crucial given the growth in numbers of female-headed households across the developing world.[14]

Recent studies have also challenged the assumptions on the lack of 'entrepreneurial' behaviour among business owners in the informal sector. A study by Voeten of female entrepreneurs in small businesses in the informal economy of Vietnam showed that 25.6 per cent of these entrepreneurs are growth-oriented. It also showed that more than half of the business owners do not consider their business simply as 'income generating', but they also take investment and development into account.[15] Another study into business management development for female entrepreneurs in Vietnam revealed that the enthusiasm for business support and training interventions has a critical impact on the success of their businesses.[16] These preliminary studies underline not only the economic significance and the ambition of female entrepreneurs in the informal sector, but also the necessity of considering factors beyond merely socio-demographic characteristics, such as personal dedication and ambition, when aiming to explain and improve the business success of small-scale entrepreneurs.

By using a psychological perspective to assess the entrepreneurial activities of street food vendors, we aim to enhance the understanding of entrepreneurship in the street food sector in present-day Vietnam by looking at the psychological motives and related actions of micro business owners.[17] Such an approach has already been successfully applied to studies of micro businesses in Africa, but it still awaits further implementation into studies on small-scale informal businesses in other parts of the world.[18] In addition, we want to contribute to a better understanding of the street food sector in contemporary Vietnam. Although the importance of small and medium-sized enterprises for the Vietnamese economy is widely recognized, studies on food hawking in the Vietnamese context, and on female food hawkers in particular, are rare.[19] To promote female entrepreneurship in the street food sector effectively, with the ultimate aim of gender equality and economic efficiency, it is important to know how women entrepreneurs perceive and do their work and what makes them successful. This is important not only for the street food sector, but also for the women who operate within it and their families. In this chapter, we therefore analyse the survival and expansion strategies of these women entrepreneurs from a psychological perspective and relate this to their economic performance. This will allow us to shed light on the importance and success of the street food sector as a source for jobs and poverty reduction for Vietnamese women and their families.

The majority of the data for this chapter is derived from a field study undertaken in 2000 and enhanced by a literature study. In the field study we collected data through observation, interviews and a survey among 102 street food vendors who owned the business and were also responsible for the daily management. Data were collected in two cities: Hue, a provincial city in Central Vietnam, and Hanoi, the capital situated in the north. In both cities, the position of the business, for example, in a marketplace, railway station, or on a busy street corner, and the time of day during which business is undertaken, for example, in the morning, afternoon or evening, were taken into account to ensure a representative sample. Furthermore, when analysing the success of the business, the city in which the vendor worked was also controlled for. We had to overcome some challenges typical for field work in informal sector settings in a developing country. Data collection took place on noisy and crowded streets during business hours, which required us to maintain the attention of the vendors while they were engaging in sales activities. This meant that the time to interview the vendors was limited. Additionally, language barriers, which required the involvement of interpreters, and different cultural predispositions between the interviewers and the vendors, may have influenced the results. Finally, none of the food vendors in our study keeps written business records; we therefore had to rely on the memories of the food vendors for information such as the length of their business careers and their business finances.

In addition to surveying 102 vendors in Hue and Hanoi, 62 vendors were interviewed to assess how their motivations and strategies are related to entrepreneurial success. To invite the vendors to give specific examples of how they undertook business we presented them with six common business goals (to show initiative, to make improvements, to find new ways to market their products, to perform better than their competitors, to expand their business, and to make more profit).[20] These goals were not important as such; they were merely a starting point to invite vendors to give a description of their activities and their goals. The interviewers rated the answers to this question on how much planning and proactiveness exists. If the answer was not clear, the vendors were invited to describe an extra goal and the procedure was repeated. Additionally, vendors were asked how they perceive the competitiveness of the sector and their relationship towards other vendors. For example, we asked, 'How many competitors do you have?' and 'Are they really competitors or are they really just friends and colleagues?'. Finally, we questioned their motives for becoming a street food vendor in order to assess their career perspectives. We used questions such as 'Why did you enter the street food sector?' and 'Do you want to leave the street food sector?'. Before we analyse the results of the in-depth interviews, we will first provide a description of the street food sector in the two cities, based on observations and the results of the survey.

The street food sector in Hanoi and Hue

The street food sector consists of vendors selling ready-to-eat foods and beverages, sometimes prepared on the spot, from stalls in streets and other public places. There is a great variety of street food on offer in the two cities under scrutiny, and despite some overlap in the products for sale we also observed clear differences between the two cities (see Figure 7.1). This is not very surprising as the cities are over 800 kilometres apart and have a very different meteorological climate.

Soup, mainly noodle or rice soup, is a very common street food in both cities. In particular, *Pho*, a noodle soup that can be found at many stalls throughout the country. Other types of soups sold in the street are *Chao* (soup with rice) or *Mien* (soup with glass noodles). Rice meals are also popular in both cities, although in Hanoi it was encountered more often than in Hue. A delicious example of such a rice meal is *Bun thit nuong*, a noodle meal with beef, herbs and a spicy peanut dressing. Another product that one encounters throughout the country is sandwiches. The bread, called *Banh mi*, is similar to a French baguette, and is a legacy from the French colonial rule which lasted until 1953. *Banh mi* can be eaten with fried eggs, cheese or different types of meat or sausages. Home-baked snacks, usually cakes, are also sold in the

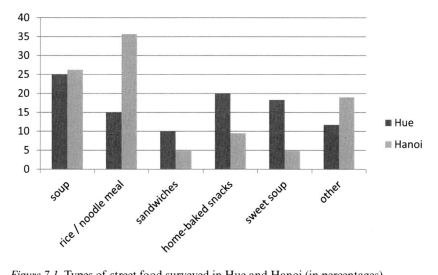

Figure 7.1 Types of street food surveyed in Hue and Hanoi (in percentages).

streets. In Hue many stationary vendors with relatively elaborate and expensive carts sell cakes. The cakes on offer at these carts are fried sweet cakes, often rolled in sesame seeds. In the evening many ambulatory vendors in Hue sold *Banh bao*, a steamed roll with meat and a small egg inside. In Hanoi there seemed to be a preference for another variety of cake, *Banh chuoi*, a fried cake filled with banana. Vendors in Hue were more often selling cold sweet soup (*che*) than those in Hanoi, despite the fact that this sweet soup made of green mung beans originates from Hanoi. *Che* is eaten from a glass with crunched ice and (if preferred) some coconut milk. A possible explanation for observing the selling of *che* more often in Hue than in Hanoi is that this research was undertaken at a time when the weather in Hue was still very hot. Hanoi was visited in October when the climate was mild. Many sweet soup vendors told us that they do not sell it during the rainy season or make less profit during that period. Finally, the 'Other' category in Figure 7.1 accounts for local specialties. Hue used to be the seat of the imperial residence and still derives fame from this heritage. The imperial Nguyen dynasty (1802–1945) also left its traces in the local cuisine. Well known in the Hue region is *Banh Khoai*, a shrimp pancake dipped in a hot peanut sauce. Other specialties are *Banh Uot* (wet rice paper with meat inside) or *Banh Beo* (wet rice paper with dried shrimp).

When we move from the food for sale in the streets to the sellers and the character of their businesses, we find that the typical form of organization of the street food businesses is that of a household enterprise. Food preparation and sales are mostly done by the same person, although sometimes the various tasks involved are divided among members of the same household.

Table 7.1 Descriptive characteristics of the street food vendors and their business in Hue and Hanoi

Descriptive characteristics	Hue (n=60)	Hanoi (n=42)
Mean age (in years)	42.85	39.22
Gender (% female)	93.33	97.62
Marital status (% married)	78.33	85.71
Working hours in street food (in hours a day)	8.91	9.06
Only job (% yes)	91.67	85.71
Child care (in hours a day)	0.83	1.39
Importance in family income (%)	69.58	76.38
Age of the business (in years)	12.16	9.38
Level of education (in years)*	5.11	8.90
Sole owner of the business (%)	88.33	73.17

Note: * indicates that the difference between Hue and Hanoi is statistically significant (test: Mann-Whitney, $\alpha < 0.05$).

Interestingly, as Table 7.1 shows, the characteristics of the street vendors and their businesses greatly overlap in Hue and Hanoi. As was stated earlier for the country as a whole, an overwhelming majority of food hawkers are women, 93 per cent and 98 per cent respectively, in these two cities. The majority of these women are married, and the sole owner of the business. Those vendors who do not work on their own usually work together with their husband or children. None of the vendors surveyed work with people who are not relatives. The average age of the food hawkers is 40 (43 in Hue, 40 in Hanoi), and on average the street food vendors have been in business for nine (Hanoi) to 12 (Hue) years, implying that most start out in their late twenties to early thirties. The level of education, expressed in the number of years the street vendors went to school, is the only significant difference between the vendors in Hue and Hanoi, with Hanoi sellers on average having attended school longer. Although we lack information on the wider context of schooling in these cities, it can be assumed that as Hanoi is a bigger city and the capital, its population has better access to education than the inhabitants of Hue.[21]

The survey furthermore revealed that for almost all of the vendors in both cities, the work at the food stall is the only paid work they do. Moreover, the income generated by these businesses accounts for more than two-thirds of the household income, confirming the importance of the street food sector for Vietnamese households as outlined in the introduction. In both Hue and Hanoi we encountered similar work patterns. About half of the surveyed vendors work all day, with an average of 11.25 hours per day. The other half of the vendors works either in the morning or in the evening, in shifts of 6–7 hours a day.[22] The group that works in the morning is larger than the group working in the evening, which is probably explained by the fact that having breakfast on the street is more popular than having dinner. Indeed, street

Table 7.2 Financial characteristics of the street food businesses in Hue and Hanoi

Financial characteristics	Hue (n=60)	Hanoi (n=42)
Price of product (VND p.p.)*	1512	2750
Sold portions (a day)	94	73
Total sales (VND a day)*	110,533	173,452
Total costs (VND a day)*	86,183	126,768
Value added (VND)*	24,350	43,598
Value added (%)	32.89	46.13
Productivity (VND/hour)*	2,980	5,852
Business value (VND)	443,448	900,902
Fixed clients (%)*	48.30	60.12
Money source – credit to start business (%)*	51.72	11.90
Money source – savings to start business (%)*	39.66	66.67
Amount of credit/saving (VND)	448,667	568,737
Business licence (%)*	3.33	24.39

Note: * indicates that the difference between Hue and Hanoi is statistically significant (test: Mann-Whitney, $\alpha < 0.05$). VND = Vietnamese Dong.

food vendors often provide the first meal of the day to many of their customers, especially to school children.

While we observed great overlap in the general character of the street food businesses and the profiles of their owners, we found that the financial characteristics of the street food sector in Hue and Hanoi differ considerably (see Table 7.2). First, the prices for the products on offer are almost twice as high in Hanoi. This also implies that the total sales and costs per day are higher in Hanoi. Furthermore, Hanoian street food vendors make significantly more profit ('value added') than those operating in Hue. However, one has to take into account that all sums of money, as presented in Table 7.2, are higher in Hanoi and that therefore the difference in relative profit ('value added %') between the two cities was smaller and not statistically significant. Vendors in Hue have an average value added of 33 per cent, while vendors in Hanoi have an average value added of 46 per cent. These financial differences can be explained by the overall financial situation in the two cities. The average income in Hanoi is higher than in Hue.[23] In 1997, the average monthly household income was calculated by the Vietnamese government at 491,000 VND ($33.86) for Hanoi and 429,000 VND ($29.59) for Hue, a difference of nearly 15 per cent.[24] The difference in average income of households between the two cities may have led the vendors in Hanoi to ask higher prices for their products, which would have enabled them to generate a higher profit in absolute terms. However, despite these financial differences, the value of street food businesses and the amount of money required setting up a business do not differ significantly between the two cities.

Second, we observed substantial differences between the two cities in how people fund the start-up of their businesses. Only a few vendors enter into business after having inherited the food stall; the majority of vendors set up the business themselves, either enabled by a loan or by savings.[25] As Table 7.2 shows, while vendors in Hue mostly use credit to initially fund their business, most vendors in Hanoi use their savings.

Third, we found that only a small minority of the food vendors, especially in Hue, hold a business licence. In Hanoi nearly a quarter of the vendors are licensed but in Hue only 3 per cent of business owners have a licence. Being in possession of a business licence, or some form of registration by a local authority, is usually considered an indicator of running a formalized business. It means that the business is registered with the authorities, and it also usually implies that the business owner pays taxes. A study by Cling and others showed that most of the business owners in the informal sector in Vietnam are reluctant to obtain a licence and as such be integrated into the formal sector. Most Vietnamese household enterprises in the informal sector, to which the street food sector belongs, either do not consider it to be compulsory or they do not know how to register.[26] This is also reflected in our findings on the Hue and Hanoi street food sector.

Finally, the observations and survey revealed that the street food vendors operate in different ways. One can distinguish three categories in Hue and Hanoi: stationary vendors, residential vendors and ambulatory vendors. The stationary vendors are those who operate from fixed spots at strategic locations. These locations are usually popular spots such as marketplaces and busy street corners. Residential vendors, like stationary vendors, prepare their food at home but sell it from their houses. Ambulatory vendors prepare their food at home but sell it in the city streets, moving from place to place, usually by bike or on foot, 'crying' their goods.

Between the three categories, we find interesting differences in the profiles of the vendors, as well as in the character of their businesses, providing a more nuanced picture of the descriptive and financial characteristics presented in Tables 7.1 and 7.2. The ambulatory vendors walk through the city 'crying' their wares, often carrying a *quang gánh*, two baskets connected with a bamboo stick that is carried over the shoulder (see Figure 7.2 and Plate 9). Others sell from their bikes. Probably as a result of their mobility they have the smallest number of fixed customers of all three groups. The ambulatory vendors in Hanoi are approximately seven years younger than the average age presented in Table 7.1, and they have the shortest careers. In Hue, on the other hand, the ambulatory vendors are the oldest group among the street vendors and have also been in business longer than the average. This is not surprising since the age of the business correlates highly with the age of the vendor. Financially, ambulatory businesses require the fewest resources, which is a plausible explanation for the attraction of younger people to these businesses in Hanoi. Strikingly, none of the ambulatory vendors in our sample has a business licence. The explanation for this is unknown, but it may be related both to a lack of financial capital, as well as their mobility, which makes the chance of detection by the authorities smaller.[27]

Figure 7.2 An ambulatory vendor with the traditional *quang gánh* selling fried tofu in Hanoi. Photo © Annemarie Hiemstra and Koen van der Kooy.

Stationary vendors sell from fixed, strategic locations such as busy street corners (see Plate 10). In Hue many stationary vendors have a cart from which they sell cakes, such as the fried sweet cakes described earlier. Each day the vendors move their carts to the location they sell from and they push them back home at the end of the working day. In Hanoi stationary vendors are more likely to have a more permanent location than in Hue, and it is some-times difficult to distinguish them from small restaurants or from residential vendors. These stationary vendors sit on the pavement in front of an indoor space resembling a garage. Inside these 'garages' one usually finds some chairs or cooking equipment and an altar (which can be found in any shop or house).[28] In Hue none of the stationaries interviewed has a business licence. They also appear to have fewer fixed customers than residential vendors oper-ating in the city. In Hanoi we observed the same pattern, but this was not sig-nificant. Stationary and residential vendors differ very little in Hanoi (there were no significant demographic or financial differences).

The third category of traders, residential vendors, operate from their homes, sometimes literally from their living room (see Figure 7.3). This is enabled by the specific design of Vietnamese houses: the front of many houses is open and only closes at night with a gate. Out of the three categories, residential

Figure 7.3 A residential vendor sitting in front of her house in Hue, selling che (sweet
soup). Photo © Annemarie Hiemstra and Koen van der Kooy.

vendors have the most fixed customers. The data from the surveys and observations also showed that the products of residential vendors are sold at higher
prices than those asked by the two other categories of traders. In Hue where,
as we saw earlier, only a very small share of the vendors holds a business
licence, this group consists only of residential vendors. Finally, the residential
street food sector is exclusively female; the few men involved in street vending
are active as ambulatory or stationary vendors.

Entrepreneurial activities and success

Having identified the street vendors and their business operations, this section will investigate which factors contribute to successful careers in the
street food sector. A Western notion of entrepreneurial success in economic
terms may not fully apply to Vietnamese business owners because of the
unique history and political-economic developments in this country.[29] The

entrepreneurial climate in Vietnam changed drastically in 1986 when the Vietnamese Communist Party introduced *doi moi* (the new market economy), allowing free market reforms without weakening the position of the communist state-party. Before 1986 the Vietnamese government encouraged state-owned enterprises and publicly discouraged enterprising values.[30] The introduction of the new market economy, however, marked the onset of rapid economic growth, averaging 9 per cent from 1993 to 1997 and 8 per cent from 2005 to 2007. It also marked the explicit encouragement by the government of entrepreneurial values, such as taking the initiative to start a business and growth orientation.[31] Because of these recent political and economic changes in Vietnamese society, Vietnamese female entrepreneurs may perceive business success differently from Western entrepreneurs. Fagenson found that American entrepreneurs wanted to be free to achieve and actualize their potential.[32] Vietnamese entrepreneurs, on the other hand, strive for happiness, a sense of accomplishment, a comfortable life, and family and national security.[33]

When assessing business success, we must also take into account that growth opportunities are limited for street food vendors. They either have to be able to move their business on a daily basis (ambulatory and stationary vendors) or they have limited space to expand (residential vendors). The vendors furthermore are restricted in the type and quantity of products they can sell. Ambulatory vendors need to be able to transport their business, so they are bound by restrictions in weight and size, and all vendors have to operate from relatively small selling spaces. As we have seen earlier, most of the business are illegal and this has an impact on the potential for business expansion; in fact, many suffer from police harassment. Even if street vendors pay some fees to the authorities, it is still uncertain whether they are allowed to operate. Finally, the weather also has a major impact on the daily success of a business. For example, in both cities business tends to drop off during the rainy season.

Following earlier work on business performance in micro- and small-scale businesses in non-Western and Western economies, we hypothesize that the strategic actions of street food vendors are related to economic success (in terms of profit and growth).[34] Furthermore, we assume that psychological factors that lead to strategic actions can be used to explain business performance, in addition to (and instead of) socio-demographic factors such as age, educational level, and type of business. Although Western notions of success may not fully apply to non-Western economies, we cannot dismiss economic measures such as profit, capital and growth. These measures can be used to assess entrepreneurial success in terms of establishing an acceptable standard of living and poverty reduction. To investigate the potential for success amongst street vendors, we first tested whether the socio-demographic indicators of age of the vendors, age of the business, working hours per day, and educational level were related to economic success. Gender was not included in this statistical analysis, because success measures were only available for four male vendors. Additionally, we tested whether the type of businesses (ambulatory, stationary or residential) differed in terms of success. Because the businesses studied in Hue and Hanoi differed significantly in terms of many financial characteristics, these differences were controlled for in our analysis (see Table 7.2).

Our results do not show that the age of the vendor and the age of the business are significantly co-related to economic success. Interestingly, the number of working hours in the street food business is negatively related to success.[35] Working more hours does not necessarily lead to an increased business performance in terms of profit and growth. Education is generally seen as a way to accumulate knowledge and skills that are important for professional life. However, contrary to our expectations, education is not related to economic success. Finally, a comparison of success levels in the three business types (ambulatory, stationary and residential) shows no significant difference. It seems that the type of business also has no influence on economic success in the way that the business growth and profit are generated. This analysis of the Vietnamese context confirms that, as has been shown in Zambia, socio-demographic factors provide limited information when trying to explain the economic success of small businesses.[36]

To test the impact of psychological factors on business success in Vietnamese street selling, we differentiated three action strategies which we have identified as planning, opportunistic and reactive strategies. These action strategies are differentiated according to the level of pre-planning by street food vendors and the extent to which they anticipate and actively deal with potential business opportunities. First, the planning strategy is characterized by a vendor who plans ahead and who actively structures the situation. This strategy implies a comprehensive understanding of the work process (i.e. the ability to describe in detail what is required to run a successful street food business), a long timeframe to plan ahead (i.e. thinking about what and where to sell, not just for a few days but also for a number of seasons, up to and sometimes even over a year), a clear knowledge and anticipation of problems (i.e. preventing and dealing with dissatisfaction among customers), and a proactive orientation. This planning strategy may take the form of a fairly comprehensive plan or the form of a critical point strategy.

A vendor applying the critical point strategy starts out with the most difficult and most important issue in the business operation and plans for this one, but does not pre-plan for all other issues. Only after solving the first critical point, she takes further steps – this can also be conceptualized as main-issue-planning. Take the example of a street food vendor who ultimately wants to start a small restaurant. After opening a small food business, this vendor identifies and plans the next steps required to accomplish her goal. First, in order to attract more customers, the vendor invests in decoration and equipment to enhance the appeal of the food and the sales premises. After saving her earnings for a while, she buys and installs a ventilator and TV to attract and retain more customers. Following on from that, she adds more tables and chairs to be able to host even more people. In addition, this vendor puts money aside to be able to pay for unforeseen costs, such as a leaking roof, whilst keeping the business running. These are all signs of a focus on expanding the business with a long-term goal in mind, which requires planning and perseverance. Second, the opportunistic strategy is characterized by looking for opportunities on the ground. This strategy has the advantage of actively recognizing and using opportunities, for instance selling different kinds of products or switching to selling durables instead of food when changes in demand occur. However, the disadvantage of this strategy is the instability of business decision-making, since planning helps to stabilize one's goals. For opportunistic business owners, all too often new opportunities are taken, without continuing with current plans. Thus, continuous learning about one aspect of the business, for example, improving one's services and products, is in constant jeopardy with this strategy. Studies on Africa show that the opportunistic strategy is positively related to success for informal business owners, but negatively for formal business owners. This implies that an opportunistic strategy can be successful in business situations where one can quickly and flexibly change one's approach (for example, selling different products, varying in locations and time) but not in kinds of more formal businesses that have to deal with administrative tasks such as bookkeeping.[37]

Third, the reactive strategy is also a non-planning strategy. In contrast to those using the opportunistic strategy, however, the vendors do not take a proactive stance. This strategy is fully driven by the situation in which the vendor finds herself: she does not plan and is not goal oriented, but is driven by immediate situational demands without influencing them.[38] For instance, a reactive food hawker may consider her income to be too low, or feel discontented about selling on the street all day. However, because she believes that she cannot do much about the situation in which she finds herself, she does not engage in any activities which could help improve her circumstances. We related each of these action strategies to the business success of the street vendors in our sample.

Our research found that the majority (69 per cent) of the street food vendors do not plan and none of them keep written business records. A possible explanation is that this is caused by a selection bias as it is likely that the 'planners' do not stay in the street food sector, but leave to start a small restaurant. At the same time, 70 per cent of the vendors in both Hue and Hanoi have the desire to expand their business. This desire for growth is evenly distributed among different types of businesses as well as among different age and educational levels. However, nearly all vendors say that they do not expect to accomplish this goal because of their situation. This could be related to either the attitude of the local authorities or to financing problems such as a lack of capital available to them. We furthermore found that the desire to expand the business is not related to business success in terms of growth and profit.

As the majority of the vendors do not plan ahead, the strategies of most vendors can be classified as using one of the two non-planning strategies: 35

per cent use a reactive strategy and 31 per cent use an opportunistic strategy. Strikingly, the type of strategy applied by the vendors is not related to the type of business (ambulatory, stationary or residential); nor is it related to age or educational level. As could be anticipated, we found that a reactive strategy is the least successful, but we also rather unexpectedly found that an opportunistic approach does not carry negative effects for street food vendors in Vietnam, despite the lack of planning. This is especially interesting as planning is generally considered the most important individual contributor to entrepreneurial success.[39] This finding may be explained by the limited opportunities for growth in the street food sector, which would enhance the earning potential of those actively searching for business opportunities on a day-to-day basis.

Connections and competitiveness

A psychological characteristic of entrepreneurial orientation is competitiveness, which makes it difficult for new vendors to enter the sector. Porter states that an understanding of the nature of competition is fundamental for small firms to be successful, in terms of growth and profit.[40] As mentioned before, a Western prototype of entrepreneurial success in economic terms may not necessarily apply to Vietnamese street food vendors. This may, as we pointed out earlier, be related to the specific economic history of the country, but it could also be specific to food selling. For instance, Tinker found in a comparative study of street food selling that food pricing was seldom competitive; rows of vendors sell the same food at the same price. To maintain a consistent price as ingredients fluctuate and to keep one's customers, vendors often reduce their own profit margin or alter proportions of ingredients, thus resulting in a lower income for the vendor.[41] Perhaps the political and cultural background of Vietnam lowers competitiveness among vendors even further. The values that stem from socialism and which are endorsed by Vietnamese entrepreneurs, such as happiness, may not be compatible with the notion of competitiveness.

To measure competitiveness amongst the street vendors in our sample, we used the number of competitors mentioned by the vendor as an indicator. Although all vendors acknowledge that there are many other vendors active in the same sector, not every vendor labelled them as competitors. Since competitiveness is generally considered to be low in the street food sector, knowing and naming the number of competitors can be seen as a sign of competitiveness.[42] Our findings confirm earlier conclusions on competitiveness in the street food sector. Sixty per cent of the vendors who participated in the survey claims to have no competitors at all. About 13 per cent claim to have six or more competitors. The rest of the vendors indicate that they have up to five competitors. Only 20 per cent claim that the other vendors form real competition to their business. The rest regard the other vendors as friends and colleagues or state that they do not have any competitors. Figure 7.4 shows

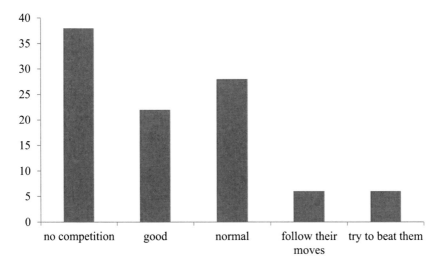

Figure 7.4 Relation towards competitors as reported by vendors (in percentages).

what the relation of the vendors is towards the other vendors operating in the same market. As can be seen in Figure 7.4, only 10 per cent of the vendors interviewed in Hue and Hanoi admit that they are following the movements of competitors or even trying actively to beat them.

Interestingly, we found that the educational level of the vendors is related to the number of competitors that the sellers identify. Vendors who had more years of education mentioned a higher number of competitors than those with a shorter time spent in school. The type of street-vending business also matters: residential vendors name the lowest number of competitors (18 on average), while the numbers mentioned by ambulatory and stationary vendors are much higher (respectively 24 and 30 on average). On the other hand, the age of the vendor and the age of the business are not related to the perceived number of competitors, and hence to competitive aggressiveness.

The extent to which competitive aggressiveness is related to the success of the business is not clear and needs to be addressed. Contrary to economic theory, however, no relation was found between competitiveness and economic success. We observed that many vendors state that large numbers of other vendors are active and that their numbers are increasing. The overall attitude towards other vendors, however, seems to be 'to live and let live'. It is not uncommon to find that a successful vendor draws other vendors to a particular selling spot, simply because that is the place where the customers go. The successful vendor who started out at that spot is usually not too pleased with this effect, but, despite a certain level of discontent, all vendors appear to be tolerated on the same selling spot.

Career perspectives

Finally, we focused on the motives for women entering the street food sector in order to shed light on the issue of whether this sector can be seen as 'entrepreneurial'. Theoretically, women can either be pushed into the sector, for example, because of fear of unemployment or they can be pulled towards it, for example, because it provides the opportunity to combine flexibly work with domestic tasks.[43] The question remains, however, whether selling street food is merely an emergency exit or a deliberate career choice.

The results from the survey show that 70 per cent of female food vendors in Hue and Hanoi previously worked in another occupation. This is distributed fairly equally among the different types of street food business owners (ambulatory, stationary, residential). Many women were wage workers, some used to sell other products on the street, some made traditional hats or clothes, and others were housewives or farmers. Of the women who had been in employment before entering the street food sector, the majority claim that their salary had increased (76 per cent). For 15 per cent, their earnings had remained equal and, for only 9 per cent, the earnings had diminished since they switched jobs. It is interesting to see that the vendors who experienced a drop in income are to be found among the ambulatory and stationary vendors. Of the residential vendors, on the other hand, only one vendor claims that her income had remained at the same level, whereas all other residential vendors had experienced an increase in their earnings.

Many women indeed state that the move into street vending was a deliberate choice because, in the street food business, vendors could make more money than in their previous jobs, and, in addition, they could be their own boss. Also, according to the vendors, the street food sector requires little financial capital to enter as only cooking utensils are needed to start a small business. Some vendors even state that street food has the image of being 'easy money': you do not need much capital to make a good living. Only 12 per cent of the vendors state that they started their street food business because they could not find another job, indicating that for these vendors food hawking is an emergency exit. There are no residential vendors in this group. Interestingly, the entry into the street food sector is not related to the age or educational level of the vendor. Among the 12 per cent that started a business because they could not find other work are vendors with the equivalent of high school education, as well as vendors with primary or no education.

Over 50 per cent of the vendors who started their working life in the street food sector say that they work in the street food sector because it is a family tradition. Usually the vendor has learned the cooking skills from her mother or sister. In Hue we spoke with a residential vendor of *banh beo* (wet rice paper with dried shrimps) who used to sell another type of street food before she married. However, her mother-in-law was skilled in making *banh beo* and therefore the vendor started to sell this product, according to her husband's family tradition. The others who started their working life in street food usually did so because it was easy to enter the market, investment costs were low, and vendors could work close to home. The move into selling street food therefore mostly seems to be a deliberate choice, further illustrated by the fact that only six vendors in the sample state that they want to leave the sector, the majority of whom are hoping to start a small restaurant.

Overall it can be concluded that many of the interviewed vendors are drawn towards the street food sector in both Hue and Hanoi as a deliberate and positive choice. When the vendor starts her career directly in street food it is usually because of a family tradition in which the mother or sister does the same work and teaches the skills to the new vendor. For many people entering the sector also means an increase in income. Although general information on the financial characteristics of informal sector activities is generally lacking due to limited registration, our findings support the idea that street food vendors do not form the poorest population of the Vietnamese economy. This confirms findings earlier put forward by Cling and others which shows that while informal sector workers in Hanoi belong to the poorer segments of society, their earnings are nearly 40 per cent above those working in agriculture.[44]

Concluding remarks

In the Vietnamese cities of Hue and Hanoi, street food selling is a lively economic sector, with a broad variety of products on offer that reflect Vietnamese cuisine. It attracts large numbers of consumers from a great variety of backgrounds, illustrating the importance of street food not only for vendors but also for Vietnamese society more widely. The purpose of this chapter was to study the survival and expansion strategies of female food vendors in Vietnam from a psychological perspective and to shed new light on the importance of the street food sector as a source of work, and therewith poverty reduction for women and their families.

First, this chapter has shown that socio-demographic and macro-level economic factors do not fully explain the successes and failures of informal businesses. We found that businesses in the Vietnamese street food sector generate decent incomes for the women involved and their families. Our findings also confirm the role of the street food sector as a so-called social 'safety valve', playing an important role in the household budgets and family nutrition. However, by assessing the motivations of women for entering and remaining in the sector we also showed that dismissing the sale of street food as marginal because it is hardly formalized and because little socio-economic information on these businesses is available is not justified. For most women, entering the street food sector meant an increase in income. Indeed we found that street vendors were generally better-off than their counterparts working in agriculture. Women were also attracted to street food selling by the prospect of being their own boss. The fact that the move into street selling is a deliberate choice for most and that it generally leads to an increase of income contradicts the notion that street food vending is no more than an emergency exit from poverty or unemployment.

This notion is further strengthened when we acknowledge that preparing and selling food requires craftsmanship. Such skills distinguish food vendors from other street vendors who sell ready-made products bought from a wholesaler, such as sunglasses. Indeed, several vendors in this study take pride in selling tasty, traditional and regional dishes. As with many other crafts, it takes time to acquire skills to prepare these foods and to build a business with returning customers. Street food vendors should therefore not be regarded as people who are simply looking for an emergency exit from poverty.

Second, our assessment of what factors explain entrepreneurial success in the street food businesses of Vietnam shows that these micro-businesses benefit from business owners who actively try to influence their situation, either through a planning or an opportunistic strategy. Vendors applying a reactive strategy in their business ventures were generally the least successful. This is in line with findings on other (Western and non-Western) countries and suggests that, regardless of cultural and economic factors, a lack of goal orientation and proactiveness is bad for business in financial terms. Strikingly, however, we found that opportunistic strategies do not affect street food businesses negatively. Contrary to reactive sellers, opportunistic vendors, while not pre-planning for business operations and development, do attempt to influence actively the success of the business. Another reason for the success of the opportunistic vendors may be that actively searching for business opportunities reduces the frustration caused by the difficulties of selling on the street.

There may also be a cultural explanation for our findings on the effects of different business strategies. Vietnamese society scores low on 'uncertainty avoidance'.[45] This means that Vietnamese people are able to deal with uncertainty fairly easily and overall do not feel the need to control the future. This may explain the preponderance of the opportunistic approach among street food vendors as opposed to a more formalized, planning approach. Finally, we found that Vietnamese food hawkers perceived competition very differently from Western entrepreneurs. Whereas a Western notion of competitiveness suggests that this is important for micro-entrepreneurs, the competitiveness expressed by street food vendors is generally low and not related to business success.

Our findings have a few important implications. The fact that female street food vendors do not belong to the poorest segment of society needs to be acknowledged when considering the facilitation of credit. Credit programmes run by NGOs usually target poverty reduction, but many street food vendors will be exempted from these as they do not live under the poverty line. For financial institutions, on the other hand, the fact that many street food vendors do not run formalized businesses means that they are denied access to credit through their channels. Education and targeted credit programmes may help to overcome this problem. Second, as our findings on entrepreneurial success show that planning and competitiveness relate differently to economic success in comparison with Western economies, it is important to take into account cultural factors, under which local ideas about gender and entrepreneurship develop, when designing training programmes with the aim to stimulate female entrepreneurship in developing countries. Similarly, future research on entrepreneurship in the street food sector needs to focus on the concept of competition and the cultural and economic factors that may influence the experience of competition among vendors. This research also needs to incorporate the effect of competition on the well-being of the business owner and on business success. In conclusion, this study shows that the Vietnamese street food sector is a serious and dynamic economic sector. In the words of the women working in this sector: the street food sector means business and it is here to stay.

Notes

* I wish to thank Jaap Voeten for his helpful comments on an earlier version of this chapter.

1 This is a line from a Vietnamese folksong by Vu Ngac Phan. The original title is *Tuc ngu ca dao dan ca Viet Nam*, as described in Wazir-Jahan Begum Karim, *'Male' and 'Female' in Developing Southeast Asia* (Oxford, 1995), p. 165.

2 Stephen O'Harrow, 'Vietnamese women and Confucianism: Creating spaces from patriarchy', in Karim, *'Male' and 'Female' in Developing Southeast Asia*, pp. 161–180.

3 See, for example, Gracia Clark, *Onions Are My Husband: Survival and Accumulation by West African Market Women* (Chicago, 1994). See also Chapter 9 in this volume.

4 Jaap Voeten, *The Street Food Sector in Hue, Central Vietnam: Baseline Study, Assessment of Possible Interventions* (Amsterdam, 2001), pp. 1–16.

5 Micro- and small-sized enterprises are defined according to their staff headcount and turnover. The definition may differ per country, depending on economic circumstances. In Vietnam, a small enterprise in trade and services is defined as an enterprise which employs fewer than 50 persons and a micro-enterprise is defined as an enterprise which employs fewer than ten persons. T.T. Vo, T.C. Tran, V.D. Bui and D.C. Trinh, 'Small and medium enterprises access to finance in Vietnam', in C. Harvie, S. Oum and D. Narjoko (eds), *Small and Medium Enterprises (SMEs) Access to Finance in Selected East Asian Economies. ERIA Research Project Report 2010–14* (Jakarta, 2011), pp. 151–192.

6 Irene Tinker, *Street Foods: Urban Foods and Employment in Developing Countries* (Oxford, 1997), pp. 147–176.

7 Jean-Pierre Cling, Mireille Razafindrakoto and François Roubaud, *The Informal Economy in Vietnam* (Geneva, 2011), pp. 11–47.

8 I. Tinker, 'Street foods: Traditional microenterprise in a modernizing world', *International Journal of Politics, Culture and Society* 16 (2003), pp. 331–348.

9 D. Smallbone and F. Welter, 'The distinctiveness of entrepreneurship in transition economies', *Small Business Economics* 16 (2001), pp. 249–262.

10 Basudeb Guha-Khasnobis, Ravi Kanbar and Elinor Ostrom, *Linking the Formal and Informal Economy: Concepts and Policies* (Oxford, 2007), pp. 1–19.

11 H. Nguyen and N. Nguyen, 'Examining personal values and entrepreneurial motives of Vietnamese entrepreneurs in the 21st century: Two empirical studies', *African and Asian Studies* 7 (2008), pp. 141–171.

12 International Labor Organisation, *Women's Entrepreneurship Development Capacity Building Guide* (Geneva, 2009), pp. 1–18.

13 R. Hisrich and S. Öztürk, 'Women entrepreneurs in a developing economy', *Journal of Management Development* 18 (1999), pp. 114–125.
14 M. Minniti, 'Female entrepreneurship and economic activity', *European Journal of Development Research* 22 (2010), pp. 294–312.
15 Jaap Voeten, *Criteria to Define Women Entrepreneurs Who Own and Manage Micro and Small Enterprises (WMSE)*, Working Paper 1 of 'Training for Women in Micro and Small Enterprises, phase 2 (TWMSE2) project' (Maastricht, 2002).
16 Jaap Voeten, 'Management development for women entrepreneurs who own and manage small businesses in Vietnam', in Rosemary Hill and Jim Stewart (eds), *Management Development: Perspectives from Research and Practice* (London, 2007).
17 This study builds on two earlier studies: A. Hiemstra, K. van der Kooy and M. Frese, 'Entrepreneurship in the street food sector of Vietnam: Assessment of psychological success and failure factors', *Journal of Small Business Management*, 44 (2006), pp. 474–481, and Nguyen and Nguyen, 'Examining personal values'.
18 M. Frese, S. Krauss, N. Keith, S. Escher, R. Grabarkiewicz, S.T. Luneng, C. Heers, J. Unger and C. Friedrich, 'Business owners' action planning and its relationship to business success in three African countries', *Journal of Applied Psychology* 92 (2007), pp. 1481–1498.
19 See, for example, Jean Pierre Cling, Mireille Razafindrakoto and François Roubaud, *The Informal Economy in Vietnam* (Geneva, 2011). For an exception, see Hoa Van Tran and Jaap Voeten, 'Household food consumption and modernisation: The street foods sectors in Vietnam', paper presented at the International Workshop on 'Socio-economic research as a tool for improving household food security and nutrition', Bogor, July 2001.
20 This is based on the use of these terms in Frese *et al.*, 'Business owners' action planning'.
21 See for instance L. Yap, 'The attraction of cities: A review of the migration literature', *Journal of Development Economics* 4 (1977), pp. 239–264.
22 This accounts for the overall average of approximately nine hours in Table 7.1.
23 This was the case in 2000 when the survey was undertaken and it remains so today.
24 *Statistics Yearbook of the Social Republic of Vietnam* (Hanoi, 1998), pp. 84–85.
25 In both cases, the time to build up these funds was on average six months, either to repay the loan or to save enough money to start the business.
26 J. Rand and N. Torm, 'The informal sector wage gap among Vietnamese micro-firms', *Journal of the Asia Pacific Economy* 17 (2012), pp. 560–577.
27 Hernando de Soto, *The Other Path* (New York, 1989), pp. 131–177.
28 See Chapter 8 in this volume.
29 Nguyen and Nguyen, 'Examining personal values'.
30 Nguyen and Nguyen, 'Examining personal values'.
31 The World Bank, *Vietnam: Laying the Foundation for Sustainable Inclusive Growth* (2010).
32 E. Fagenson, 'Personal value systems of men and women entrepreneurs versus managers', *Journal of Small Business Venturing* 8 (1993), pp. 409–430.
33 Nguyen and Nguyen, 'Examining personal values'.
34 M. Frese, M. Van Gelderen and M. Ombach, 'How to plan as a small-scale business owner: Psychological process characteristics of action strategies and success', *Journal of Small Business Management* 38 (2000), pp. 1–18.
35 A significant Pearson correlation of -0.35, $p < 0.01$.
36 M. Keyser, M. de Kruif and M. Frese, 'The psychological strategy process and socio-demographic variables as predictors of success for micro- and small-scale business owners in Zambia', in Michael Frese (ed.), *Success and Failure of Micro-Business Owners in Africa: A Psychological Approach* (Westport, 2000), pp. 31–53.
37 Based on Frese *et al.*, 'Business owners' action planning'.

38 Hiemstra *et al.*, 'Entrepreneurship in the street-food sector of Vietnam'.

39 This is similar to findings in Zambia, but opposite to some findings among micro-business owners in several other African countries such as Namibia and Zimbabwe, as described in Frese *et al.*, 'Business owners' action planning'.

40 Michael Porter, *Competitive Advantage: Creating and Sustaining Superior Performance* (New York, 1985).

41 Tinker, *Street Foods*, pp. 149–176.

42 The notion that competitiveness is generally low is based on Tinker's comparative study on street foods in seven countries (Tinker, *Street foods*). Campion, on the other hand, observed high levels of competitiveness among female food vendors in Mozambique, in M. Campion, 'Commodities and competition: The economic marginalization of female food vendors in Northern Mozambique', *Women's Studies Quarterly* 38 (2010), pp. 163–181.

43 K. Hughes, 'Pushed or pulled? Women's entry into self-employment and small business ownership', *Gender, Work and Organization* 10 (2003), pp. 433–454.

44 Cling *et al.*, *The Informal Sector in Vietnam*, pp. 11–47.

45 Geert Hofstede, *Cultures Consequences: Comparing Values, Behaviors, Institutions, and Organizations across Nations* (Thousand Oaks, 2001), pp. 145–199.

8 Rethinking street foods

Street food hospitality in contemporary Calcutta*

Manpreet K. Janeja

'Street foods' are not so easy to define. Some of the challenges in defining what can be classified as street foods have been highlighted by Tinker when she asks, for instance, whether to include fresh fruits, chewing foods that are not nutritious and not meant to be swallowed such as betel nut with lime and spices, and 'invisible street foods', that is 'ready-to-eat food that (is) carried through the streets by the preparer rather than the purchaser, for eating at home or to office, and (is) not for sale *on* the street' called *rantangan* (Indonesia) or *tif-fin* boxes (India) (original emphasis).[1] Studies of street hawkers and vendors that focus on the urban 'informal' economy, labour protection policies, street vending regulations, and gender, ethnicity and geographies of urban food distribution tend not to problematize the processual delineations of street foods.[2] In contrast to such studies, this chapter describes what emerge as street foods in hospitality transactions in the city of Calcutta in the Indian state of West Bengal. Through an ethnographic analysis of taut negotiations of what constitute street foods vis-à-vis normal home foods in Bengali Hindu middle-class households, it explores the ways in which current hospitality practices of preparation, consumption, marketing and distribution are reconfiguring formations of the inside/outside. In so doing, it treats street food hospitality as an event for negotiating differences across scale in collaborative forms.

Calcutta: city, foodscape and street food vendors

Calcutta, dating back more than 300 years when three settlements were combined by Job Charnock of the British East India Company, was the capital of India under British colonial rule until 1912. After the partition of India in 1947, Calcutta remained in the Indian Union as the capital of West Bengal – the western part of the divided region of Bengal – while Dhaka became the capital of East Bengal which joined Pakistan as its eastern wing but later gained independence to become the present-day nation-state of Bangladesh. These various political divisions generated large numbers of displaced people across borders, with Calcutta being at the crossroads of constant flows of migrants into and out of the city. In the late 1960s and early 1970s, the decline of Calcutta's jute mills and engineering industries led to the unemployment of thousands of workers, and further reinforced the city's transformation into a 'peripheral city' when compared to the vibrant energies that animated it especially in the early nineteenth century. Many unemployed workers and migrants turned to street vending and hawking to earn a livelihood. However, with economic liberalization reforms set into motion by the Union government in the mid-1990s focusing on urban centres and urban renewal initiatives, the then long-standing Left Front government in power in the state of West Bengal aspired to reshape Calcutta as a 'world-class' city, a paradigm which excluded street vendors and hawkers. It consisted of constructing satellite townships, special economic zones and 'beautification' drives over the years to 're-order' the city, e.g. Operation Sunshine in 1996 to 'cleanse' the streets of vendors 'responsible' for the dirty and disordered city.[3] Periodic cleansing drives and changing forms of regulations to manage the 'hawker problem' have continued over the years, e.g. a recent state government (now headed by the All India Trinamool Congress Coalition) order banning street vendors from heating and cooking food on pavements levied in December 2013.[4] The variegated genealogy of Calcutta's street foods and Bengali food relationships has to be described in the nexus of such flows, circulations, movements and stoppages.

The city foodscape is constituted by regular supplies of fresh foods such as fish, milk, vegetables, fruits and poultry from its hinterland, as well as rice, pulses and cooking oils. This is supplemented by food, raw and cooked, that is gifted by kin relations who come from other regions, districts, towns or villages associated as *desh*.[5] The food travels by bullock carts, boats, buses, trains and sometimes planes from various places at different times of the day. Fresh foods are often sold in 'temporary' 'makeshift' (*kachcha*) road-side and street stalls and open-air bazaars conveniently located near bus terminals, train stations and the banks of the river, to middle-class customers returning home from work and to the poor classes.[6] These street food stalls offer to their customers the advantages of lower prices, quicker transactions since they are on the way home, informal arrangements and purchases on credit, and familiar and trusted interactions.

Within the city, many middle-class neighbourhoods have their own *kachcha* and *pukka* bazaars where fresh foods and groceries are sold, with the *pukka* bazaars often consisting of a large complex of fixed shops made of concrete (in contrast to makeshift stalls) and rows of food vendors who display their wares on a sackcloth or plastic sheet spread out on the floor. Engaging in skilful price negotiations with fishmongers, fruit, vegetable and flower sellers is a part of these bustling bazaar transactions that invite the senses with their myriad sights, sounds, smells, textures and tastes on offer. Prices of fresh foods in particular vary widely depending on the neighbourhoods they are sold in. Compared to the large numbers of street food vendors, there are fewer shops organized on the lines of departmental stores – selling pre-packaged, labelled and frozen meats, fruits and vegetables at fixed prices – like Spencer's, located in swanky high rise shopping malls such as Mani Square or South City Mall and with 'neighbourhood stores' in various parts of the city, or Food Bazaar, a two-storey food hall located on the Eastern Metropolitan Bypass and with branches elsewhere in the city as well. These manicured department stores, characterized by a distinctive seductive aesthetic of 'imagery, illumination, and design, whether of packaging, shop floor arrangement, or storefront display' contrast with the aesthetics of the vendors' display of a small variety of foods on a sackcloth or handcart together with his/her bodily hygiene and mode of dress.[7]

There are peripatetic food sellers waxing lyrical about the virtues and varieties of their wares, sometimes in the form of limericks, as they either walk bearing a basket on their heads or cycle past the houses. Often they have established routes, zigzagging through the lanes and by-lanes of middle and upper class areas into adjacent slums, which they traverse every day at a set hour, so that the fishmonger extolling the freshness of the different fish in his basket proclaims to the inhabitants the hour of the day. There are itinerant specialists who sharpen kitchen implements such as knives and grinding stones (*shil*), and food vendors clanging their ladles against their *koras* (bowl-shaped frying pans with two handles) on the street in front of the house, who compose the temporal calibration of this foodscape too. Such street food vendors are often also found outside/inside the market in the neighbourhood, by the riverside, railway stations, bus-stops, major crossings, under some of the city's major flyovers, outside shopping malls, and in moving trains, trams and buses. Those travelling in cars, taxis, three-wheeled auto-rickshaws, and hand-pulled or bicycle-driven rickshaws, are constantly being entreated to buy anything ranging from peanuts and strawberries to incense sticks and roses at the traffic lights at several major city crossings, especially during rush hour traffic jams. The traffic snarls are partly caused by jaywalking in turn partly accounted for by the pavements crowded with hawkers selling anything ranging from cut fruit slices and *mudi* (puffed rice) to slippers and buckets, street tea stalls, and *machch-bhat* (fish and rice) hotels.

The street food hawkers set up 'temporary' shack-like structures, with small wooden benches, that are not dismantled at night so as to hold on to street space which is a scarce resource in a crowded city such as this. Some even sleep overnight in these structures to reassure themselves that 'their' space will not be 'appropriated' by another vendor. It is not unusual for vendors in these 'makeshift' stalls to make informal arrangements, steeped in strategic calculations, with owners of nearby *pukka* shops or *chowkidars* (watchmen) of state government and municipal buildings to store their glass jars of comestibles, cooking pots and implements in lieu of 'rent'. At times these hawkers run these street enterprises on behalf of the *pukka* shopkeepers who are thereby able to maintain their middle-class 'respectability' by not selling on the street, and are also able to control the use of pavement space outside their *pukka* shops. It is also 'normal' for food vendors to set up 'not-permanent' stalls near public buildings such as the Indian Museum, the Alipore Zoological Gardens, the Victoria Memorial, behind municipal and state government administrative buildings. For instance, a makeshift stall behind Writers' Building, the colonial era building which now houses state government offices, sells the famed sweets of Krishnanagar, the headquarters of the West Bengal district of Nadia, and 100 km north of Calcutta, associated with sweets such as Sarbhaja and Sarpuria that were invented there. The state government officials and employees working in Writers' Building throng this stall during their lunchtime and tea breaks. Hospitals (including the new swanky ones such as Columbia Asia), schools (e.g. Loreto Bowbazar, Heritage), and universities (e.g. the West Bengal National University of Juridical Sciences) are also focal points that gather food hawkers at their gates.

Most itinerant and stationary food hawkers, indeed other street vendors selling non-food wares too, are men in Calcutta, more so than in other Indian cities.[8] The predominant presence of street vendors who are men in Calcutta, and indeed other Indian cities, contrasts with the greater visibility of street vendors who are women in cities in south-east Asia, e.g. Thailand, Philippines, Cambodia and Vietnam.[9] Women in Calcutta tend to take up mobile rather than stationary vending, since they are harassed by the police and municipal officials, and by vendors who are men who 'appropriate' almost all the pavement spots because 'fixity' brings forth a higher turnover of customers.[10] However, most of the foods, sold by hawkers who are men, require labour-intensive modes of cooking and are prepared by women, like in Bengali middle-class households where most cooks employed are women. The women who prepare the foods vended by men are either non-family members who are employed to do so, or wives, daughters, mothers and sisters, who provide unpaid labour, with food vending thereby becoming a family enterprise.[11] Around 60 per cent of the hawkers on the streets of Calcutta claim to be Forward Caste Hindus, with the rest mostly claiming other Other Backward Class status, and less than 10 per cent Scheduled Caste status, which has significant implications especially for food transactions entangled in complex networks of class, caste, religious, ethnic and regional forms of differentiation.[12]

Worship, cleanliness and street foods

Almost all vendors perform some *puja* (worship) rituals and oblations twice a day.[13] Before they start their hawking in the morning, they clean their work space of dirt: they dust their pushcart, sweep the stall and pavement area around it, or if that is not possible sprinkle drops of water so that the dust particles do not fly. They then burn incense sticks and stick them into a boiled potato or a heap of peanuts, for example, garland photographs of deities, images sometimes painted on the wooden lid of the pushcart (Plate 11), or the machine itself (e.g. the manually operated sugarcane juicer), and touch either the right hand or both palms enfolded together to their forehead in a gesture of reverence and thanksgiving to the heavenly gods. Some of them pay Oriya Brahmins a monthly salary to come to their stands to sprinkle drops of the sacred waters of the river Ganga from a sparkling brass receptacle (*kamandala*) and give them a sacred flower and a *bel pata* (leaf of the wood apple tree used in rituals of worship performed for the mother goddess Durga). Similar rituals of auspiciousness are performed at dusk, at the hour of conjunction of light and darkness, when the candles are lit or the electric lights, drawing electricity illegally from overhead wires (see Figure 8.1) or from a collectively operated generator, are switched on. This recalls the *puja* ritual, especially at nightfall, of lighting the auspicious lamp, performed by women in Brahmin households described by Kaviraj and discussed later on in the chapter.[14]

These rituals of cleanliness and piety offer a striking contrast to the sometimes adjacent open drains and small heaps of rubbish (see Figure 8.2) generated by the collective sweeping of 'designated' pavement spots by the street vendors, and of the shop interiors and the shop front areas by the owners of *pukka* shops. This is joined by rubbish bins – normally old rusty tin containers now emptied of their former contents – with their distinctive olfactory and visual display of food waste, wooden spoons (used for some street foods), biodegradable cones or bowls made of *shaal pata* (leaves of the sal or *shorea robusta* tree held together by toothpicks), and old newspaper sheet cones in which the food is served. Given that often there are no communal taps nearby, water has to be carried and stored in suspect containers. This is the case with both potable water, and water for washing hands. Even though some street food vendors now offer paper napkins as well, one continues to observe a frequent washing of hands, before and after eating, which together with the washing of hands before preparing and serving food, constitutes an important element of classical Hindu cosmological understandings of ritual purity and cleanliness.

The street food vendors of Calcutta offer a rich and immensely variegated repertoire of foods, unrivalled at least by those of any other Indian city: *phuchka* (tamarind water and spicy potato-filled balloons made of flour), *aloo kabli* (spicy mix of boiled potatoes and whole yellow peas), *shingara* (triangular fried pastries containing spiced mashed potatoes, and often cauliflowers and peas in the winter), *jhal muri* (puffed rice mixed with chopped green chillies, various spices, tamarind and lemon juice, boiled potatoes, and red onions), *telebhaja* [*peyaji* (deep-fried onions in a gram flour batter), *phuluri* (deep-fried balls of spiced chickpea batter), *potoler pata bhaja* (wax gourd leaves deep-fried in a gram flour batter), *beguni* (deep-fried aubergines in a gram flour batter)], and *ghoogni chaat* (dried yellow peas cooked with potatoes, ginger and other spices, and garnished with chopped coconut, green chillies, red onions, and tamarind/lemon juice). Joining their ranks are the foods which are 'not-Bengali' or 'not-purely Bengali': the cutlets and 'chops' (croquettes),[15] rolls (omelettes or spicy kebabs, mixed with sliced onions, lemon juice, chopped green chillies, and rolled into a *paratha* or fried bread, wrapped in a piece of paper),[16] *chowmein* (a fried greasy spicy 'Bengali-ized' version of Chinese noodles), *momos* (Tibetan and Nepalese vegetable and meat dumplings), stews (chicken, lamb, vegetable), *bhel puri* (puffed rice mixed with red onions, boiled potatoes, spices, fresh

Figure 8.1 Overhead wires from which electricity is drawn illegally, hanging above street food (*bhel puri* and *phuchka*) vendors and their vending carts. Photo © Manpreet K. Janeja.

coriander leaves, a tangy tamarind sauce, and *sev* (small thin noodle-like crispy curls made from chickpea flour)), and Bombay *vada pao* (potato patty wedged inside a bun slit in the middle), and newer additions such as 'Chinese *samosas*' (the older *shingara* or triangular fried pastries described above filled with Chinese noodles instead of the usual spiced mashed potatoes and vegetables). Many of these street foods are tailored to the preferences and predilections of their customers: '*ar ektu shukno morich dao*',[17] '*aar ektu tok dao*',[18] '*koda korey bhajben*',[19] constitute an oft-heard chorus of requests and instructions from groups of adolescents, young couples, women and men, oblivious to the snarling traffic, the smoke and dust, and the jostling crowds passing by. Increasingly, though, there are street food vendors offering 'home delivery' and 'takeaway' services, including hot food in aluminium foil containers (Plate 12), or wheeling their mobile pushcarts laden with foods to the doorstep of the inward-turning middle-class houses. There are also the food vendors near the 'local pubs' (*bhati khana*), who recognize the regular pub clientele – predominantly men, including food vendors, with some *basti* women (women from the slums) – and serve them highly charged foods to which chillies and other spices have been added in greater proportions. They prepare these foods, labelled as '*moder thek*' (the

Figure 8.2 A heap of rubbish behind a street food stall selling rolls. Photo © Manpreet
K. Janeja.

alcoholic's support), in this manner because the regular consumption of large
quantities of alcohol and 'country liquor' by these clients has desensitized their
taste buds.[20] These food vendors come to anticipate the tastes of their of regular
clientele, and like others also selling perishable foods, come to acquire over time
the skill of thrift, of approximating with considerable accuracy the number of
'regulars' and the 'correct' quantities of food to be prepared fresh daily, which
would otherwise spoil due to the lack of refrigeration, and therefore be wasted.

In addition to these genres of street foods sold by hawkers, there are the
aforementioned fruit (whole and sliced) and fruit juice (sugarcane, orange,
lime, lemon, coconut) and the *kulfi* (indigenous ice cream) sellers. Adding further to the repertoire of foods sold by street vendors, are those offered in the
'*bhat-machch* (rice-fish) hotels' (see Figure 8.3) – shack-like structures with
wooden benches that serve rice, fish (*machcher jhol*), *aloor dom* (potato curry),
luchi (small deep-fried breads), *shobji* (vegetables) and the aforementioned
ghoogni (dried yellow peas cooked with potatoes and spices). These food offerings of the *bhat-machch* hotels are intrinsic components of normal 'Bengali
home food' (*Bangali ghoroa khabar*) rather than 'street foods', and yet they
are served and consumed on the streets. They are sometimes even prepared
on the streets though many of these hotels serve food that has already been

Figure 8.3 A *bhat-machch* (rice-fish) roadside hotel. Photo © Manpreet K. Janeja.

cooked at home by their wives or daughters, as described before, thereby rely-ing on female labour. They cater to 'office-goers', predominantly men, in the 'office *padas*' (neighbourhoods where offices are concentrated) like Decker's Lane/James Hickey Sarani, and relatives of hospital patients who have trav-elled from towns and villages near Calcutta. Middle-class women sitting in *bhat-machch* hotels rubbing shoulders with men from various classes are not a common sight. Rickety kiosks selling *paan* (a preparation of betel leaf with areca nuts and various other ingredients such as slaked lime paste, fennel and anise seeds), cigarettes and *bidis* (thin Indian cigarettes with tobacco flakes) are similarly gendered – frequented mostly by men, though the kiosk vendors themselves might occasionally be women.

Makeshift stall or tea-shops (*chayer dokan*) on the street pavements where tea is often served with 'local teacakes' and 'Britannia English Mairi' arrow-root biscuits, and sometimes coffee too, also have groups of men (rather than women) seated together on benches or standing around, engaged in *adda* ('idle-talk') or merely watching passers-by. Such tea-shops are frequently erected on pavements against street walls with prominent displays of graf-fiti or cinema posters. The shop assistants, usually boys aged six upwards, often carry the kettle around high-rise office buildings at a predetermined hour, for the mid-morning and mid-afternoon tea breaks. Such tea-shops are especially crowded in the evenings as most people prepare to go home after a day's work, when the inviting sights, sounds, smells, tastes and textures of the rich and enchanting array of street foods also lure passers-by. The street food vendors residing on pavements, commuting from the suburbs and nearby villages, or living in slums are, like the cooks (*rannar lok*) who go to cook every day in Bengali middle-class households, significant 'silent service providers' or invisible veiled presences that effectuate the foodscape in middle-class neighbourhoods in the city, a theme to which I return later.

Networks of regulations and conventions: street food and 'public/private'

The food vendors on the streets of Calcutta described above have not been legal entities. The city has had laws that define street vending as an illegal activity, and hawking a cognizable and non-bailable offence in order to prevent 'encroachment' of public places.[21] The various regulations that could be used to control street foods and their vendors include:

> the Indian Penal Code regulating public nuisance, negligent or malignant acts leading to dangers of life, fouling of water and adulteration of food and beverages. This regulation is executed by the enforcement branch of the police, if necessary, with the help of the forensic laboratory. The second is the Calcutta Municipal Act (1980, mentioned above) regulating urban environmental and sanitary conditions, the sale of food and drink and the authorization for operating under the Prevention of Food Adulteration Act (1954). The municipal authorities deal with these matters with the General Calcutta Police assisting and supporting the municipal council. The third regulation is the Prevention of Food Adulteration Act and Rules, which is a very comprehensive set of regulations providing details of procedures for food inspectors and for food analysis by a *public agent*. It is the responsibility of the food or health authority designated under the act. The Calcutta Municipal Corporation Health Officer is the designated local health authority for Calcutta.[22]

More recently, with the Indian Parliament enacting the Street Vendors Act 2014 – with a view to providing a uniform national legal framework to regulate street vendors in public spaces as well as protecting their livelihood and rights – the present West Bengal government is in the process of delineating new strategies to implement various provisions of the Act, though the Bill itself has been criticized for legal ambiguities and other drawbacks.[23] A policy proposal that seeks to formalize hawking by registering street vendors and hawkers, issuing vending certificates, identity cards and other benefits such as insurance and pension, and setting up a 'vending committee' to oversee the process of registration, collection of registration fees and fines for violating norms governing designated vending zones is in the works.[24]

Despite all this, street food hawkers have been, and continue to be, ubiquitous in Calcutta.[25] The historical genealogy of this phenomenon can be traced back to the fraught negotiations of the nineteenth-century Bengali middle classes or *bhadralok* (respectable people) and the poor classes with the colonial laws, governing conventions and constant interventions of the British colonial administration, seeking to produce a sanitized urban order and discipline everyday conduct in the public sphere.[26] As Kaviraj reminds us, the idea of the public is historically specific, referring to 'a particular configuration of commonness that emerged in the capitalist democratic West in the course of the eighteenth century (with) … associations … like universal access and *öffentlichkeit* (openness), which might not be expected to exist universally in ideas of common space'.[27] Entangled in networks of European Enlightenment, bourgeois publicity, with its characteristic features of proper authorization, a recognizable source, impersonality, legality, state sanction, clear ascription of individual responsibility and distinction from 'the private' as encapsulated by bourgeois domesticity resting on a companionate yet paradoxically contractual marriage, differed from indigenous Bengali perceptions of common responsibility, obligation, action and domesticity. The public/private distinction was placed on a pre-existing conventional grid in Bengal, *gharey/bairey*, which Kaviraj points out, translates as inside the house/outside (as opposed to literally the world).[28] The Bengali distinction *gharey/bairey* is 'closely linked to *apan/par* (or *apna/paraya* in Hindi) (mine/not-mine or self/not-self)'. Thus, particular configurations of the 'inside' and the 'outside' emerged from the combined mapping of these pairs that were neither autonomous nor in a dialectical relation; each becomes 'the starting point for the form which the other takes'.[29]

On the one hand, the Bengali middle-class English-educated elites were strongly drawn to the European model of the public sphere in that it offered newer possibilities of generating forms of personhood free from the narrow confines of caste restrictions. Yet, at the same time, they were not inclined to readily accept the bourgeois practices of companionate marriage and the nuclear family that contradicted indigenous forms of domesticity hinging on the practices of the joint-family with the ideal housewife as a 'good cook/mistress' as its lynchpin, and a paternalistic, supervised, comfortable home-inside for women that constituted a realm of stable, predictable and secure relationships in contradistinction to the volatile, dangerous, disorderly outside.[30] Thus, the outside became ambiguous: turgid with the perpetual threat of uncertainty and unpredictability yet holding out the promise of possibilities of freedom. The Bengali middle-class city, separated from the centre where the colonial offices and European quarters were concentrated, and from the slums of the poor that emerged both outside it and in its interstices, contained the inward-turning affluent private houses that stood in a relation of reciprocity to the immaculately maintained 'public' parks they surrounded, in that the latter were used by the middle classes as virtual extensions of their *pada* (neighbourhood), with the poor being allowed restricted access as child minders, municipal gardeners and sellers of food snacks. That is, the Bengali middle-class *pada* exercised quasi-proprietary rights over the 'internal public sphere' as distinguished from the ' "outer", more universalistic one, which concerned everybody, (where) nothing could be done without the explicit sanction or consultation of the colonial administration'.[31]

On the other hand, the 'deeply traditional' Brahmin and upper-caste groups, who rejected English education, and the poor, who could not access such education given their paucity of financial resources, did not perceive European forms of the *civic* in the same way as the English-educated Bengali middle-class elites. The startling contrast, for instance, between the spotless interiors of Brahmin households and the heaps of household garbage, collected from the constant house-cleaning performed with care and as a quasi-religious duty by their household members (mostly women),[32] can be traced back to the difference between Brahmanical cosmological understandings of cleanliness and *purity* and European notions of *hygiene*. House-cleaning activities, as part of housekeeping, are indexical of, as Chakrabarty points out, 'the auspicious qualities of the mistress of the household, her Lakshmi (the goddess of well-being)-like nature that protects the lineage into which she has married … Auspicious acts protect the habitat, the inside, from undue exposure to the malevolence of the outside. They are … cultural performance(s) through which this everyday "inside" is both produced and enclosed', with household rubbish emerging as a marker of the boundary of this enclosure.[33] As Kaviraj succinctly describes further:

> When the garbage is dumped, it is not placed at a point where it cannot casually affect the realm of the household and its hygienic well-being. It is thrown over a conceptual boundary. The street was the outside, the space for which one did not have responsibility, or which was not one's own, and it therefore lacked any association with obligation, because it did not symbolize any significant principle, did not express any values.[34]

Furthermore, with the rise of nationalist mass politics which included vast numbers of the poor classes, the influx of destitute people displaced by Partition in 1947 (the 'refugee problem') who built shacks and slums, and the rise of hawkers since the mid-1960s unable to afford *pukka* shops, the city's streets, public parks and railway stations came to acquire a 'soiled' and 'filthy' character. For the poor, hawking on the streets by day, and sleeping on the pavements by night, 'public' came to mean that which is not-private property, not owned by individual property owners with exclusive rights. This perception also became intertwined with conventional notions of *bairey* or the outside as not one's own: it is precisely because there is no indigenous conception of the civic as equated with the public, 'the idea of publicity in its altered Bengali version can mean merely empty, valueless negative of the private. It comprizes assets that are owned by some general institution like the government or the city municipality', and in which, as poor people, they have a quasi-claim to settle.[35] Thus, in contemporary Calcutta the street as *pablik* co-exists uneasily with the idea of a 'civic space with norms and rules of use of its own',[36] being enforced by the city's municipal authorities who seek to control the food hawkers squatting in *public* places and streets and threatening public health, hygiene and order.[37]

Normal Bengali home food (*ghoroa khabar*)[38]

Many middle-class Bengali households in Calcutta employ part-time cooks (*rannar lok*): women from poor migrant households, who speak some Bengali dialect, dress mostly in saris, were born on either side of the West Bengal-Bangladesh border, and also "know how to cook Bengali food" (*Bangali khabar randhtey janey*). Furthermore, the cook's *desh* is often taken into consideration as well, with an *East Bengali* Hindu family in Calcutta aspiring to employ an *East Bengali* Hindu cook whose *desh* is, or was, "originally" East Bengal (now Bangladesh). However, many families are now also willing to employ the services of a West Bengali Hindu cook, insofar she has the perceived capacity or skill to cook "food like ours" (*aamader moton ranna*). Symmetrically different preferences often characterise the deployment of such part-time cooks in West Bengali Hindu households as well.

> '*Desh* can be distinguished as narrowly or broadly as the transactions demand…it is relational and fluid. It could refer to the country…region… district or *zillah*, sub-district, town or village. It is one's "native birthplace", one's "local homeland", the *place* whose land, soil, air, water, trees, food, people, and things (*jinish*) are one's own (*nijer*)…to which one belongs, and which belong to one'.[39]

One *cares* for one's *desh*, and one's *desh cares* for one. Thus, what is illuminated is that people and *desh* as place engage with each other, enmeshed in spatio-temporal-affective 'networks'.[40]

It is food that gathers for the recipient in most immediate, intimate and continuous ways the forms of relating and relatedness that are assembled as *desh* in everyday life. I develop the term 'foodscape' further in an attempt to describe the capacity of food, its depth, reach and scale, to bring forth a sense of place as a particular configuration of relations or form of engagement, *desh*. *Desh* as foodscape then is an 'event'. It captures the 'interanimation' of food, and other thing-, person-, and place-actants.[41] It emerges as a hybrid entity that is a 'condensed network' of multiple and spatio-temporally distributed humans and non-humans.[42] The 'good cook' is one who can emulate for the patron in a continuous manner (everyday) the foodscape that is normal for the latter: the way food is normally cooked in *desh* or the ways in which food normally deploys and redeploys the various actants that are associated as *desh*. In other words, the good cook is one who has the 'hand' or unceasing (everyday) capacity to prepare food which is efficacious in recalling, retaining, and projecting the modes of relating with all kinds of others which is perceived as *desh*. On the other hand, the dis-capacity of the cook to uninterruptedly bring forth the normal foodscape for the patron household – such dis-capacity being perceived as "not-normality" – can reveal itself in myriad ways that help to evoke what normality is for such households. *Desh* as foodscape then becomes a trope for perceiving normality.

The household of the Rays

In one such Bengali middle-class Hindu household (the Ray household) in south Calcutta, the doorbell rings, and Shayanti's cook, Nupur, enters the house. Nupur enters the kitchen after washing her hands and feet in the bathroom, and seeing the fish on the worktop, asks her mistress: '*Aajkey machch ki bhabey ranna korbo?*'.[43] Shayanti:

> *Jey bhabey roj koro! Beshi jhaal diyo na! Aar shono! Aajkey bikeley Kamala aar tar bor ashbey, tai jal khabar korey ditey hobey. Aami school thekey pherar pothey, padaye konaye Tapan dar dokan thekey goda machcher chop niye aashbo, tumi bikeley gorom gorom bhejey diyo. Beshi tel diyo na kintu, thik aandaj korey diyo. Aami salad korey nobo.*
>
> [The way you cook it *every day*. Don't add too much chilli! And listen! This evening Kamala and her husband will come, so you will need to prepare the snacks (*jal khabar* = lit. food that is partaken with water (and tea)). On the way back from school, I will get *goda* (lit. that which has been given form or shape to) 'fish chops' from Tapan *da*'s shop at the (street) corner in the neighbourhood, you (that is, with your hand) will fry them hot (that is, fresh so that they can be served hot) in the evening.[44] Don't give (use) too much oil, use the oil in correct approximation (that is, use oil thriftily). I will make the salad.]

Nupur drags the *shil bata* (grinding stone and pestle) from its normal designated spot, and sitting on her haunches, begins to grind the spices laid out for the fish for the lunchtime meal.

Measuring normality

Normally, the cook grinds the spices and chops ingredients with the *bonti* while sitting on her haunches, while the cooking of the food on the gas stove necessitates standing. During the process of cooking, the clattering and banging of steel and aluminium utensils *above* a certain 'normal' level – delineated as such by the mistress – is a measure of the time invested by the cook. It also embodies the cook's discontentment, which annoys the mistress and embarrasses her insofar as it indexes to her middle-class neighbours that she is not a 'good mistress' who has the skill to run her house efficiently and keep her employee satisfied. On the other hand, a lack of noise, or noise which is below the 'normal' level, elicits suspicions and assumptions of theft. Thus the sounds engendered by the preparation of everyday normal food enmesh both the cook and the mistress in a web of surveillance. Not-normality then emerges as the dis-capacity of both the cook and the mistress to bring forth in a smooth and unceasing manner the everyday foodscape perceived as normal.

Other measures of normality include exercising the requisite culinary skills in the process of cooking normal food which embody knowledge of diffuse sensuous calibrations such as 'when (the food) will become somewhat crispy to touch', 'when (you) will see it has become slightly reddish'. Given the diffuse nature of these sensual measures, as indexed by words such as 'somewhat', 'reddish', the capacity to exercise the skill of approximation is significant. Furthermore, memory is critical to effective approximation: the proficient cook with a 'good hand' is one who has the aptitude to retain and project the ways of configuring various elements that constitute normal food, and the capacity to approximate, emulate or project such relations uninterruptedly on an everyday basis. 'Like everyday', then, emerges as a continuous process of emulation that evokes normality as a 'temporally extended field'.[45] The dis-capacity to do so is not-normality. For instance, in the Ray household described above Shayanti reminds Nupur to exercise restraint in her use of chillies (and oil). Not-normality here entails the cook's dis-capacity to excise her class characteristics, since the poor are perceived as those who normally eat very hot food. As Mukhopadhyay points out, in the new Bengali *haute cuisine* which emerged in the late nineteenth century, the extremes in the spectrum of Bengali taste hierarchy – chilli (and tamarind) – were considered taboo, as unfit for polite cuisine, and increasingly came to be recognized as markers of the 'subaltern';[46] hence 'the 'civilizing' project of Bengali nationalism tried to eliminate these extreme tastes perceived as excess. Normal Bengali home food in respectable middle-class households aspires to be faithful to this historical genealogy.

The work of food in eliciting normality, then, is turgid with apprehension, and taut with ambiguity, distrust and mistrust. Normality emerges as a tenuous negotiation with not-normality in everyday food transactions in middle-class Bengali Hindu households in contemporary Calcutta.

Normal everyday food as emulation

In the description rendered above home food (*ghoroa* khabar) gathers various spatio-temporally distributed actants – persons, things, and places – to create *desh* as normal foodscape in the everyday lives of middle-class Bengalis.[47] It performs the work of translating human intentions – for instance preparing and eating normal Bengali everyday food – into efficacious action. In the process of mobilising these human and non-human actants into collective associations or attachments called networks in everyday interactions food acquires agency, delineated as the relational capacities to act and be acted upon simultaneously.[48] Agency thus emerges as collective and mixed in character. There are no pure forms, only mixtures that embrace both humans and non-humans, as also depicted by Latour, and other proponents of Actor Network Theory (ANT).[49] This act of mobilising multiple actants that food performs in translating human intentions is continuous and precarious. It is also collaborative, understood as both (a) working jointly on an activity; (b) cooperating traitorously with an enemy.[50] This is because these networks are fragile and dynamic – humans and non-humans have the capacity to betray - and the act of translation is *not faithful* always, and can have unanticipated effects. However, the unexpected character of networks is reined in by simultaneous historical acts of 'purification' in the very process of translation, purification into relatively stabilised forms: Nature/Society, Object/Subject, Normal/Not-Normal.[51] Discerning specific forms of dispersed agency and configurations of distributed actants are thus events.

Everyday home food (*ghoroa khabar*) then is an event which displays the agency that food exercises through the claims it makes on people, and the manner in which it gathers those around itself in all kinds of roles inside and outside the house. For instance, everyday food makes the utensils within the house and the cook from outside the house, with the mistress as manager, collaborate together. Food, therefore, conducts the continuous fragile balance between this inwardness and outwardness. In the relentless process of mediating this tenuous balance, it emerges as a specific mixed entity containing various measures of coherence of normality and not-normality: temporal-spatial-corporeal-moral-affective. That is, home food as an event effectuates normality as a particular form of relations between distributed actants engaged in taut and ambiguous negotiations with not-normality. Normality is elicited through an ongoing mimetic process – *everyday* – which indexes a degree of cognized or intentional emulation of taken-for-granted normality. Given the critical role of memory, approximation, retention and projection, in this process, however, there are modifications. These modifications combine with changes that occur through unexpected acts of betrayal committed by the everyday normal foodscape: contentions of its capacity for not-normality. The phrase "like everyday" then illuminates a relentless process of emulation that yearns to be everyday but can *never* exactly be everyday. It is this unfinished quality or process of continuous becoming that also gives normality its taken-for-granted quality. Everyday food thus emerges as a *collaborative* relational and transformational field which is evoked in its very performance. The fragile and animated networks of retentions, projections, and collaborations that '"cohere" as normality acquire a cognized objectified and emplaced form in *desh* as foodscape', and the very practices of everyday home food (*ghoroa khabar*), still perceived as pivotal to Bengali middle-class domesticity.[52]

Street food hospitality: mediating ambiguities

Now, normal Bengali hospitable food served to guests in a Bengali middle-class household would be cooked in the same manner as everyday home food (*ghoroa khabar*) as described above. However, in the Ray household described above, the preparation of hospitable food violates various measures of normality. The fish chops that Shayanti instructs her cook to fry 'fresh' and serve 'hot' when her guests arrive for evening tea and snacks, have already been prepared in Tapan *da*'s shop around the corner in the *pada* (neighbourhood) where she intends to buy them.53 The time and labour-intensive chops have been 'formed' (*goda*) in the shop: the de-boned mashed and spiced fish fillet, in an envelope of mashed potatoes and (sometimes) whipped egg, has been rolled in bread or biscuit crumbs,54 given shape (oval or spherical) using the pressure of finger tips, and dried by being left uncovered (that is, by the air circulating around). The chops are formed outside the house: on the street, with its associations of disorder, filth and lurking dangers of all kinds, rather than in the orderly, clean and safe kitchen inside the middle-class house. The cleanliness of the cooking area in the shop on the street where the chops are formed, of the cooking implements, utensils and other things, and the origins and attributes of the food ingredients used, including oil and water, are not known. Nor are the cook, his/her *desh* and caste origins, and his/her fingertips (his/her 'hand') and touch known,55 with this anonymity of touch feeding into *chunchibiou* or the phobia of pollution through touch and eating.56

Shayanti seeks to navigate the degree of ambiguity of these persons, places and things by intending to purchase the formed (*goda*) chops from Tapan *da*'s shop around the corner in the neighbourhood. The familiarity and intimacy generated by the use of the kinship term *da* (short for '*dada*' or elder brother), is in this case also reinforced by Tapan *da*'s shop being located at the familiar street corner near the house, which facilitates frequenting it, and offers the possibility of building up trusting relationships with their concomitant negotiations of risks.57 Shayanti also attempts to navigate the taut ambiguities by instructing her cook to fry the already-formed chops, with her own hand, so that it mediates the anonymous touch of unknown fingers. Shayanti carefully instructs her cook to fry the chops, formed outside the house, in the oil in the kitchen inside the house in 'correct approximation' (that is, thriftily) and serve them 'fresh' and 'hot', with the warmth and freshness of the (trusted) oil perhaps also intended to fill the gap of the missing affective dimensions of *desh* as normal foodscape.58 She also intends to prepare the salad to be served with the chops herself. Shayanti's performance here as a normal West Bengali 'good hostess', and therefore, her capacity to gather various dispersed persons, places and things normally, entails a creative tempering of not-normality or the betrayal of various indices of normal hospitality through anxious and ambiguous negotiations of the 'inside' and 'outside' while maintaining her middle-class status.

On the other hand, what of the street food vendor, Tapan *da*, who sells the formed (*goda*) fish chops? He, like many other street food hawkers, has the cleanliness of the utensils, the quality of the foods, his bodily hygiene, and mode of dress (which in conjunction with his name mark him off as a Bengali Hindu) on display. He exercises the skills of 'correct approximation' and thrift, and performs rituals of cleanliness and piety every day in the morning before he starts work and at dusk, e.g. sweeping the workspace of dust and dirt, lighting candles/lamps and garlanding photographs of deities: everyday performances and skills – continually eliciting a ritually enclosed inside – that are gendered as female and entrenched in historical understandings of the ideal Bengali housewife described earlier. The enactment of these female skills and the quasi-religious performances by vendors who are predominantly men on the streets of Calcutta, together with their activities of preparing, serving and selling food, seeks to emulate and appropriate the form of interiority evoked as normal domesticity in Bengali middle-class houses (*gharey* – inside the house which is one's own (*apan*) as described earlier). It is through such performances of enclosure eliciting normal Bengali domesticity that the food vendors who are men appropriate, as 'their own', street and pavement spots, part of the 'outside' (*bairey*) that is 'not one's own'. These quasi-proprietary rights are forever 'temporary', indexed by the 'makeshift'/'not-permanent' character of their 'shops' sitting uneasily on 'public' streets regulated by the civic authorities. But it is these very precarious spatio-temporal engagements of the food vendors with public streets that also enable the respectable middle classes to continue to use public space as virtual extensions of their private neighbourhoods and inward-turning flats and houses with kitchens where the work of 'normal' Bengali everyday and hospitable food continues. Thus the public streets – that can be rubbished as *bairey* (not one's own) – make possible continued contextual engagements with values of middle-class domesticity by offering foods that lend themselves to being prepared and sold on them. Bengali street food hospitality in contemporary Calcutta, entangled in colonial and post-colonial networks, then emerges as an event: bringing forth emergent configurations of interiority and exteriority that negotiate differences across scale in collaborative forms.

Notes

* This chapter draws on fieldwork conducted in Calcutta during periods from December 2009 to January 2013. I would like to acknowledge with gratitude the many culinary excursions and engaging discussions I have had with the interlocutors of my study. This chapter has also been enriched by succinct comments from Prasanta Ray at Presidency University, Calcutta, and the editors of this volume, Melissa Calaresu and Danielle van den Heuvel. It has further benefited from the discussions at the 'Food Hawkers: Selling in the Street from Antiquity to the Present' Conference (22–23 April 2010, CRASSH University of Cambridge); the Centre for India and South Asia Seminar (15 January 2014, University of California Los Angeles); and the 'Focus Asia: Foods in Asia' Symposium (15–16 April 2014, Lund University).

1 I. Tinker, *Street Foods: Urban Food and Employment in Developing Countries* (Oxford, 1997), pp. 15–16. The Food and Agricultural Organization (FAO), on

the other hand, defines street foods as 'ready-to-eat foods and beverages that are prepared and/sold by itinerant or stationary vendors, especially on the streets and in other public spaces ... For many people with limited means, street foods are often the least expensive and the most accessible way of obtaining a nutritionally balanced meal outside the home, provided the consumer is informed and capable of choosing an appropriate combination of foods.' FAO, *Good Hygienic Practices in the Preparation and Sale of Street Food in Africa: Tools for Training* (Rome, 2009).

2 S. Bhowmik, *Hawkers and the Urban Informal Sector: A Study of Street Vending in Seven Cities* (Patna, 2000); S. Bhowmik, 'Street Vendors in Asia: A Review', *Economic and Political Weekly* 28 (May 2005), pp. 2256–2264; S. Bhowmik, *Street Vendors in the Global Urban Economy* (New Delhi, 2010); J. Cross and A. Morales (eds), *Street Entrepreneurs: People, Place and Politics in Local and Global Perspective* (London, 2007); S. Lloyd-Evans and R.B. Potter (eds), *Gender, Ethnicity and the Informal Sector in Trinidad* (Aldershot, 2002).

3 As Rajagopal mentions, '(t)he drive was allegedly launched to make the city look attractive for foreign investment on the eve of the visit of the then British PM John Major'. A. Rajagopal, 'The Violence of Commodity Aesthetics: Hawkers, Demolition Raids, and a New Regime of Consumption', *Social Text 68* 19(3) (2001), p. 105.

4 'Kolkata Street Food Vendors Face Govt. Heat', *Indian Express*, 17 December 2013, http://archive.indianexpress.com/news/kolkata-street-food-vendors-face-govt-hcat/1208580/, accessed on 17 October 2014.

5 Literally one's 'native birthplace', one's 'local homeland', and the spatio-temporal and affective attachments, amongst others associated with it, to which I return later. Also see K. Gardener, *Global Migrants, Local Lives: Travel and Transformation in Rural Bangladesh* (Oxford, 1995).

6 The poor classes (*daridra jati or garib lok*) include the part-time cooks (*rannar lok*) and domestic helps, roadside *bhat-machch* (rice-fish) hoteliers, tea stall operators, vegetable and fishmongers, and other street food vendors described later, living in slums, as well as the paper/rag pickers, casual and daily labour, and beggars who are homeless and destitute street dwellers. The poor classes thus include a range of multiple elements, and other (than place of residence) perceived differences that mark them off from the middle and upper classes include education, wealth, food, dress, verbal violence and speech (often dialect too), general demeanour (*aacharan*) and 'lack of *bhadrata*' (the perceived quality of cultivatedness or gentility).

7 Rajagopal, 'Violence', p. 99.

8 Bhowmik also points out that about 50 per cent of the street hawkers in Calcutta were previously employed in the 'formal' sector, and are now engaged in street vending after having lost their jobs due to industrial decline and factory closures described earlier. Bhowmik, *Street Vendors in the Global Urban Economy*, p. 25. Kuppusamy describes a similar development in Kuala Lumpur since the 1998 financial crisis and economic slowdown. B. Kuppusamy, 'Vendors Fear City Hall, but Watch New Policies', *Terraviva, Special Edition on Informal Economy: Street Vending in Asia* (2006).

9 G. Yasmeen, '"Plastic-bag Housewives" and Postmodern Restaurants? Public and Private in Bangkok's Foodscape', in C. Counihan and P. Van Esterik (eds), *Food and Culture: A Reader* (London and New York, 2008); I. Tinker, 'Street Foods: Traditional Microenterprise in a Modernizing World', *International Journal of Politics, Culture and Society* 16(3) (2003), pp. 331–349; Bhowmik, 'Street Vendors'.

10 Bhowmik, *Hawkers*, p. 26. Harassment of female street vendors in Vietnam (Hanoi) also, for example, is pointed out by Bhowmik, 'Street Vendors', p. 2261.

11 Tinker's study of street food in Bangladesh (Manikganj) also provides a similar insight, as do Bhowmik's observations on street food vending in Dhaka. Tinker, *Street Foods*; Bhowmik, 'Street Vendors'.

12 The Indian Constitution describes the Other Backward Classes (OBCs) as 'socially and educationally backward classes'; they are entitled to 27 per cent reservations in public sector employment and higher education to ensure their social and educational development. Scheduled Castes are recognized by the Indian Constitution as groups that were previously called the 'depressed classes' by the British. According to the 2001 Census, over 16 per cent of the Indian population can be described as belonging to the Scheduled Castes, some of whom are also known as *dalits* or the former 'untouchables', who were historically associated with ritually impure and polluting occupations like waste removal and leather work, and were segregated from the other castes as the pollution was considered contagious and capable of being transmitted through touch. Fifteen per cent of all vacancies in government-aided educational institutions and jobs in the public sector are now reserved for the Scheduled Castes. Bhowmik, *Hawkers*, p. 26.

13 *Puja* or the act of worship, performed regularly, is 'the core ritual of popular theistic Hinduism'. C.J. Fuller, *The Camphor Flame: Popular Hinduism and Society in India* (Princeton, 1992), p. 57.

14 S. Kaviraj, 'Filth and the Public Sphere: Concepts and Practices about Space in Calcutta', *Public Culture* 10(1) (1997).

15 These are made from minced fish/chicken/goat meat. Cutlets and chops are served with salad, *kasundi* (Bengali mustard sauce) and tomato ketchup, and are not included in '*telebhaja*' even if fried in the same oil. This is attributed to their origins in the 'interaction between indigenous and colonial cuisines', as a result of which they still retain a 'different class character' in contrast to the humble *telebhaja*, explained one of my interlocutors.

16 Nizam Restaurant, located in the New Market area of Calcutta, is credited with inventing the roll.

17 Add some more chilli powder.

18 Add some more 'sour', that is, tamarind or lemon juice.

19 Fry it until it is crisp.

20 Country liquor is made from fermented rice, jaggery (*gur*), to which chemicals are often added for a 'kick'. At times the addition of spurious chemicals causes blindness and death.

21 Calcutta Municipal Corporation Act, Second Amendment Bill 1997. The Bill later became an Act, and Section 371 of the Act that originally prevented the use of any pavement for hawking goods was amended to include 'any basket, receptacle or goods on pavement, street, park or garden for display or sale' (Section 371, sub-section 1, as quoted in Bhowmik, *Hawkers*). As Rajagopal points out often the 'problems of urban space (are) devolved entirely onto street vendors' who are described as 'both illegitimate competition (for legitimate shopkeepers) and a drain on the legitimate economy'. Rajagopal, 'Violence', p. 106.

22 Emphasis mine; I. Chakravarty and C. Canet, *Street Foods in Calcutta*, FAO Corporate Document Repository (1996), p. 34 (www.fao.org/docrep/W3699T/w3699t06.htm).

23 For a review of the Street Vendors Bill 2012, which came into force on 1 May 2014 as the Street Vendors Act 2014, see A. Srivastava, V. Ram, M. Kurpad, S. Chatterjee, P. Vora and M. Bose, 'Formalising the Informal Streets: A Legislative Review of the Street Vendors (Protection of Livelihood and Regulation of Street Vending) Bill 2012', *Journal of Indian Law and Society* 4 (2014), pp. 247–274.

24 See 'Street-Legal Strategy for Hawkers', *The Telegraph*, Calcutta, 1 March 2014, www.telegraphindia.com/1140301/jsp/calcutta/story_18033826.jsp#.VENt-1e0BhU, accessed on 17 October 2014.

25 Historically, Mukhopadhyay contends, street food is a relatively recent phenomenon in Bengal, with the earliest literary reference to it dating back to only the late nineteenth century in a novel, *Sachitra Guljarnagar* (1871), about the 'mysteries' of the big city. B. Mukhopadhyay, 'Between Elite Hysteria and Subaltern Carnivalesque: The Politics of Street-Food in the City of Calcutta', *South Asia Research* 24(1) (2004), p. 39.

26 For more on the *bhadralok*, see S. Banerjee, *The Parlour and the Streets: Elite and Popular Culture in Nineteenth Century Calcutta* (Calcutta, 1998); P. Chatterjee, *The Nation and Its Fragments: Colonial and Postcolonial Histories* (New Delhi, 1993); Rabindra Ray, *The Naxalites and their Ideology* (Oxford, 2002), p. 55.

27 Kaviraj, 'Filth', p. 86.

28 Kaviraj, 'Filth', p. 93.

29 M. Strathern, 'Environments Within: An Ethnographic Commentary on Scale', in K. Flint and H. Morphy (eds), *Culture, Landscape and the Environment: The Linacre Lectures* (Oxford, 1997), p. 48.

30 The portrait of the ideal housewife (*sugrihini*) that emerges in nineteenth- and early twentieth-century published Bengali tracts on family, personhood and domesticity, analysed by Chakrabarty, is of one who does not neglect the routine of *grihakarya* (domestic work) and the rituals of auspiciousness that were meant to intimately tie women to concern for the *mangal* (well-being) of the *kula* (lineage). As Bose points out, Bipradas Mukherjee's *Paak Pranali* (Cooking Methods) (1885), the first widely popular cookbook on 'family cooking' (cooking at home for the family), which continues to be an authoritative reference point for the Bengali middle classes, describes the Bengali housewife as a 'good cook/mistress' with her well-ordered, spotless kitchen, her presentation of the normal Bengali meal and hospitality arrangements, and her capacity to address the demands of potential monotony by incorporating 'changing tastes' embodied in 'foreign/*bideshi*' foods, thereby encompassing the threat of the latter. Thus, the delineation of the 'normal' Bengali foodscape, in a constant threat of collapse into not-normality, came to index the fraught negotiations of the middle classes with the 'traditional' and the 'modern'. D. Chakrabarty, 'The Difference-Deferral of a Colonial Modernity: Public Debates on Domesticity in British Bengal', in D. Arnold and D. Hardiman (eds), *Subaltern Studies VIII: Essays in Honour of Ranajit Guha* (New Delhi, 1994); P. Bose, 'Aadarsha Poribarey Aadarsha Randhanpranali', *Anushtup* 32(1) (1997), pp. 14–40.

31 Kaviraj, 'Filth', p. 101.

32 Delineating the connection between these cleaning chores and the religious calibrations of the hours of the day, Kaviraj writes 'the household's internal space had to be cleaned at the hours of the conjunction between light and darkness, at dawn and dusk, which coincided with time for worship (*puja*). The form of this puja, especially at nightfall, was to light the auspicious lamp, which had an understated piety about it and was performed by women, who shared a strong connection with the symbolism of the interior'. Kaviraj, 'Filth', p. 98.

33 D. Chakrabarty, 'Open Space/Public Place: Garbage, Modernity and India', *South Asia* XIV(1) (1991), p. 20.

34 Kaviraj, 'Filth', p. 98.

35 Kaviraj, 'Filth', pp. 104, 108.

36 The English word 'public' pronounced as such when incorporated into a Bengali sentence. It is noteworthy that there is no indigenous Bengali word for 'public' that

is exactly equivalent to it. However, as explained, the middle-class usage of the term would be more faithful to its meaning in English, in contrast to its usage by the poor classes.

37 More than 100,000 hawkers were forcibly evicted from the streets during Operation Sunshine on the night of 16–17 November 1996 for example. The police and municipal authorities dismantled shacks and stalls built on the street pavements in some parts of the city to 'clean' them up and 'restore' their middle-class character. Also see Tinker, 'Street Foods', for similar street cleansing operations in e.g. Manila.

38 Parts of some of the following sections mobilize arguments made in my monograph *Transactions in Taste: The Collaborative Lives of Everyday Bengali Food* for purposes anew.

39 Janeja, *Transactions*, p. 50.

40 B. Latour, *We Have Never Been Modern* (London, 1993); B. Latour, *Reassembling the Social. An Introduction to Actor-Network-Theory* (Oxford, 2005).

41 On 'interanimation' see K. Basso, 'Wisdom Sits in Places: Notes on a Western Apache Landscape', in S. Feld and K. Basso (eds), *Senses of Place* (Santa Fe, 1996), p. 55. The use of the term 'actants' has been explained later.

42 M. Strathern, 'Cutting the Network', *Journal of Royal Anthropological Institute* (N.S.), 2(3) (1996), p. 523.

43 How do I cook the fish today?

44 'Fish chops' are deep-fried fish croquettes. Bengali fish (chicken/goat meat) 'chops' and cutlets are foods that emerged from the 'interaction of indigenous and colonial cuisines'. The making of these fish chops has already been described earlier. *Da* = short for '*dada*' (elder brother), a common mode of addressing men, excluding one's (grand)father and husband, by Bengali Hindu men and women.

45 Compare with A. Gell, *Art and Agency: An Anthropological Theory* (Oxford, 1998) p. 239.

46 Mukhopadhyay, 'Elite Hysteria', p. 46.

47 The term 'actants' is used, rather than 'actor' which in English is often limited to humans, to embody the mixed character of agency that encompasses both humans and non-humans.

48 Compare with A. Gell, *Art and Agency: An Anthropological Theory* (Oxford, 1998); Latour, *We Have Never Been Modern*; Latour, *Reassembling the Social: An Introduction to Actor-Network-Theory*.

49 Latour, *We Have Never Been Modern; Latour, Reassembling the Social*.

50 The *Concise Oxford Dictionary* (Oxford, 1999), p. 280.

51 Latour, *We Have Never Been Modern*.

52 Janeja, *Transactions*, p.66.

53 'Tapan *da*'s shop round the corner' is a shack-like structure like the innumerable other such street food vending 'shops' described in the first part of this chapter.

54 These are crumbs obtained from crushing large coarse biscuits that are cheaper than the finer tea biscuits that are sold in branded packs consumed normally by the middle and upper classes that are able to afford them more so than the poor classes.

55 As mentioned earlier, male street food vendors such as Tapan *da* rely on women for these labour-intensive modes of cooking and food, either non-family members employed in this capacity or family members who provide unpaid labour.

56 Mukhopadhyay, 'Elite Hysteria', p. 39.

57 Compare Ostor, who describes the use of such kinship categories as expressing 'a continuing relationship and enjoin(ing) a code of conduct'. A. Ostor, *Culture and Power: Legend, Ritual, Bazaar and Rebellion in a Bengali Society* (Delhi, 1984), p. 135. For more on the relation between familiarity and trust,

see N. Luhmann, 'Familiarity, Confidence, Trust: Problems and Perspectives', in Diego Gambetta (ed.), *Trust: Making and Breaking Cooperative Relations* (Oxford, 1988).

58 West Bengal has been plagued by spurious oil scandals. The oil used for cooking food outside the house, particularly by street food vendors, is not be trusted, since they are unlikely to use the packaged oils of the trusted brands (more expensive) that meet the standards of the food regulating authorities.

9 Negotiating gendered spatial boundaries

Women's food hawking in Penang, Malaysia

Anja K. Franck

Introduction

Small-scale food vending, or food hawking, represents an important part of the informal economy of twenty-first-century Malaysia.[1] The importance of food hawking in Malaysia can partly be attributed to the local food system. Public eating is part of everyday life and Malaysian families spend an increasing amount of their household expenditure on take-away food.[2] Anyone who has visited Malaysia can testify to the plurality of dishes being cooked up and consumed in all sorts of locations during all hours – in local market sites, by the roadside or in front of people's houses – in the major cities as well as small *kampungs* ('villages').[3] It has been suggested that food retailing is especially sensitive to cultural and religious influences.[4] In Malaysia the majority population are Malay, but there are also two large ethnic minority groups: the Chinese and Indians. Each of the ethnic groups have their own languages religious beliefs and cultural practices, and the ethnic differences in food preparation, vending and consumption are visible everywhere. Studies from various parts of the world have also illustrated the importance of gender in food hawking – partially revealed through gendered spatial divisions of labour in various food hawking activities.[5] In Malaysia these divisions are visible through women and men (of diverse ethnic belongings) performing different forms of food hawking, in different places and during different times of the day. That said, there is no comprehensive study of gender in food hawking in Malaysia and this study therefore attempts to contribute to such knowledge-building through its focus upon food hawking as a gendered spatial practice. Empirically this is examined through qualitative research interviews with female and male hawkers in the northern Malaysian state of Penang.

This chapter suggests that gendered spatial divisions in food hawking are not incidental. Instead, they reflect place-based gender relations in Malaysian society. This, in turn, produces a gendered outcome of contemporary hawker policies. This chapter will further propose that while women's food hawking, especially in developing or emerging economies, seems to be stuck in discourses of 'victimization', female hawkers are far from a homogenous group.[6]

Amongst the women food hawkers encountered in Penang, a few run flourishing businesses with several employees while many others struggle to make ends meet. In investigating their decisions to venture into food hawking we can therefore not rely on generalized assumption that hawking constitutes a 'last resort'. Instead, necessity and choice may well be co-present.[7]

Gender as a spatial practice

Gender relations are part of our everyday lives and the 'arrangement' of gender is so common that we often perceive it as 'natural' or 'given'. However, being a woman or man is not a fixed state. Instead, as suggested by Connell: 'It is a becoming, a condition actively under construction.'[8] Through our lives we acquire femininity and masculinity and a study of gender relations, therefore, involves inquiry into an active social process; a process through which power relations are established, maintained and negotiated in particular places.[9] Gender relations embody both the material and the ideological. They are, in other words, revealed both through divisions of labour and resources as well as through the representations and ideas of what is male or female.[10] It needs to be noted, however, that what it means to 'act like' a woman or man has a variety of meanings to different groups of people in different places, and may also mean a different thing to the same group at a different point in time.[11]

Feminist geographers recognize that gendered relations have particular spatialities. These spatialities create place, construct identities and affect material practices.[12] 'Place' is here not understood as a set of coordinates on a map, but rather as made up of power relations. Such power relations are central to construct various kinds of boundaries. In other words, they influence the 'rules' which tells who belongs in a certain place and who should be excluded. The idea that women and men occupy particular and different places is central to the social organization of homes, workplaces, labour markets and political institutions.[13]

Of particular relevance to this study are constructions of concepts such as 'work' and 'workplaces'. 'Work' is largely perceived as gendered – as 'men's work' or 'women's work' – and assumptions about the 'natural' affinities of men and women shape these definitions.[14] This, Peterson and Runyan suggests, is not entirely surprising considering that the way we think about who people *are* is often 'inextricable from what we expect them to *do*' (my emphasis).[15] The spatial separation of work, expressed through the public/private, workplace/home dichotomies, are important to the gendering of work*places* as well as for its definition as 'work' or 'non-work'.[16] The household/home/private realm has traditionally not been regarded as a site of production or even as part of 'the economy'. The economic contributions of women's work taking place here are therefore typically overlooked.[17]

Food hawking provides an interesting case for analysis of spatial boundaries in the work sphere for several reasons. Not only do women and men perform different types of hawking in different places, but previous studies have also illustrated how food hawking seems to dissolve the traditional (Western) constructions of public/private, home/workplace as dichotomous.[18] In fact, food-hawker sites (such as street kitchens) have been found to function as sites 'where gendered identities are negotiated, established and performed, between shifting, ambiguous, contingent definitions of public and private'.[19] Studies of hawking can therefore, I argue, reveal new insights about the way that gender is constructed in the world of work at the intersection of gender, work and place but also the way that women, through their daily activities and decisions, (re-)negotiate the meaning of public/private and workplace/home constructions.

Importantly, gender intersects other structures of social hierarchy (such as class, ethnicity, age, locality and nation).[20] The women who feature in this study are Malay and, hence, Muslim. Their role as economic agents, as well as the spatial boundedness of their everyday lives, are constructed at the intersection of their ethnic and religious identities: Malay culture and Islam.[21] This, as Lie and Lund propose, can explain their somewhat 'paradoxical' role when it comes to work and income-earning. On the one hand, Malay women have held jobs outside the home 'from the time of the Prophet'.[22] On the other, their role is still strongly connected to their responsibility for the home and children.[23] Yusof explains that while Islam provides incentives for women to engage in income-earning, their right to work is subject to certain basic principles. For married women this involves that the husband must agree to his wife working – as her job should not be the cause of the breakdown of the family unit. There are also restrictions in the spatial characteristic of the workplace:

> the workplace should not expose women to physical or moral dangers. There should not be a mixing of the sexes which might lead to '*fitnah*', '*khalwat*' or '*zina*', loosely translated as backbiting or gossip, close proximity and adultery. The main aim of this rule is to protect the woman's reputation so that there is no loss of respect for her.[24]

In their study of the role of Malay women Abdullah, Noor and Wok further find that Malay women perceived as part of their role to 'not compete with men, nor show off their ability'.[25] This, as we will see in sections to come, has important implications for the way that female and male hawking is perceived as well as for the way that women and men construct their identities as food hawkers.

Malaysian food hawking and its related policies

As stated in the introduction, food hawking represents an important informal economic activity in Malaysia. Informal workers can be found in a wide range of sectors and occupational categories. They can be casual and temporary workers, employees, own account, unpaid family and home-based workers – in both formal and informal enterprises.[26] Importantly, while hawkers (as well as other categories of informal workers) may work in licensed businesses – the work that they perform generally lacks legal recognition, regulation and protection.[27] As workers, they thus form part of the informal labour force. This has implications for their entitlements to, for example, pensions and social security.

Hawking in the street is still a common practice in Penang, however, the spatial organization of food hawking has been profoundly affected by contemporary hawker policies. These policies include a number of measures. For one, all hawkers are required to obtain a license from the Penang Municipal Council (MPPP) in order to conduct their business. Second, the MPPP is seeking to move hawkers from the streets into *designated hawker sites*.[28] These designated sites can be day/morning-markets, night-markets, food complexes, temporary hawker sites and sites for mobile hawkers. Based on surveys conducted throughout Penang, a large number of new hawker sites have therefore been put in place – mainly in residential areas. The objective of relocating hawking activities, the MPPP suggests, is to tackle the commonly cited sanitary and health problems associated with street-food vending as well as the obstruction to traffic caused by road-side hawkers.[29] While the above policies have caused public debate, its gendered implications are rarely – if ever – mentioned.[30] However, as will be argued here, neither licensing requirements nor the relocation of hawker activities have a gender-neutral outcome. Instead, due to place-based gendered relations, female and male hawkers may be differently affected by these policies.

Data on the number of licensed hawkers in Penang tells us that the majority of licence-holders are men. MPPP officials, however, estimate that there are in fact more female hawkers vending in market sites.[31] This reflects the common practice that a male member of the family is the licence-holder – while it is a female member of the family who actually performs the hawking on site.[32] Also, studies from for example Bangladesh and Indonesia, have shown that male-owned or run small-scale enterprises generally rely on women's home production of the goods sold, a pattern which is particularly striking in Muslim countries.[33] Thus, while the food may be sold by the husband in the street, the wife has commonly prepared it or taken part in the preparations at home. Also, while some studies from Malaysia have found that a majority of the hawkers are male, I would argue that the gender composition of the hawker workforce is not so easily determined from studies focusing upon one hawker location.[34] A key reason for this is that women and men perform hawking in different places and during different times of the day. When surveying hawker sites, we may therefore get significantly different results depending on where the market is located (urban/suburban/village), its opening hours (morning/day/night) and what goods are sold (cooked/raw food). From observation we can, for example, establish that in designated morning markets throughout Penang's residential areas women dominate the food-court sections (where cooked food is served) – whereas male vendors are in the majority in sections where fresh food, such as vegetables, fish and meat, is sold. Morning markets, in general, are sites with many women – whereas night markets are male-dominated spaces.

In discussions around divisions of labour and spaces in Malaysian food hawking one cannot disregard the importance of ethnicity. The three main ethnic groups in Malaysia, Malay, Chinese and Indian, all have their own food cultures and preferences – including what to eat and when.[35] As mentioned above, the Malay population is Muslim and the *Syariah* Laws (which apply to the Muslim part of the population) contain requirements with regard to hygiene, sanitation and safety of foods.[36] According to Islam, Muslims are allowed to consume food that is *Halal* (lawful) and, according to Golnaz, the Halal concept 'is essentially a way of life and not solely confined to types of food that Muslims are allowed to consume'.[37] As such, it has a wide range of implications for how food products are prepared, sold and consumed. One specific example is that the Muslim population does not consume pork and many Malays therefore, in fear of coming into contact with pork-polluted food or things, feel uneasy eating food from Chinese vendors who often serve pork dishes.[38] In food markets, pork vending therefore takes place in a separate section contained from the rest of the market and it is run exclusively by Chinese men. The Indian Hindus, on the other hand, do not eat beef. However, while many Muslims prefer not to eat together if non-Halal food is consumed, most Indians would not have a problem eating together when other people consume beef.[39] Beef is also sold in the open section of the market. In sections to come we will return to the issue of how food-vending and its related policies intersect with gender and ethnicity.

The outline of the study

This study builds upon interviews conducted with 33 Malay women and 12 Malay and Indian Muslim men in Penang. These hawkers work in five different locations throughout the island: *Batu Ferringhi, Balik Pulau, George Town, Tanjung Bungah* and *Teluk Bahang*. The different interview sites were selected taking into account the ethnic and as well as the different socio-economic settings of the community. All of the respondents were approached during working hours in their place of work. The choice of respondents was made by randomly walking between the different hawker stalls in the chosen locations. While many respondents spoke English, all interviews were conducted together with a Malay interpreter. The interviews were structured around an interview guide which, apart from basic data (such as the respondents' age and education level) contained open-ended questions focusing upon work-life history, the relationship between work and family, current status of employment and conditions of work.[40] The depth of the information retrieved from the interviews varied significantly depending on the respondent's willingness to talk. Some interviews were brief (30 minutes) while others lasted longer with questions being added as the conversation proceeded (an hour or more). The empirical part of this chapter deals with two main themes. First, gendered constructions and boundaries within food hawking and, second, the gender implications of hawker policies. The inquiry however starts by investigating what forms of food hawking the respondents engaged in the different sites visited.

The respondents and vending sites

The female respondents interviewed in Penang sell a wide variety of food. Vending of cooked and prepared food was most common – such as noodle or rice dishes, pancakes, porridge, finger-food (snacks), fresh coconut milk, dried fish and cookies. A smaller number also sell fresh vegetables and herbs and various kinds of dry goods such as packaged rice, noodles, spices, tinned food and candy. The women mostly perform their hawking inside – or in close proximity to – designated morning markets. As seen in Figures 9.1, 9.2 and 9.3 the hawkers working inside the market building operate their business from a fixed stall. In the food-court section of the market all vendors have their own separate space (see Figure 9.1) and there is a joint open eating area in the middle (see Figure 9.2). In all of the surveyed markets, although the ethnic composition of the vendors varies, this area is female-dominated. To the contrary, the vending of fresh produce, fish and meat (except pork and chicken) is conducted in big open hall where the stalls are distributed over the room (see Figure 9.3). The stalls here are generally bigger and the majority of the vendors are male.

Some of the women also operate mobile stalls in the streets surrounding the market. Most commonly these businesses are run from pushcarts like the ones seen in Figure 9.4 but some also perform the vending from a portable table or piece of fabric on the floor. The mobile hawkers mostly sell various forms of snacks (finger-food, pancakes, dried fish, etc.).

All of the markets are morning markets and while opening hours vary slightly, in general, business hours are from early morning until noon. Business hours of those operating mobile stalls in the nearby streets usually coincide with the market opening hours. Only a few women perform their hawking in the afternoon and evening.

All of the male hawkers work in the Chow Rasta market located in Penang's main urban centre George Town.[41] The area where this market is located was once the settlement for Tamils from southern India and the vending of fish, beef and chicken in the market is by tradition dominated by Indian Muslim petty traders. The Chinese still call the market *Kelinga Ban San* ('the Indian market').[42] All of the hawkers surveyed in Chow Rasta are fish and beef vendors on the ground floor of the market building. All but a few vendors in this section are male and the vast majority are of Muslim Indian and Malay origin. The vending, as seen in Figure 9.5, takes place in a large open market hall.

Figure 9.1 Food-court stall, Teluk Bahang. Photo © Anja K. Franck.

In the empirical sections which follow we will take a closer look at why the respondents have opted for food hawking, gendered spatial divisions of work, and how the above influences the outcome of hawker policies.

Reasons to enter food hawking

Almost all of the male vendors interviewed in Penang had entered food hawk-ing as a result of family tradition – taking over their fish or beef stalls from their fathers or grandfathers. And, only a very limited had any experience of other jobs or the formal labour market. Several of the men underlined that their families had been involved with the trade for generations. One man stated: 'From my grandfather until now – 100 years!' However, for some this was not necessarily their first choice – but rather something which was expected of them as sons or grandsons. In contrast with the male hawkers, who had largely entered the trade at a relatively young age, the women had entered food hawking at a later stage in the life-cycle. The large majority had, prior to marriage and child-birth, held jobs in export-factories or in the tour-ism industry. For the most part, they had stayed at home while their children

Figure 9.2 Joint seating area in food-court, Teluk Bahang. Photo © Anja K. Franck.

Figure 9.3 Fresh food hall, Teluk Bahang. Photo © Anja K. Franck.

Figure 9.4 Mobile street stall, Teluk Bahang. Photo © Anja K. Franck.

Figure 9.5 Fish stall, Chow Rasta market. Photo © Anja K. Franck.

were small and then taken up food hawking when their children were old enough to attend school. Given their previous experiences from the formal labour market, an interesting question with regards to the women hawkers is therefore what motivated their choice not to re-engage with formal work but rather to opt for informal work like food hawking.

A reoccurring theme in the women's stories was that hawking, as opposed to formal employment (in factories and hotels), allowed them to combine income-earning with their roles as wives and mothers. This illustrates that the general lack of institutional support offered to working mothers in Malaysia, particularly the lack of affordable and reliable child-care facilities, restricts their ability to (re-)engage in waged formal work after child-birth.[43] One woman, who used to work in a hotel, explained the reasons for why she entered hawking by exclaiming:

> [Because of] family la'! I wanted to control my children! Then I got this stall ... [In the hotel] you work in shifts and there is nobody to look after the children ... My husband only works at night so when I had to do the night shifts then it's not possible.

Many of the women cited the working conditions of their former jobs (including the shift work, long working hours, lack of flexibility, insecure contracts, hiring practices and hierarchies in formal workplaces) as the reason for why they were either unwilling or unable to return to such work. However, an issue which kept reoccurring during the interviews was the fact that formal work opportunities are largely found outside the village and commuting where they live. For many this was associated with both practical difficulties (such as lack of access to transportation) as well as resistance on behalf of their families. As a central difference, food hawking could be performed in closer proximity to the home – which was an issue of central importance in their choice to take up hawking. Unlike the male hawkers in Chow Rasta, where the majority of the traders lived at least five kilometres away from the market, an overwhelming majority of the female food hawkers interviewed lived within walking distance of their workplace. In fact, none of female food hawkers lived outside the community where they worked. Selling *kuih-muih* ('finger-food') from a pushcart in the street, one hawker answered that she chose her specific location because it was close to the designated market. Asked why she had chosen that particular market she simply exclaimed: 'Because I live here!' Another woman, a former factory worker explained that: '[Here] I can get home early and cook for my husband ... I was working for 12 hours [in the factory] and when I came back I had to cook and do the dishes ... and my house was not organized.' While the time factor is certainly relevant, commuting also requires access to transportation. And, while all of the male vendors in Chow Rasta drove to work using their own vehicle (most commonly a motorbike), only around half of the women had access to a vehicle. Instead, many walked to their workplace or had someone else (mostly their husbands) drop them off at the site. Some women commented that while they would like to trade also in other places the lack of transport made this impossible. Answering whether she could imagine travelling a distance to work a woman stated:

> It is going to be difficult for me because I can't drive. I depend on my husband and my son ... I could take a bus but the bus is not reliable ... Being in your fifties you don't want to go far. It is different when you are young.

For hawkers, access to transportation is also an important aspect when it comes to getting supplies for the business. In the morning markets in residential areas, where most of the women run their hawker stalls, they have access to most necessary supplies. The stock needed for cooking can be purchased in the fresh food-hall, preparations (like the chopping, cooking of foundation and sauces) can be done at home and easily transported in pots to the vending place.

The choice to work in close proximity to the household was, however, not only motivated by material conditions (such as the lack of child-care and transportation) – but also by normative constructions around gender, work and place.[44] In several cases the possibilities of the women to take up formal work after marriage and child-birth was restricted by the wishes of their husband or other family members who did not approve of them leaving home for formal work. One woman, now selling dried fish from a portable table outside the market, stated that 'My husband won't let me! If it was up to me then I really want it! I have had lots of job offers but he never let me. I went to work for a day and he came to ask me to come back.' In this case the husband's unwillingness to let the wife work was linked to the perception that married women 'should not work'. In other cases, however, the decision of the husband was directly linked to the lack of affordable child-care. One woman, for example, explained that out of her Ringgit Malaysia (RM) 1,200 monthly wage, RM 800 would have to be paid to child-care and her husband had therefore decided that it was not worth it. Instead, she decided to take up hawking in the nearby market during the hours that her children attended school. These findings are consistent with the study of Abdullah *et al.* who found that support of the husband and other family members is crucial for Malay women's labour market choices.[45]

The female respondents expressed quite differing views regarding how the intra-household decision-making was made as well as the restrictions it placed upon their ability to work. While some expressed explicit criticism towards the norm of the husband as the decision-maker in the family, others accepted or supported it, making reference to their faith or to Malay culture. One of the women explained that it was her husband who made the decision that she should leave her former job in the factory. When asked why she explained:

> How can my husband stay at home and cook? ... He is the leader of the house ... Because he is the husband! It's not like we are going to listen to someone else – other than our husband ... it's the Malay culture.

To several women the social aspects of performing food hawking in the market – relative to what they perceived as quite 'lonely' and 'boring' life as a housewife staying at home – was mentioned as a reason to enter this work. One woman, asked why she started hawking, for example stated, 'To pass my time. Nothing to do at home. To get some new relationships with other people here, to mix around.' And several women emphasized that they found staying at home, as their husband and children all went to work and school during the day, outright 'boring'. What were they expected to do at home all day, they asked, watch TV? A further illustration of this is, perhaps, that in the Teluk Bahang market some of the women gather after closing hours to sing karaoke together in a small room at the back of the market before returning to the house.

In conclusion, the male and female hawkers had quite different motivations for entering food hawking. While the men were largely motivated by family tradition, the women's decisions to enter food hawking reflected, on the one hand, their inability or unwillingness to (re-)engage with work in the formal economy and, on the other, their need for more freedom and flexibility in order to meet their double role as breadwinners and mothers. The hawking currently performed by the male and female respondents of this study, however, differed and in the following section we take a look at some of the reasons why.

Gendered constructions of food hawking and place

As discussed earlier, the gendered (ethnic) divisions of labour in food hawking are clearly visible when visiting various Penang hawker sites. In the interviews with the male hawkers these divisions kept resurfacing as an issue of importance. The fish and meat section of the Chow Rasta market, where all of the male respondents work, is a heavily male-dominated space. Almost all of the men underlined that this was neither a job nor a place suitable for Muslim women. The most commonly mentioned reasons were that the work performed here was too 'hard' and 'heavy' – and the market a 'too dirty' environment. One of the male vendors, for example stated:

> Women like to work in their house. Very hard work here – they wouldn't like to work here … It's hard work. Very hard. Only men can do this work … They [women] like to work in the office, or factory. Very light work. It's easy for them to handle the documents, to treat the papers.

Another man said, 'The women don't want to work here. It's heavy work. Dirty! And their husbands say: You don't want to work here. It's dirty. It's not classy. It's dirty. It smells bad. And you will feel ashamed.' The fact that women were not able to handle the butcher's knife was also an issue mentioned by several of the respondents. It was too heavy, they explained, for women to cut the heavy meats handled in the market. When asked if women

Figure 9.6 Beef stall, Chow Rasta market. Photo © Anja K. Franck.

did not do the same at home – chopping of the meat for cooking – several men responded that women wanted their heavy meat chopped in the market as it was not 'fit for ladies'. One man also stated that women were too lazy. However, as seen in Figure 9.6, not all meat handled in the market involved heavy meats – instead, much of the work also involved 'light cutting'.

Instead, the construction of this type of work as male rested as much upon the idea of what the work *signified* – rather than the actual tasks performed. This is very well illustrated in the responses by this beef vendor:

Question: Why do the women not like being here?
Answer: They don't feel comfortable with all this meat. Look at it! There are no women here.
Q: But … once it comes home the women cook it right?
A: Yes, cooking is fine.
Q: But not chopping?
A: They just feel like that. They have never been exposed to the market. And if you have never been exposed then they don't know. On the 'light stuff' in front there are some women [points towards the section selling rice and other food-items].
Q: So, this is the heavy stuff?

A: *Yes*
Q: Why?
A: *It's heavy because you have to deal with the butcher's knife and heavy meat.*
Q: But that's not so heavy [points to the pieces of beef being chopped]?
A. *They [women] are just not used to it. The Malaysian says it's heavy – foreigner says it's light.*
Q: But a sack of rice is heavier than that?
A: *Yes, true.*
Q: So, is it more an idea that it's heavy work – it feels heavy?
A: *Yes! It's the understanding.*

Apart from the work being 'too heavy' – the exclusion of women from this market was also much related to the perception of the market space. Several men commented that this market was not a suitable place for Muslim women because it represented what one man called 'a social life', which would not be appropriate for Malay or Indian Muslim girls. This is linked to the idea that women may, in the market, be exposed to both physical and moral dangers.[46] What is interesting about this assumption is that the residential areas are undeniably also social and outdoor places (see, for example, Figures 9.2 and 9.3). However, the residential area markets were perceived quite differently and the interviews revealed some interesting reasons why. One of the male vendors in Chow Rasta, for example, explained that the residential area markets were a good place for women to work because there they can do cooking. This, he stated, as difference to his own workplace, would not feel as dirty. What type of food – fresh or prepared – being sold in the market therefore seemed to be significant for whether hawking in such places was perceived as suitable or not for Muslim women. However, while the meat and fish vending was here described as making the market site 'more dirty', fish and beef is, nonetheless, sold also in the residential area markets (see Figure 9.7). And, it thus seems that the explanation to its gendering can be found at the intersection of what goods are sold and the construction of the place where the selling takes place.

One factor, discussed earlier, for why the residential area markets were perceived as more suitable for women is likely the close proximity between the home and the market. This proximity is both geographic and social – and these sites seemed to be perceived and constructed as part of the community – rather than as public workplaces. The proximity to the home guarantees some form of 'social control' – which would avoid putting women at risk of moral danger and/or being the subject of gossip.[47] This lends some support to Loh-Luhder's contention that women's informal work in Malaysia is viewed as an extension of their domestic work.[48] Their hawking is, as such, placed somewhere in-between the public and the private – illustrating the inadequacy of the public/private dichotomy as a framework.[49] However, there were also additional spatial aspects raised by the male Chow Rasta hawkers with regards to why residential area market vending was appropriate for

Figure 9.7 Fish stall, Teluk Bahang. Photo © Anja K. Franck.

Muslim women. One of the male hawkers, for example, explained that the actual design of the market halls played a significant role:

> Because this [room] is too open ... You have got to mix and you have to talk to a lot of strangers. Sometimes some have got the wrong comments – wrong thinking ... That's why the Malay girls they don't go around like this in the open places. They go for stalls, they sell clothes. If you go inside [points to the other part of the market] there will be a lot of Malay girls. That is different. They bargain and do business with women. This one you have to do business with all races. Mostly the Malay and Indian girls they don't come in.[50]

The open room referred to here is the large open hall where beef and fish are sold. And, the same man explained, a room with separate more restricted spaces would be more appropriate – such as in the food-court sections in the residential area markets where each hawker has their own separate space (see Figure 9.1). The residential area markets are thus considered to be 'safer' for women – because they are 'less social'. It needs to be noted, however, that although the residential area market food-courts are dominated by female vendors – the customers are of both genders. Therefore, women working here also need to mix with both men and women. But the spatial organization of the market – the actual architecture of the market building – seems to facilitate a different understanding of this space relative to vending in a large open hall.

The gendered divisions of labour and spaces described above are clearly related to gendered spatial relations and practices in Malaysian society. However, as will be argued in the next section, gendered relations – and its consequent spatial boundaries – are not fixed. Instead, they are continuously under negotiation – and, I argue, women actively participate in this process through their actions and spatial strategies.[51]

Negotiating boundaries

As discussed above, a number of women stated that their husbands objected to them 'working'. This was generally a reference to 'formal work' – and mostly to work in factories and hotels. Interestingly, while 'working' in the formal economy was seen as out of place for these women – some had been actively encouraged by their husbands to do business in their local market. Food hawking in the local market did, therefore, not seem to fall within the category of 'work'. One way to find out how the women themselves characterized their hawking was to ask which 'job title' they would use to describe themselves. The majority of the women responded that they would use titles such as 'business woman', 'self-employed', 'hawker' or 'market worker'. A considerable number of the women, however, stated that they would use the title 'housewife' or, in some cases, 'helper'. The practice that female hawkers do not report their hawking activities in surveys was also noted by the MPPP. One MPPP official stated that female hawkers would not normally declare their work but rather fill out 'housewife' in official forms. Some of the women stated practical or 'pragmatic' reasons to call themselves housewives – such as declaring 'housewife' for fear of losing benefits or having to pay (higher) taxes.[52] Other women argued that the hawking they performed would not really qualify as 'work'. One respondent, selling beef in one of the residential markets for example, stated: 'I just help my husband.' When asked how long she had worked in the market she emphasized again that she did not consider herself a worker in the market: 'I help only. Twenty-four years. He is selling for 30 years already.' In other cases, the women perceived their businesses as 'too small' to be considered 'proper' businesses or 'work'. Some also made reference to their husband as the main providers – whereas the work they performed was more an 'add-on' or extra.[53] One way to interpret the way that women's hawking is constructed as 'helping out' or just an 'add-on' is that women's food hawking is devalued relative to that of male hawkers. However, describing their income-earning activities as 'housework' could also be understood as a deliberate choice. In other words, it was a way for women to avoid looking as if they were competing with their husbands as the breadwinner of the family.[54] It is, of course, difficult to deter from women's covert strategies why they (seem to) comply with gendered norms. However, as Agarwal reminds us: 'Compliance need not imply complicity.'[55] It is thus, I argue, quite possible that the women strategically use the title 'housewife' as a way to create some space to manoeuvre. By describing their remunerative activities as 'housework' rather than 'work' they avoid putting into question norms they are expected to comply with. And, through this, they are able to secure extended access to remunerative work outside the household realm. As we shall see, gendered constructions and boundaries within of food hawking, such as described here, are also important when evaluating the outcome of hawker policies.

Gendering Penang hawker policies

In the following section we will take a closer look at how contemporary hawker policies are gendered – and in particular the policy of relocating hawker activities to designated market sites. For the female hawkers interviewed in this study, the possibility of being able to perform hawking in their residential area – in and around the designated market sites – provided the very incentive for them to enter food hawking. It provided, as argued above, the possibility to combine their reproductive responsibilities with the need and desire for remunerative work. For the male hawkers at Chow Rasta the policy of setting up markets in residential areas had quite the opposite effect – as it limited their ability to make a living from hawking. The latter is very much related to the dramatic changes that have taken place in inner-city George Town over the last few decades. These changes involved the development of legislation around housing which, as Jenkins and King argue, has been designed 'to bring capital and development into formerly controlled urban areas' and has 'aimed at removing working class tenants to new low-cost, high rise housing schemes' in suburban areas.[56] While many older heritage buildings in George Town have been preserved, certain parts of the city have had to give way to 'modernization' and the erection of, for example, massive shopping complexes. The implications for social and economic life in the city have been extensive and, according to Jenkins and King, most hawkers in the affected areas have either been displaced or relocated into hawker food-courts. Many of the hawkers in Chow Rasta described how the changes to the surrounding environment have had a detrimental impact upon their businesses. The most important reason for that is, as one hawker explained, 'There are no more people in town … People have moved out'. A concern for the male hawkers is therefore that the people who used to inhabit the central parts of the city have now been relocated (displaced some would perhaps argue) to low-cost housing projects in suburban areas. In each of these areas there are designated markets put in place. Many of the Chow Rasta hawkers expressed criticism towards this policy – as they believed it deprived them of customers. When speaking to their elected chairman, he stated:

The government should do something to avoid a lot of markets ... Because whenever you create storage flats for the residents they make it compulsory that they need a Mosque, a temple and a market ... so they already have all their necessities there. So, this is the problem ... Because most of the buyers they won't come to town because it is far away.

Similarly, a beef vendor remarked:

It [the market] has changed a lot. Customers have changed. What we sell has also changed. Prices have changed ... Previously the costumers they used to stay around this area. Due to development they have left. They went to decent places. That is development! Development drove the people away from the town. So a lot of my customers have left, to decent places. And there are markets everywhere and when people move to some of the decent places there are markets also so they never come back.

The lack of costumers has forced the Chow Rasta hawkers to alter their business strategies and today they mainly cater to restaurants. Several of the men stated that restaurants currently constituted almost 90 per cent of their business. One man exclaimed: 'If there is no restaurant – close up and go back! Do something else!'

The male and female hawkers in this study thus have quite differing experiences of the policy of relocating hawkers from streets and the inner city to designated sites in residential areas. The fact that in this case study the male hawkers work in a market in the city centre while the female hawkers work in the suburban or village areas is one aspect of this. However, as has also been argued above, this division of labour and place is not incidental. Instead, it reflects specific gendered spatial norms and practices in Malaysian society – where Malay (and Indian Muslim) women's mobility and access to work are framed and constructed according to both tradition and religious beliefs. For example, a survey of female Chinese hawkers operating in the city centre may generate a different result in terms of how they view hawker policies and the implications this has for their possibilities to conduct business. The point here is thus not to make a generalized assumption about ethnicity and gender and their relation to work and place – but rather to illustrate that hawker policies are gendered and that due analysis is needed regarding how different groups of hawkers in Malaysia (female, male, Malay, Chinese, Indian) are affected.

Conclusions

This study set out to investigate food hawking, and its related policies, at the intersection of gender, work and place. It has illustrated that gender is essential to both divisions of labour and places within food hawking in Penang. These divisions, as is argued in the introduction, are not incidental. Instead, they reflect gendered spatial practices that are essential to upholding gendered power relations.

Many of the women interviewed in Penang expressed both unwillingness and inability to return to waged formal labour. In contrast, food hawking offered them the possibility to combine earning an income with their roles as wives or mothers. However, not all types of food hawking or food-hawker places were considered acceptable for married Malay/Muslim women. In interviews with the male Malay and Indian Muslim hawkers, it became clear that while the vending of cooked food in residential area markets signified a 'proper' activity for women, vending meat and other raw foods in city centre markets did not. The belief that residential area markets are good places for married women to work was also visible in the stories told by the female hawkers. Several of them had faced resistance with regards to formal work; instead, hawking in residential markets was acceptable and, in some cases, also encouraged by their husband or other family members. Important to this acceptance was the construction of the residential area markets as 'safe' places for women where they would not face moral or physical dangers. The geographic proximity between home and workplace is one potential reason for this, as well as the social proximity, which would imply some form of social control. The work performed here is also not perceived as 'dirty' or 'dangerous'.

This study further suggests that women themselves actively participate in constructions of women's food hawking as an extra or add-on to their 'main' (read: child-care and household) duties as a way to secure self-interest – in this case, their will and need to work for money outside the vicinity of the home. Labelling their hawking as 'non-work', 'home-work' or 'helping' they seem to be complying with male-breadwinner and housewife norms while at the same time securing their possibilities for remunerative public work. As such, food hawking represents a means by which they are able to renegotiate spatial boundaries and extend their access to public places of work.

The above also has significant implications for the outcome of hawker policies. The study has illustrated how gendered divisions of labour and places within food hawking are essential to the way that the male and female hawkers experienced, for example, the policy of designated residential area markets. For the male hawkers in Chow Rasta this change meant competition for customers – often with a detrimental effect upon their ability to make a profit. For the women, on the other hand, this policy has worked as an incentive to enter hawking, as it provided the opportunity to perform hawking in close proximity to their house, where the lack of transportation is compensated by the possibility to get their supplies on site, and where the market is considered both safe and appropriate as a place of work for Muslim women.

Notes

1 M.R. Agus, 'Integrating the Informal Sector in Planning for Low-Income Settlements: The Malaysian Experience', *Thai Journal of Development Administration*

27/3 (1987), pp. 436–448; N. Hassan, 'Accommodating Street Hawkers into Modern Urban Management in Kuala Lumpur', paper presented at 39th ISoCaRP Congress, 17–22 October, Cairo (2003); SERI [Socio-Economic Research Institute], 'The Performance of the Informal Sector in Penang', *Economic Briefing To the Penang State Government*, 5/6 June 2003.

2 H. Lee Siew Heng and A. Tan Khee Guan, 'Examining Malaysian Household Expenditure Patterns on Food-Away-From-Home', *Asian Journal of Agriculture and Development* 4/1 (2007), pp. 11–24.

3 It is estimated that in the state of Penang street food alone has generated around 20,000 jobs (which is the equivalent of 12 per cent of employment in the island), see: R.V. Bhat and K. Waghray, 'Profile of Street Foods Sold in Asian Countries', *World Review of Nutrition and Dietetics* 86 (2000), pp. 53–99.

4 T.F. Lam, 'Food for the City: The Role of the Informal Sector', *GeoJournal* 4/1 (1982), pp. 49–59.

5 L.E. Bass, 'Enlarging the Street and Negotiating the Curb: Public Space at the Edge of an African Market', *International Journal of Sociology and Social Policy* 20 (2000), pp. 74–95; Narumol Nirathron, *Fighting Poverty from the Streets: A Survey of Street Food Vendors in Bangkok* (Bangkok, 2006); S. Teltscher, 'Small Trade and the World Economy: Informal Vendors in Quito, Ecuador', *Economic Geography* 70/2 (1994), pp. 167–187; I. Tinker, 'Street Foods: Traditional Microenterprise in a Modernizing World', *International Journal of Politics, Culture and Society* 16/3 (2003), pp. 331–349; Gisele Yasmeen, *Bangkok's Foodscape: Public Eating, Gender Relations, and Urban Change* (Bangkok, 2006).

6 In a study of street vendors in Asia, Bhowmik, for example, writes: 'Women vendors form the lowest rungs amongst street vendors. In most cases they take to this trade because of poverty and because the male members in the family do not have jobs.' S.K. Bhowmik, 'Street Vendors in Asia: A Review', *Economic and Political Weekly*, May 28–June 4 (2005), p. 2264.

7 C.C. Williams, 'Informal Entrepreneurs and their Motives: A Gender Perspective', *International Journal of Gender and Entrepreneurship* 1/3 (2009), pp. 219–225.

8 Raewyn Connell, *Gender* (Malden, 2002).

9 Connell, *Gender*.

10 B. Agarwal, '"Bargaining" and Gender Relations: Within and Beyond the Household', *Feminist Economics* 3/1 (1997), pp. 1–51.

11 V. Spike Peterson and Ann S. Runyan, *Global Gender Issues* (Boulder, 1993).

12 Ann M. Oberhauser and Amy Pratt, 'Women's Collective Economic Strategies and Political Transformations in Rural Africa', *Gender, Place and Culture* 11/2 (2004), pp. 209–228.

13 Linda McDowell, *Gender Identity and Place: Understanding Feminist Geographies* (Minneapolis, 1999).

14 Mona Domosh and Joni Seager, *Putting Women in Place: Feminist Geographers Make Sense of the World* (London, 2001).

15 Peterson and Runyan, *Global*, p. 18.

16 Peterson and Runyan, *Global*, p. 12.

17 L. Benería, 'The Enduring Debate over Unpaid Labour', *International Labour Review* 138/3 (1999), pp. 287–309; Domosh and Seager, *Putting Women in Place*.

18 See: L.B.W. Drummond, 'Street Scenes: Practices of Public and Private Space in Urban Vietnam', *Urban Studies* 37/12 (2000), pp. 2377–2391; A.K. Franck, 'Factors Motivating Women's Informal Micro-Entrepreneurship: Experiences from Penang, Malaysia', *International Journal of Gender and Entrepreneurship* 4/1 (2012), pp. 65–78; S. Huang and B.S.A. Yeoh, 'Gender and Urban Space in the Tropical World', *Singapore Journal of Tropical Geography* 17/2 (1996), pp. 105–112; Yasmeen, *Foodscape*.

19 J. Wardrop, 'Private Cooking, Public Eating: Women Street Vendors in South Durban', *Gender, Place and Culture* 13/6 (2006), p. 677.

20 Devasahayam therefore proposes that we make use of the term 'gendered' rather than 'gender' identities because as term can capture plurality and difference – without abandoning the importance of gender in constituting the subject. T.W. Devasahayam, 'Power and Pleasure around the Stove: The Construction of Gendered Identity in Middle-Class South Indian Hindu Households in Urban Malaysia', *Women's Studies International Forum* 28/1 (2005), pp. 1–20.

21 Merete Lie and Ragnhild Lund, *Renegotiating Local Values: Working Women and Foreign Industry in Malaysia* (Richmond, 1994).

22 See also: R. Yusof, 'Interpreting How Religious Values Affect Entrepreneurial Behaviour among Muslim Businesswomen: The Case of Businesswomen from the District of Pendang, Kedah in Malaysia', paper presented at the 2nd Congress of the Asian Association of Women's Studies (CAAWS), 9–11 December (2010), Penang.

23 K. Abdullah, N.M. Noor and S. Wok, 'The Perception of Women's Roles and Progress: A Study of Malay Women', *Social Indicators Research* 89/3 (2008), pp. 439–455. It should further be noted that there is an ongoing debate around how the roles of Malay women have been influenced by the Islamization projects in Malaysia, see: Sylva Frisk, *Submitting to God: Women and Islam in Urban Malaysia* (Copenhagen, 2009); A. Ong, 'State versus Islam: Malay Families, Women's Bodies, and the Body Politics of Malaysia', *American Ethnologist* 17/2 (1990), pp. 258–276; M. Stivens, '"Family Values" and Islamic Revival: Gender, Rights and State Moral Projects in Malaysia', *Women's Studies International Forum* 29/4 (2006), pp. 354–367; K.-C.J. Tong and B.S. Turner, 'Women, Piety and Practice: A Study of Women and Religious Practices in Malaysia', *Contemporary Islam* 2/1 (2008), pp. 41–59.

24 Yusof, 'Interpreting How Religious Values', pp. 6–7.

25 Abdullah *et al.*, 'The Perception of Women's Roles and Progress', p. 453.

26 As a difference to the traditional approach towards the informal 'sector' – more recent scholarship have shown the need to focus upon the informal 'economy'. This reflects the need to place emphasis upon 'workers' and 'employment relationships' that are not legally regulated – rather than the traditional approach which focuses on the not legally regulated *enterprises*. See: M. Chen, 'Rethinking the Informal Economy: Linkages with the Formal Economy and the Formal Regulated Regulatory Environment', *DESA Working Paper 46* (2007); S. Lloyd-Evans, 'Geographies of the Contemporary Informal Sector in the Global South: Gender Employment Relationships and Social Protection', *Geography Compass* 2/6 (2008), pp. 1885–1906.

27 Lloyd-Evans, 'Geographies', p. 1885.

28 Annual Report of the Municipal Council of Penang Island (MPPP) (Penang, 2008).

29 See: F. Pang and P.S. Toh, 'Hawker Food Industry: Food Safety/Public Health Strategies in Malaysia', *Nutrition & Food Science* 38/1 (2008), pp. 41–51; P.S. Toh and A. Birchenough, 'Food Safety Knowledge and Attitudes: Culture and Environment Impact on Hawkers in Malaysia. Knowledge and Attitudes are Key Attributes of Concern in Hawker Food-Handling Practices and Outbreaks of Food Poisoning and their Prevention', *Food Control* 11/6 (2000), pp. 447–452.

30 See for example: *The Star*, 2 March 2009; 27 October 2009; 30 October 2009; 28 December 2009.

31 Interview with the MPPP, 2009.

32 Some of the women who feature in this study are the licence-holders while others work in stalls where the licence is held by someone else. However, the actual name on the licence (their own, a relative or friend) was, by many women, seen as a mere 'formality' which did not have any great influence upon the actual

work performed in the stall. In other words, many women regarded the stalls as theirs – although it was formally registered to someone else. What was significant, however, was whether the stall where they perform their hawking was licensed at all – i.e. whether the stall was legal or illegal. But issues relating to the difficulties associated with performing illegal hawking are beyond the scope of this chapter.

33 M. Cohen, 'Women Street Vendors: The Road to Recognition', SEEDS 20 (2000).
34 See for example Hassan, 'Accommodating Street Hawkers'.
35 Tan Chee-beng, 'Food and Ethnicity with Reference to the Chinese in Malaysia', in David Y.H. Wu and Tan Chee-beng (eds), *Changing Chinese Foodways in Asia* (Hong Kong, 2001), pp. 125–160.
36 On Malaysian Halal food see: *Standardization for Halal Food, Standards and Quality News*, 11(4), available at: www.sirim.my/f_corp/july04.pdf; and for a shorter introduction to Halal food in Malaysia see: www.malaysiahalalfoods.com.
37 R. Golnaz, M.R. Zainalabidin, M.S. Nasir and E.F.C. Chiew, 'Non-Muslims' Awareness of Halal Principles and Related Food Products in Malaysia', *International Food Research Journal* 17 (2010), pp. 667–674.
38 Chee-beng, 'Food and Ethnicity', p. 148.
39 Chee-beng, 'Food and Ethnicity'.
40 There were some differences in the questions between the February/March and the September surveys. The questions in the September survey were based partly on the results of the previous survey and upon the development of the ongoing global economic crises.
41 The word *Chow Rasta* is Urdu and means 'four crossroads' – signalling the location of the market in-between the four roads: Chow Rasta Street, Tamil Street, Kuala Kangsar Road and Penang Road.
42 Khoo Su Nin, *Streets of George Town Penang* (Penang, 2007).
43 See also: Abdullah *et al.*, 'The Perception of Women's Roles and Progress'; Franck, 'Factors Motivating Women's Informal Micro-Entrepreneurship'.
44 Although it should be noted that the material and discursive reasons/practices are not so easily separated.
45 Abdullah *et al.*, 'The Perception of Women's Roles and Progress'.
46 Yusof, 'Interpreting How Religious Values'.
47 Yusof, 'Interpreting How Religious Values'.
48 L. Loh-Luhder, 'Women in the Informal Sector in Malaysia', *Bahá'í Topics* (not dated).
49 See also: Yasmeen, *Foodscape*.
50 The restrictions in the working environment were, however, not applicable to all women. Instead, several hawkers made reference to the fact that for Chinese women the market was an acceptable workplace.
51 See also: Anja Franck, *From Formal Employment to Street Vending: Women's Room to Maneuver and Labor Market Decisions under Conditions of Export-Orientation – the Case of Penang, Malaysia* (Gothenburg, 2012), PhD Dissertation, pp. 97–99.
52 See also: A.K. Franck and J. Olsson, 'Missing Women? The Underrecording and Underreporting of Women's Work in Malaysia', *International Labour Review* 153 (2014), pp. 209–221.
53 Abdullah *et al.*, 'The Perception of Women's Roles and Progress'.
54 Abdullah *et al.*, 'The Perception of Women's Roles and Progress'.
55 Agarwal ' "Bargaining" and Gender Relations', p. 25.
56 G. Jenkins and V.T. King, 'Heritage and Development in a Malaysian City: George Town under Threat?' *Indonesia and the Malay World* 31/89 (2003), p. 49.

Select bibliography

Abad, Reynald, *Le grand marché. L'approvisionnement alimentaire de Paris sous l'Ancien Régime* (Paris: Fayard, 2002).

Abreu-Ferreira, Darlene, 'Fishmongers and shipowners: Women in maritime communities in early modern Portugal', *Sixteenth Century Journal* 31 (2000): 7–23.

Ago, Renata, *Gusto for Things: A History of Objects in Seventeenth-Century Rome*, trans. Bradford Bouley and Corey Tazzara with Paula Findlen (Chicago: University of Chicago Press, 2013).

Aron, Jean-Paul, *Essai sur la sensibilité alimentaire à Paris au 19e siècle* (Paris: Harvard University Press, 1967).

Atkinson, Niall, 'The republic of sound: Listening to Florence at the threshold of the Renaissance', *I Tatti Studies in the Italian Renaissance* 16/1–2 (2013): 57–84.

Balme, M., 'Attitudes to work and leisure in ancient Greece', *Greece and Rome* 31 (1984): 140–152.

Bass, Loretta, 'Enlarging the street and negotiating the curb: public space at the edge of an African market', *International Journal of Sociology and Social Policy* 20 (2000): 74–95.

Beall, Karen F., *Kaufrufe und Straßenhändler/Cries and Itinerant Trades* (Hamburg: Dr Ernst Hausdwedell & Co, 1975).

Benedetta, Mary, *The Street Markets of London*, with photographs by Laszlo Moholy-Nagy (London: John Miles, 1936).

Béraldi, Henri (ed.), *Paris qui crie. Petits métiers* (Paris: Georges Chamerot, 1890).

Beurdeley, Michel, *Les petits métiers de la France d'autrefois* (Paris: Solar, 1992).

Bhowmik, S.K., *Hawkers and the Urban Informal Sector: A Study of Street Vending in Seven Cities* (mimeo) (Patna: National Alliance of Street Vendors of India NASVI, 2000).

Bhowmik, S.K, 'Street vendors in Asia: A review', *Economic and Political Weekly* 30/22–23 (2005): 2256–2264.

Bhowmik, S.K., *Street Vendors in the Global Urban Economy* (New Delhi: Routledge, 2010).

Boutin, A., *City of Noise: Sound and Nineteenth-Century Paris* (Urbana: University of Illinois Press, 2014).

Brunt, P.A., 'Aspects of the social thought of Dio Chrysostom and of the Stoics', *Proceedings of the Cambridge Philological Society* 19 (1973): 9–34.

Buijnsters-Smets, Leontine, *Straatverkopers in beeld. Tekeningen en prenten van Nederlandse kunstenaars circa 1450–1850* (Nijmegen: Vantilt, 2012).

Burford, A., *Craftsmen in Greek and Roman Society* (Ithaca, NY: Cornell University Press, 1972).

Burke, Peter, 'The Virgin of the Carmine and the revolt of Masaniello', in Peter Burke, *The Historical Anthropology of Early Modern Italy: Essays in Perception and Communication* (Cambridge: Cambridge University Press, 1987), pp. 191–206 (first published in *Past and Present* 99 (1983): 3–21).

Calabi, Donatella, *The Market and the City: Square, Street and Architecture in Early Modern Europe* (Aldershot: Ashgate, 2002).

Calabi, Donatella and Christensen, Stephen Turk (eds), *Cities and Cultural Exchange in Europe, 1400–1700* (Cambridge: Cambridge University Press, 2007).

Calaresu, Melissa, 'From the street to stereotype: Urban space, travel, and the picturesque in late eighteenth-century Naples', *Italian Studies* 62/2 (2007): 189–203.

Calaresu, Melissa, 'Collecting Neapolitans: The representation of street life in late eighteenth-century Naples', in Melissa Calaresu and Helen Hills (eds), *New Approaches to Naples c.1500-c.1800: The Power of Place* (Farnham: Ashgate, 2013), pp. 175–202.

Calaresu, Melissa, 'Costumes and customs in print: Travel, ethnography and the representation of street-sellers in early modern Italy', in Joad Raymond, Jeroen Salman and Roeland Harms (eds), *'Not Dead Things': The Dissemination of Popular Print in England and Wales, Italy, and the Low Countries, 1500–1900* (Leiden/Boston: Brill, 2013), pp. 181–209.

Calaresu, Melissa, 'Making and eating ice cream in Naples: Rethinking consumption and sociability in the eighteenth century', *Past and Present* 220/1 (2013): 35–78.

Calaresu, Melissa, 'Street "luxuries": Food hawking in early modern Rome', in Ivan Gaskell and Sarah Anne Carter (eds), *The Oxford Handbook of History and Material Culture* (Oxford, forthcoming).

Calaresu, Melissa (with Vicky Avery and Mary Laven), *Treasured Possessions from the Renaissance to the Enlightenment* (London: Philip Wilson, 2015).

Carlin, Martha, 'Fast food and urban living standards in medieval England', in Martha Carlin and Joel T. Rosenthal (eds), *Food and Eating in Medieval Europe* (London: Hambledon 1998), pp. 42–43.

Cassani, Silvia, *Capolavori in festa: Effimero barocco a Largo di Palazzo (1683–1759)* (Naples: Electa, 1997).

Clark, Alice, *Working Life of Women in the Seventeenth Century* (London: Routledge, 1992).

Clarke, Georgia and Nevola, Fabrizio, 'The experience of the street in early modern Italy', *I Tatti Studies in the Italian Renaissance* 16/1–2 (2013): 47–55.

Clarke, J.R., *Art in the Lives of Ordinary Romans* (Berkeley: University of California Press, 2003).

Clemente, Alida, *Il lusso 'cattivo': Dinamiche del consumo nella Napoli del Settecento* (Rome: Carocci, 2011).

Cling, Jean-Pierre, Razafindrakoto, Mireille, and Roubaud, François, *The Informal Economy in Vietnam* (Geneva: ILO, 2010).

Cohen, Thomas V. and Laitinen, Riita, *Cultural History of Early Modern Streets* (Leiden/Boston: Brill, 2008).

Corbin, Alain, *Le temps, le désir et l'horreur. Essais sur le XIXe siècle* (Paris: Aubier, 1991).

Cowan, Brian, *The Social Life of Coffee: The Emergence of the British Coffeehouse* (New Haven/London: Yale University Press, 2005).

Crum, Roger J. and Paoletti, J.T. (eds), *Renaissance Florence: A Social History* (Cambridge: Cambridge University Press, 2006).

Cuno, James, 'Violence, satire, and social types in the graphic art of the July Monarchy' in George Weisberg and Petra Chu (eds), *The Popularization of Images: Visual Culture under the July Monarchy* (Princeton: Princeton University Press, 1994), pp. 10–36.

D'Alessio, Silvana, *Masaniello: La sua vita e il mito in Europa* (Rome: Salerno, 2007).

D'Arms, J. H., *Commerce and Social Standing in Ancient Rome* (Cambridge, MA: Harvard University Press, 1981).

Daprà, Brigitte, *Micco Spadaro, Napoli ai tempi di Masaniello* (Exhibition Catalogue, Naples, 2002).

Day, Ivan, 'Ox roasts – from "frost fairs to mops"', in Ivan Day (ed.), *Over a Red Hot Stove: Essays in Early Cooking Technology* (Totnes: Prospect Books, 2009), pp. 55–82.

Deceulaer, Harald, 'Dealing with diversity: Pedlars in the Southern Netherlands in the eighteenth century', in Bruno Blondé, Peter Stabel, Jon Stobbart and Ilja Van Damme (eds), *Retail Circuits and Practices in Medieval and Early Modern Europe* (Turnhout: Brepols, 2006), pp. 171–198.

De Soto, Hernando, *The Other Path: The Invisible Revolution in the Third World* (New York: Harper & Row, 1989).

Di Grazia, Donna M. 'New perspectives on Thomas Myriell's Tristitiae remedium and Add. Ms.29427', *Early Music* 28/1 (2010): 101–112.

Domosh, Mona and Seager, Joni, *Putting Women in Place: Feminist Geographers Make Sense of the World* (New York: Guilford Press, 2001).

Dorey, Margaret, 'Controlling corruption: Regulating meat consumption as a preventative to plague in seventeenth-century London', *Urban History* 36 (2009): 24–41.

Drummond, Lisa, 'Street scenes: Practices of public and private space in urban Vietnam', *Urban Studies* 37 (2000): 2377–2391.

Ehrman, Edwina, Forsyth, Hazel, Peltz, Lucy and Ross, Cathy (with a preface by Loyd Grossman), *London Eats Out: 500 Years of Capital Dining* (London: Philip Wilson, 1999).

Favro, Diane, 'Meaning and experience: Urban history from antiquity to the early modern period', *Journal of the Society of Architectural Historians* 58/3 (1999): 364–373.

Fiensy, D.A., 'What would you do for a living?', in A.J. Blasi, J. Duhaime and P.-A. Turcotte (eds), *Handbook of Early Christianity: Social Science Approaches* (Walnut Creek: AltaMira Press, 2002), pp. 555–576.

Fontaine, Laurence, *History of Pedlars in Europe* (Durham, NC: Duke University Press, 1996).

Fontaine, Laurence (ed.), *Second-Hand Circulations from the Sixteenth Century to the Present* (Oxford: Berghahn, 2008).

Forsyth, Hazel, 'Street food – gingerbread, sugar-loaves and mechanical vending machines', in E. Ehrman, H. Forsyth, L. Peltz and C. Ross (with a preface by Loyd Grossman), *London Eats Out: 500 Years of Capital Dining* (London: Philip Wilson, 1999), pp. 28–29.

Franck, Anja, '"I am too old! Who is going to give me a job?": Women hawkers in Teluk Bahang, Penang, Malaysia', *Journal of Workplace Rights* 15 (2011): 111–132.

Freedman, Paul, 'Eating out', in Ken Albala (ed.), *A Cultural History of Food in the Renaissance* (London/New York: Berg, 2012), pp. 101–115.

Frese, Michael, Krauss, Stephanie, Keith, Nina, Escher, Susanne, Grabarkiewicz, Rafal, Luneng, Siv Tonje, Heers, Constanze, Unger, Jens and Friedrich, Christian, 'Business owners' action planning and its relationship to business success in three African countries', *Journal of Applied Psychology* 92 (2007): 1481–1498.

Gaillard, Jeanne, *Paris la ville: 1852–1870* (Paris: L'Harmattan, 1997).

Garnsey, Peter, *Cities, Peasants and Food in Classical Antiquity* (Cambridge: Cambridge University Press, 1998).

Gautier, Alban, 'Eating out in the early and high Middle Ages', in Massimo Montanari, *A Cultural History of Food in the Medieval Age* (London/New York: Berg, 2012), pp. 91–106.

George, M., 'Social identity and the dignity of work in freedmen's reliefs', in Eve D'Ambra and Guy P.R. Métraux (eds), *The Art of Citizens, Soldiers, and Freedmen in the Roman World* (Oxford: Archaeopress, 2006), pp. 19–29.

Gibbs, Kristine Forney, 'A study of the cries of London as found in the works of the English Renaissance composers', unpublished masters thesis (University of Kentucky, 1974).

Gill, Miranda, *Eccentricity and the Cultural Imagination in Nineteenth-Century Paris* (Oxford: Oxford University Press, 2009).

Gouriet, Jean-Baptiste, *Personnages célèbres dans les rues de Paris, depuis une haute antiquité jusqu'à nos jours* (2 vols, Paris: Lerouge, 1811).

Guha-Khasnobis, Basudeb, Kanbur, Ravi and Ostrom, Elinor (eds), *Linking the Formal and Informal Economy: Concepts and Policies* (Oxford: Oxford University Press, 2006).

Guzzo, P., 'Sul fregio figurato *praedia* di Giulia Felice di Pompei (II, 4. 3)', in M.S. Ragni (ed.), *Studi di archeologia in memoria di Liliana Mercando* (Turin: Soprintenda per i beni archeologici del piemonte e del Museo antichita egizie, 2005), pp. 102–113.

Harding, Vanessa, 'Shops, markets and retailers in London's Cheapside, c.1500–1700', in Bruno Blondé, Peter Stabel, Jon Stobart and Ilya van Damme (eds), *Buyers and Sellers: Retail Circuits and Practices in Medieval and Early Modern Europe* (Turnhout: Brepols 2006), pp. 155–170.

Hart, Keith, 'Informal income opportunities and urban employment in Ghana', *Journal of Modern African Studies* 11/1 (1973): 61–89.

Hawkins, Cameron, 'Labour and employment', in Paul Erdkamp (ed.), *The Cambridge Companion to Ancient Rome* (Cambridge: Cambridge University Press, 2013), pp. 336–351.

Hiemstra, Annemarie, van der Kooy, Koen and Frese, Michael, 'Entrepreneurship in the street food sector of Vietnam: Assessment of psychological success and failure factors', *Journal of Small Business Management* 44 (2006): 474–481.

Holleran, Claire, 'Migration and the urban economy of Rome', in C. Holleran and A. Pudsey (eds), *Demography and the Graeco-Roman World: New Insights and Approaches* (Cambridge: Cambridge University Press, 2011).

Holleran, Claire, 'Street life in ancient Rome', in Laurence, R. and Newsome, D. (eds) *Rome, Ostia, Pompeii: Movement and Space* (Oxford: Oxford University Press, 2011), pp. 245–61.

Holleran, Claire, *Shopping in Ancient Rome: The Retail Trade in the Late Republic and the Principate* (Oxford: Oxford University Press, 2012).

Holleran, Claire, 'Women and retail in Roman Italy', in Emily Hemelrijk and Greg Woolf (eds), *Gender and the Roman City: Women and Civic Life in the Western Provinces* (Leiden/Boston: Brill, 2013), pp. 313–330.

Huang, Shirlena and Brenda Yeoh, 'Gender and urban space in the tropical world', *Singapore Journal of Tropical Geography* 17 (1996): 105–112.

Hughes, Karen, 'Pushed or pulled? Women's entry into self-employment and small business ownership', *Gender, Work and Organization* 10 (2003): 433–454.

Husson, Armand, *Les consommations de Paris* (Paris: Corbeil, 1856).

International Labor Organization, *Women's Entrepreneurship Development Capacity Building Guide* (Geneva: ILO, 2009).

Jackson, Kevin, *Fast: Feasting on the Streets of London*, with photographs by Richard Heeps (London: Portobello, 2006).

Janeja, Manpreet K., *Transactions in Taste: The Collaborative Lives of Everyday Bengali Food* (London/New Delhi: Routledge, 2010).

Johnson, Richard, *Street Food Revolution: Recipes and Stories from the New Food Heroes*, with photographs by Laura Edwards (London: Kyle Cathie, 2011).

Joshel, S.R., *Work, Identity, and Legal Status at Rome: A Study of the Occupational Inscriptions* (Norman: University of Oklahoma Press, 1992).

Kampen, N., *Image and Status: Roman Working Women in Ostia* (Berlin: Mann, 1981).

Kampen, N., 'Social status and gender in Roman art: The case of the saleswoman', in Eve D'Ambra (ed.), *Roman Art in Context: An Anthology* (Englewood Cliffs: Prentice Hall, 1993), pp. 115–132.

Kastner, Georges, *Les voix de Paris: essai d'une histoire littéraire et musicale des cris populaires de la capitale, depuis le moyen âge jusqu'à nos jours, précédé de considérations sur l'origine et le caractère du cri en général* (Paris: G. Brandus, Dufour, 1857).

Kaviraj, S., 'Filth and the public sphere: Concepts and practices about space in Calcutta', *Public Culture* 10/1 (1997): 83–113.

Kock, Paul de (ed.), *La grande ville: nouveau tableau de Paris, comique, critique et philosophique* (2 vols, Paris: Maresq, 1844).

Korda, Natasha, 'Gender at work in the cries of London', in Mary Ellen Lamb and Karen Bamford (eds), *Oral Traditions and Gender in Early Modern Literary Texts* (Aldershot: Ashgate, 2008), pp. 117–135.

Korda, Natasha, *Labor's Lost: Women's Work and the Early Modern Stage* (Philadelphia: University of Pennsylvania Press, 2011).

Koslofsky, Craig, *Evening's Empire: A History of the Night in Early Modern Europe* (Cambridge: Cambridge University Press, 2011).

Kraig, Bruce and Carroll, Patty, *Man Bites Dog: Hot Dog Cultures in America* (Lanham: AltaMira Press, 2012).

Krohn, Deborah L., 'Picturing the kitchen: Renaissance treatise and period room', *Studies in the Decorative Arts* 16/1 (2008–2009): 20–34.

Krohn, Deborah L., *Food and Knowledge in Renaissance Italy: Bartolomeo Scappi's Paper Kitchens* (Farnham: Ashgate, 2015).

Kümin, Beat, 'Eating out before the restaurant: Dining cultures in early modern times', in M. Jacobs and P. Scholliers (eds), *Eating Out in Europe: Picnics, Gourmet Dining and Snacks since the Late Eighteenth Century* (Oxford: Berg, 2003), pp. 71–87.

Kümin, Beat, *Drinking Matters: Public Houses and Social Exchange in Early Modern Central Europe* (London: Palgrave Macmillan, 2007).

Kurke, L., 'Kapeleia and deceit: Theognis 59–60', *American Journal of Philology* 110 (1989): 535–544.

Les Français peints par eux-mêmes (4 vols, Paris: Furne et cie, 1840–1842).

Magaldi, E., *Il commercio ambulante a Pompei* (Naples: Tipografia Ospedale psichiatrico provinciale L. Bianchi, 1930).

Marin, Brigitte, 'Sur les traces de la via Marina: Embellissements urbains et aménagements portuaires à Naples au XVIIIe siècle', *Rives méditerranéennes* 39 (2011): 33–44.

Marshall, C.R., '"Causa di stravaganze": Order and anarchy in Domenico Gargiulo's Revolt of Masaniello', *The Art Bulletin* 80/3 (1998): 478–497.

Massin, R., *Les cris de la ville: commerces ambulants et petits métiers de la rue* (Paris: Gallimard, 1985).

Mayhew, Henry, *London Labour and the London Poor* (Oxford: Oxford University Press, 2012).

McDowell, Linda, *Gender Identity and Place: Understanding Feminist Geographies* (Minneapolis: University of Minnesota Press, 1999).

Merriman, John, *The Margins of City Life: Explorations on the French Urban Frontier 1815–51* (Oxford: Oxford University Press, 1991).

Migliorini, Luigi Mascilli, *Il sistema delle arti: Corporazioni annonarie e di mestiere a Napoli nel Settecento* (Naples: A. Guida, 1992).

Milliot, Vincent, *Les cris de Paris, ou le peuple travesti: les représentations des petits métiers parisiens (XVIe-XVIIIe siècles)* (Paris: Publications de la Sorbonne, 1995).

Milner, Stephen J., '"Fanno bandire, notificare, et expressamente comandare": Town criers and the information economy of Renaissance Florence', *I Tatti Studies in the Italian Renaissance* 16/1–2 (2013): 107–151.

Monson, Craig, 'Thomas Myriell's manuscript collection: One view of musical taste in Jacobean London', *Journal of the American Musicological Society* 30/3 (1977): 419–465.

Monson, Craig, *Voices and Viols in England, 1600–1650: The Sources and the Music* (Ann Arbor: UMI Research Press, 1982).

Montenach, Anne, 'Formal and informal economy in an urban context: The case of food trade in seventeenth-century Lyons', in Thomas Buchner and Philip R. Hoffmann-Rehnitz (eds), *Shadow Economies and Irregular Work in Urban Europe: 16th to Early 20th Centuries* (Vienna: LIT, 2011), pp. 91–106.

Moore, A.P., *The Genre Poissard and the French Stage of the Eighteenth Century* (New York: s.n. 1935).

Muto, Giovanni, 'Le tante città di una capitale: Napoli nella prima età moderna', *Storia urbana* 123 (2009): 19–54.

Naddeo, Barbara, 'Topographies of difference: Cartography of the city of Naples, 1627–1775', *Imago Mundi* 56/1 (2004): 23–47

Nappo, S., 'Fregio dipinto dal *praedium* di Giulia Felice con rappresentazione del foro di Pompei', *Rivista di studi pompeiani* 3 (1989): 79–96.

Nevola, Fabrizio, 'Street life in early modern Europe', *Renaissance Quarterly* 66 (2013): 1332–1345.

Nguyen, Hannah and Nguyen, Nhung, 'Examining personal values and entrepreneurial motives of Vietnamese entrepreneurs in the 21st century: Two empirical studies', *African and Asian Studies* 7 (2008): 141–171.

Ogilvie, Sheilagh, 'Consumption, social capital, and the "Industrious Revolution" in early modern Germany', *Journal of Economic History* 70 (2010): 287–325.

Owens, Jessie Ann, *'Noyses, sounds and sweet aires': Music in Early Modern England* (Seattle and London: University of Washington Press for The Folger Shakespeare Library, 2006).

Pane, Giulio and Valerio, Vladimirio (eds), *La città di Napoli tra vedutismo e cartografia* (Naples: Grimaldi & C., 1987).

Pennell, Sara, "Great quantities of gooseberry pie and baked clod of beef": Victualling and eating out in early modern London', in P. Griffiths and M.S.R. Jenner (eds), *Londinopolis: Essays in the Cultural and Social History of Early Modern London* (Manchester: Manchester University Press, 2000), pp. 228–249.

Pennell, Sara, 'Four hundred years of keeping food hot', in Philippa Glanville and Hilary Young (eds), *Elegant Eating: Four Hundred Years of Dining in Style* (London: V&A Publications, 2002), pp. 68–71.

Pennell, Sara, 'Family and domesticity: Cooking, eating, and making homes', in Beat Kümin (ed.), *A Cultural History of Food in the Early Modern Age* (London/ New York: Berg, 2012), pp. 123–142.

Peterson, Lauren Hackworth, *The Freedman in Roman Art and Art History* (Cambridge: Cambridge University Press, 2006).

Power, Henry, 'Virgil, Horace, and Gay's art of walking the streets', *Cambridge Quarterly* 38/4 (2009): 338–367.

Prévost, Augustin, *La marchande d'amadou et la marchande de gâteaux de Nanterre, folie-parade, caricature du jour, en un acte* (Paris: s.n., 1803).

Reddé, M., 'Les scènes de métier dans la sculpture funéraire Gallo-Romaine', *Gallia* 36 (1978): 43–63.

Réné, 'La marchande de gâteaux de Nanterre', in Alfred Nettement (ed.), *La semaine des familles: Revue universelle hebdomadaire* (Paris: J. Lecoffre, 1866–1867), pp. 7–9.

Revel, Jacques, 'A capital's privileges: Food supplied in early-modern Rome', in R. Forster and O. Ranum (eds), *Food and Drink in History* (Baltimore/London: Johns Hopkins University Press, 1979), pp. 37–49.

Rich, Rachel, *Bourgeois Consumption: Food, Space and Identity in London and Paris, 1850–1914* (Manchester: Manchester University Press, 2011).

Rieger, Dittmar, 'Ce qu'on voit dans les rues de Paris: marginalités sociales et regards bourgeois', *Romantisme* 59 (1988): 19–29.

Riello, Giorgio, '"Things seen and unseen": The material culture of early modern inventories and their representation of domestic interiors', in Paula Findlen (ed.), *Early Modern Things: Objects and their Histories, 1500–1800* (London/New York: Routledge, 2013), pp. 125–150.

Rinne, Katherine W., 'The landscape of laundry in late Cinquecento Rome', *Studies in the Decorative Arts* 9/1 (2001–2002): 34–57.

Roche, Daniel, *The People of Paris: An Essay in Popular Culture of the Eighteenth Century* (Berkeley: University of California Press, 1987).

Schmiechen, James and Carls, Kenneth, *The British Market Hall: A Social and Architectural History* (New Haven: Yale University Press, 1999).

Scholliers, Peter, 'Eating out', in Martin Bruegel (ed.), *A Cultural History of Food in the Age of Empire* (London/New York: Berg, 2012), pp. 108–114.

Scola, Roger, 'Food markets and shops in Manchester, 1770–1870', *Journal of Historical Geography* 1 (1975): 153–168.

Scola, Roger, *Feeding the Victorian City: The Food Supply of Manchester, 1770–1870* (Manchester: Manchester University Press, 1992).

Sestieri, Giancarlo, and Dapra, Brigitte, *Domenico Gargiulo detto Micco Spadaro: Paesaggista e 'cronista' napoletano* (Milano: Jandi Sapi, 1994).

Sewell, William H., 'Visions of labor: Illustrations of the mechanical arts before, in, and after Diderot's *Encyclopédie*', in Steve Kaplan and Cynthia Koepp (eds), *Work in France: Representations, Meaning, Organization and Practice* (Ithaca: Cornell University Press, 1986), pp. 258–288.

Shaw, James, 'Retail, monopoly and privilege: The dissolution of the fishmongers' guild of Venice, 1599', *Journal of Early Modern History* 6 (2002): 396–427.

Shesgreen, Sean, *The Criers and Hawkers of London: Engravings and Drawings by Marcellus Laroon* (Palo Alto: Stanford University Press, 1990).

Shesgreen, Sean, 'The cries of London in the seventeenth century', *Papers of the Bibliographical Society of America* 86 (1992): 269–294.

Shesgreen, Sean, *Images of the Outcast: The Urban Poor in the Cries of London* (Manchester: Manchester University Press, 2002).

Simopolous, A.P. and Bhat, R.V. (eds), *Street Foods*, vol. 86 of *World Review of Nutrition and Dietetics* (Basel, 2000).

Smith, Bruce R., *The Acoustic World of Early Modern England: Attending to the O-Factor* (Chicago: University of Chicago Press, 1999).

Spang, Rebecca, *The Invention of the Restaurant: Paris and Modern Gastronomic Culture* (Cambridge, MA: Harvard University Press, 2000).

Spary, Emma, *Eating the Enlightenment: Food and the Sciences in Paris* (Chicago: University of Chicago Press, 2012).

Spinosa, Nicola, and Di Mauro, Leonardo, *Vedute napoletane del Settecento* (Naples: Electa Napoli, 1996).

Stabel, Peter, 'From the market to the shop: Retail and urban space in late medieval Bruges', in Bruno Blondé, Peter Stabel, Jon Stobart and Ilya van Damme (eds), *Buyers and Sellers: Retail Circuits and Practices in Medieval and Early Modern Europe* (Turnhout: Brepols, 2006), pp. 79–108.

Stewart, P., *The Social History of Roman Art* (Cambridge: Cambridge University Press, 2008).

Tangires, Helen, *Public Markets* (New York: W.W. Norton, 2008).

Tanzer, H., *The Common People of Pompeii: A Study of the Graffiti* (Baltimore: Johns Hopkins Press, 1939).

Théaulon, Emmanuel and Dartois, Achille, *Le boghey renversé, ou un point de vue de Longchamps; croquis en vaudevilles* (Paris: Mme Masson, 1813).

Thirsk, Joan, *Food in Early Modern England: Phases, Fads, Fashions 1500–1760* (London/New York: Continuum, 2007).

Tinker, Irene, *Street Foods: Urban Foods and Employment in Developing Countries* (Oxford: Oxford University Press, 1997).

Tinker, Irene, 'Street foods: Traditional microenterprise in a modernizing world', *International Journal of Politics, Culture and Society* 16 (2003): 331–349.

Treggiari, S. M., 'Urban labour in Rome: *Mercennarii* and *tabernarii*', in Peter Garnsey (ed.), *Non-Slave Labour in the Greco-Roman World* (Cambridge: Cambridge Philological Society, 1980), pp. 48–64.

Van den Heuvel, Danielle, *Women and Entrepreneurship: Female Traders in the Northern Netherlands c.1580–1815* (Amsterdam: Aksant, 2007).

Van den Heuvel, Danielle, 'Partners in marriage and in business? Guilds and the family economy in the urban food markets in the Dutch Republic', *Continuity and Change* 23/2 (2008): 217–236.

Van den Heuvel, Danielle, 'The multiple identities of early modern Dutch fishwives', *Signs: Journal of Women in Culture and Society* 37 (2012): 587–594.

Van den Heuvel, Danielle, 'Selling in the shadows: Peddlers and hawkers in early modern Europe', in Marcel Van der Linden and Leo Lucassen (eds), *Working on Labor: Essays in Honour of Jan Lucassen* (Leiden/Boston: Brill, 2012), pp. 125–151.

Van den Heuvel, Danielle, 'Guilds, gender policies and economic opportunities for women in early modern Dutch towns', in Deborah Simonton and Anne Montenach (eds), *Female Agency in the Eighteenth-Century Urban Economy: Gender in European Towns, 1640–1830* (London: Routledge, 2013), pp. 116–133.

Van den Heuvel, Danielle, 'Depictions and perceptions of street vending in the Northern Netherlands 1600–1800', in G. Nigro (ed.), Il commercio al minuto tra economia formale ed economia informale. Secc. XIII–XVIII (Florence: Firenze University Press, 2015), pp. 249–259.

Van den Heuvel, Danielle, 'Policing peddlers: The prosecution of illegal street trade in eighteenth-century Dutch towns', *Historical Journal* 58/2 (2015): 367–392.

Vinçard, Pierre, *Les ouvriers de Paris: alimentation* (Paris: Gosselin, 1863).

Watts, Sidney, *Meat Matters: Butchers, Politics and Market Culture in Eighteenth-Century Paris* (Rochester: University of Rochester Press, 2006).

Wardrop, Joan, 'Private cooking, public eating: Women street vendors in South Durban', *Gender, Place and Culture* 13 (2006): 677–683.

Wassyng Roworth, Wendy, 'The evolution of history painting: Masaniello's revolt and other disasters in seventeenth-century Naples', *Art Bulletin* 75/2 (1993): 219–234.

Welch, Evelyn, *Shopping in the Renaissance: Consumer Cultures in Italy, 1400–1600* (New Haven/London: Yale University Press, 2005).

Wilson, Eric, 'Plagues, fairs and street cries: Sounding out society and space in early modern London', *Modern Language Studies* 25/3 (1995): 1–42.

Woodfill, Walter L., *Musicians in English Society from Elizabeth to Charles I* (Princeton: Princeton University Press, 1953).

Yasmeen, Gisèle, *Bangkok's Foodscape: Public Eating, Gender Relations, and Urban Change* (Bangkok: White Lotus Press, 2006).

Yriarte, Charles, *Paris grotesque: les célébrités de la rue* (Paris: Dupray de la Maherie, 1868).

Yusof, Rohana, 'Interpreting how religious values affect entrepreneurial behaviour among Muslim businesswomen: The case of businesswomen from the District of Pendang, Kedah in Malaysia', unpublished paper presented at the 2nd Congress of the Asian Association of Women's Studies, 9–11 December 2010, Penang.

Index

Printed and bound by CPI Group (UK) Ltd, Croydon, CR0 4YY
01/05/2025
01858605-0001